THE SCHOOLS HISTORY PROJECT
· S·H·P ·
OFFICIAL TEXT

BRITAIN 1851–1918

A LEAP IN THE DARK?

Michael Willis
Series Editor: Ian Dawson

Hodder Murray
A MEMBER OF THE HODDER HEADLINE GROUP

In the same series

Communist Russia Under Lenin and Stalin	Chris Corin and Terry Fiehn	ISBN 0 7195 7488 9
Fascist Italy	John Hite and Chris Hinton	ISBN 0 7195 7341 6
Weimar and Nazi Germany	John Hite and Chris Hinton	ISBN 0 7195 7343 2
Britain 1783–1851	Charlotte Evers and Dave Welbourne	ISBN 0 7195 7482 X
The Early Tudors: England 1485–1558	David Rogerson, Samantha Ellsmore and David Hudson	ISBN 0 7195 7484 6
The Reign of Elizabeth: England 1558–1603	Barbara Mervyn	ISBN 0 7195 7486 2
England 1625–1660: Charles, the Civil War and Cromwell	Dale Scarboro	ISBN 0 7195 7747 0
Modern America: The USA, 1865 to the present	Joanne de Pennington	ISBN 0 7195 7744 6

This book is dedicated to my students and Skippy, the bush kangaroo.

The Schools History Project

The Project was set up in 1972, with the aim of improving the study of history for students aged 13–16. This involved a reconsideration of the ways in which history contributes to the educational needs of young people. The Project devised new objectives, new criteria for planning and developing courses, and the materials to support them. New examinations, requiring new methods of assessment, also had to be developed. These have continued to be popular. The advent of GCSE in 1987 led to the expansion of Project approaches into other syllabuses.

The Schools History Project has been based at Trinity and All Saints College, Leeds, since 1978, from where it supports teachers through a biennial Bulletin, regular INSET, an annual conference and a website (www.tasc.ac.uk/shp).

Since the National Curriculum was drawn up in 1991, the Project has continued to expand its publications, bringing its ideas to courses for Key Stage 3 as well as a range of GCSE and A level specifications.

Papers used in this book are natural, renewable and recyclable products. They are made from wood grown in sustainable forests. The logging and manufacturing processes conform to the environmental regulations of the country of origin.

Orders: please contact Bookpoint Ltd, 130 Milton Park, Abingdon, Oxon OX14 4SB. Telephone: +44 (0)1235 827720. Fax: +44 (0)1235 400454. Lines are open from 9.00 a.m. to 5.00 p.m., Monday to Saturday, with a 24-hour message answering service. You can also visit our website www.hoddereducation.co.uk

© Michael Willis 2006

First published in 2006
by Hodder Education, part of Hachette Livre UK
338 Euston Road
London NW1 3BH

Impression 5 4 3 2

Year 2009 2008

Layouts by Eric Drewery
Illustrations by Oxford Designers and Illustrators Ltd
Typeset in 10/12pt Walbaum by Fakenham Photosetting, Fakenham, Norfolk
Printed and bound in Britain by Martins The Printers Ltd

A catalogue entry for this title is available from the British Library

ISBN: 978 0 7195 7489 4

Contents

Acknowledgements

Text credits

Text extracts reproduced by kind permission of:
p.15 *Source 1.6* statistics from *The Making of the Second Reform Bill*, Francis Barrymore, Cambridge University Press, 1966; **p.103** *Source 6.7* verses from 'Vitaï Lampada' by Henry Newbolt, by permission of Peter Newbolt; **p.124** *Sources 7.6–7.8* statistics from *The Rise of Anglo-German Antagonism 1860–1914*, Paul M Kennedy, Allen and Unwin, 1980; **p.139** *Source 11A* statistics reprinted from *Explorations in Economic History* 31.2, NFR Crafts and TC Mills, 'Trends in Real Wages in Britain 1750–1913', copyright 1994, with permission from Elsevier, *Source 11B* statistics from *National Income, Expenditure and Output of the United Kingdom 1855–1965*, C. H. Feinstein, Cambridge University Press, 1972; **p.147** *Source 8.8* graph 'Real Earnings 1892–1914' from 'Edwardian Britain: Empire, income and Political Discontent' by Wardley in *Twentieth Century Britain: Economic, Cultural & Social Change*, Johnson (ed), Pearson Education Limited; **p.182** *Source 11.12* statistics from *Liberal Landslide: The General Election of 1906* (David & Charles 1973) by kind permission of the publishers; **p.191** *Sources 12.3 & 12.4* statistics from *Poverty: A study of Town Life*, Seebohm Rowntree, The Policy Press, 2000; **p.270** *Source 15.15* extract from *The Classic Slum*, Robert Roberts, Manchester University Press, 1971.

Photo credits

The Publishers would like to thank the following for permission to reproduce copyright material:

Cover *main* Mary Evans Picture Library, *inset* Courtesy of the Museum of London; **p.2** Mary Evans Picture Library; **p.5** *tl* Getty Images, *tr & b* Mary Evans Picture Library; **p.6** *tl* Private Collection, The Stapleton Collection/Bridgeman Art Library, *tr* Mary Evans Picture Library, *b* Getty Images; **p.7** Mary Evans Picture Library; **p.18** *t & b* Mary Evans Picture Library; **p.19** *l & r* Mary Evans Picture Library; **p.22** Getty Images; **p.24** Mary Evans Picture Library; **p.26** *l & br* Mary Evans Picture Library, *tr* Mary Evans/The Women's Library; **p.32** *l & r* Courtesy of the Museum of London; **p.37** *tl* National Portrait Gallery, London (detail, NPG 4034), *tc* Time Life Pictures/Getty Images, *tr, bl, bc & br* Getty Images; **p.39** Getty Images; **p.49** Getty Images; **p.57** Private Collection/Bridgeman Art Library; **p.60** *tl* TopFoto, *tr* National Portrait Gallery, London (NPG 3241), *bl* © Punch Ltd.; **p.74** *l & r* Getty Images; **p.76** © Punch Ltd.; **p.83** *l & r* St Deiniol's Library, Hawarden, Flintshire; **p.85** The Illustrated London News Picture Library; **p.86** © Punch Ltd.; **p.100** Getty Images; **p.101** *t & b* Getty Images; **p.102** *t* Mary Evans Picture Library, *bl* The Advertising Archive Ltd., *br* V&A Images/Victoria and Albert Museum; **p.106** The Illustrated London News Picture Library; **p.109** Getty Images; **p.119** *t & b* Mary Evans Picture Library, *c* © National Maritime Museum, London; **p.121** Mary Evans Picture Library; **p.127** Mary Evans Picture Library; **p.135** © Punch Ltd.; **p.136** *t & br* Getty Images; **p.137** *tl & tr* Getty Images, *cl, cr & b* Mary Evans Picture Library; **p.143** *t & b* Mary Evans Picture Library, *c* Getty Images; **p.148** Getty Images; **p.150** © Corbis; **p.152** *l* Getty Images; **p.153** *t* Private Collection/Bridgeman Art Library , *b* By permission of People's History Museum; **p.157** *t & b* Getty Images; **p.162-163** V&A Images/Victoria and Albert Museum; **p.169** Getty Images; **p.170** Popperfoto; **p.174** TopFoto; **p.179** *l* V&A Images/Victoria and Albert Museum, *r* With permission of the Director of Information Services, University of Bristol; **p.183** Getty Images; **p.184** TopFoto; **p.188** Getty Images; **p.189** Mary Evans Picture Library; **p.199** Mary Evans Picture Library; **p.200** Mary Evans Picture Library; **p.203** Getty Images; **p.204** *t & b* Getty Images; **p.210** © Punch Ltd.; **p.227** Getty Images; **p.233** Getty Images; **p.234** *t, c & b* Getty Images; **p.235** *t, c & b* Getty Images; **p.239** *l* © Punch Ltd.; **p.242** V&A Images/Victoria and Albert Museum; **p.244** Getty Images; **p.245** *l & r* Getty Images; **p.251** © Courtesy of the Council, National Army Museum, London, UK/Bridgeman Art Library.

Using this book

This is an in-depth study of Britain 1851–1918. It contains everything you need for examination success and more. It provides all the content you would expect, as well as many features to help both independent and class-based learners. So, before you wade in, make sure you understand the purpose of each of the features.

Focus routes

On every topic throughout the book, this feature guides you to produce the written material essential for understanding what you read and, later, for revising the topic (e.g. pages 11, 67 and 121). These focus routes are particularly useful for you if you are an independent learner working through this material on your own, but they can also be used for class-based learning.

Activities

The activities offer a range of exercises to enhance your understanding of what you read to prepare you for examinations. They vary in style and purpose. There are:

- essay titles (e.g. pages 133, 173)
- source investigations (e.g. pages 19, 60)
- examination of historical interpretations, which is now central to A level history (e.g. pages 159, 175)
- decision-making exercises which help you to see events from the viewpoint of people at the time (e.g. pages 46, 65)
- exercises to develop Key Skills such as communication (e.g. page 95).

These activities help you to analyse and understand what you are reading. They address the content through the key questions that the examiner will be expecting you to have investigated.

Overviews, summaries and key points

In such a large book on such a massive topic, you need to keep referring to the big picture. Each chapter begins with an overview and each chapter ends with a key-points summary of the most important content of the chapter.

Timelines showing different governments are on page 41 (to cover the whole book) and on pages 38, 164 and 205 for the different parts of the period.

Learning trouble spots

Experience shows that time and again some topics cause confusion for students. This feature identifies such topics and helps you to avoid common misunderstandings (e.g. page 29). In particular, this feature addresses some of the general problems encountered when studying history, such as explaining contemporary ideas (e.g. pages 75, 178).

Charts

The charts are our attempts to summarise important information in note or diagrammatic form (e.g. pages 9, 21). There are also several grid charts that present a lot of information in a structured way (e.g. page 70). However, everyone learns differently and the best charts are the ones you draw yourself! Drawing your own charts in your own way to summarise important content can really help understanding (e.g. page 14).

Glossary

We have tried to write in an accessible way but occasionally we have used advanced vocabulary. These words are often explained in brackets in the text but sometimes you may need to use a dictionary. We have also used many general historical terms as well as some that are specific to the study of Britain 1851–1918. You won't find all of these in a dictionary, but they are defined in glossary boxes close to the text in which they appear. The first time a glossary word appears in the text it is in SMALL CAPITALS like this.

Talking points

These are asides from the normal pattern of written exercises. They are discussion questions that invite you to be more reflective and to consider the relevance of this history to your own life. They might ask you to voice your personal judgement (e.g. pages 20, 92); to make links between past and present (e.g. pages 102, 182); or to highlight aspects of the process of studying history (e.g. pages 33, 101).

Nineteenth-century British history is one of the most popular A level history topics. The content is deeply relevant to the modern world. But the actual process of studying history is equally relevant to the modern world. Throughout this book you will be problem solving, working with others, and trying to improve your own performance as you engage with deep and complex historical issues. Our hope is that by using this book you will become actively involved in your study of history and that you will see history as a challenging set of skills to be mastered rather than as an inert body of factual material to be learned.

Introduction

A LEAP IN THE DARK.

SOURCE 1 A cartoon by John Tenniel for *Punch*, 3 August 1867. The horse's head is Disraeli

DISCUSS

Look carefully at the cartoon in Source 1. Britannia, the symbol of British power, is riding the horse into a dense and dark field.
a) Judging from her gesture, how does she feel about it?
b) What do you think is meant by 'A Leap in the Dark'?

The Conservative Prime Minister, Lord Derby, described the Second Reform Act of 1867 as a 'leap in the dark'. The Act nearly doubled the number of men who could vote and large numbers of town workers voted for the first time. What would happen? How would Britain change? How would government change?

Looking back today it is easy to see a pattern of progress – an inevitable movement towards democracy and a bigger state. People at the time could not see it this way. Politicians were groping towards democracy, feeling their way, uncertain and often fearful of what change would bring. Power in government was shifting as factory towns grew and the Empire expanded. Were politicians right to be afraid? Were their fears realised?

This book helps you decide as you investigate five interrelated sections.

Your pathway

Section 1

Who should vote?
You examine why and how Parliament gave the vote to working men and women over 30. How far did they really get power in government? You may not look at all the detail, but it is essential background to what follows.

You look at the consequences of this in later sections. Sections 2 and 4 in particular ask how Britain's political parties appealed to working men.

Section 2

How did politicians appeal to the new voters?
William Gladstone and Benjamin Disraeli were the first party leaders to face the new voters. They were bitter rivals who came to hate each other yet often followed similar policies. In this section you compare their achievements as prime ministers, their policies and their personalities.

Section 3

How did Britain maintain its empire?
Gladstone and Disraeli both faced this problem; Section 2 describes their successes and failures. Section 3 explains how the Empire dominated Britain's relations with other countries and how British worries about other European powers led the country into the First World War.

Section 4

Who should the working classes vote for?
Section 4 returns to domestic politics and picks up the themes from Section 1. Extending the franchise did not just mean *more* voters – it meant *different* voters. For the established parties – the Conservatives and the Liberals – one of their biggest challenges was how to respond to these new voters. For the new voters on the other hand, particularly working men, the issue was whether they were best represented by these old parties or whether they needed a new one of their own. This section examines the changing fortunes of the new and old parties in this period. How did they respond? And how did they help change life for ordinary people in Britain?

Section 5

Ireland and the First World War
How to govern Ireland troubled all British political leaders and the Irish problem comes up in Sections 2 and 4. In Section 5, Chapter 14 tackles it head on. Finally Chapter 15 examines how the First World War changed almost every aspect of British life.

How was Britain changing 1851–1918?

Most of this book is about political change but there were other changes taking place as well.

THE ECONOMY

In 1851 Britain was the world's leading industrial nation. This was largely because of just two industries – cotton cloth and iron – but they were the most important ones in clothing and mechanising the world. Nearly half the country's workmen were manufacturing goods in 1851. The proportion was about the same at the start of the First World War but the methods changed. Most of the manufacturing workmen in 1851 were making goods in small workshops, using their hands. Steam power was generally used to make cotton cloth and iron in 1851, but in the next 50 years it spread to a great range of trades like sewing cloth, making boots and milling flour.

While this sounds like great technological advance, in other ways Britain fell behind. British industry and the whole British economy grew at a slower rate than before and grew more slowly than several other industrial countries. The USA overtook Britain as the leading industrial producer in the 1880s and Germany overtook Britain as the second largest before the First World War. Both countries had more resources, especially the USA, but they also did better in developing new and complex industries like chemicals and electrical engineering.

Britain still developed as the greatest trading nation in the world. It had the money to finance development in other countries and, while it exported a lower value of goods than it imported, it also got money from other countries in return for its services and investments. This did not stop people worrying about the way Britain was falling behind.

TELEGRAPH
System of wires for sending and receiving messages electronically.

QUIZ

How much do you know about Britain in 1851?

Choose a), b) or c) for each question. You can find the answers on page 276.

1 How many people lived in Britain?
 a) 11 million
 b) 21 million
 c) 51 million.

2 What proportion lived in towns?
 a) 34 per cent
 b) 44 per cent
 c) 54 per cent.

3 What proportion went to church?
 a) 50 per cent
 b) 70 per cent
 c) 80 per cent.

4 How fast could you travel?
 a) 15–20 mph
 b) 35–40 mph
 c) 60–65 mph.

5 What do you think people could look forward to which might be exciting? Think of as many ideas as possible.

Faster, bigger, cleaner, brighter...

1851 was an exciting time to be young. Britain was changing...

- Railways meant you could travel fast for the first time. There were 15,500 route miles by 1870, and they were cheap enough for ordinary people to use them. The TELEGRAPH, which generally ran alongside railway lines, now brought national news quickly as well. Photography was in its early stages, bringing accurate pictures of distant places and national leaders.
- In 1851 one of the most popular spectator events had been a public hanging. By 1914 it was more likely to be football. Professional football grew rapidly after the Football League began in 1888.
- Popular entertainment was booming too. Music halls soon attracted thousands every night. The first films appeared in the early 1900s, with accompanying music, but no speech. Shopping had changed as well – not only with big window displays and department stores in large towns, but also through nationally advertised brands stocked in village shops.
- Britain was changing from a land where most people lived in the countryside and worked at their own pace to one where most people lived in towns and were regulated by clocks.
- By 1918, as well as railways, there were bicycles, electric trams and a few motor vehicles. Many homes had replaced candles with gaslight. Most wealthy households already had electricity. There was running water in almost all homes and normally a lavatory which flushed instead of a privy which stank.
- Of course you might not live to see all these changes. Many babies still died in infancy. How long you lived depended a lot on whether your family was rich or poor and whether you lived in a country village or a city slum. But if you were born in 1851, with luck, you might just live long enough to be an old man or woman in 1918.

SOURCE 2 (above) Horse-drawn vehicles and motor cars share the roads: Piccadilly, 1910

SOURCE 3 (right) Cover sheet for a popular song about train travel, c. 1860

SOURCE 4 A cartoon commenting on the enthusiasm for seeing criminals hanged in public: from the *Tomahawk*, 1867

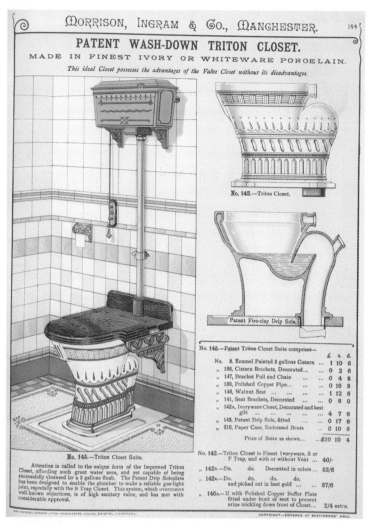

SOURCE 5 Extract from a catalogue of sanitary wares, c. 1890

SOURCE 6 Marie Lloyd (1870–1922) was a popular music hall entertainer, here featured on a postcard

SOURCE 7 Football matches had large attendances: Tottenham Hotspur v Manchester City, 1912

How far did Britain move towards democracy 1851–1918?

SOURCE 1 The atmosphere at an election in the mid-nineteenth century: a drawing in the *Illustrated London News* showing candidate Lord Robert Grosvenor going to the hustings (a platform where he would speak) at Brentford, 1847

Does this look like democracy to you?

Most Europeans now believe in democracy and therefore tend to judge past political systems by how democratic they were. There are different definitions of democracy but most people would argue that it involves at least:

- all adults having the right to vote
- freedom of speech and freedom of the press so people can know about the alternatives on offer in order to choose between them
- government in line with what the majority want.

By these criteria democracy in Britain was severely limited in 1851. This section examines how far Britain moved towards these features by the end of the First World War.

- Chapter 1 examines how working men got the right to vote.
- Chapter 2 examines how this right was extended to women (although only women over 30) in 1918.

By 1918 more people in Britain could vote than ever before but did that really make it democratic? That is for you to decide. So the key enquiry in this section is: *How far did Britain move towards democracy 1851–1918?*

Orientation: What you need to know about nineteenth-century government and elections

■ A Jobs in government and who did them

NATIONAL GOVERNMENT

Queen Victoria was reigning monarch. In theory the government was made up of her ministers, she called Parliament and the law was applied in her courts. In practice, Parliament was much more powerful than the monarch. As the journalist Bagehot put it, the queen would have to sign her own death warrant if Parliament insisted.

Legislative
Making laws and deciding what taxes should be levied.

DONE BY

House of Lords
Peers were HEREDITARY but new ones were created as well. Church of England bishops also sat in the Lords.

House of Commons
MPs belonged to political parties. Party WHIPS tried to persuade MPs to support party leaderships but had little control over how they voted.
 The House of Commons was now clearly the more powerful house in deciding laws and taxes. As more people elected it, as a result of further Reform Acts, the Commons could claim more power. But the Lords could and did reject its BILLS. However, after the 1911 Parliament Act, the Lords could only delay any bills the Commons wanted for two years.

Executive
Running the country on a day-to-day basis. This included defending the country and keeping law and order but governments did a growing amount beyond this.

DONE BY

Prime Minister
The prime minister was generally leader of the party that had the majority of MPs in the House of Commons. His job was to form a government. If no party had a clear majority he had to keep the support of enough MPs to win crucial votes about the budget and to defeat any motion of no confidence in the government.
 The prime minister's powers were not clearly written down, and how he governed depended on his personal style. Although the role varied, premiers of that time generally had less power over their governments than those in the twenty-first century.

Cabinet
The Cabinet consisted of about fifteen of the most important government ministers. The prime minister could appoint and dismiss these ministers, but had to get their agreement for important government decisions.
 The Cabinet increasingly determined how Parliament spent its time. It put forward many bills. In the mid-nineteenth century there was an understanding that government ministers' business had priority on two days a week. From the 1880s it had priority on well over 80 per cent of the days when the Commons sat. It was therefore getting much of the legislative power as well as the executive.
 In practice, ministers had to be in Parliament and defend their decisions there but they could come from either the Lords or the Commons. Many Cabinets drew most of their members from the House of Lords.

Balance of prime minister's and Cabinet's powers
- The Cabinet seems to have made more of the decisions than now, though it is hard to be certain as there were no formal records of Cabinet meetings until the First World War.
- Prime ministers normally let government ministers run their own departments with less central direction than in the twenty-first century.
- Lloyd George increased the prime minister's powers considerably in 1916–18 because of wartime needs but there was much criticism of this later.

Judicial
Judging and punishing those who may have broken the laws.

DONE BY

Judges
Judges in the House of Lords made final decisions at the head of a series of law courts.

LOCAL GOVERNMENT

Most people living in the nineteenth century would have been more aware of local than national government. There were a large number of local councils and boards acting to provide education, improve public health and help the poor.
 These local authorities used about 25 per cent of the total spent by the government around 1850, about 40 per cent by 1890 and about 50 per cent by 1910.
 National government's role increased from 1906 with the Liberal government's welfare reforms and increased government control in the First World War.

■ B Who could vote and how were elections organised?

MID-NINETEENTH CENTURY

1 About a fifth of men in England could vote (around a seventh in the UK as a whole) but no women.
2 The country was divided into county areas and boroughs (towns) to elect MPs. The number of voters varied a great deal among the different areas (constituencies) electing MPs. Generally each constituency elected two MPs.
In boroughs anyone *occupying* a house worth £10 a year in rent could vote. In counties there were various qualifications. Men could vote if they owned property worth 40 shillings (£2) a year in rent or they *rented* property worth £10 a year on a long-term agreement or £50 a year on a short-term one.
3 Candidates in elections spent as much as they wanted and there were no effective rules against bribery.
4 Electors voted in public. Their friends, neighbours, enemies, employers and landlords knew how they voted.
5 Most candidates stood as Liberals or Conservatives. People often voted for local reasons and followed the wishes of employers or landowners, though parties were becoming more important in elections.
6 There were contests for about half the seats in Parliament when general elections were held. There were no contests in other constituencies because it was so expensive to stand as a candidate and it was often obvious that one candidate had the power and influence to win.
7 Most of the MPs were landowners and all were comparatively wealthy.

TWENTY-FIRST CENTURY

1 All men and women over 18 can vote, with a few exceptions (e.g. some criminals in prison at the start of the 21st century).
2 The country is divided into constituencies (areas electing MPs) with roughly equal numbers of voters. Each constituency elects one MP. (There are different arrangements for European and regional assembly elections.)
3 There are limits to spending on local and national campaigns.
4 Electors vote secretly by ballot.
5 There are many parties. Nearly all MPs stand for one of the parties. People generally vote for national reasons and vote for a party leader whom they want to be prime minister.
6 The main parties contest almost all the constituencies in the country.
7 MPs come from varied backgrounds though they are predominantly middle class.

■ C How mid-nineteenth-century election campaigns differed from those of today

MID-NINETEENTH CENTURY

- Local candidates put on a big show. Politics involved a lot of street theatre.
- Handbills were given out which often included candidates' speeches, but they printed songs, rude poems and cartoon-style pictures as well.
- Local newspapers gave information about the candidates and their meetings, and newspapers could be read out to people who could not read themselves.
- Laws against bribery did not have much effect. There was plenty of free beer offered by the candidates to encourage people to vote for them.

TWENTY-FIRST CENTURY

- TV is the most important way in which electors learn about politics.
- National, regional and local newspapers all have an important influence.
- Political parties issue advertisements and send leaflets to electors' homes.

FOCUS ROUTE

Study Chart A and, using your own knowledge of modern politics, note
a) one significant similarity
b) one significant difference
between mid-nineteenth-century government and government in present-day Britain.

BILLS
Drafts of proposed laws which are debated in Parliament. If they are approved they become laws, known as acts or statutes.

HEREDITARY
Passed from parent to child. Peers' titles and lands were passed from father to son.

WHIPS
MPs appointed by the party leaders who try to persuade other MPs to support the leadership and its policies.

TALKING POINT

Can you see any advantages in the nineteenth-century style of campaigning apart from the opportunities for getting drunk?

How democratic was Britain by 1900?

CHAPTER OVERVIEW   Most politicians in the mid-nineteenth century thought democracy dangerous. They were cautious about extending voting rights.

There was a big shift in opinion from the 1850s to the 1880s. Parliament gave most male workers in large towns the vote in 1867 and most men elsewhere in 1884. This chapter examines how this happened:

A Why was there a Second Reform Act in 1867? (pp. 11–14)

B How much did the Second Reform Act change the electoral system? (pp. 14–15)

C How far did the Second Reform Act lead to a more modern type of politics? (pp. 16–17)

D How far did the conduct of elections change? (pp. 18–19)

E How important was the Third Reform Act of 1884–85? (pp. 20–23)

■ 1A Different views on who should vote in the mid-nineteenth century

MODERATES or CONSERVATIVES

1 The Vote is a Privilege, people need to earn it.
2 People need education to vote. Otherwise they will not know what they are doing and can easily be misled.
3 Only people who hold land or houses should vote as they have a stake in the country. If the masses get power they may want much higher taxes on the rich or they will try to seize property which will lead to anarchy.
4 Citizenship involves duties as well as rights. People should vote only if they make a contribution to society such as by paying rates (local taxes based on property value). The vote should go only to respectable and responsible householders.
5 If the poor voted, they could be easily bribed with money and drink.

6 We should avoid the mistakes made in other countries.
 ■ In the USA politicians have often gained power through controlling their parties' organisations and manipulating people.
 ■ In France the French Revolution shows how dangerous radical change can be.

EXTREME RADICALS

1 The Vote is a Right, all men should have it.
2 Government affects all adults, so all should have a say in who governs the country, whether educated or not.
3 Working men should vote because they contribute to the country by their labour.

4 Everyone should vote because we are equal human beings. Everyone pays taxes on some of the goods they buy (see page 44) and should therefore have a say in government.

5 The rich use the existing system to their own advantage. Governments use patronage (giving well paid jobs to friends and supporters) and organise the tax system so that they benefit.
6 We should learn from other countries that democracy can strengthen a state.
 ■ The USA has a democratic system (at least for white citizens) and is growing into a great power.
 ■ There is manhood suffrage (voting rights) in white settler colonies in Canada and Australia.
 ■ All adult men have had the vote in France since 1848.

ACTIVITY

Look at Chart 1A. Work in pairs to role play a discussion between a radical and a conservative in the 1850s. Try to bring in as many points from your side of the chart as possible. Swap roles to argue the opposite point of view.

FOCUS ROUTE

Make notes about the following:
1 What has been the main controversy between historians about the reasons for the Second Reform Act?
2 What reasons had both Liberals and Conservatives for wanting reform?
3 How much public pressure was there for reform up to 1866?
4 a) What did Disraeli's reform bill propose in 1867?
   b) How did it differ from Gladstone's?
   c) How was it altered in Parliament?
5 Look at the timeline in Chart 1B.
   a) In what ways did
      i) public agitation
      ii) the situation in Parliament
      appear to have influenced the Conservative government?
   b) Which do you think was more important and why?

The story so far

Many working men demonstrated for a parliamentary REFORM BILL to extend the vote in 1831–32. A few rioted when it was blocked, and there were widespread celebrations when it was later passed in Parliament even though it gave the vote to a comparatively small number of people. Later the Chartist movement, which wanted **all men** to have the vote, got massive support from workers in the 1840s. Over 3 million signed a petition for manhood suffrage (all men to have the vote) in 1842 and about 2 million in 1848.

But in 1851 most politicians still thought democracy was dangerous. Even Liberals arguing for parliamentary reform generally wanted only a limited increase in the number of electors. After the failure of a big Chartist petition in 1848 there was less interest in reforming Parliament until the 1860s.

Why did this change?

There has been particularly active historical debate on the reasons why reform returned to the agenda in the 1860s. On one side are historians who explain changes by what was happening in the economy and society and who emphasise how agitation by the masses put pressure on the MPs to take action. This is in line with the Marxist approach and was widely argued in the 1950s and 1960s. On the other side historians taking the 'high politics' line argue that the manoeuvres of leading politicians probably mattered more. This was the argument of Maurice Cowling (1967) in *1867: Disraeli, Gladstone and Revolution*, which in many ways started the 'high politics' approach to history.

1 The actions of politicians

Both Liberal and Conservative politicians saw some advantages in reform, but there were opponents in both parties too.

- Many RADICAL Liberals wanted to reduce the landowners' power and Church of England privileges. They therefore wanted to redistribute MPs around the country so fewer came from small boroughs where landowners often controlled the voting. They thought worthy skilled working men would support the Liberals if more of them got the vote, and the pollbooks listing how people voted in the mid-nineteenth century suggest they were probably right.
- Conservatives saw themselves doing very badly under the existing system (see page 9) which the Liberals had set up in 1832. This was partly because the English counties where Conservatives were strong had fewer MPs than the boroughs in proportion to their population.

Consequently several bills to reform the electoral system were introduced in Parliament. Lord Russell, one of the most prominent Liberals, introduced bills in the 1850s. Disraeli introduced one when the Conservatives were in government in 1859. They came to nothing as there was no agreement about reform and Lord Palmerston, the Liberal prime minister in 1855–58 and 1859–65, was against significant change.

RADICALS
People who wanted extensive reforms in government. *Radix* means root; radicals wanted change from the roots, i.e. total change.

REFORM BILL
Draft of a law to change the way Parliament was elected and which Parliament would then debate.

CHARTISTS

Largely working-class men and women who campaigned for democracy. They demanded the vote for all adult men, a secret ballot, annual general elections and other changes in the law to allow working men to get into Parliament. In 1839, 1842 and 1848 their organisations got millions of signatures for petitions to Parliament, putting forward very radical political and economic demands

CONSTITUTIONAL MOVEMENTS
Groups trying to change the ways countries were governed.

ARISTOCRATIC
Belonging to a privileged group, generally inheriting land and wealth and often having titles.

PAUPERS
People getting help from local taxes because they were too poor to maintain themselves.

The position altered rapidly in the mid-1860s. Gladstone, who was emerging as a Liberal leader at this time, came out in favour of reform (see page 44). He was impressed by the responsibility of working men who avoided agitation in times of hardship and workers who invested in the post office savings bank. Skilled workers looked safe people to have the vote. They also seemed to support his tax-cutting policy.

When Palmerston died in 1865 Russell took over as prime minister, and Gladstone introduced a reform bill to give a vote to householders in boroughs if they occupied a house worth £7 a year instead of £10. It was a very moderate proposal, but it started a battle in Parliament and raised interest outside.

2 Agitation by the people

The large numbers of Chartists (see box, left) who agitated in the 1840s had not disappeared. Many clearly gave up politics, but some pressed for educational and other social reforms. A number supported CONSTITUTIONAL MOVEMENTS abroad, such as the Italian nationalists who were struggling for self-government. The Italian commander, Garibaldi, was a particularly inspiring symbol for the people's struggle against corrupt, ARISTOCRATIC rulers. Vast crowds greeted him when he visited England in 1864, and the London Working Men's Garibaldi Association formed the core of the Reform League set up the next year. A more middle-class Reform Union began in Manchester in 1864, while the Reform League largely came from the trade unions and gained about 60,000 members. They wanted manhood suffrage, though only for men who had been living in their houses for a year, and they did not think PAUPERS should vote. Fathers of households and breadwinners for families should vote as full citizens. It was a very masculine idea, and it was based on a sense of pride and respectability (see Sources 1.1–1.3).

■ IB Steps towards the Second Reform Act 1866–67

1866	March	Gladstone introduces reform bill
	June	Russell's Liberal government resigns after defeat on an amendment to the bill
		Derby forms a Conservative government
	July	Disturbances in London at Hyde Park when demonstrators try to hold a meeting in favour of reform
	August onwards	Mass meetings in favour of reform, particularly in the North and Midlands
	November–December	Conservative government decides to introduce reform proposals
1867	March	Disraeli introduces reform bill in the House of Commons
	May	Reform League holds successful mass meeting in Hyde Park
		Disraeli accepts Hodgkinson's amendment
	August	Reform bill becomes law and forms the Second Reform Act

The struggle over reform in 1866–67

Gladstone's bill failed when right-wing Liberals and Conservatives voted together for amendments which would destroy it. Then Russell's Liberal government lost a crucial vote in June 1866, resigned and was replaced by a Conservative government with Lord Derby as prime minister and Disraeli as Leader in the House of Commons. The Conservative government did not have a majority in the House of Commons and could keep going only with some assistance from MPs on the Liberal side.

There was then increasing support for reform outside Parliament. The Reform League decided to hold a mass meeting in London's Hyde Park in July; the government banned it, but crowds went anyway and tore down some of the park railings. There were large reform demonstrations in some northern and Midland towns in the autumn.

ARTISANS

Skilled craftsmen.

COMPOUNDERS

Tenants (people holding land or a house for a set time) who paid money to a landlord to cover local rates (taxes) as well as rent.

SOURCE 1.1   *The Times* described a big Reform League demonstration in Hyde Park in July 1866

The processions did, indeed, contain a certain number of decent mechanics [skilled craftworkers], and some persons who, from their dress and appearance, seemed to belong to the middle class; but these were almost lost in a surrounding and interpenetrating mass of the coarsest mob. The great majority of the people in the crowded streets were the usual slouching, shambling man-boys who constitute the mass of the ordinary London multitude.

SOURCE 1.2   The trade union newspaper, the *Bee-Hive*, was supportive of the demonstration

[T]he greatest order and good humour prevailed amongst the people, and any tendency on the part of unthinking lads, or disorderly boys, to create a disturbance, was promptly checked by the mass of working men present.

SOURCE 1.3   The *Newcastle Weekly Chronicle* reported a statement by Robert Warden, a brass founder at a local locomotive works, in early 1867

[The working classes] were able to build leviathan [huge] ships to carry the commerce of the world across the mighty oceans; they were able to construct mighty iron warps [metal ropes] to connect two distant continents together; but the opponents of Reform did not consider that those same ARTISANS were able to choose their representatives in Parliament.

The demonstrations clearly had some impact on the Conservative government, but they were only one factor. Disraeli had already mentioned taking up reform in a letter in June before the Hyde Park disturbances. Later in 1866 Derby came 'reluctantly to the conclusion' that the Conservatives should introduce reform proposals. Source 1.4 shows how he put it in a letter to Disraeli in December.

SOURCE 1.4   Derby in a private letter to Disraeli, 22 December 1866

Of all possible hares to start I do not know a better than the extension of household suffrage, coupled with plurality of voting (electors having more than one vote).

In 1867 Disraeli introduced a Conservative government reform bill. Three ministers, including Lord Cranborne (who was later Foreign Secretary and Prime Minister), resigned because they disagreed with it. The bill would give the vote to all householders in boroughs who paid rates, which Disraeli suggested made them responsible citizens, but they would get it only when they had lived in their homes for at least two years (a so-called two-year residence qualification).

This already went further than Gladstone had proposed, but Disraeli then went on to accept amendments from Radical MPs which would give the vote to many more people. He seemed more concerned with who had introduced the amendments than what they actually proposed. For example, he opposed an amendment from Gladstone to give lodgers the vote and then accepted the same idea a month later when it was proposed by the radical Liberal MP, W.T. Torrens. It gave the vote to people who did not pay rates (local taxes), though Disraeli had previously suggested that this was a key qualification to vote. He opposed an amendment to give the vote to COMPOUNDERS when it came from Hugh Childers, a close personal supporter of Gladstone's. Then he accepted a worse drafted amendment to do this from the Radical MP, Grosvenor Hodgkinson. This would give the vote to something like 400,000 people – a massive number when the existing electorate was just over one million. What was he up to? Source 1.5 shows some of Disraeli's likely motives.

SOURCE 1.5   From a private letter Disraeli wrote to another Conservative minister, Gathorne Hardy, explaining why he accepted Hodgkinson's amendment, 18 May 1867

[W]e might take a step which would destroy the present agitation and extinguish Gladstone and Co.

One can read Disraeli's actions as the response to the set of problems outlined in Chart 1C.

- If the Liberal MPs reunited they could defeat the Conservative government in the House of Commons and turn it out of office.
- Disraeli needed to keep the Liberals split, and backing Radicals against Gladstone was an effective way of doing it.
- Disraeli was desperate to stay in power. The Conservatives had been out of power for most of the last twenty years. They wanted to show that they could govern, and they wanted to keep at least some control over the details of parliamentary reform, not to hand the initiative to their political opponents.
- As for the extra voters: most boroughs returned Liberal MPs anyway, so the Conservatives had little to lose there. The new Act gave the vote to far fewer people in the counties where the Conservatives had their main strength (see Source 1.6). Disraeli also knew it was not so much the number of voters in each constituency that mattered but how MPs were distributed around the country. That decided who got power.

ACTIVITY

Make your own copy of Chart 1C and add notes to show how the Second Reform Act helped Disraeli to solve each problem.

B How much did the Second Reform Act change the electoral system?

FOCUS ROUTE

Study page 15 and make notes about the following:
1 To what extent did the Second Reform Act increase the number of electors in
   a) the boroughs
   b) the counties?
2 How extensive was the redistribution of parliamentary seats (MPs elected in different areas)?
3 How did the number of electors in Scotland and Ireland compare with the number in England and Wales?

SOURCE 1.6 Who could vote under the 1867–68 Reform Acts (the Scottish and Irish Acts were passed in 1867–68)

	Who could vote in the boroughs?	Proportion of borough population who could vote	Who could vote in the counties?	Proportion of county population who could vote
England and Wales	Householders who paid rates and £10 LODGERS if they had been resident for at least a year	English boroughs 1 out of 8 Welsh boroughs 1 out of 8	40-SHILLING FREEHOLDERS; COPYHOLDERS and long LEASEHOLDERS paying at least £5 rent a year; property holders who paid POOR RATES and whose land had a rateable value of £12 a year	English counties 1 out of 15 Welsh counties 1 out of 13
Scotland	Householders who paid rates (lodgers had already been given the vote in Scotland as they had legal status as tenants)	1 out of 9	Same as in England	1 out of 24
Ireland	Men occupying property which officials calculating poor rates reckoned was worth £4 rent a year	1 out of 16	Men occupying property which officials calculating poor rates reckoned was worth £12 rent a year	1 out of 26

£10 LODGERS
People paying at least £10 per year to live in others' houses. Men who could afford £10 rent would be middle class or skilled craftsmen, but it was often difficult for them to get on the register to vote anyway (see below).

40-SHILLING FREEHOLDERS
People owning land or houses worth 40s [£2].

COPYHOLDERS
People holding land from another owner by a traditional type of agreement, normally for a long period.

LEASEHOLDERS
People holding land and buildings for a specific period, according to an agreement known as a lease.

POOR RATES
Local taxes charged on land and houses and used to provide help for the poor.

ROYAL COMMISSION
Group set up by the government to investigate and report on an issue.

The terms of the Second Reform Act

About a fifth of adult men in Britain could vote before the Second Reform Act and about a third after. Historians estimate the number of voters in English and Welsh boroughs grew by 134 per cent but it only grew by 46 per cent in the counties – an increase of 89 per cent overall.

Vast differences remained between the numbers of voters in each constituency.

Only 52 parliamentary seats were redistributed in England and Wales (a few more than Disraeli intended). Several small boroughs lost their MPs. Some were allocated to large towns, but more were given to the counties. The ROYAL COMMISSION on boundaries, which decided how seats were to be distributed, was mainly made up of Conservative landowners and they did a good job for their party. Many suburbs and industrial villages were put within borough boundaries so that the counties could remain more solidly Conservative. A parliamentary committee later modified this, but in the 66 seats where boundary alterations took place the Conservatives made a net gain of 25 MPs at the next election in 1868.

The Second Reform Act did not make the voting qualifications clear. Hodgkinson's amendment said that the compounders – tenants who had previously paid rates through their landlords as part of their rent – were now to pay rates directly and have a vote. When this did not work effectively a new Act in 1869 said they could still pay rates through their landlords but have a vote as well.

It was very difficult for lodgers to register themselves to vote. Political parties would dispute whether men likely to support their opponents had the qualifications to vote, and it could be difficult and time-consuming to argue this out in the registration courts which decided on claims. The situation changed in 1878 when a further Act allowed men occupying rooms and flats in a larger house to vote. These subsequent Acts led to a 40 per cent increase in the numbers of borough voters between the Second Reform Act and the next one in 1884–85 – a much bigger increase than there was in population over the period.

ACTIVITY

Write two short paragraphs to argue that the Second Reform Act
a) was a very important step towards democracy
b) did very little to make the UK more democratic.

How far did the Second Reform Act lead to a more modern type of politics?

FOCUS ROUTE

Chart 1D compares the situation with the modern equivalent in the twenty-first century. As you read through Section C, fill out the middle column on your own copy.

Then write your answer to this question: Was politics after the Second Reform Act more like what came before, or more like the present day? Note evidence that supports your answer.

■ 1D Differences between nineteenth-century politics and modern politics

	Before Second Reform Act	After Second Reform Act	Modern politics
Issues	• Election contests often about local issues and personalities, although national party labels (Liberal and Conservative) were used and national issues were important		• Election contests about national issues and leaders. National leaders' image, competence and policies are much more important than local party candidates
Campaign techniques	• Campaigning mainly involved street theatre, handbills and local newspapers		• National media, particularly TV and newspapers, are vital
Influences	• Landowners and employers had important influence on the result		• National party campaigns and organisations matter most

British politics did alter from 1867. The combination of lots of new voters and many more newspapers helped produce a modern kind of politics with national party organisations and national newspaper coverage gradually dominating election campaigns. Yet historical change is complicated.

- Changes took place at varying speeds around the country. The 1950s historian H.J. Hanham described how landowners' influence stayed strong in many English counties after the Second Reform Act. The new type of party politics came faster in towns than in the countryside.
- New political influences grew, but they were very different from twentieth-century ones. Industrial employers often controlled or influenced electors. The historian Patrick Joyce (1980) found cotton factory workers in some Lancashire towns, such as Blackburn, voted in line with their employers' wishes.
- Political campaigning developed from the old street theatre, but in distinctively Victorian ways. The Conservatives made effective use of new images (see page 63) and music halls had political songs and displays (see page 79).
- Newspaper circulation grew, but local and regional papers were probably more important than the national ones immediately after 1867. Sixteen English towns had a daily paper in 1868, rising to 71 by 1901.
- National issues became more important, but they were often based more on religious divisions than on the economic and social welfare issues that dominated much of twentieth-century politics. Education and controls on the sale of alcohol raised issues connected with religion, but there was fierce controversy about religious beliefs and worship for their own sake.
- The 1867 Act gave the vote to many town workers, but they still voted in public until the 1872 Ballot Act.

Party organisation

The number of voters in the UK grew from about 1.3 million before the Second Reform Act to 2.4 million in 1868 and 3.1 million by 1883. Each man had to make the effort to get himself registered to vote. This was not just a matter of filling in a form, as today, but of applying to register and sometimes having a lengthy legal argument to prove his property qualifications.

Parties started working men's clubs. These boosted political support by providing a social life, with entertainment, outings and general camaraderie. Research by Garrard (1988) and Joyce (1980) shows an extensive range of political clubs in Lancashire (see Sources 1.7 and 1.8), offering not only entertainment but also welfare benefits. For example, the Bolton Conservative Sick and Burial Society expanded rapidly from 1867. Local clubs and party branches also joined together to fight elections. By the 1880s both main parties had local organisations in almost all the constituencies.

DISCUSS

1 Are any of the facilities or activities listed in Sources 1.7 and 1.8 directly connected with politics?
2 Why do you think political clubs provided this range of facilities and activities? You could also refer to page 86, describing a Salford Liberal Association outing in 1877, and page 168, showing how the Conservative Primrose League developed activities from 1883.

SOURCE 1.7 The *Salford Weekly News* indicated the Broughton Liberal Club's facilities when reporting on a branch meeting in February 1872

[I]t was further intended, if the funds were forthcoming, to erect a commodious billiard room, which should be replete with every convenience, and contain a full-sized table. This, combined with a reading room, smoke room, chess, draughts, a good supply of papers and periodicals, and the opportunity for obtaining tea, coffee, cigars etc., at fixed charges on the premises, would, it was confidently hoped, offer such advantages as should induce all Liberals of the district to enrol themselves as members.

SOURCE 1.8 The *Salford Weekly Chronicle* gave an attractive description of the Salford Constitutional (Conservative) Association's annual picnic and sports in August 1872

At five o'clock the racing sports commenced ...
 After the last deciding heat had been run, the party assembled near the refreshment tent, and the prizes to the successful competitors were distributed ... Prior to the distribution the new 'Conservative Gallop', composed by Mr J.A. Gifford, the bandmaster of the Salford Volunteers ... was played (for the first time publicly) by the band.

Both parties developed national organisations. The Conservative National Union developed from small beginnings in 1867 and by 1877 had 791 affiliated associations (see page 64). The National Liberal Federation was formed in 1877 to improve Liberal electoral organisation (see page 92). These central organisations were run by professionals who developed more efficient national campaigns. The two main parties now fought nearly all constituencies in general elections. The number of uncontested elections fell from 194 to 39 between 1865 and 1885.

National campaigns by party leaders

Chapters 3, 4 and 5 describe the roles of Gladstone and Disraeli as national leaders (see especially pages 71 and 86). A new kind of national political debate developed over foreign policy issues in the late 1870s (see page 83). The *Annual Register* estimated that 'more speeches had been made by Cabinet ministers' while Parliament was in recess (not sitting) in 1879 'than in all the recesses of other Parliaments put together'. There were much fuller national party campaigns at the 1880 election than ever before.

The two main parties did not yet issue MANIFESTOS to the country promising what they would do; these came after the First World War. All the same, a party leader's election address to his constituency was seen as a kind of national policy statement. Politicians thought this gave them a mandate (instruction) to carry out their policy if their party won.

MANIFESTO
Public statement of what a party will do if it has power after an election.

The press

Newspaper sales grew rapidly in the mid-nineteenth century. The steam press printed papers quickly and cheaply. Taxes on papers were scrapped so that prices fell. Telegraph lines transmitted news fast, and railway trains distributed papers speedily. Thirty times as many newspapers were sold in 1870 as in 1830. Most were local, but the London press grew rapidly. The *Daily Telegraph* sold 190,000 copies by 1870, mostly around London. Weekly papers went further afield, and *Lloyd's Weekly* sold about 600,000 copies from the 1860s. Newspapers were vital in the development of national politics.

FOCUS ROUTE

1 List changes and continuities
  following
  a) the 1872 Ballot Act
  b) the 1883 Corrupt and Illegal
  Practices Act.
2 Note which Act you think brought
  about most significant change and
  why.

D How far did the conduct of elections change?

1872 Ballot Act

Why? There had been much discussion about introducing the secret ballot in the mid-nineteenth century. There was a small majority in favour of it in the House of Commons in 1848 and 1859. Later, threats and bribes increased when more workers voted in the boroughs after the 1867 Reform Act, and many politicians who had opposed the ballot changed their minds after the 1868 election.

■ 1E The argument over the ballot

SOURCE 1.9 Drawing from Cassell's *History* showing men voting on an open platform. Their votes would be publicly recorded

SOURCE 1.10 Drawing in the *Graphic* showing how men would take a ballot paper and vote secretly in a cubicle

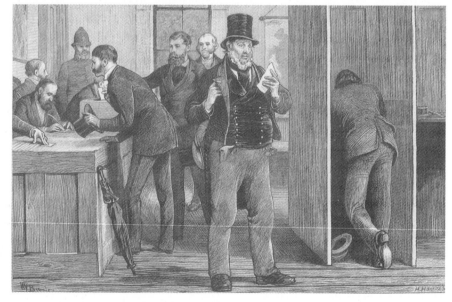

Case for open voting
- Men cast votes not only for themselves but also for the whole community. People should know how the electors voted on their behalf. Voting was a public duty which affected everyone and should be done publicly.
- It was unmanly to sneak into a ballot box. Why should a man be ashamed of his vote?

Case for secret ballot
- Electors could be threatened by employers, landlords or trade unions to vote in a particular way, and public voting encouraged people to bribe others.
- The atmosphere around the hustings where men voted was often riotous or drunken. This was not the right setting for someone to carry out a serious public duty.

Effects of the Act
Secret balloting was now to be used in all elections. Elections generally got quieter, but some bribery continued. People were still willing to pay others for

their votes even though they could not check up on them. Employers could no longer threaten their workers or landlords their tenants. Landlord threats had apparently been most important in Ireland, and the HOME RULE PARTY there benefited from the ballot in the 1874 election. Many English tenants still seemed happy to follow the wishes of their landlords and employers.

1883 Corrupt and Illegal Practices Act

Why? Several laws were passed in the mid-nineteenth century to stop candidates bribing the voters with food, drink and money, but they had little effect. Bribery was most obvious in some small boroughs which still kept their MPs but had few voters, such as Bewdley (Worcestershire) and Sandwich (Kent). Commissioners investigating bribery there in the 1880 election produced a strong case for reform.

Effects of the Act
The Act limited the number of paid election workers and the total amount candidates could spend.

Evidence suggests it reduced bribery considerably:

- Officially recorded election spending at the 1885 election was about 25 per cent of that in 1880
- There were far fewer petitions to Parliament about election bribery
- Parties now relied much more on volunteers than paid election workers.

THE PARTY WHO, ETC.   FREE AND INDEPENDENT, ETC.

THE ORDINARY LEGAL EXPENSES OF AN ELECTION.

SOURCE 1.11   A cartoon in *Punch* commented on bribery in 1853

KING CASH!—THE BOSS OF EVERY ELECTION.

SOURCE 1.12   Despite evidence of reduced corruption, the cartoonist Cheffins in *Illustrated Bits* suggests that candidates' wealth was still important in 1885

FOCUS ROUTE

Note your answers to the following questions:

1 Why was further reform needed?
2 Why did Liberal politicians take up the issue?
3 What part did public pressure play?
4 How did the Act make Britain more democratic?
5 How did the Act change party organisation and national campaigning?

TALKING POINT

Is it a problem that politicians sometimes support a cause for selfish reasons? Does that devalue the support?

E How important was the Third Reform Act of 1884–85?

What was the need for reform?

The Second Reform Act in 1867 had given the vote to householders in boroughs but not in the counties. There was an idea that townsmen were more knowledgeable about government and society and therefore better able to vote than country people. Even if this were true, it was impossible to make a clear distinction. Borough constituencies included some villages with agricultural labourers. County ones included medium-sized towns and about 500,000 coalminers who seemed much like industrial workers. The terms of the 1867 Reform Act had resulted from manoeuvres in Parliament, and it was impossible to defend the anomalies.

There was also a strong argument for redistributing MPs, as about a quarter of the voters elected two thirds of MPs, but this did not generally trouble the politicians so much at the time.

Why did Liberal politicians take up the issue?

From 1872 Gladstone said publicly that the difference between county and borough voting rights should not continue. The Liberals became more enthusiastic for reform when the Conservatives won many county seats in the 1874 election. Many Liberal MPs, including Gladstone, supported it in their addresses for the 1880 election.

Radical Liberals pressed for the change during Gladstone's second ministry (1880–85). Gladstone himself saw the opportunity to achieve a major reform and thought giving workers the vote in the counties would undermine Conservative strength there and help future Liberal election success. He was not so keen on redistributing House of Commons seats.

What part did public pressure play in 1884–85?

The reform was introduced because of a government decision, not public demand. As Gladstone put it in the Commons: he was not concerned whether or not agricultural labourers wanted the vote; 'the State wants it for them'. Conservatives in the Commons agreed to the bill to extend voting rights in 1884 and did not vote against it. Conservatives in the Lords defeated it because there was no scheme to redistribute seats. While Liberals were likely to benefit from extending the vote, Conservatives saw they could gain from the redistribution.

There were then public demonstrations in favour of reform and against the Lords. It is estimated that protesters held 1200–1300 meetings, many of which were large demonstrations. Over 100,000 men from nearby counties were reported to have marched to a big meeting at Hyde Park. There were similarities with the pressure on Parliament in 1867.

It is hard to assess the impact because the Lords were bargaining with the Liberal government about the terms of the reform, not trying to stop the change taking place.

In 1867 politicians debated whether there should be reform at all. In 1884 there was general agreement between the parties about extending the vote. Politicians haggled over the details as they attempted to gain most advantage for their own party.

The terms of the Third Reform Act

The Second Reform Act in 1867 had given the vote to householders and £10 lodgers in boroughs (see page 15). The Third Reform Act extended the same qualifications to the counties. Whereas there had been separate acts for Scotland and Ireland in 1867–68, there was now one measure for the whole UK, including Ireland.

Who could vote?
- Rate-paying householders and £10 lodgers if they had been resident for at least a year
- A few voters in certain boroughs who still had ancient rights to vote dating from before the First Reform Act in 1832.

Who could vote more than once?
- Men with degrees from any of five universities with the right to elect MPs
- Men who lived as householders in one constituency and qualified for a vote by occupying or owning property in another – generally business premises.

Who could not vote?
- Men who moved and had not been in their homes long enough
- Men who were not householders, e.g. soldiers and sailors in the armed forces, servants living with employers, sons living with their families
- Men receiving poor relief
- All women
- Anyone under 21.

Who could vote under the new Act?

- The electorate grew from about 3½ million to 5½ million. Overall the increase was about 60 per cent, but in Ireland it was about 230 per cent.
- The main qualification to vote was still to be a householder, whereas Radicals wanted manhood suffrage. An amendment to give women the vote was rejected in the House of Commons.

  Gladstone's view of voting qualifications was based more on nineteenth-century traditions than democratic ideas. The numbers registered to vote fluctuated around 63–66 per cent of all adult men. As some people had second votes, this meant that around 60 per cent of men were electors.

Who could not vote?

What about the other 40 per cent?

- Most men who could not vote were off the electoral register because they had not been in their homes long enough. An elector had to live in an area for a year before he could go on the register, and this did not come into force for another six months, so moving house often meant 18–24 months without a vote. Such men were not permanently excluded – they just went on and off the register.
- About 12 per cent did not vote because they were not householders or lodgers (see Chart 1F).
- Many lodgers had difficulty in getting themselves registered and might have to defend their right in electoral registration courts.
- About 7 per cent of the votes were extra ones belonging to men who already had a vote as householders. These plural voters were mainly wealthy men, and there was no limit to the number of votes they could have (see Chart 1F).

How were MPs distributed under the new Act?

Previously there was a divide between county and borough constituencies, and most areas sent two MPs to Parliament. This system was largely replaced by smaller areas with roughly equal population, each electing a single MP. Towns with 50,000–165,000 population still kept two MPs each in the traditional way. The population of the largest constituency was now only eight times that of the smallest, instead of 250 times as before, but that still left large differences. Ireland kept over 100 MPs, so the average Irish constituency had just over half as many voters as the average English one.

What were the effects of reform?

For the first time in British history, there was now a big working-class majority in the electorate, though historians have debated how significant this was. Some workers were excluded because they received poor relief, moved house or had lodgings which were not worth £10 a year. Accordingly, historians used to assume that the working-class proportion of the electorate was much smaller than the proportion in the country as a whole. More recently Duncan Tanner (1990) has used local research to suggest that these factors actually reduced the working-class proportion of electors by no more than 4–5 per cent. The group most affected by the residency requirement were young men (both working class and middle class) because they tended to move around more than older men.

The working man had to think twice before he spent a halfpenny; perhaps he would only buy a daily paper once or twice a week, perhaps not at all … Sunday papers were very popular in those days. Many people who could not afford a daily paper depended upon the Sunday papers for their news … they contained a re-hash of the news of the whole week.

ACTIVITY

Compare Source 1.14 with Source 1 on page 7 and Chart C on page 9. How far does this suggest political campaigning on the streets changed or stayed the same from the mid-nineteenth century to the First World War?

SOURCE 1.14 How street campaigning had developed by the early 1900s: a travelling Conservative van in 1907

A working-class majority was, however, slow to produce working-class politicians. (You will return to this story in Chapters 9 and 13.) In the short term there was a gradual shift in political power from the landowners to the middle class. Whereas about two thirds of MPs had come from landowning families in 1865, under a third did in 1900.

The social make-up of the Cabinet changed gradually, and there was a shift from a landowning to a middle-class majority among ministers in the early twentieth century. New Conservative MPs as well as Liberal ones were mainly middle-class industrialists or professionals after 1885, and even most British county MPs were no longer from the traditional landed class by 1914.

The redistribution of seats at first seemed to help the Conservatives. Having done badly in the towns before, they were able to win new constituencies in middle-class suburbs, but it is not clear that they benefited so much in the long run, and they lost out through Ireland being over-represented.

Party organisation and national campaigns became still more important. Both the main parties continued to develop a national network of clubs and associations, but the Conservatives had most success. This was partly because getting funds was so vital, and they had far more wealthy supporters. (Source 1.14 shows one way in which funds were spent.)

Having grown rapidly through the century, the sale of daily newspapers roughly quadrupled from 1896 to 1914, and national newspapers became much more important in the early 1900s (see Source 1.13). The *Daily Mail* occasionally sold a million copies a day in the excitement of the Boer War around 1900, and the *Daily Mirror* achieved a regular sale of a million in 1912.

ACTIVITY

This chart shows the various ways that electors could influence politicians and politicians could influence voters. Which direction do you think the influence runs in 1900? Redraw the chart with arrows and labels to explain your view. In your labels include evidence from the chapter.

You can keep this chart and return to it or add to it as you find out more about:
a) the development of trade unions (Chapter 8)
b) the development of the national parties (Section 4).

```
                    Public meetings
                   Local organisations
                    Election campaigns
   VOTERS                                    POLITICIANS
                     Pressure groups
                      Newspapers
              New parties to replace the old
```

CHAPTER I REVIEW ACTIVITY

How democratic was Britain by 1900?

The diagram on the right shows various ways people might measure democracy.

Work in pairs with one person arguing that Britain was democratic in 1900 and the other arguing that it was not. Before you start note your own ideas about the key questions in the diagram. Below are some key points that you might include in your arguments. You can find much more evidence through the chapter to support your argument, whichever side you are taking.

❶ What proportion of people can vote?

❷ Do electors have enough information to vote knowledgeably?

❸ Are electors bribed or intimidated?

Measures of democracy

❹ Is anyone able to stand for election regardless of wealth or social class?

❺ Are votes of equal value – i.e. do all MPs represent an equivalent number of voters?

❻ ?

After the Third Reform Act roughly 60 per cent of all men could vote	In 1900 no women were allowed to vote in Parliamentary elections	Constituencies were rearranged in 1885 but they still had very different populations	MPs were not paid so only people who had some other income could become an MP
The 1883 Corrupt and Illegal Practices Act worked well to stop bribery and corruption	Circulation and readership of national and regional newspapers grew massively in the second half of the century. They covered election campaigns in detail	Trade unions had started to sponsor working-class candidates for Parliament	Secret balloting had replaced the open vote
By 1880 education was compulsory so by 1900 most of the young population could read and write	Parties developed national organisations and sponsored local clubs to run their local campaigns	Factional and religious views influenced discussion of some key political issues	The main political parties did not publish a national manifesto before an election.

KEY POINTS FROM CHAPTER I

How democratic was Britain by 1900?

1 Only a minority of men could vote in the mid-nineteenth century. They voted openly, and election campaigns involved significant bribery.

2 Politicians' changing beliefs, party political manoeuvres and public pressure may all have contributed to getting the Second Reform Act in 1867, although historians have disagreed about which factors were most important.

3 The 1867 Act gave the vote to most working men in boroughs and led to important developments in party organisation and campaigning.

4 The Ballot Act (1872) and Corrupt and Illegal Practices Act (1883) did much to change election campaigning.

5 There was some pressure to give the vote to working men in the counties on the same terms as in the boroughs, and this was done in the Third Reform Act in 1884–85.

6 There was also a large-scale redistribution of MPs to ensure that the electors in different areas were more fairly represented in 1885.

7 Only about 60 per cent of men and no women could vote for Parliament before the First World War.

Why did it take so long for women to get the vote?

CHAPTER OVERVIEW

As you studied the extension of voting rights in Chapter 1 you may have been surprised at the lack of reference to women. None of the Reform Acts extended the vote to women. Indeed women had actually lost rights in the early nineteenth century. The 1832 Reform Act and 1835 Municipal Corporations Act, stating who could elect the House of Commons and borough councils, specifically said that only males could vote even though women had sometimes voted before that, particularly in council elections.

A few women campaigned for the vote from the mid-nineteenth century, and they gained support, slowly. Indeed by 1897 they had a majority of MPs on their side. Why then did it take another 21 years and a world war for women to win the right to vote? That is the theme of this chapter.

You will examine:

A How much did women's position change from 1851 to 1914? (pp. 25–26)

B Why was there so much controversy about women having the vote? (pp. 26–28)

C How much did women's suffrage movements achieve by 1903? (pp. 29–30)

D Did the Suffragettes' activities after 1903 help or hinder women getting the vote? (pp. 30–33)

E Why did women get the vote in 1918? (pp. 34–35)

F Review (p. 35)

SOURCE 1 The atmosphere at an election after the First World War: photos from the *Graphic* showing prominent politicians meeting voters in 1923, including Lady Astor (top right), the first woman to enter Parliament as an MP after the First World War

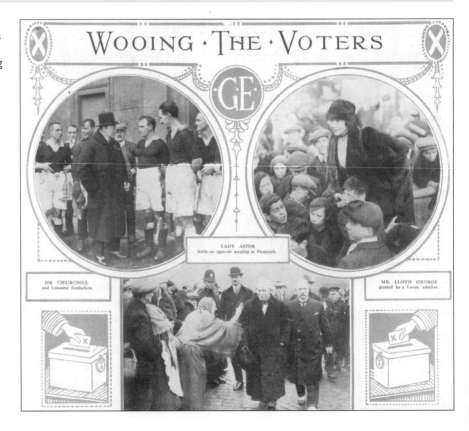

FOCUS ROUTE

Make notes as follows:
1 Between 1851 and 1914 what were the most important gains in women's
   a) legal rights
   b) educational and job opportunities
   c) power in local government?
2 How significant would you judge each gain to be?

TALKING POINT

What do the changes in women's rights suggest about changing attitudes to their roles in politics and society?

A How much did women's position change from 1851 to 1914?

In 1851 even middle- and upper-class girls had few opportunities for advanced education and, apart from teaching, there were no obvious opportunities for them in the professions or in business when they grew up. They were increasingly seen as ornaments in the home who did charity work and managed the servants. Working-class women, in contrast, usually had paid jobs because the family budget required it.

Neither middle-class nor working-class women had what we today regard as basic civil rights. Between 1851 and 1914 this situation changed slowly. Women did gain more rights and opportunities in different ways.

DISCUSS

1 Among women, which social groups appear to have gained the most rights and opportunities between 1851 and 1914?
2 Why were there differences between married and unmarried women in terms of political rights?
3 How would greater education and opportunities for work increase the demand for women to have the vote?

Legal rights

Before 1870 a woman's property became her husband's on marriage. The Married Women's Property Acts in 1870 and 1882 allowed women to have their own property and income after they married.

The repeal of the Contagious Diseases Act in 1886 stopped the forcible medical examinations of women whom the police suspected of being prostitutes. The original Act of 1864 had been designed to stop the spread of sexually transmitted diseases, especially among soldiers and sailors, but both the aims and methods used were seen as an insult to women.

Education

More elementary schools were founded to educate girls in the working class. North London Collegiate School and Cheltenham Ladies' College, founded in 1850 and 1854, provided an academic secondary education for the middle and upper classes. The Girls' Public Day School Trust was established in 1872 to extend this. More girls' grammar schools were established and more women went to universities from the late nineteenth century.

Employment

Many working-class women had paid employment in manual jobs such as making textiles, and there were about 2 million women employed as domestic servants.

Secretarial work and elementary school teaching were the main non-manual jobs for women. A small but increasing number got into skilled professions. For example, the number of female doctors grew from 20 in 1881 to 447 in 1911.

Local government

Women's participation in local administration depended on customs and individual court decisions as well as laws. The main developments were:

1834 Women could be POOR LAW GUARDIANS as the law did not stop them, but no woman seems to have been elected until 1875
1869 Unmarried women who paid rates could vote in town council elections
1870 Women ratepayers could vote for and join school boards
1888 Unmarried women ratepayers could vote for county councils
1894 Married as well as unmarried women ratepayers could vote for parish and district councils and could belong to them as councillors
1907 Women could be county councillors.

Under the 1902 Education Act, county council education committees had to have at least one female member. Under the 1905 Unemployed Workmen's Act, there had to be one woman on each local distress committee.

POOR LAW GUARDIANS
People elected by the ratepayers in a local area, known as a Poor Law union, to fix rates (local taxes) there and organise relief (help) for the poor.

TALKING POINT

Women were required to be members of education and distress committees because of the type of work they did. Is this a sign of gender stereotyping or increasing equality?

CANVASSING
Trying to persuade people to vote for a particular political party or issue.

Party politics

Women did much of the work for political parties, including CANVASSING, getting voters out to vote in elections and sometimes public speaking. Women eventually made up 49 per cent of the members in the Conservatives' Primrose League and were leaders of a quarter of the branches (see page 168). The Women's Liberal Federation was formed in 1887.

FOCUS ROUTE

The case for women voting was based on several different types of argument:
a) women's **rights** as equal citizens
b) women's **need** to overcome disadvantages
c) women's **wish** to participate
d) **positive impact** – a good effect on the country as a whole.
List the points made on pages 27–28 that would support or counter each of these arguments.

B Why was there so much controversy about women having the vote?

DISCUSS

1 Many prominent women opposed women's suffrage. Which arguments from Chart 2A do you think they were most likely to use against it?
2 Compare Source 2.2 with 2.1.
   a) How does their impression of women differ?
   b) Which do you think is the more effective piece of propaganda? Give reasons.
3 How would you explain the different impressions of the role of women given in Sources 2.2 and 2.3?

SOURCE 2.1 A postcard in favour of women having the vote, 1912

SOURCE 2.2 An anti-Suffragist postcard from 1905

SOURCE 2.3 Women at work in a Kidderminster carpet factory, 1902

FOR

AGAINST

- Women should vote because of their **individual rights** as human beings. Nineteenth-century laws prevented women from voting but a few had apparently voted in the past.

- MPs claim to represent non-voters but in reality they are not likely to look after non-voters in the same way as voters.

- Working men are struggling to get representation for their interests in Parliament. Women need representation to get rid of discrimination against them.

- Giving the vote to uneducated male agricultural workers and unskilled labourers has not damaged the country. How could giving the vote to educated women harm the country?

- Women who pay rates and taxes have a right to representation like other taxpayers.

- Men can have sex with women and walk away from the consequences too easily, leaving the women stigmatised and forced to look after illegitimate children. Women need political power to change men's attitudes to sex.

- If women can be doctors, lawyers and town councillors, they are capable of voting sensibly. Britain has grown great under a female ruler – Queen Victoria.

- Health, welfare and education are becoming more important in politics. Women have a different understanding of these from men.

- According to the 1911 census, 55 per cent of single women and 10 per cent of married women are in paid employment. Our **sphere** is already outside the home.

- Women have voted in New Zealand from 1893 and in the Australian federation from 1902. The system works well in these essentially British societies. Women also have the vote in some states of the USA.

- If women can canvass for political parties and run political campaigns, why should they not vote?

- Women are represented by men. Men who vote act on behalf of the whole community, including women and those men who do not have the vote. This virtual representation is a longstanding part of the British constitution.

- The current system works well. Victorian Britain had unparalleled economic and imperial achievements. Don't risk changing it.

- Women having the vote may split families and divide society as a whole.

- If all adults have the vote, women will be in a majority.

- Most national taxes are paid by men. Women who pay local rates already vote in local elections.

- There are better ways of improving men's morals than by giving women a vote.

- Women are too emotional and sentimental to have power, and they are biologically different – they are not well balanced when they are having their periods. As for Queen Victoria, she detested the idea of women voting.

- Women might be well suited to take part in local government which deals with social welfare but they are not fitted to manage foreign affairs and defence. The knowledge that women had power in Britain could weaken the Empire in the East where Orientals see things differently from us.

- There are **separate spheres** for men and women. The woman's role is in the home, not in public life.

- So far giving women the vote has only been tried in smaller and less powerful countries without the same imperial and economic problems as Britain.

- Women already have much influence in politics and society. Why do they need a vote as well?

DISCUSS

4 Which of the arguments in Chart 2A are used in Sources 2.1 and 2.2?

5 Which argument against women voting do you think was strongest in the circumstances before the First World War and why?

TALKING POINT

Few, if any, of the arguments against women's suffrage would be taken seriously in western societies today. To what extent is this because of experience over the last century and/or changed beliefs about what is right and wrong.

ACTIVITY

Sources 2.4–2.6 use a range of arguments for and against women's voting rights.
a) Read each source and give it a headline summing up its key point(s).
b) Compare Sources 2.4 and 2.6. How do they use different values in judging foreign policy?
c) Compare Sources 2.4 and 2.5. Which do you think is the strongest argument and why?
d) How do you think the authors of Sources 2.4 or 2.5 might respond to the point made in paragraph 1 of Source 2.6?

SOURCE 2.4 Mrs Fawcett, the Suffragist leader, in a lecture delivered in the early 1890s

Up to the present, my belief is that the home side and political side of things have been kept too far apart, as if they had nothing to do with one another. We have before us the picture of the whole of Europe armed to the teeth, and the great neighbouring nations ready to spring like wild beasts at each other's throats, all for the sake of fancied political advantage, while the true domestic interests of the nations concerned would be almost as much injured by victory as by defeat ...

[Women] will not so often be led away by the gunpowder and glory will-o-the wisp, which is really alien to the womanly nature, but will much more certainly than now cast their influence on whatever side seems to them to make for peace, purity and love.

SOURCE 2.5 Mrs Pankhurst, the Suffragette leader, 1908

[I]t is important that women should have the vote in order that in the government of the country the women's point of view should be put forward ... [An MP's] time is fully taken up by attending to the needs of the people who have sent him to Parliament ... you cannot take up a newspaper, you cannot go to a conference, you cannot even go to church, without hearing a great deal of talk about social reform and a demand for social legislation. Of course, it is obvious that that kind of legislation ... is of vital importance to women ... We are hearing about legislation to decide what kind of homes people are to live in. That surely is a question for women ... Since 1870 men have been trying to find out how to educate children. I think they have not yet realised that if they are ever to find out how to educate children, they will have to take women into their confidence.

SOURCE 2.6 Lord Curzon, a leading Conservative opponent of women's suffrage, in 1912

The whole life of the working man is a political school. The papers which he reads every day, the public meetings which he attends, the debating societies to which many belong, the enormous influence of the Press – all of these are a mechanism for familiarising the working man with his duties ... it is a different question when you come to women ...

Issues sometimes arise in public affairs – you can see them on the horizon now – great issues of peace and war, of treaties and alliances, of the treatment to be adopted to our Colonies and dependencies. An unwise, and still more an emotional, decision of those issues might in circumstances which it is easy to imagine lead to the disruption and even to the ruin of the Empire ... Suppose that it was a question of instituting national compulsory military training in this country. I ask you, are those the sort of questions that in a reflective mood you would wish to be decided by a majority of women? ...

What is the good of talking about the equality of the sexes? The first whiz of the bullet, the first boom of the cannon, and where is the equality of the sexes? When it comes to fighting, war has to be decided, always has been decided, and always will be decided, by one sex alone.

Suffrage, Suffragist and Suffragette

Suffrage means the right to vote.

Suffragist was used to describe people who worked to get women the right to vote, usually by peaceful and legal methods.

Suffragettes belonged to the Women's Social and Political Union started in 1903. This used 'militant' methods to help their cause, including some which broke the law and some involving force (which left-wingers often call 'direct action' and right-wingers describe as illegal, unconstitutional or violent).

Historians have often drawn a distinction between the Suffragettes, who believed in physical methods, and Suffragists, who stayed within the law, but campaigners often changed their methods according to circumstances.

Key dates
Suffragists
1897   National Union of Women's Suffrage Societies (NUWSS), founded by a merger of several societies under the leadership of Millicent Fawcett

Suffragettes
1903   Women's Social and Political Union (WSPU), founded by Emmeline Pankhurst. They used increasingly militant tactics which led to some splits in the WSPU:
1912   Mr and Mrs Pethick-Lawrence, who had been important members, set up the Votes for Women Fellowship
1914   Sylvia Pankhurst formed the East London Federation for working-class women

C How much did women's suffrage movements achieve by 1903?

FOCUS ROUTE

Copy and complete this table summarising the suffrage movement up to 1903.

	Up to 1903	
Achievements		
Failures		
Problems it faced		

Although some women had struggled for more rights in the mid-nineteenth century, a stronger women's suffrage movement developed from discussion over the Second Reform Act in 1866–67. Suffragist organisations came and went and found it difficult to work together. They concentrated on petitioning Parliament and finding BACKBENCH MPS who would introduce bills to give women the vote. Unfortunately it was more and more difficult for ordinary MPs to get parliamentary time for their bills, which had little chance of becoming law. The best prospect was getting or amending a government bill, but there was not yet enough support. Individual Liberal MPs tried to change the Second and Third Reform Acts, but their leader, Gladstone, was against them. He even said he would drop the 1884 bill, rather than agree to women's voting. John Stuart Mill's amendment to the Second Reform Act, to give women the vote on the same terms as men, was turned down by 196 to 73 in 1867 and William Woodall's amendment to the Third by 273 to 137 in 1884.

Historians have generally suggested that the movement declined in the 1890s, but Martin Pugh (2000) stresses the gains it achieved. The different Suffragist groups successfully joined in the National Union of Women's Suffrage Societies (NUWSS) in 1897. More importantly in 1897 they won the first majority they had achieved for women's voting rights when there was a substantial attendance of MPs in the House of Commons. This majority remained in the early 1900s. Their problem was that while Suffragist MPs could get a majority for their bills, they could not get enough time in parliament to get them passed into law. It was the government of the day that effectively controlled the parliamentary timetable, and governments did not want to take up the cause of women's suffrage.

The suffrage movement had a big tactical problem in deciding the terms on which they should try to get the vote. They had two main options.

Option 1
To win voting rights on the same terms as men, so that the vote would go to rate-paying householders and £10 lodgers
Comment: It was usually the man, not his wife, who paid the rates (local taxes), so most married women would not qualify to vote under this option. It would mean about 300,000–400,000 women voting in the 1870s and about 1 million in the early 1900s. These women would then be a small addition to an electorate of nearly 8 million men.

Option 2
To win voting rights on the basis of adult suffrage, so that all men and women could vote
Comment: This would involve a far greater change and produce a female majority in the electorate.

BACKBENCH MPS
MPs who are not ministers in government or leading spokespersons for their parties. Government ministers and the MPs in an opposition party who would be ministers if their party were in government sit on the front benches in Parliament; other MPs sit on the back benches.

The Suffragists looked for support wherever it could be found in the Commons. Most thought Option 1 was more practical and tended to concentrate on it. But Martin Pugh and another leading historian of women's suffrage, Brian Harrison, think women would have had a better chance if they had gone for the more radical Option 2.

The Suffragists got a majority in the Commons largely through winning support from Conservative MPs. Indeed successive Conservative leaders – Disraeli, Salisbury and then Balfour – favoured some women having the vote (although only a small number of women ratepayers who they thought likely to support the Tories). Women's concern with religion, morals and home life fitted in well with Conservative beliefs. Nevertheless, many of the Suffragists' strongest opponents were Conservative MPs and especially Conservative peers.

Individual Liberal MPs had generally given them the most useful support, but their leaders were divided. Liberals feared that giving the vote to women ratepayers on the same terms as men would benefit the Conservatives at their expense. The Liberal Party was also often divided between MPs who worked for narrow, specialised reforms, and Gladstone saw women's suffrage as another troublesome issue dividing the party.

FOCUS ROUTE

Add a third column to your chart from Section C summarising the situation 1903–14.

D Did the Suffragettes' activities after 1903 help or hinder women getting the vote?

After 1903 the Suffragettes adopted more militant tactics.

■ 2B Suffragette tactics

ACTION

Heckling politicians at meetings

AUTHORITIES' RESPONSE

Threw hecklers out of meetings. The Liberal Party banned Suffragettes from attending their election meetings

Demonstrations and protest marches

Arrested and imprisoned demonstrators for short periods if they broke the law

Window breaking. Mary Leigh broke the first window in Downing Street in 1908. Subsequently the Suffragettes targeted government offices, newspapers, gentlemen's clubs and shops

Arrested window breakers and imprisoned them for short periods

Hunger strikes in prison. (Hunger strikers refuse to eat as a protest.) Marion Wallace Dunlop was the first hunger striker in 1909

Force-fed the hunger strikers. After this caused an outcry, they passed the 'Cat and Mouse' Act (1913). This allowed them to release hunger strikers until they regained their strength and then re-arrest them

Attacks on property. For example Suffragettes set fire to post office letter boxes (from 1911) and empty buildings. The Chancellor of the Exchequer's new house was fire-bombed in 1913

Imprisoned law-breakers

As a result of their actions:

- The Suffragettes got much more **publicity** for the women's cause.
- This led to far bigger **membership**. WSPU numbers grew. At the same time women also joined several non-militant suffrage organisations. These groups used different means but worked in the same direction, and the number of local societies affiliated to the National Union of Women's Suffrage Societies (NUWSS) increased from 16 in 1903 to over 300 in 1911. They had over 50,000 members by 1914.
- The Suffragettes got far more **money** than other groups and their paper *Votes for Women* sold about 30,000 copies a week.

Despite this they did not achieve the political result they were after.

In Parliament

In 1910 an all-party committee of MPs came up with a scheme known as the Conciliation Bill to give the vote to women householders on the same terms as men. It would give about one million women a vote. As this looked like progress the Suffragettes suspended militant action. Unfortunately the Liberal government of the time saw it as a real problem. First, the prime minister, Asquith, was against women getting the vote anyway. Even Liberal ministers who were in favour, such as Lloyd George and Churchill, feared that these million would generally be wealthy Conservative supporters. One Independent Labour Party survey suggested over 80 per cent were working class, but it is hard to know. In such situations what politicians think is true is more influential that what is actually true, and Lloyd George thought they would 'add hundreds of thousands of votes to the strength of the Tory Party'.

The Conciliation Bill got a massive majority in the Commons in 1911 but it was not a government bill and had little hope of progressing without government support. In November, the Liberal government announced it would introduce a new bill of its own. This would give all adult men a vote. Ministers said an amendment could be introduced by MPs to extend the vote to women as well, but as this was likely to propose a vote for **all** adult women it was a very different matter from the Conciliation Bill. At this point the Suffragettes restarted their campaign of violence.

The SPEAKER of the House of Commons said he would not allow an amendment to the government's bill, giving women the vote, because that would alter its character. In these changed circumstances the Conciliation Bill was defeated in 1912. The government also abandoned its proposed bill because of the controversy.

Reaction to militancy

Suffragette militancy may well have been partly responsible for the failure in Parliament (see Sources 2.7–2.9). Certainly there was a sense that the issue for many influential people was not whether women should have the vote but how to deal with the militancy.

SPEAKER
Chairperson in the House of Commons who makes decisions on procedure.

SOURCE 2.7 In a letter to *The Times*, March 1912, Sydney Buxton, a Liberal Cabinet minister, explained why he was voting against the Conciliation Bill after supporting it before

I feel convinced that to pass the Bill just now might appear to be, and would undoubtedly be claimed by the militants and their admirers to be, a justification for and an endorsement by the House of Commons of their methods and actions.

SOURCE 2.8 In a letter to the *Evening Standard*, August 1912, Millicent Fawcett, leader of the NUWSS, which believed in using legal methods alone, explained the Conciliation Bill's defeat

[The militants were now] the chief obstacles in the way of the success of the Suffrage movement in the House of Commons, and far more formidable opponents of it than Mr Asquith or Mr Harcourt (anti-Suffragists in the Cabinet).

SOURCE 2.9 In a private letter, Christabel Pankhurst, referring to the situation in Ireland, claimed the Liberal government was giving way to violence

The Liberals can no longer say that the Government will not yield to violence because [they] are doing so. Unionists [Conservatives supporting the union with Ireland and backing Ulster Protestants] ... can no longer say that violence is not legitimate when used by women because they have threatened it themselves.

DISCUSS

1 In what ways do Sources 2.7 and 2.8 suggest militancy may have harmed the cause of women's suffrage?
2 In 1912 the Liberal government had to deal not only with Suffragette protest but also with military preparations by Unionists resisting Home Rule in Ireland (see page 244) and with widespread strikes by trade unionists (page 147). How might this have affected the way ministers responded to the Suffragette campaign?
3 How does Christabel Pankhurst argue in Source 2.10 (page 32) that violence is necessary to gain votes for women?
4 What aspects of the situation in 1908, apart from past experience, could be used to justify women using force?

TALKING POINT

'Violence is justifiable in order to achieve constitutional change.' Discuss.

FENIAN
Fenians were members of an Irish Republican Brotherhood, started in Ireland and the USA in 1858, who believed in using force to overthrow British rule.

DISESTABLISHMENT
Disestablishing a Church meant removing the privileges it had through being connected with the State, particularly land and other wealth. See also page 41.

SOURCE 2.11 Annie Kenney, the most famous Suffragette with a working-class background, photographed in 1907 in her mill girl's clothes

SOURCE 2.12 Three Suffragette women photographed in 1909 just before they chained themselves to some railings

SOURCE 2.10 Christabel Pankhurst puts the case for militant methods in 1908

Magna Carta was secured because of the fear that the people succeeded in implanting in the mind of King John. We must make Mr Asquith as much afraid of us as King John was of the Barons ... The Reform Bills – how were they obtained? Were they obtained by milk-and-water methods? Were they obtained by coaxing the Government, by trying to win their sympathy? No. They were got by hard fighting, and they could have been got in no other way.

Some forty years ago there were FENIAN outrages in Manchester, and the blowing up of Clerkenwell Gaol. What did those two terrible events prompt Mr Gladstone to say? He said that they had drawn the attention of England to the fact that there were grievances in Ireland. What did those two events prompt him to do? He DISESTABLISHED the Irish Church! How anybody after that can say that militant methods are not effectual, I do not know.

The Suffragettes had frequently focused their campaigning on by-elections (when voters choose a single MP). In 1912 there was a by-election at Bromley and Bow in the East End of London that was clearly about women's suffrage. George Lansbury, the sitting Labour MP, resigned his seat to campaign on the women's suffrage issue and the Suffragettes worked hard for him. He had one opponent – an anti-Suffragist Conservative. When Lansbury lost his seat it looked like a Suffragette defeat and in particular a vote against Suffragette militancy.

There was more hostility to the Suffragettes between 1912 and 1914. Their meetings were often violently broken up and they needed police protection.

As the violence escalated, by 1913 Suffragette membership subscriptions were falling, while the peaceful Suffragist movements took new initiatives and apparently still grew.

What sort of movement was the Suffragette movement?

The Pankhurst family ran the WSPU without any democratic arrangements for the members to make decisions. They needed a clear chain of command to plan and use physical action successfully, but could this be justified in a movement trying to win democratic rights for women? Certainly it led to lots of splits. Mr and Mrs Pethick-Lawrence, who had provided much of the Suffragettes' money, were expelled in 1912, and Mrs Pankhurst's daughter, Sylvia, was thrown out in 1913.

The Pankhursts
Mrs Emmeline Pankhurst was married to a Radical lawyer. She worked for the Independent Labour Party (ILP) in the 1890s, campaigned for women's rights and was a Poor Law guardian (see page 25) for several years. After her husband's death she started the WSPU in 1903 to fight actively in favour of votes for women. Her three daughters – Christabel, Sylvia and Adela – all supported the movement. **Christabel** worked closely with her mother and particularly championed militant methods (see Source 2.10). The two of them eventually split with **Sylvia** who, in 1914, developed an East London Federation for women's rights and insisted on working with the Labour Party when her mother wanted to be independent of political parties. Adela fell ill, gave up campaigning, took up gardening and went to Australia.

Was is it a socially unrepresentative middle- and upper-class movement?

There were working-class Suffragettes. The most prominent was the Lancashire mill girl Annie Kenney (see Source 2.11). There were WSPU branches in working-class areas of London and a significant worker membership in Glasgow and Liverpool. Evidence of some working-class members has turned up by chance in historians' researches suggesting there may well be more. Yet the general tone of the movement was clearly middle or upper class. Suffragettes held lots of 'At Homes' and drawing room meetings, and expensive West End shops advertised regularly in their paper *Votes for Women*. There was a substantial workers' movement for women's rights in Lancashire, described by Liddington and Norris, but it was largely separate from the Suffragettes. Other areas did not apparently have so many women factory workers or such strong organisations.

ACTIVITY

1 How do Sources 2.11 and 2.12 give a very different impression of the Suffragette movement?

2 The picture of Annie Kenney was taken in a photographic studio and she was by then a full-time paid organiser for the Suffragettes. Why do you think she dressed like this and what use could be made of the picture?

TALKING POINTS

The Suffragettes' struggle is linked with two important and controversial twenty-first-century issues:

- women's rights and role in politics
- how far street demonstrations and other physical action can or should bring changes.

Their campaign is linked with strong images. Their enemies caricatured them as sex starved, lesbian, mentally unbalanced or neglecting their families. They countered with images of heroic sacrifice. Emily Davison, who was killed by horses running in the Derby in 1913, was soon presented as a martyr. The images make historical judgement harder.

1 To what extent are you influenced by traditional images or modern controversies when studying the Suffragettes?

2 How far do you think you can study them in an objective or unbiased way?

In summer 1914 Asquith and Lloyd George made contact with the East London Federation, a more working-class organisation than either the NUWSS or the WSPU. It was also much more moderate than the WSPU. It did not support the use of violence. Asquith may have been hoping to win left-wing support but also to show that he was willing to deal with a group that did not use the extreme tactics of the Suffragettes. The discussions were making progress but the outbreak of the First World War altered the whole situation.

■ 2C Historians' views of the Suffragettes

Masculinist historian

Judges the Suffragettes by how effective they were in persuading men to give women the vote. This leads to criticisms of their methods – that they did not use the most effective means possible in the existing political system. They failed to play the political game and so showed their naïvety.

Feminist historian

Considers the suffrage movement was part of a broader struggle for women's rights and helped change the way women see themselves. The delay in getting the vote can be seen as the fault of the men who denied it rather than the women who did not follow the men's rules about political debate.

ACTIVITY

Work in pairs, with one person writing an account of Suffragette activity from a 'masculinist' viewpoint and one from a 'feminist' viewpoint. Male students should if possible attempt this from a feminist viewpoint and female ones from a masculinist viewpoint.

Feminist historians emphasise less the Suffragettes' own violence, more the way hostile men attacked them. In *Votes for Women* (Holton and Purvis, eds, 2000) June Purvis, a leading feminist historian, ends an article on 'Daily life in the WSPU' with a ringing declaration: 'Their courage, bravery and faith, particularly when enduring repeated imprisonments and the torture of forcible feeding, remain an inspiration to us all.'

E Why did women get the vote in 1918?

After all the campaigns of the previous decades the way that women finally got the vote seems almost an anti-climax. This is how it happened.

As soon as war broke out in 1914 the Suffragettes called off their campaign of violence. Both Suffragette and Suffragist leaders gave full support to the war effort. As the demands of wartime production led to a shortage of workers they also backed the government in recruiting a large number of female workers to fill the jobs vacated by men who had joined the army. This story is covered on page 268–269.

Meanwhile the government had a different problem. In 1916 the government needed to make plans for a general election. If they used the existing register of electors then soldiers who were serving their country by fighting in the Great War would not be allowed to vote because they would not qualify as householders or lodgers, and they were not even in the country. Something had to be done and the government set up a committee drawn from all parties in the Lords and the Commons, under the chairmanship of the Speaker (who was not aligned to any party) to suggest solutions.

The Suffragists saw their chance. With Suffragette violence before the war an increasingly distant memory, the Suffragists resumed their campaign of deputations and letter-writing to MPs. When the Speaker's committee put forward its proposals in 1917, they included not only measures to allow soldiers to vote but also a proposal to give the vote to women over 30 who were ratepayers or the wives of ratepayers. It received cross-party support in Parliament and duly became law as the Fourth Reform Act in 1918.

> **PROPORTIONAL REPRESENTATION**
> Arrangements for electing an assembly so that the number of members for each party is in proportion to the votes for the party.
>
> **ALTERNATIVE VOTE**
> System of voting where voters number candidates 1, 2, 3, etc. in order of preference.

■ 2D The Fourth Reform Act, 1918

	Terms	Significance and effects
Who could vote?	• All adult men provided they had been resident in one place for six months • Women over 30 who were ratepayers or wives of ratepayers	• 95% of adult men could vote • Women formed 42–43% of the electorate
Who had more than one vote? (Nobody was allowed more than one extra vote)	Those with business premises in a constituency where they did not live or degrees from some universities	Second votes made up just over 1% of the total
How were MPs distributed and elected?	A boundary commission created constituencies with more equal numbers of voters. Suggestions of different electoral systems, including PROPORTIONAL REPRESENTATION and ALTERNATIVE VOTE, were eventually rejected	The strongest party generally did disproportionately well in elections even if it did not have the support of most voters
Election arrangements	Local councils now ensured electors were registered. Polling at general elections took place everywhere on one day instead of over 3–4 weeks as before. Election expenses were more restricted, and candidates got a free mail delivery to all electors	It was cheaper to fight elections

This was a significant turnaround from the situation in 1914. So the question arises as to why this happened. Historians have debated the significance of the different factors that contributed to the change of heart:

• the suspension of the Suffragette campaign of violence
• the support of the women's leaders for the war effort
• the work that hundreds of thousands of women were doing in wartime industries
• the Suffragist lobbying in 1916.

SOURCE 2.13 Asquith speaking in the House of Commons, March 1917

I think that some years ago I ventured to use the expression 'Let the women work out their own salvation'. Well, Sir, they have worked it out during this War: How could we have carried on the War without them?

This famous statement from Lord Asquith (Source 2.13), one of the pre-war opponents of female suffrage, points towards the significance of women's war work but it is undoubtedly more complicated than that. For example, the suspension of Suffragette violence in 1914 would have had no meaning if there had been no campaign of violence in the first place, so any explanation needs to consider the impact of the campaign of violence before the war as well as its suspension. Furthermore the war work argument has an ironic twist in that the vote was granted to women over 30 while more young women had taken up wartime jobs than older women. If Parliament had intended to reward the war workers it partly rewarded the wrong women.

F Review

Historians do not agree about the relative importance of the Suffragists, the Suffragettes and the First World War. It is the Suffragettes who get the most attention from historians. Since the 1970s there has been intense debate about their role and in particular about their campaign of violence. Andrew Rosen presented a strongly critical view in *Rise up Women!* (1974), suggesting how Suffragettes harmed the women's cause. Martin Pugh, who has researched the women's movement extensively, takes a more balanced but still critical line, well developed in *The March of the Women* (2000). Other historians, writing from a feminist viewpoint, emphasise the Suffragettes' positive contribution to the campaign and their long-term role in helping women to gain rights. Sandra Holton took this more favourable view in *Feminism and Democracy* (1986) and more recently with June Purvis in *Votes for Women* (2000).

As for the relative importance of women's war work, this is returned to in Chapter 15 where it can be examined in context. Most agree it was undoubtedly an important factor in gaining women the vote, but most would also argue this depended on other factors. Maybe its most critical significance was that it gave politicians a valid excuse for doing what they wanted to do anyway – give some women the vote – but which the strained atmosphere of the pre-war period had made impossible.

CHAPTER 2 REVIEW ACTIVITY

1 Look back over pages 25–35. Make a list of all the factors that helped lead to women getting the vote in 1918.
2 Now make a separate list of factors that slowed down progress towards women winning the vote.
3 From each list choose your two most important factors.
4 Discuss your chosen factors with others and try to reach agreement on which were most important.

KEY POINTS FROM CHAPTER 2

Why did it take so long for women to get the vote?

1 There was extensive discrimination against women in the nineteenth century. Although women gained some more rights and opportunities from 1851 to 1914, they did not get the vote until 1918.

2 There were big differences within the Conservative and Liberal parties over whether women should get the vote.

3 A late-nineteenth-century campaign for women's voting rights gained significant support, but women had the vote only for local council elections, not parliamentary ones.

4 The Suffragette movement campaigned vigorously from 1903, but its militancy became very controversial, and it is hard to assess its effects.

5 In 1918 the vote was eventually extended to all adult men and most women over 30.

How far did **Britain** move towards democracy 1851–1918?

There is more to democracy than how you run elections but as that has been the main focus of this section that is what we are focusing on in this review. In the table below we compare different features of British electoral politics in the 1850s, in 1918 and in the early twenty-first century.

■ **A Ways of comparing the political system and assessing democracy from the nineteenth century to the twenty-first century**

	Mid-nineteenth century	1918	Twenty-first century
Voters	• About 20 per cent of adult men had the vote and no women	• Men over 21 and most women over 30 had the vote	• Adults over 18 have the vote
Constituencies	• Constituencies electing MPs had very unequal populations	• Constituencies were roughly equal in population	• Constituency boundaries are adjusted according to population every 8–10 years so that they remain roughly equal
The ballot	• Electors voted openly, so employers and landowners could influence them, and there was extensive bribery	• There was a secret ballot, and there were laws against bribery and corruption	• As in 1918
Campaigns	• Elections were fought on national and local issues. Newspapers were important, but many electors heard candidates' speeches	• Elections were fought predominantly on national issues. Newspapers and pamphlets were the main way of learning about issues, but some electors went to local meetings. There was concern about the influence of newspaper owners	• National issues generally dominate elections. TV is the most important way of reaching electors, but there is still concern about the impact of newspaper owners. 'Spin doctors' have developed methods to influence the media on behalf of political parties
Corruption	• Wealthy men used their influence locally, and this affected government policies and parliamentary debates. There was little scope for politicians to use patronage – giving people jobs for personal and political reasons, rather than on merit	• There was still little opportunity for politicians to use patronage, though there was soon to be a controversy about how agents of the prime minister (Lloyd George) seemed to be selling honours	• There are strict laws against corruption, but there are queries about the influence of wealthy men who contribute to political party funds and whether money spent on government advertising benefits the governing party

1 Draw a continuum like this:

1851 ── today

2 For each row of the table decide whether the situation in 1918, at the end of the First World War, was more like 1851 or more like today. Mark each feature at the point on your continuum where you think it belongs.

3 Write some paragraphs to explain your chart.

4 What are the main features on this chart that suggest
   a) Britain was not fully a democracy in 1918
   b) Britain is not fully a democracy in the twenty-first century?

5 Finally, write a paragraph to summarise your answer to the question: How far did Britain progress towards democracy 1851–1918?

The Section 4 Review on page 222 also examines progress towards democracy through political parties.

TALKING POINT

From the Second World War to the early twenty-first century no political party in government in Britain has won the support of over half the electors who voted. For example, Labour won 36 per cent of the votes in the 2005 election but gained 56 per cent of the MPs. Is modern Britain therefore a democracy or not?

Gladstone and Disraeli – how great were the differences between them?

William Gladstone (1809–98)

1832
Entered Parliament as a strong Tory

1868–74
In his sixties, led a great reforming Liberal government

1886
Aged 76, split the Liberal Party over the issue of who should govern Ireland, and weakened it for the rest of the nineteenth century

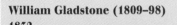

Benjamin Disraeli (1804–81)

1820s
Fell deeply into debt. Later tried to enter Parliament as a Radical, but eventually got in as a Conservative in 1837

1852
Led the Conservatives in the House of Commons

1874
Aged 69, was Prime Minister with a majority in the House of Commons for the first time; later became a Conservative hero

Gladstone and Disraeli dominated British politics between the 1860s and the 1880s. They were fierce rivals, they led opposing parties, and each was keen to criticise the policies and the character of the other. It was a classic political struggle that caught the imagination of Parliament and the wider public. However, looking deeper you quickly find the contradictions in their own lives and some surprising similarities in what they actually did as prime ministers.

- Chapter 3 investigates Gladstone's career up to 1874.
- Chapter 4 investigates Disraeli's career up to his death in 1881.
- Chapter 5 returns to Gladstone from his re-entry to politics in 1876 through to the split in the Liberal Party in 1886.

Through these chapters:

- You will examine how Gladstone and Disraeli became political heroes and how their character, their political skills and an element of luck helped each man to build his reputation.
- You will compare their policies on the important international and domestic issues they both faced.
- You will investigate the contradictions in both men and consider their all too evident failures.

And through it all one key line of enquiry as you study the interlocking lives of these two apparently opposite characters will be: **Gladstone and Disraeli – how great were the differences between them?**

■ A Government ministries 1866–85

DATE	PARTY	PRIME MINISTER
1866–68	Conservative	Lord Derby (3rd ministry)
1868	Conservative	Disraeli (1st ministry)
1868–74	Liberal	Gladstone (1st ministry)
1874–80	Conservative	Disraeli (2nd ministry)
1880–85	Liberal	Gladstone (2nd ministry)

3

Why did the 'People's William' lose the 1874 election?

CHAPTER OVERVIEW　Rogerson's shipyard at Newcastle-upon-Tyne was a nasty, ugly, smelly place to work. The River Tyne beside the yard was blackish grey and fumes from Allhusen's Chemical Works hung in the air, but on 8 October 1862 it was the most exciting place in England to be a worker.

All Newcastle seemed to be down at the riverside or on the river itself. There were large steamers carrying businessmen in top hats, small boats painted with stars and stripes and manned by fantastically dressed keelmen and little wager-boats carrying anybody who could squeeze on to them. Everywhere had flags – the walls of the shipyard, the entrance to Johnson's Cement works, even the chimneys at the chemical plant. Church bells rang, cannons fired, ladies waved handkerchiefs, men shouted hurrahs. There were people everywhere. You could even see them on hillsides two or three miles downstream. All because a government minister, the Chancellor of the Exchequer, was sailing down the Tyne.

This was no ordinary minister. It was William Gladstone, the first politician to become a big popular hero. He was already used to more modest photo opportunities (see Source 3.1 below) but the reception at Newcastle was by far the biggest he had yet received. It was confirmation of the status that he had achieved. In the twenty-first century sexy pop idols, glamorous royals and national football heroes may get this sort of reception, but not British politicians. This chapter examines how Gladstone built up his reputation, becoming known as the 'People's William' yet, despite this massive personal popularity, still led his Liberal Party to defeat in 1874.

SOURCE 3.1　Gladstone is photographed visiting the world's first underground line with directors and engineers of the Metropolitan Railway Company, London, 24 May 1862

This chapter asks:

A　What did the Liberal Party stand for? (pp. 40–41)

B　Gladstone: idealist or opportunist? (pp. 42–43)

C　How did Gladstone become the 'People's William'? (pp. 43–45)

D　What did the Liberals achieve in Gladstone's first ministry, 1868–74? (pp. 45–51)

E　Did Gladstone's government fail abroad? (pp. 52–55)

F　Review: Why did the 'People's William' lose the 1874 election? (pp. 55–56)

FOCUS ROUTE

1 Draw a Venn diagram with two spheres for the Whigs and Radicals which overlap. Show which beliefs all Liberals had in common in the overlapping part. Then show other Whig and Radical beliefs which were held by different people in the Liberal grouping but not shared by others.
2 List the main strengths and weaknesses of the Liberals.
3 Note the main reasons people supported the Liberals.

■ **Learning trouble spot**

Whigs and Radicals

The Whigs were great landowning families who believed in reforming government and reducing privileges for the Anglican Church. The word was also sometimes used more broadly to include their supporters and to describe moderate Liberals who did not want as much reform as Radicals.

Radicals were those who wanted large-scale reform from the roots, not just a few surface changes. The word comes from the Latin *radix*, meaning a root, and is a general description for those wanting change, not any precise group. Radicals wanted very different kinds of reform. In the late nineteenth century the description is often used for those who wanted reform in government, giving people more freedom and political rights rather than economic change to redistribute wealth.

Whigs often found that they could get a majority in the House of Commons and form a government if they joined with various Radicals who wanted more drastic reform. Whigs and Radicals could work together to an extent because they shared Liberal ideas and beliefs about some kinds of freedom and progress (see Chart 3A).

DISESTABLISH
Disestablishing a church meant removing the privileges it had through being connected with the state, particularly land and other wealth.

A **What did the Liberal Party stand for?**

Political parties in the 1850s and 1860s were very different from modern ones. Today we see a political party as a centralised, national organisation. The Liberal Party in the late nineteenth century was very different.

You could not join a national Liberal Party, although you could sometimes join a local club or association supporting Liberal MPs. MPs who called themselves Liberals sometimes did not vote for Liberal leaders in Parliament. The Liberal Party was more a loose alliance of people and groups who shared a few common goals as expressed in Chart 3A.

Back in the 1830s people used the term Whig to describe the Liberal Party and government, but the Whigs gradually became known as Liberals during the 1830s–50s.

■ **3A Liberal ideas and beliefs**

1 **Free trade.** Goods move between countries with few taxes and no restrictions.
2 **More say in government for people who were responsible and respectable.** This was judged by their property, education and behaviour.
3 **The spread of British Liberal ideas.** They hoped to spread their ideas about government and trade elsewhere in Europe and the world.
4 **More freedom and more equal rights for people with different religious beliefs.** This meant removing various privileges which the Church of England had as an established church and giving more rights to people with other beliefs.

Two of these beliefs are particularly important in this period: religion and free trade.

Religion

The Liberals gained their most important support from Nonconformists because of their policies on religion. A count of the people attending church services in 1851 found that nearly half were Nonconformists, and they made up about a quarter of the population. Nonconformists supported Liberals because of resentment about Church of England privileges. They hated the way they had to pay church rates (taxes to keep up the local parish churches) and could not have their own graveyards. Most Liberal MPs and all their leaders were Anglicans, but they at least accepted a need for change which Conservatives rejected. The Liberation Society, a Nonconformist group fighting to DISESTABLISH the Church of England, often worked for Liberal candidates who supported some reform, even if it were not radical enough for them. The Liberals gave the Nonconformists their best hope of removing Anglican privileges.

Free trade

The main belief uniting the different elements of the Liberal Party was free trade. After governing in the 1830s the Liberals were replaced by a Conservative majority in the House of Commons and a government led by Sir Robert Peel. When Peel's Conservative Party broke up over the repeal of the Corn Laws (removing taxes on imported corn) in 1846, the Liberals had a big opportunity. Most Conservatives opposed the abolition of the Corn Laws but a minority of the party, including most ministers, supported Peel's reform. This minority, know as the Peelites, were now separated from other Conservatives. The Conservative Party was therefore weakened for a generation and the Liberals had possible new allies among those who had left the Conservatives over the issue of free trade.

The Liberals agreed with each other on free trade but it was difficult to work together otherwise. Liberals had varied ideas about reform, and Liberal MPs were often elected on the basis of local issues, on how well they served the voters or according to how much money they spent bribing them. The Radicals

FREE TRADE

This meant removing restrictions on trade and getting rid of all taxes on imports except for a very few which the government needed to raise money. Its supporters thought it would not only lower prices but also encourage more trade and so bring greater prosperity.

differed among themselves on what they wanted. For example, two of the most prominent, Cobden and Bright, who had fought together against the Corn Laws, wanted free trade, low taxes and every effort to stay out of war. Other Radicals, such as Roebuck, were all in favour of fighting the evil, dictatorial Russian government.

Whigs had other ideas and also differed among themselves. Russell fought for parliamentary reform and introduced a number of bills for it. Palmerston supported people struggling for greater freedom abroad but opposed parliamentary reform in Britain.

Consequently it was difficult for ministers to work together as a government or keep a parliamentary majority and so governments changed quite frequently (see Chart 3B).

■ Learning trouble spot

Different types of churches

Protestants were all those who had broken away from the Roman Catholic Church in the sixteenth century. Generally they favoured plainer services with less ceremony and more emphasis on teaching the Bible. Protestants included groups such as Anglicans, Methodists, Quakers and Presbyterians. Protestants were divided roughly equally between Anglicans and Nonconformists in late-nineteenth-century England and Wales. There were rather more Anglicans in England, and there were a lot more Nonconformists in Wales.

Anglicans accepted the kind of compromise between Roman Catholic and Protestant teachings found in the Church of England. The Church of Ireland and Church of Wales were organised in the same way.

Nonconformists would not conform to Anglican worship. This group included Quakers, Presbyterians, Baptists and Congregationalists.

Established churches are linked to the state, which has some control over them and gives them support. The Church of England is still an established church, which means that the monarch is its head and appoints leading churchmen. (In practice the prime minister has much of this power.) Parliament can pass laws regulating the Church. In the nineteenth century the Church of England had large estates and was also able to collect taxes from citizens whatever their religious beliefs. The main taxes were tithes (originally a tenth of the produce of land, but changed to a set sum of money by 1836) and church rates to keep up church buildings.

■ 3B Government ministries 1846–68

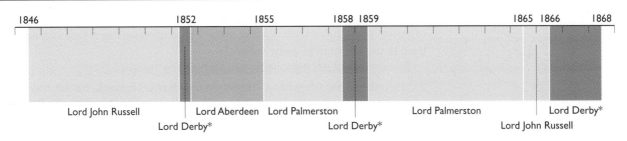

Key:
- Liberal
- Conservative
- COALITION of Whigs and Peelites

* Minority government: had no majority in the House of Commons, so would have difficulty in getting laws passed.

COALITION

A government or other group combining people from different parties.

Outside Parliament, though, many groups thought the Liberals provided the best hope of achieving their aims. Many intellectuals saw them as more progressive and rational than their opponents. Manufacturers saw they would safeguard free trade and might reduce the landowners' privileges.

Whatever its failings, the Liberal Party was a success story from the 1850s, and it gained massive support from British workers.

B **Gladstone: idealist or opportunist?**

■ **3C Gladstone's career**

Gladstone's party	Date	Gladstone's life
	1809	Born
CONSERVATIVE	1832	Entered Parliament as a Conservative
	1841–45	Vice-President and then President of the Board of Trade in Peel's Conservative government
	1845–46	Colonial Secretary in Peel's government
PEELITE	1846–52	Out of government
	1852–55	Chancellor of the Exchequer in Aberdeen's coalition government of Peelites and Liberals
	1855–59	Out of government
	1859–65	Joins Liberals and is Chancellor of the Exchequer in Palmerston's government
	1865–66	Chancellor of the Exchequer in Russell's government and introduces reform bill which is defeated in the Commons
	1868–74	First ministry
	1875	Retires as Liberal leader
LIBERAL	1876–80	Comes back into politics to fight against the foreign policy of Disraeli's government, but is not part of the Liberal leadership
	1880–85	Second ministry
	1886	Third ministry
	1886–92	Leader of the Liberals in opposition
	1892–94	Fourth ministry
	1898	Dies

FOCUS ROUTE

Summarise in notes the different motives for Gladstone's policies and actions shown in this section.

Background

Gladstone's father was a Liverpool merchant, but William had the most upper-class education possible at Eton and Oxford before starting his political career as a Conservative. After entering Parliament in 1832, he wrote the book *The State in its Relations with the Church* in 1838, taking an extreme position on how the government should support the Anglican type of religion in the Church of England and not encourage different beliefs. He became President of the Board of Trade in Peel's Conservative government, working out the moves towards free trade. After 1846, when Peel's party split, Gladstone was labelled as a Peelite or moderate Conservative.

Character

He was extraordinarily clever, hard-working and religious. He not only was a great politician but also studied and wrote about Greek classics and Christian theology. He consciously linked all his actions and decisions with his Christian beliefs and throughout his life kept diaries as a kind of spiritual accounting exercise. The entries show how he weighed up decisions in religious terms and tried to use his time in godly ways.

Two aspects of his personality are particularly puzzling.

1 Like other keen Christians, Gladstone did charitable work, but he chose reclaiming prostitutes as his task, walking the streets at night to find them. He was married and had eight children, but, for a prominent politician with plenty of sexual drive, this was living dangerously. When he read pornography or got sexually excited by the prostitutes he would go home and whip himself, recording the 'discipline' with a drawing of a little whip in his diary. When someone tried to blackmail him Gladstone took the man straight to a police station, but he was taking unnecessary risks.

2 Gladstone showed a mixture of strong impatience and impressive self-control, but he sometimes appeared really angry when he spoke in Parliament and attacked opponents such as Disraeli. In modern terms Gladstone seemed seriously stressed.

Motivation

For the historian the big issue is motivation. Near the end of his life Gladstone suggested that his greatest political talent was a sense of right timing. For him,

IDEALIST
One who follows strong beliefs and aims at achieving these rather than accepting something which may be easier or more practical.

OPPORTUNIST
One deciding policies according to circumstances and political opportunities rather than following principles.

this did not mean opportunism (taking up policies according to circumstances because they would be popular and win support), but understanding when it was practically possible to do the right thing.

Here comes the big dilemma about Gladstone's motives. How far was he an IDEALIST, guided by deep religious beliefs and conscience, or an OPPORTUNIST, making decisions to advance his own career? Think how far both could be true. Most people do things for a variety of reasons. What we genuinely believe often fits in with our self-interest. Gladstone had a complex mind, and it is important to work out how different beliefs and ambitions fitted together in his thinking.

Historians have different emphases. Two great biographies have come out on Gladstone in the last 25 years – one by Colin Matthew, who edited the vast diaries Gladstone left, and the other by Richard Shannon. Matthew broadly accepts Gladstone's sincerity and gives a favourable view of him. For example, he accepts that Gladstone went into politics to help protect the Church of England.

Shannon takes a more cynical line, giving painstaking explanations of Gladstone's actions which often suggest self-interest and ambition were important. Both Shannon and John Vincent (1990) have suggested that political calculation played a big part in Gladstone's decisions. Roy Jenkins (1995) and Eugenio Biagini (2000) have also written very readable biographies showing great admiration for Gladstone as well as some criticism.

Why join the Liberals?

There has been a lot of debate about Gladstone's decision to join the Liberal Party. These are the circumstances. In 1859 he was almost 50. He had been a successful Chancellor of the Exchequer in Aberdeen's Peelite government for nearly three years but had then been out of office for four. He was invited to join Palmerston's Liberal government. Should he? The main political issue at the time was whether the Italians should be allowed to throw off Austrian rule and unite under a government of their own. Gladstone agreed with Palmerston that they should. He said he would join the Liberals but there was a condition: he insisted on being Chancellor of the Exchequer.

ACTIVITY

You are a journalist sent to interview Gladstone about his beliefs and ambitions in 1860.
  List the questions you would like to ask him.

Historians see that his beliefs were shifting from Conservative to Liberal, but they also point out that joining the Liberals was much the best career decision for Gladstone. He hated Disraeli, who was likely to be Conservative leader in the Commons for a long time as he was only five years older than Gladstone. The current Liberal leaders were old men. Palmerston was 74 and Russell 67, so Gladstone had a good prospect of becoming leader. Shannon and Matthew both stress that he wanted his old job back as Chancellor of the Exchequer. Matthew says his decision 'was the hard-headed response of an able politician with a programme for action'. Roy Jenkins comments that if Italy was 'his dominating concern it was not clear why he had insisted on being Chancellor or nothing'.

FOCUS ROUTE

1 Make brief notes on Gladstone's policies to 1868 under these headings:
  a) Finance
  b) Foreign policy
  c) Religious freedom
  d) Parliamentary reform.
2 Add to each section any motives you identify for the policies.
3 Explain how the policies would have gained Gladstone popularity.

C How did Gladstone become the 'People's William'?

A Liberal candidate at the 1868 election explained what he did if he had forgotten what to say next in a speech:
  'I say "Gladstone", and then they are sure to cheer, and I have time to think.'
  How had Gladstone become so popular?

1 Gladstone was a brilliantly successful Chancellor of the Exchequer in 1852–55 and 1859–66

Luckily for him these were boom times. A Chancellor could keep tax rates the same or lower them and still get more money.

Old money

Before decimalisation, Britain's money was divided into shillings and pence as follows:

£1 = 20s (shillings)

1s = 12d (pence; 'd' from the Latin word *denarii*)

- He had long-term tax-cutting plans, including the abolition of income tax. The cost of the Crimean War (1852–55) put an end to that, but he reduced the rate from 10d to 4d per £ between 1861 and 1866. This helped wealthier people.
- He also made food cheaper. Two-thirds of taxes were on goods, and everybody paid these. A lot of food items were taxed. Gladstone scrapped most of these taxes and lowered those that remained on items such as sugar and tea which working people used.

Gladstone was a brilliant publicist and briefed newspapers to get good coverage of his tax cuts. He was the first to make the Budget into a big annual event and he explained how his tax changes would work. He knew when he could look good by having a political fight. When the Lords rejected a proposal to scrap the tax on paper in 1860, he included it in his 1861 Budget bill which they dared not reject. This made newspapers cheaper and helped the growth of a free press.

Gladstone believed that states would benefit from free trade between each other and therefore be less likely to go to war. Maintaining peace kept defence costs down and might make tax cuts possible. Though the peaceful foreign policy was not always popular, tax cuts were. Unfortunately the Crimean War upset Gladstone's long-term plans, as the government spent more and taxes had to increase. But when there were war scares with the French in 1860, Cobden (in consultation with Gladstone) negotiated a free trade treaty with them. Both countries would lower taxes on each other's goods. This helped British trade and reduced tension.

2 Gladstone appealed to Nonconformists

There were almost as many Nonconformists as Anglicans, and for many voters religion was a main election issue. Nonconformists wanted equal rights with Anglicans. Gladstone was a strong Anglican, and at the beginning of his career he believed the government should support the Church of England and discriminate against other churches. During the 1840s and 1850s he changed his mind as he took up liberal ideas about freedom and equal rights for people with different religious views. In 1863 he spoke in favour of Nonconformists being allowed to have their own kind of burial services in Anglican graveyards. When out of government, before the 1868 election, he pushed a bill through Parliament to abolish the compulsory payment of church rates. Gladstone had declared himself a 'lover of liberty' which he valued 'for every human being', and Nonconformists generally believed him.

3 Gladstone had tried to give the vote to more working men

In 1864 he came out in Parliament with a striking statement that every man was 'morally entitled' to have a vote unless disqualified by 'personal unfitness' or 'political danger'. He then added lots of qualifications to the statement, but opponents of parliamentary reform were horrified. *The Times* described Gladstone's declaration as 'the language of sweeping and levelling democracy', which was not bad for his popular image.

Two years later, in 1866, Gladstone did introduce a reform bill in the House of Commons to give the vote to more workers (see page 12) but it was on a very restricted basis. The Second Reform Act introduced by Disraeli gave the vote to far more people than Gladstone's would have done, but it is easy to see why many workers saw Gladstone as their champion.

4 Gladstone went on speaking tours to big towns

Traditionally political leaders spoke in Parliament and in their constituencies. Palmerston seems to have been the first leader to go on speaking tours round the country. Other Cabinet ministers started speaking outside Parliament as well, but not with quite so much effect as Gladstone. He spoke to audiences of working men from the early 1850s. He got his first really big reception when he went to Newcastle in 1862 and people lined the banks of the River Tyne for more than 30 kilometres (described on page 39). This is partly explained by his recent tax-cutting budgets and his high-profile fight with the Lords over paper taxes the year before.

Image

Gladstone's popularity was not just the sum of these four factors. Together they helped create a powerful image. Many historians doubt whether workers had much sense of being a working class at this time. They probably saw themselves more as independent citizens and part of a free people, especially after many more of them got the vote in 1867. Gladstone's speeches played up to this increasing self-respect. Working men did not generally expect the state to provide a range of social services such as schools and hospitals, but they wanted lower taxes and more equal rights. Biagini (2000) sees the large workers' movements in the early nineteenth century as struggles for more freedom and political power against landowners and aristocratic privileges, and he believes this thinking continued in popular liberalism. Gladstone offered more freedom, greater dignity and a general sense of moral uplift.

ACTIVITY

The 1867 Reform Act gave the vote to many working men in boroughs, and they voted for the first time in 1868. Many had high hopes of religious and economic reforms.

You are a working man about to vote in 1868. Write a short speech for a local election meeting in which you explain your reasons for supporting Gladstone and the Liberals.

Gladstone becomes Liberal leader and prime minister

The Liberals in the House of Commons split over parliamentary reform in 1866, allowing the Conservatives to get into government (page 12). Following the Second Reform Act in 1868 Gladstone introduced resolutions to disestablish the Church of Ireland. He argued that the Church helped maintain the collective power of Protestant landowners who dominated the country and had a poisonous influence.

It was an issue on which the Liberals in the Commons could unite. As Colin Matthew (1995) put it, the resolutions were not merely an 'initiative on a single Irish issue' but 'part of a general move by the Liberal leadership to solve both their party and their policy problems'. They defeated the Conservative government and a general election followed.

The Liberal leader, Lord John Russell, had retired, and Gladstone was now the most prominent Liberal in Parliament. The Liberals won the election. Gladstone became prime minister and formed his first ministry.

D What did the Liberals achieve in Gladstone's first ministry, 1868–74?

FOCUS ROUTE

1 What evidence is there that Gladstone was still conservative in his thinking?
2 Why might Nonconformists have been dissatisfied with him as Prime Minister?

What were Gladstone's aims?

Gladstone privately said his 'mission' was 'to pacify Ireland'. The disestablishment of the Irish Church was the key election issue in 1868 and Gladstone set to work on Irish Church and land reforms in 1869–70. He and his ministers also agreed that they must provide efficient government and give value for money. Gladstone wanted a minimalist state – a government which did only what was necessary and spent as little as possible.

His ministry was not there to introduce a lot of radical social or constitutional reforms. From the 1840s to the 1860s Gladstone had come to believe in far more freedom and equal rights for people with different religious beliefs. But in many other ways his ideas were much the same as when he was a Conservative minister in Peel's government. Like the Conservatives, he wanted to preserve:

• the monarchy – Queen Victoria came to loathe him, but he still did his best to strengthen her family's position

■ **Learning trouble spot**

Social and constitutional reforms
Social reforms are changes which affect the way people live together. The main areas of social reform in the late nineteenth and twentieth centuries were housing, education, poor law and welfare benefits and, later, health care.

Constitutional reform involves changes in the way the country is governed. This includes parliamentary reform, but also changes in other parts of government, alterations in their power and changes in their relationships.

VOLUNTARY ORGANISATIONS
Organisations set up by people on their own initiative and using their own money.

RATES
Tax payments, based on the value of land and houses, made to local authorities.

- the landowning aristocracy – he still thought it had a big role in government, and Whig aristocrats had important jobs in his ministries; Gladstone later described himself as an 'out and out inequalitarian'
- the Church of England – he was a dedicated member, believed passionately in its teaching and thought it must remain as an established church.

Many of his reforms were designed to strengthen these institutions by dealing with justified criticisms. For Gladstone, the UK's way of government after the Second Reform Act was largely good. Although he later decided that much more change was necessary, he thought it needed comparatively small-scale alterations in 1868. As Colin Matthew (1995) puts it: 'Gladstone saw his first government not as the new dawn of thorough going liberalism emancipated [freed] by democracy, but as the setting of the sun at the end of the day of the building of the mid-nineteenth century edifice.'

What did the public expect?
Obviously public expectations varied. Some Nonconformists had high hopes of what Gladstone would do to improve their position and reduce the privileges of the established Anglican churches. The record number of 64 Nonconformist backbench Liberal MPs would put forward their views in Parliament.

Looking back from the twenty-first century we might have expected the new working-class voters to want extensive social reform from a new government. In 1868 the public expected much less of this. Local and VOLUNTARY ORGANISATIONS dealt with services such as education, help for the poor, sewerage and general public health. Workers were probably more likely to complain at paying RATES for these than about any lack of provision.

What were the big difficulties the government faced?
- There were now more **voters** with very varied beliefs. It was hard to please them all.
- **Party organisation** mattered more when there were more people to persuade. The Nonconformists who dominated the Party often wanted different things from most of the voters.
- Any government had to maintain support in the **House of Commons**. It had to get its bills through both the Commons and the **House of Lords**.

ACTIVITY

What should the Liberal government do?
Make your own copy of the table on the right. Fill in the third column with what you think the Liberal government should do. (You will complete the fourth column in Chapter 4.)

Remember: if you increase government spending on the army, navy or education, you must raise more money by increasing taxes in one of the top two rows.

	Political issues	Options	Gladstone	Disraeli
INCOME	Customs duties (charged on goods entering the country)	a) Increase them to provide more money b) Keep taxes on a few items imported into the country which could not be provided at home as at present c) Reduce taxes on goods further and abolish some		
INCOME	Income tax (only levied on the higher income earners)	a) Keep it at 6d in the £ b) Raise it c) Lower it to 4d in the £ d) Abolish it		
SPENDING	Spending on the Army	a) Increase it b) Keep it the same c) Reduce it		
SPENDING	Spending on the Navy	a) Increase it b) Keep it the same c) Reduce it		
SPENDING	Education	a) Leave schooling to voluntary organisations as at present, accepting that most schools are Anglican b) Increase government money for voluntary schools (generally run by religious societies) which will mainly benefit schools teaching the Anglican religion c) Set up local authority schools financed from rates (local taxes on property) as Nonconformists want		
SPENDING	What social reform should you introduce?	a) Laws which **compel** local councils to improve housing and sanitation so as to improve public health b) Laws which **allow** local councils to improve housing and sanitation if they wish to spend ratepayers' money on this c) Take no action because reforms may well be unpopular with ratepayers		

What did the Liberals do at home?

Over the next six years the Liberals introduced a wide range of reforms. You are going to study the main ones.

> **FOCUS ROUTE**
>
> Here are five aspects of life which were affected by Liberal reforms between 1868 and 1874. Copy and complete the table to show the main changes and who was most affected. This is a summary chart so keep your notes brief. Use column four to record your judgement as to who this was popular or unpopular with. This will be useful when you come to review your work on this chapter.
>
> | | Main Acts with dates | Main effects | Popularity |
> |---|---|---|---|
> | Education | 1870 Education Act | | |
> | Pubs | | | |
> | Trade unions | | | |
> | Civil service | | | |
> | The army | | | |

Education

■ 3D The education system in the 1860s

Social class	Type of school	Who paid?	Problems
Upper-class and upper middle-class boys	Public schools	Often had endowments (property or funds to provide a regular and permanent income); parents paid fees	Often inefficient, with growing criticism of the lack of science teaching in the late nineteenth century, but there was some reform
Middle-class boys	Grammar schools	Usually had endowments to provide education for local boys; parents usually paid fees	Many criticisms that the endowments were wasted; local parents often resented boarders from families outside the neighbourhood
Upper-class and middle-class girls	Governesses at home; after 1850, a few girls' grammar schools	Parents paid governess or school fees	Too few opportunities for girls to receive a good quality education
Working-class boys and girls	Elementary schools, which taught reading, writing and arithmetic, mainly run for religious reasons, and most were Anglican	Many run by religious societies, but some were founded by local landowners; parents usually paid a few pence a week in fees; after 1833, the schools received government grants; after 1862, these were based on test results	Teaching generally limited and extremely boring, intended for children who would do physical work; many children did not attend at all, others attended irregularly

1869 Endowed Schools Act for grammar schools

Commissioners were to go round the country drawing up schemes to ensure that the money from endowments was used well. Grammar schools were to provide good quality academic teaching for the middle class.

1870 Education Act for elementary schools (introduced by William Forster)

Why? As more working-class men voted after the Second Reform Act it was more important to educate them. As Robert Lowe, Gladstone's Chancellor of the Exchequer, put it, politicians must get their 'future masters to learn their letters'. There was growing concern about foreign industrial competition, and a better educated workforce might help Britain become more competitive. People were worried that the German education system was better than the English one. They were also concerned that many children had no opportunity to attend school. If they built more schools, children would be taught useful skills and there would be strong emphasis on Christian morals. Young people would then be better able to find jobs, less likely to ask for poor relief and less likely to commit crimes.

SOURCE 3.2 Terms of the 1870 Education Act

> ### Terms of the 1870 Education Act
> 1 Religious societies and wealthy individuals were to continue to run their own schools (voluntary schools).
> 2 Where there were no elementary schools ratepayers would elect school boards.
> 3 School boards could:
>   • levy rates (local taxes) to build schools
>   • charge school fees, but also pay the fees of poor children at their own or voluntary schools
>   • compel children to attend school between 5 and 13.
> 4 Religious teaching at school board schools must be based on the Bible and not the ideas of any particular denomination (Christian group or church).

ACTIVITY

1 What would be the likely results of the funding for the board schools coming from local rates?

2 The National Education League campaigned for changes in elementary education and had extensive Nonconformist support by 1870. It was fighting for education to be 'national, compulsory, unsectarian (not linked to any particular Christian church) and free'.
How far did the 1870 Education Act meet these demands?

3 Both Anglicans and Nonconformists condemned the Act. You can work out why. Continue the word bubbles for the Anglican and the Nonconformist by using evidence from the Act.

4 Whereas nineteenth-century controversy about the Act focused on the issue of religion, twenty-first-century historians focus on the advance in education. Continue the historian's argument using information about the Act.

Anglican

These school board schools are godless ...

Nonconformist

Many places have no school boards, and Anglican schools are the only ones available ...

Twenty-first-century historian

The 1870 Act began the system of state education ...

Abolition of religious tests for teachers at Oxford and Cambridge, 1871

This meant Nonconformists as well as Anglicans could teach there. Although Gladstone did not like this, he thought it necessary in response to criticism and introduced a government bill to abolish the restrictions after the Lords had turned it down.

Other social reforms

1872 Public Health Act

Every area of the country had a council or board for public health which had to appoint a Medical Officer of Health.

ACTIVITY

1 How would the 1872 Licensing Act be unsatisfactory both to temperance reformers and to drinkers?
2 Study Source 3.3. What was the Conservative spokesman's view of the Act?
3 How does Source 3.4 suggest the Act roused feelings about
   a) class divisions
   b) public freedom?
4 How far do Sources 3.3–3.6 suggest that the Act was a major reason for the Liberals' defeat at the 1874 election?

1872 Licensing Act

Why? Pubs were important as meeting places in Victorian Britain, but there was a strong TEMPERANCE movement, which got much support from Nonconformists. Temperance organisations had strong support among Liberals and campaigned for the 'Permissive Bill' to allow local votes about closing pubs and drink shops.

Effects of the Act The Act was a compromise which limited pub opening hours. When the Liberals were losing MPs in the 1874 general election, Gladstone told a colleague they had 'been swept away, literally, by a torrent of beer and gin', but recent historians emphasise how much responses to the Act varied.

TEMPERANCE
Belief in self-restraint and in not drinking alcohol.

PUBLICAN
Person running a public-house which sells alcohol.

SOURCE 3.6   Outside a London pub in the 1870s

SOURCE 3.3   A Conservative spokesman, Sir Henry Selwin-Ibbetson, at the second reading of the 1872 bill

[h]e hailed the Bill of the Government with the greatest satisfaction ... he also regretted that the present Bill ... laid down no rule limiting the number of public-houses to the amount of the population of a district ... there was nothing he dreaded so much as that a question of this sort should be made a subject of political agitation at an election.

SOURCE 3.4   The closing hours applied to pubs but not to clubs, which often tended to have wealthy members. There are many reports of bad reactions when the Act was first enforced. This is a report from the *Licensed Victuallers' Guardian* of a disturbance in Coventry

[A] large concourse of persons assembled in the Broadgate ... The most favourite song seemed to be, 'Britons never shall be slaves'. Stones were also thrown, several of the police officers being struck. There is in Little Park-street a building used by the City Club, and the cries were raised, 'Down with the City Club', 'Smash the windows', 'Down with the Government', and others of a similar kind.

SOURCE 3.5   An editorial in *The Economist* in December 1873 may have exaggerated the Act's effects, but it apparently came from a well informed journalist

No Ministry, however strong, and however pressed from the outside by fanatical agitators, would willingly provoke an opposition so formidable as that with which the PUBLICAN interest threatens every Administration that dares to meddle with the traffic in strong drinks ... It turns elections and shakes Administrations.

ROYAL COMMISSION
Group set up by the government to investigate and report on an issue.

PICKETING
Standing outside a workplace where there is a strike to show others that the strike is taking place and to discourage them from working.

DISCUSS

How might the Licensing Act and the two Acts concerning trade unions have affected working men's support for Gladstone?

SUBSERVIENCE
Being under other people's orders, possibly in a humiliating way.

Trade union reforms

Trade unions did not have any status in the law courts to protect their funds. At the same time, there was concern about how they might intimidate other workers into joining strikes. A ROYAL COMMISSION reported on trade union reform in 1869, and the government prepared a new law for 1871. This contained different measures which the trade unions did and did not want. They therefore got the proposed bill split into two:

- **1871 Trade Union Act** – what the unions wanted. It gave them status in the law courts to protect their funds.
- **1871 Criminal Law Amendment Act** – what the unions did not want. It stopped peaceful PICKETING.

Reforms to make the state more efficient

Competitive exams for the civil service, 1871

Why? The Trevelyan–Northcote report had recommended this move in 1853. Gladstone also wanted efficiency and appointment on the basis of merit.

Effects of the reform Exams were introduced for the civil servants who administered all government departments except the Foreign Office. (It was argued that more personal qualities were needed for diplomacy, and the Foreign Secretary opposed any change.) The exams were designed for people with a university or public school education, and Gladstone believed they would 'strengthen and multiply the ties between the higher classes and the possession of administrative power'. Clerks who did the routine paperwork were recruited separately.

Army reforms, 1869–72

Why? Britain had a small army compared with continental countries, but it was vital to defend different parts of the empire. There were increasing doubts about army efficiency. The Crimean War (1854–56) had shown serious faults in getting supplies to the troops, and some officers had made tactical mistakes. The Austro-Prussian and Franco-Prussian Wars in 1866 and 1870 showed the efficiency of the Prussian army which now served the new German empire. After the war in 1870 many people were anxious about the state of the British army and expected the government to act.

Ordinary recruits tended to come from poor families, as richer men were put off by the living conditions and SUBSERVIENCE associated with the army. Officers bought their positions rather than being promoted on the basis of skill and experience. The reforms were intended to produce more efficient officers and a better type of recruit.

SOURCE 3.7 Gladstone explained the advantages of copying the Prussian system in an anonymous magazine article in 1870

[The Prussian system] works by short service and large reserves. It interferes very little with domestic ties. The system it employs for the choice of officers secures the highest efficiency ... without being open to the objections that attach to mere promotion from the ranks ... Lastly, Parliament and the country will, without doubt, remember that among the features of the German system none is more marked than its economy.

SOURCE 3.8 In the Commons in 1871 Gladstone supported changes in recruitment and promotion

[The officers] are the brains of the Army ... I hold that without the very best system for our officers all other improvements must be looked upon as dust in the balance ... The idea is to have the very best men and the very best officers.

ACTIVITY

1 Read Source 3.7. List the things that Gladstone admired about the Prussian army system.
2 What does the final sentence of Source 3.7 suggest about Gladstone's aims for army reform?

• Men could enlist for a shorter period than previously, with six years full time in the army and then six years in the reserves.

• Regiments were linked with different regions of the country to help local recruiting.

• Administration in the War Office (the government department running the army) was improved.

• The Commander-in-Chief (the Duke of Cambridge, who was Queen Victoria's cousin) was formally placed under the Secretary for War, the Cabinet minister in charge of the army.

• Officers could no longer buy their COMMISSIONS.

COMMISSIONS
Posts in the armed forces of or above the rank of lieutenant.

BOERS
People descended from Dutch settlers in southern Africa.

Effects of the reforms Historians studying the late-nineteenth-century army have found little change in the type of troops recruited or officers appointed. Officers still came largely from the upper class, and they were promoted because of length of service rather than merit. The army fought many successful colonial wars, but defeats in the BOER War, 1899–1902, showed that a lot of important defects were still there.

ACTIVITY

Imagine that you were a working-class Victorian lad, thinking of joining the army. List reasons why Cardwell's reforms might make joining more attractive.

1873 Judicature Act
This remodelled the law courts to get a more efficient and economical system.

Constitutional reform
1872 Ballot Act
This was another reform which Gladstone had previously opposed, but then he changed his mind. A bill for the ballot had failed in 1871, but Gladstone put one forward in 1872 and fought successfully against Lords' opposition. It was important in allowing men to vote freely (see page 18).

E Did Gladstone's government fail abroad?

Any British government had to run a vast empire as well as governing at home (see Map 3F). Most British governments were also concerned about the future of the Turkish Empire – what was called the Eastern Question. First let's explain the background before we examine Gladstone's performance.

The British Empire

■ 3F British Empire in Gladstone's first ministry 1868–74

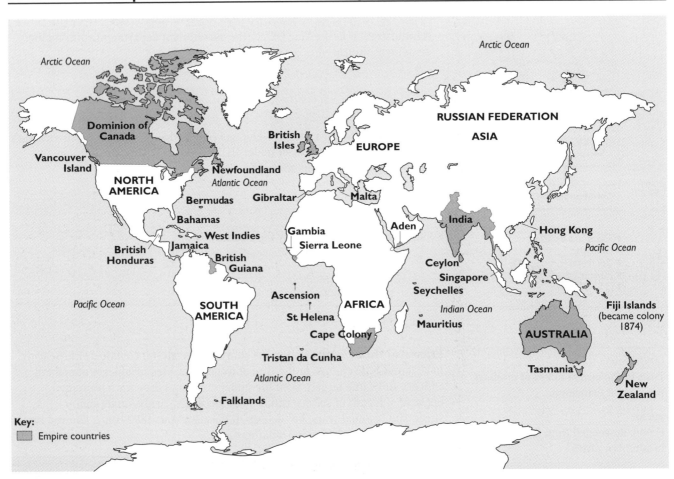

Britain's wealth and strength depended greatly on its empire. Although this included lands and bases across the world, economically India was the most important part. Until 1857 the East India Company had a big role in running it, though Indian princes ruled much of the country guided by British representatives. Britain relied on an army largely made up of Indian troops. When some of these rebelled in the Indian Mutiny of 1857 they had support from many Indian people. There was a year's fighting followed by extensive reform in Indian government, which took away control from the old company.

The empire was expanding in the 1850s and 1860s, but it grew faster from the 1870s. Canada, Australia and New Zealand, with large numbers of British settlers, were treated differently from other areas and had more power to govern themselves.

The Eastern Question

The Turkish Empire had grown hugely in the 1400s–1600s, then declined in the 1700s–1800s, but still included large areas of south-eastern Europe and the Middle East.

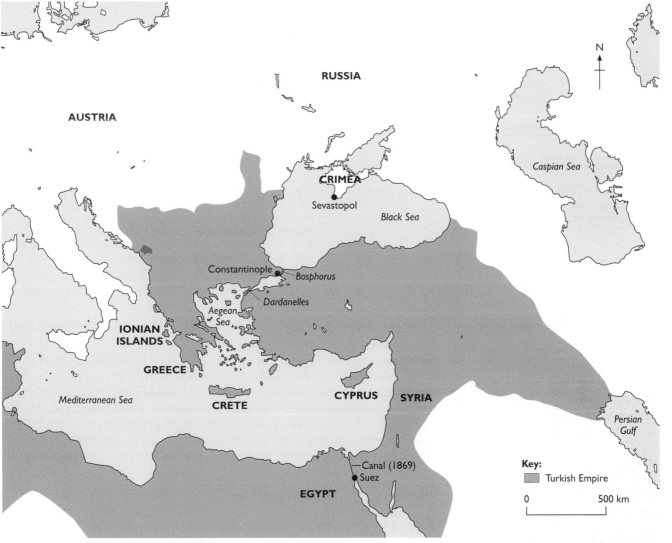

From a British viewpoint, the big issues involved in the Eastern Question were:

1 What would happen to the empire as Turkish power declined? European countries, such as France and Russia, might fight over it and upset the Balance of Power between major countries.

2 Russia, in particular, might gain large amounts of land and get access to the Mediterranean Sea. Right-wingers feared Russia because it might get too powerful and threaten the British Empire. Left-wingers hated it because the Russian Tsar's government denied people basic freedoms.

3 Russian power might threaten India. Russian ships in the eastern Mediterranean could interfere with routes to India that had become more important after the Suez Canal opened in 1869. As the Russians expanded in Asia they might also reach India's north-west frontier.

4 Muslim Turks ruled Christians in south-east Europe. Did they govern them fairly? The Russian government complained about Turkish misrule there, but Britain did not know how far it was aiming to protect Christians or to get more power.

In 1854–56 Britain fought the Crimean War to take the Russian naval base of Sevastopol on the Black Sea. The aim was to safeguard Turkey against future Russian threats. The Treaty of Paris, at the end of the war in 1856, therefore banned any warships or naval bases on the Black Sea, but the Eastern Question continued to plague Gladstone's and Disraeli's ministries in 1868–80.

■ 3H What Gladstone wanted in foreign policy

AIMS
- Free trade around the world

- To settle disputes by using the Concert of Europe. This meant the great powers (normally Britain, France, Germany, Austria-Hungary and Russia) working out agreed solutions to problems and using their power to enforce them

OBSTACLES
- Other industrial countries and self-governing colonies (like Canada and Australia) wanted to tax imports to help their own industry
- Bismarck, the chief minister of the powerful German empire, had different ideas. He was prepared to use the concert system, but thought more in terms of power politics

■ 3I What Gladstone wanted in the empire

AIMS
- Self-government for peoples who could run their own affairs

- Britain should rule India as long as the Indians wished it and eventually leave the country in a good state
- Cut spending on empire defence

OBSTACLES
- No obstacles. This had largely been granted in colonies with white settlers
- The men running India did not see it like this, but fortunately they did not know too much of Gladstone's thinking
- The government would have to resist attacks by hostile forces. Men on the spot or even Cabinet ministers in charge of the army and colonies had more knowledge than Gladstone and might take action he could not prevent

---

BRITAIN'S ECONOMIC RIVALS

Britain had the greatest empire in the world, but the USA and Germany emerged as big industrial rivals. After the American Civil War (1861–65) the USA grew fast into a great power, and in 1870 the north German state of Prussia smashed the French to create a new German empire with a bigger population and a much larger army than Britain. Both brought problems for Gladstone's government.

FOCUS ROUTE

Create a table to summarise the government's performance in foreign policy 1870–74.

Problem	Action	Success

Fill it in as you study pages 54–55. In the success column record your score out of five and the reason for it.

Foreign policy problems and what the government did

The Franco-Prussian War

Problem In 1870 France and Prussia (the main state in northern Germany) were preparing to fight each other. There was a danger that either state might march through Belgium to attack the other. In 1839 Britain, together with other powers, had signed the Treaty of London, guaranteeing that Belgium should remain neutral (have no other country's troops on its land).

Government action Gladstone warned both countries that Britain would act against either if it invaded Belgium. He had the War Office working out how to send 20,000 men over there, but neither side invaded.

Russian action in the Black Sea

Problem In the Treaty of Paris, at the end of the Crimean War in 1856, Russia and Turkey agreed with Britain and France that neither would have any warships or naval bases on the Black Sea. When the French were being smashed up by the Prussians in 1870, Russia took the opportunity to say it would no longer keep this part of the agreement.

Government action Although Gladstone had always thought this clause was a nonsense, the Russians could not be allowed to break international treaties. Gladstone got them to come to a conference in London. First they signed a declaration that treaties could not be altered by just one of the states that signed them. Then Britain and the other states signed another agreement cancelling the clause that the Russians had just broken anyway.

The American Civil War and the *Alabama* dispute

Problem The American Civil War (1861–65) had ended with a victory for the North (federal government) over the South. During the war a British shipyard had built the *Alabama* for customers in the South. Although apparently a merchant ship, it could be used for fighting. At the last minute the American government asked the British government to stop the ship being sent to the South, but the British did nothing until it was too late. The ship reached the southern side and proceeded to attack northern shipping. Subsequently the American government claimed for the damage the *Alabama* had done to northern shipping and for the way the ship had strengthened the southern side and so kept the war going longer.

The dispute was important because it upset British relations with the USA. The Americans might attack Canada along a lengthy land border which the British could not defend, especially as Gladstone's government withdrew troops from Canada in 1871.

ARBITRATION
Procedure for judging and making a decision in a dispute by a person or group not directly involved.

Government action The government eventually got an agreement with the USA for the dispute to go to ARBITRATION. The Americans dropped some of the claims, but in 1872 the arbitrators awarded the USA £3.25 million compensation. See Chart 3J for an assessment of the Alabama agreement.

■ 3J Was the Alabama agreement good or bad for Britain?

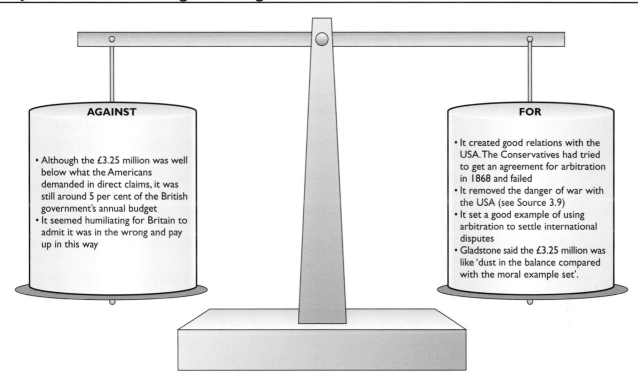

AGAINST

- Although the £3.25 million was well below what the Americans demanded in direct claims, it was still around 5 per cent of the British government's annual budget
- It seemed humiliating for Britain to admit it was in the wrong and pay up in this way

FOR

- It created good relations with the USA. The Conservatives had tried to get an agreement for arbitration in 1868 and failed
- It removed the danger of war with the USA (see Source 3.9)
- It set a good example of using arbitration to settle international disputes
- Gladstone said the £3.25 million was like 'dust in the balance compared with the moral example set'.

SOURCE 3.9 Lord Clarendon, Gladstone's Foreign Secretary, who also tried to get an agreement with the USA over the *Alabama*, explained the government's problem in 1869

It is the unfriendly state of our relations with America that to a great extent paralyses our action in Europe. There is not the slightest doubt that if we were engaged in a Continental quarrel we should immediately find ourselves at war with the United States.

TALKING POINT

To what extent does the handling of the *Alabama* dispute suggest idealism or opportunism?

ACTIVITY

Look back to the table you began on page 46.

1 What differences are there between your ideas and what Gladstone did?
2 Why are there differences?

F Review: Why did the 'People's William' lose the 1874 election?

Gladstone decided to have an election suddenly in early 1874. Most people just assumed the Liberals would remain the dominant party. After all the Conservatives had not actually won an election since 1841. At worst Liberals thought they might lose their overall majority in the House of Commons. Few expected the Conservatives would win but that is exactly what happened.

One reason lies in how voters were distributed between constituencies – the Liberals actually got 189,451 more votes than the Conservatives yet gained fewer seats. But this was partly because the Liberals did not put up candidates in many English counties and so some Conservatives were sent to Parliament in strong Tory areas without any votes being cast.

Politicians at the time and historians since largely explained the defeat by the way the government's reforms upset so many different people. As the Conservative Lord Derby put it, 'Ministers have managed to offend nearly every important interest in the country.' The most obvious way of explaining the defeat therefore is to look at how different classes and groups were offended by reforms in Gladstone's First Ministry.

CHAPTER 3 REVIEW ACIVITY

1 Copy this table. Use the third column to explain why the groups listed in the first column might be dissatisfied with the reforms listed. You can add other reforms if you wish.

Group affected	Reform	Reasons for dissatisfaction with Gladstone and the Liberals
Upper class	Officers could no longer buy commissions in the army	
Middle class	1870 Education Act 1872 Public Health Act introducing new regulations and extra rates (local taxes)	
Working class	1871 Criminal Law Amendment Act 1872 Licensing Act	
Anglicans	1870 Education Act	
Nonconformists	1870 Education Act 1872 Licensing Act	

2 Now look at your summary table about the government's foreign policy on page 54 and find what actions or failures might account for electors turning against the government.

Of course this is only part of the story. In later chapters you will look at two other significant contributors – the unpopularity of Gladstone's policies in Ireland (see Chapter 14 in particular) and the changes taking place in the Conservative opposition under Disraeli's leadership. That is the focus of Chapter 4.

Write this essay: To what extent did Gladstone lose the 1874 election because of his government's reforms?

KEY POINTS FROM CHAPTER 3 — Why did the 'People's William' lose the 1874 election?

1 The Liberal Party stood for free trade, giving people more political rights, and more equal treatment for people with different religious beliefs.

2 The Liberals were much stronger than the Conservatives in the House of Commons from 1846 to 1874.

3 Gladstone's work as Chancellor of the Exchequer, his reform policies and emphasis on the dignity of the working man brought him extensive popular support.

4 Gladstone's first ministry was responsible for many important changes, particularly in Ireland.

5 His foreign policy was sometimes criticised as weak.

6 Many of the reforms brought opposition from Liberal supporters and played a part in the Liberals' surprise defeat in the 1874 election.

4

Did Disraeli offer a practical alternative to Liberalism?

CHAPTER OVERVIEW Disraeli was of Jewish origin, never went to a major public school or university, looked unusual and was widely distrusted by Conservative MPs. He was, in short, a very unlikely nineteenth-century Conservative prime minister. Yet he had a talent for using words, a brilliant wit, flashes of perception and great style, so he later became a romantic hero for many Conservatives. People saw his high-flown statements leading to important reforms at home and actions abroad.

Historians in the 1960s largely demolished Disraeli's reputation, particularly Lord Blake whose biography of Disraeli was published in 1966. They saw Disraeli as wholly self-interested and ambitious (Source 4.1), but others have taken a more sympathetic approach. John Vincent (1990) and Paul Smith (1996) have examined the novels he wrote; some are largely nonsense but others show insights and ideas which inspired him throughout his career. Disraeli saw the importance of image and presentation in a way that compares with twenty-first-century politicians. There is something fascinating about this bizarre man, but did he offer anything worthwhile and different from the Liberals?

SOURCE 1 Disraeli photographed in 1878

This chapter asks:

A What did Disraeli offer the Conservative Party? (pp. 58–60)

B What had the Conservatives achieved by 1874? (pp. 61–63)

C Why did the Conservatives win the 1874 election? (pp. 63–64)

D What did Disraeli's second ministry achieve at home? (pp. 65–68)

E How different were the home policies of the Gladstone and Disraeli ministries, 1868–80? (pp. 69–71)

F What did Disraeli's second ministry achieve in the empire? (pp. 71–75)

G How successfully did Disraeli's second ministry deal with the Eastern Question? (pp. 75–80)

H Why were the Conservatives defeated in 1880? (p. 80)

FOCUS ROUTE

1 What suggests Disraeli might make a strong and effective Conservative leader?
2 What were the main problems in having him as leader, from the viewpoint of Victorian Conservatives?

SATIRISING
Criticising and making fun of (ridiculing).

CORN **L**AWS
Laws which taxed corn imports to keep prices higher and therefore benefit British farmers and landowners.

SOURCE 4.1 Opinion of Ian Machin, in his biography *Disraeli*, 1995

Disraeli never took up and pursued a policy which might not aid his political interest.

TALKING POINT

How important an accusation is Source 4.1 against a politician?

A What did Disraeli offer the Conservative Party?

What sort of man was Benjamin Disraeli?

Disraeli's Jewish father inherited a large amount of money and so set himself up as a country gentleman, collected a library and wrote books. Benjamin was baptised in the Church of England and went to small private schools near London where he did not get on very well. He left school at fifteen, educated himself by reading in his father's library and then went to train as a solicitor until he got bored with it. He played the stock market, buying South American mining shares, lost money and fell heavily into debt. A first attempt at novel writing, SATIRISING high society, made him a laughing stock. He had a nervous breakdown and recovered on a journey to the eastern Mediterranean where he was fascinated by the Turkish empire.

He had an active sex life, apparently caught a sexually transmitted disease, seems to have known at least one London brothel-keeper and, for a time, lived openly with an aristocratic mistress.

He stood for Parliament as a Radical in the early and mid-1830s, looking round for some wealthy man who would help his career. After playing off the Radical Lord Durham against the Tory Lord Lyndhurst, he became a Tory MP on his fifth attempt in 1837.

Disraeli generally preferred older women and eventually married Mary Anne Lewis, a widow twelve years older than himself, who paid off many of his debts, though he was not fully honest with her about them. His debts remained a big problem, and he had some narrow escapes from arrest.

He continued with novel writing and his seventeenth attempt, *Coningsby* in 1844, was the first one generally considered to have much merit. When the Conservatives got into government in 1841 he asked the Prime Minister, Peel, for a job in the Cabinet, but was turned down. He later joined with three other MPs in the Young England group, which put forward a conservatism urging landowners to do more for the poor in their own areas. When Peel took up policies which many Conservative MPs disliked, Disraeli attacked him, using satire (see Source 4.2). His big opportunity came when Peel set about abolishing the CORN LAWS, which the Tory landowners thought safeguarded their position. Many Conservative MPs felt they had been betrayed but none could express this nearly as well as Disraeli, who played a key role in bringing down Peel's government.

SOURCE 4.2 Disraeli showed he was a master of sarcasm and clever word play in attacking Peel in the House of Commons in 1845

The right honourable gentleman caught the Whigs bathing, and walked away with their clothes. He has left them in the full enjoyment of their liberal position, and he is himself a strict conservative of their garments.

What were Disraeli's beliefs?

It is easy to argue that Disraeli was a complete opportunist, taking up whatever ideas would help his next career move. This would explain his switches from Radical to Tory or from supporting Peel to being his most damaging critic. Disraeli was an outsider from a Jewish family who had to make his way in a world dominated by English aristocracy. His strategy for doing this was to emphasise how Jews were a natural aristocracy, how outsiders could be brilliantly perceptive and that imagination was important in government. There was, then, a big role for a perceptive, imaginative man of Jewish background like himself.

Beginning as an outsider, it also made sense to start as a Radical in favour of change. Yet Disraeli's radicalism was not as opposed to conservatism as it sounds. There were many different kinds of Radicals, and Disraeli was not the kind who wanted to bring down old institutions or reconstruct society on the basis of reason and progressive ideas. He believed in popular privileges rather than democratic rights and in aristocrats who helped and led the people, avoiding class divisions and uniting the English nation. Many Conservatives had these sorts of ideas. In 1849 Disraeli wrote to Charles Attwood, brother of a famous Radical leader, saying how he agreed 'that an union between the Conservative party and the Radical Masses offers the only means by which we can preserve the Empire'. This and other statements from Disraeli in the 1830s and 1840s express ideas he championed throughout his political career.

Three novels he published in 1844–47 outlined his key political, social and religious ideas. These are summarised in Chart 4A.

■ **4A Three novels by Disraeli, 1844–47**

CONINGSBY
Attacks Peel's leadership of the Conservatives as 'an attempt to construct a party without principles', a party combining 'Tory men and Whig measures'

SYBIL
Describes social divisions and says England is divided into Two Nations

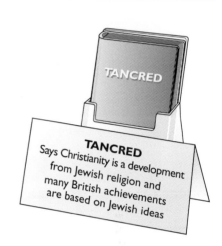

TANCRED
Says Christianity is a development from Jewish religion and many British achievements are based on Jewish ideas

SOURCE 4.3 In *Sybil* a stranger explains to the young aristocrat, Egremont, how England has not one nation, but two

'Two nations between whom there is no intercourse [communication] and no sympathy; who are as ignorant of each other's habits, thoughts, and feelings, as if they were dwellers in different zones or inhabitants of different planets ...'
'You speak of –' said Egremont hesitatingly.
'The Rich and the Poor.'

Disraeli's mixture of ideas remains a puzzle. He wrote movingly about the sufferings of the poor in slums and factories, but in 1850 he voted against more government inspectors in coal mines to please his friend Lady Londonderry and because he disliked extending national government power. Was he therefore a hypocrite?

On the other hand, in 1847, just when he wanted to become leader of the Conservatives in the Commons and needed Conservative MPs' support, he made a striking speech in favour of Jews who followed the Jewish religion being able to enter Parliament. His arguments about similarities between the Jewish and Christian religions repelled many of the MPs he needed to win over. These were not the actions of a political opportunist.

How important was Disraeli's Jewish identity?

Some recent historical discussion has focused on the problems Disraeli had because he was ethnically Jewish. Early in his career he faced racist taunts, and people waved pieces of pork in front of him. (Disraeli was Christian, but pork is an unclean meat in the Jewish religion.) Cartoonists and commentators still emphasised his Jewishness when he became prime minister.

SOURCE 4.4 Journalist E.M. Whitty described Disraeli in 1853

[He is] the least English-looking man I ever saw.

SOURCE 4.5 Cartoon of Disraeli in *Vanity Fair*, 30 January 1869

SOURCE 4.6 Portrait of Disraeli by Sir John Millais, one of the greatest Victorian artists, 1881

"MOSÉ IN EGITTO!!!"

SOURCE 4.7 Cartoon in *Punch* showing Disraeli's success in buying Suez Canal shares, 1875

SHYLOCK AND HIS "POUND OF FLESH"

SOURCE 4.8 Cartoon showing Disraeli as Shylock (the Jewish money-lender in *The Merchant of Venice*) in the Liberal magazine *Fun*, 18 February 1880

ACTIVITY

1 Is there anything in Source 4.6 to support Whitty's judgement in Source 4.4?
2 How is Disraeli's Jewishness emphasised, used in his favour or used against him in Sources 4.5, 4.7 and 4.8?
3 In what ways did Disraeli use his Jewish background to his advantage?

FOCUS ROUTE

I What were the main strengths and weaknesses of the Conservatives in 1846–66?

2 What did Disraeli contribute to their strengths?

B What had the Conservatives achieved by 1874?

ACTIVITY

Use the following information to write your own definition of nineteenth-century Conservatism in not more than 50 words.

The Conservative Party existed to conserve (preserve) the way Britain was governed. This meant defending institutions (organisations with well-established power) such as the monarchy, the Established churches (the Anglican churches in England, Wales and Ireland and the Presbyterian Church of Scotland) and Parliament (both the House of Lords, with its hereditary peers, and the House of Commons).

Conservatives thought these institutions had developed in the same way as the nation had developed over centuries. They therefore provided a uniquely appropriate way of government and a barrier against dangerous revolutions.

Conservatives also wanted to preserve landowners' power and leadership and thought they should continue to run their local areas. They wanted to preserve property rights because these seemed essential for order in the country.

PROTECTIONISTS
People who wanted taxes on imported goods to make them more expensive, so that people would buy home-produced goods because they were cheaper than foreign ones. This would protect the competitive position of home industries.

When the Conservatives split over Peel's abolition of the Corn Laws in 1846, most of the ministers supported Peel. They and their supporters were known as the Peelites – a group of around 85–90 which then fell in numbers as they joined other parties, retired or died. Over two-thirds of Conservative MPs opposed Peel over the issue and were known as PROTECTIONISTS. They generally lacked much ability or government experience, and one Radical intellectual called them 'the stupid party'. They had a very able leader, Lord Derby, who had left Peel's government after years of ministerial experience, but he sat in the Lords. Although the Protectionists did their best to avoid having Disraeli as their leader in the Commons, they eventually accepted him in 1852 as they had no-one else with similar debating talents.

First Derby ministry, 1852
This was largely made up of inexperienced men, lasted only ten months and was mainly notable for Disraeli's first budget. Despite being one of the leaders of the Protectionists, Disraeli did not actually want to reintroduce protection. He had not used economic arguments against Peel, but had attacked him for betraying his party. Disraeli accepted free trade but wanted to put forward a Conservative alternative to the Liberals' financial policy. Historians now see his proposals as clever and ingenious, but unfortunately for him the Conservatives did not have a majority in Parliament. Gladstone launched a furious attack, and the budget was defeated.

Second Derby ministry, 1858–59
Government of India Act, 1858 Following the 1857 Indian Mutiny (see page 52) this transferred power from the East India Company to the British government on the same lines as the previous Liberal government had proposed, with a Secretary of State for India in London and a VICEROY in India.

VICEROY
One given authority by a monarch to govern in his/her place. The viceroy of India was effectively appointed by the prime minister but represented the Queen there.

Third Derby ministry, 1866–68
Two important social reforms were introduced:

- **1867 Factory Act** Women and children in textile factories had already had their working day limited to 10½ hours. The restriction was now extended to other factories, as recommended by the Children's Employment Commission.
- **1867 Metropolitan Poor Act** This improved health care for people in London who depended on POOR RELIEF.

Parliamentary reform bills, 1859 and 1867
The Liberal leader, Lord John Russell, proposed reform bills in the 1850s, and Disraeli thought that the Conservatives should put forward proposals of their

POOR RELIEF
Help given to the poor paid for out of local taxes.

own which would help them win elections. He argued that reform was likely to come soon, and it was best for the Conservatives to settle the issue in a way that did not damage their own interests. As they did not have a majority in the Commons, it might be their best hope of achieving and staying in power. Disraeli therefore argued for action, and bills were introduced in 1859 and the winter of 1866–67.

Disraeli accepted having more voters but, like most politicians at the time, wanted to avoid real democracy. He made this clear when debating the Second Reform Act in Parliament in 1867: 'We do not, however, live – and I trust it will never be the fate of this country to live – under a democracy.'

Their first reform bill, in 1859, was defeated. Disraeli's 1867 bill was the basis for the Second Reform Act. He had to accept radical amendments, but getting the bill through and keeping some control over the distribution of MPs when the Conservatives had no majority in the Commons was an extraordinary parliamentary triumph. The success was an important reason for Disraeli's becoming Conservative leader and prime minister when Derby retired in 1868.

Disraeli v. Gladstone

Through the period 1852–68, personal rivalry between Gladstone and Disraeli developed privately and publicly. Gladstone distrusted the way Disraeli had helped bring down Peel and what he saw as an absence of political principles (see Sources 4.9 and 4.10). The parliamentary battle between Gladstone and Disraeli was often intense. In 1852 Disraeli gave a strong defence of his budget, followed by a furious attack from Gladstone which led to its defeat (see Source 4.11). The most intense fight was probably over parliamentary reform in 1866–67 (see pages 12–14), and this time Disraeli won by supporting Radicals against Gladstone.

SOURCE 4.9 In 1849 Gladstone complained privately about having to deal with Disraeli

[I]t is a very unsatisfactory state of things to have to deal with a man whose objects appear to be those of personal ambition and who is not thought to have any strong convictions of any kind upon public matters.

SOURCE 4.10 Edward Hamilton, Gladstone's private secretary, later recorded how Gladstone saw Disraeli

[Disraeli] was 'laughing in his sleeve', and was playing a game of politics as if it were a game of chance; and this want of sincerity engendered a feeling of distrust.

SOURCE 4.11 Journalist E.M. Whitty described the contest between Disraeli and Gladstone over the 1852 Budget

[I]t was the most superb parliamentary duel I ever witnessed ... it was real debate, in which speech did affect votes.

■ 4B Gladstone and Disraeli: a comparison up to 1868

	GLADSTONE	**DISRAELI**
The economy	Gladstone made his name as a tax-cutting Chancellor of the Exchequer, 1852–55 and 1859–66:	Disraeli was Chancellor for a much shorter time in 1852, 1858–59 and 1866–68:
	1 Abolished taxes to get free trade	1 Argued that the Conservatives should give up protection before 1850 because it would no longer be generally acceptable
	2 Reduced income tax as much as possible	2 Reduced income tax from 7d to 5d in 1858 and planned complete abolition in 1860
	3 Fought to keep defence spending down	3 Tried to resist demands for extra spending on the navy in 1858–59 and 1866–67
	4 Wanted to cut government spending as much as possible	4 Was prepared to increase spending if the government's income went up
	5 Managed the economy in periods of boom during 1852–55 and 1859–66, carried out his policies and got the credit.	5 Had to deal with slumps after a minor financial crisis in 1857 and a much larger one in 1866 and did not have much longer in office.
Religion	1 Had once defended all Anglican privileges but later fought for more rights for Nonconformists.	1 Developed a campaign to defend the rights of the Church of England from the early 1860s.
	2 Introduced the bill to abolish church rates (taxes to keep up Anglican church buildings) in 1868.	2 Changed his line on church rates when it was clear his government could not stop their abolition against a Liberal majority in 1868.
Parliamentary reform	1 Changed his position on electoral reform and suggested in 1864 that working men should have the vote as a right.	1 Argued that the vote was a privilege which suggested he would give it to fewer people.
	2 Proposed giving the vote only to better-off working men in his 1866 reform bill.	2 Proposed giving the vote more widely to all rate-paying householders in 1867.

What did the Conservatives offer that was different from the Liberals?

As Blake (1966) suggests, Disraeli established the tradition that opposition leaders should oppose the government as much and as often as possible. We take it for granted these days that this is what oppositions do, it is their job, but before Disraeli the opposition was generally more passive. He had a long time to do this job as the Conservatives were in opposition for most of the period up to 1874. The Conservatives only got into government when their Liberal opponents split for one reason or another. Disraeli had three short spells as a minister under Lord Derby in 1852, 1858–59 and 1866–68, as Chancellor of the Exchequer and Leader of the House of Commons.

The Conservatives had the problem which all long-term opposition parties face. The Liberals in government made many of the changes in taxes and administration that Disraeli himself wanted to carry out. The Conservatives had to find other policies, emphasise their traditional opposition to change or use more general patriotic ideas. How did Disraeli respond?

While Palmerston was prime minister, throwing Britain's weight around abroad and opposing constitutional reform at home, it was difficult for the Conservatives to offer anything very different. They had much more opportunity after Palmerston died in 1865, when the Liberal government took up parliamentary reform, and Gladstone emerged as a reforming Liberal leader in 1868. The Conservatives, as always, defended the CONSTITUTION. Disraeli emphasised **social reform** as it seemed a positive, undamaging alternative to constitutional reforms and reforms in Ireland.

Politics was not only about issues and policies but also about personal dignity, community and leadership, and Conservatives had something to offer here. Gladstone emphasised the working man's freedom and dignity, but Nonconformists in the Liberal Party also attacked the working man's right to enjoy drink and traditional sports. Conservatives were therefore able to defend these rights.

Disraeli and other leaders emphasised 'Englishness' and how the Queen and the Church of England could bind the nation together (see Source 4.12). They used symbols such as the Anglican Bible or banners showing 'Altar, Throne and Cottage' united in one great nation.

> **CONSTITUTION**
> Arrangements for government.

SOURCE 4.12 In 1836 Disraeli had suggested some of the features necessary to make a nation

[A] love of home and country, fostered by traditionary manners and consecrated by customs that embalm [carefully preserve] ancestral deeds ... and above all, a national character, serious and yet free.

SOURCE 4.13 Disraeli describing the Church of England, 1861

Broadly and deeply planted in the land, mixed up with all our manners and customs ... part of our history, part of our life, part of England herself.

> **DISCUSS**
>
> Do you think Gladstone would have disagreed with Disraeli's views as expressed in Sources 4.12 and 4.13?

> **FOCUS ROUTE**
>
> 1 List the main Conservative policies put forward before the 1874 election.
> 2 How far was the Conservative victory in the 1874 election due to Conservative strengths or Liberal mistakes?

C Why did the Conservatives win the 1874 election?

Disraeli was 64 when defeated by the Liberals at the 1868 election. He remained Conservative leader, but by 1872 other Conservatives doubted whether he should continue. Disraeli himself had no intention of retiring. Later that year he put forward the key principles of his Conservatism in two famous speeches to supporters at Manchester and London's Crystal Palace (see Source 4.14).

SOURCE 4.14 From Disraeli's speech to Conservatives at the Crystal Palace, June 1872

[T]he Tory party has three great objects. The first is to maintain the institutions of the country ... there is another and second great object of the Tory party ... to uphold the Empire of England ... another ... and one not inferior ... is the elevation of the condition of the people.

Of the three, Disraeli placed most emphasis on maintaining national institutions. This was what the Conservative Party had always been about, and Disraeli saw these as a focus for national sentiment. Later historians have emphasised his points on empire and social conditions because they were more novel and look like guidelines for future Conservative government, but this was not clear at the time. For example, he had no specific reform proposals to back up his reference to social reform ('elevation of the condition of the people') and was therefore creating an image rather than stating a programme for action.

SOURCE 4.15 Disraeli speaking at Manchester, March 1872

A land may be covered with historic trophies … but … if the population every ten years decreases, and the stature of the race every ten years diminishes, the history of that country will soon be the history of the past.

ACTIVITY

Explain what Disraeli meant in Source 4.15.

As you saw on pages 55–56 the Conservatives won a surprising victory in the 1874 election, through a combination of Conservative success and Liberal failure. You have already studied how Liberal reforms had upset a great variety of people including many Liberal supporters (see pages 47–51). The Conservatives offered fewer new laws rather than more social reform. Disraeli's election address argued against 'incessant and harassing legislation'.

The Conservatives had improved their organisation in many large towns and made substantial gains there. They appear to have been most successful in winning middle-class supporters. Even in the 1868 election, despite losing overall, they had made gains in Westminster and Middlesex, which had many wealthy middle-class voters. They made far more extensive gains in middle-class London suburbs in 1874. Middle-class electors seem to have particularly responded to the promise of less reform rather than more.

THE CONSERVATIVE ORGANISATION

National organiser: John Gorst, appointed by Disraeli

↓

Started Conservative Central Office, 1870

↓

Worked with National Union of Conservative Associations, started in 1867

↓

Together built up organisation in large towns

ACTIVITY

Refer to pages 16, 47–56 and 62–63. The 1872 Ballot Act meant that the 1874 general election was the first where electors voted secretly instead of doing so in public. Explain why you might vote either Conservative or Liberal in 1874 if you were:

a) an Anglican manual worker earning wages
b) a Nonconformist manual worker earning wages
c) an Anglican employer
d) a Nonconformist employer.

ACTIVITY

1 Look back to the Activity on page 46 and the table about governing Britain in the 1860s. Now fill in the fourth column to show what you would do as a Conservative.
2 How do your policies differ between the two parties?

ACTIVITY

You are Disraeli choosing your Cabinet in 1874. The men here are some of your likely ministers; most of them were in the Conservative Cabinets that you and Derby formed back in 1866–68. You are getting a bit old yourself, so you will need able ministers. You do not much like 'middle-class' men with business backgrounds, who have become more prominent in the party recently, but you do need the votes of people like this, and you are keen to get ability as well as the right social background in your government. Other appointments can wait, but you must decide whom to appoint to the following top jobs in your Cabinet:

Top jobs
- Foreign Secretary
- Chancellor of the Exchequer
- Home Secretary

Other jobs
- Colonial Secretary
- Secretary for War
- Secretary for India

- First Lord of the Admiralty (in charge of the navy)

1 Read the descriptions.
2 Decide which of the nine candidates you will discard altogether.
3 Allocate the top three jobs (in the first column), then the other four.

You can find out who Disraeli appointed on page 276.

Marquis of Salisbury, aged 44, educated at Eton and Oxford
MP from 1853 and in the Lords since 1868. Has an intellectual approach to politics and strong opposition to democracy. Secretary for India in Derby's government 1866–67. Resigned in opposition to your parliamentary reform bill.
    Strong opponent of yours, arguing that you abandoned Conservative principles with your reform bill and opened the way to dangerous and destructive democracy. Very able, will be a strong critic outside the government but difficult to work with inside

Duke of Richmond, aged 56, educated at Westminster and Oxford
MP from 1841 and in the Lords since 1860. President of the Board of Trade in last Conservative government, 1867–68, and Leader of the Conservatives in the Lords since 1870. Your relations with him were not good at first but have improved since. Opposed the introduction of the secret ballot in 1872, arguing that people should be able to vote publicly if they wished. Well known as an expert on agricultural matters

George Ward Hunt, aged 48, educated at Eton and Oxford
Lawyer. MP since 1857. Financial Secretary to the Treasury 1866–68 and then Chancellor of the Exchequer in your first government in 1868. Has an interest in agriculture and local government, which appeals to MPs and supporters in the English counties who are the main basis of Conservative electoral strength

Earl of Caernarvon, aged 42, educated at Eton and Oxford
Has never sat in the Commons. Made his reputation as Colonial Secretary in 1866–67. Created a federal Canada from the former French and British colonies, which seems to have worked well. Resigned from the government in protest at your parliamentary reform bill in 1867, then supported Gladstone's government in disestablishing the Irish Church and passing the 1870 Land Act when you and the rest of the party leadership opposed the changes. Something of an expert on colonial and Irish government

Earl of Derby, aged 47, educated at Rugby and Cambridge
MP from 1848, sitting in Lords since 1869. His father was party leader for over twenty years and Prime Minister three times. Has been a generally successful Foreign Secretary in recent Conservative governments. Believes in improving living conditions in towns. Had some notably Liberal views, but is a strong friend of yours

Richard Cross, aged 50, educated at Rugby and Cambridge
Lancashire lawyer and businessman from a long-established banking family. MP 1857–62 and again since 1868, when he defeated Gladstone in South Lancashire. Lacks top level ministerial experience, but has local government experience in Lancashire. Would help to keep Conservative support in industrial Lancashire where the party has done much better in recent elections

Gathorne-Hardy, aged 59, educated at Shrewsbury and Oxford
Lawyer from a Yorkshire family. MP since 1856. President of the Poor Law Board 1866–67. Introduced a reform to improve care for the poor in London. Home Secretary 1867–68. Active champion of the Church of England's position. A good performer in the House of Commons where the Conservatives need talent. Occasionally acted as opposition leader; loves a good clash with Gladstone

Lord John Manners, aged 55, educated at Eton and Cambridge
MP since 1841. Was with you in the Young England movement. Is a political follower of yours. Had a minor job in Cabinet in 1866–68. A strong supporter of the Church of England and concerned to improve workers' conditions. Good at debating, though not a great Commons speaker, and does not have a good reputation as an administrator

Sir Stafford Northcote, aged 55, educated at Eton and Oxford
Gladstone's private secretary in the 1840s when Gladstone was a Conservative. MP since 1855. Served on a number of government commissions and played a key part in drawing up reports on reforming the civil service and friendly societies. President of the Board of Trade 1866–67 and Secretary for India 1867–68. A useful speaker in the Commons. Has been your confidential adviser for the last ten years. A good administrator. Gladstone used him to settle disputes with the USA in 1871, and he has been Governor of the Hudson's Bay Company dealing with the Canadian fur trade since 1871

Why did Disraeli's government introduce social reforms?

QUEEN'S SPEECH
Speech read by the Queen at the opening of a session of Parliament but written by government ministers. It outlines the government's plans for new laws to be introduced in Parliament during the next year.

TALKING POINTS

1 How wise was it for an opposition leader to have a reform programme to present to the electorate?
2 Civil servants worked out the details of the ministry's social reforms. They had already drawn up some of them to deal with practical problems before Disraeli became prime minister. What would be the advantages and disadvantages of producing laws like this?

SOURCE 4.16 Richard Cross had not been in a Cabinet before. He described discussion on the QUEEN'S SPEECH and Disraeli's absence of ideas just after the Conservatives got into power in 1874

From all his speeches, I had quite expected that his mind was full of legislative schemes, but such did not prove to be the case; on the contrary, he had to entirely rely on the various suggestions of his colleagues, and as they themselves had only just come into office, and that suddenly, there was some difficulty in framing the Queen's speech.

SOURCE 4.17 Lord Derby, a long-standing friend of Disraeli's, recorded in November 1875

He dislikes detail, is easily wearied by it, and cares little about the preparation of bills while the [parliamentary] session is still distant.

SOURCE 4.18 Historian Paul Smith's judgement in his biography of Disraeli, 1996

If Disraeli had no pre-formed legislative programme [plan for new laws], he had a conceptual compass to guide him. Set in the 1830s, it had been readjusted only slightly in the 1872 speeches, which had defined, not what a Conservative ministry would do, but by what stars it would steer.

Reasons why the reforms were introduced and why they were limited

Historians and students have sometimes interpreted Disraeli's social reforms as steps towards a modern welfare system. Disraeli's government could not see them in this way. These were probably the key concerns for ministers in the 1870s:

- Social reforms (see learning trouble spot, page 46) would show the government cared about ordinary workers and their families. They were important as **gestures**. People would expect some action after what Disraeli had said about social reform.
- A government was now expected to present bills (proposals for laws) to Parliament. Social reforms would help **fill up the parliamentary session** without 'harassing' the middle and upper classes very much.
- The government could make down-to-earth practical changes and often extend reforms the Liberals had already made. The changes would be **non-controversial**.

PERMISSIVE LEGISLATION
Laws allowing local authorities to do things but not compelling them to act.

- Local councils or other authorities would generally carry out the reforms. **Government should not interfere** too much in people's lives, and the initiative should normally be left to local people or individual landowners and employers. Disraeli emphasised in 1875 that 'PERMISSIVE LEGISLATION' is 'the characteristic of a free people'.
- **Cutting taxes** was more important than social reform. That was what their middle-class supporters wanted. In 1874 they cut income tax by 1d to 2d in the £.
- Local authorities would pay for the reforms from **rates** (local taxes), though the government might offer loans. The government had surplus money following a boom in the early 1870s, and it gave some of this to local councils to help them cut rates.
- The government must not seriously upset the way the **free market** worked. No government enterprises should be started in competition with ordinary commercial ones.

FOCUS ROUTE

List Disraeli's social reforms, indicating:

a) the importance of each for the working class

b) how far they were permissive or used compulsion

c) what effects each reform would have for employers and property owners.

DISCUSS

Why would an Act which compelled local councils to clear slums have been unacceptable to many voters?

Social reform

Disraeli's government soon embarked on a series of social reforms. These were the main Acts.

1874 Factory Act

Why? A traditional worker's demand for a 10-hour maximum working day had not been fully carried out.

Effects of the Act Reduced working hours in factories for women and children from 10½ to 10 hours a day, with a half-day on Saturdays – a maximum of 56½ hours a week. In practice, this generally limited the time factories operated and therefore reduced men's working hours as well as women's.

1878 Factory Act

Why? Government inspectors went only to factories with more than 50 employees, so existing Factory Acts were not properly enforced in smaller workshops.

Effects of the Act Inspectors now visited workshops as well as factories to enforce the laws.

1875 Artisans Dwelling Act

Why? Disraeli had highlighted town slum conditions in his novel *Sybil* in 1845. A committee of Conservative and Liberal MPs from the influential Charity Organisation Society had suggested a measure.

Effects of the Act The Act was permissive: it allowed (but did not compel) local councils to:

- draw up improvement schemes for areas of their towns
- compel owners of slums to sell them, though the councils must pay compensation
- get loans from the government at lower than normal interest rates
- demolish slum areas.

New houses or other buildings would then be put up by commercial builders, not the local councils. By 1879 the Act had been used in London and only ten out of the other 87 towns where it applied.

1875 Public Health Act

Why? What local councils had to do for public health was listed in a wide range of laws and regulations and needed to be brought together in one law. Civil servants were working on this.

Effects of the Act It did not introduce new regulations, but stated clearly what councils and other organisations were required to do to provide sewerage, drainage and water supply and to look after public health. There were long-term improvements in the following years, but it is hard to assess the contribution of the Act.

1875 Sale of Food and Drugs Act

Why? Food was frequently adulterated (mixed up with) substances which lowered its quality and might be harmful (e.g. chalk in bread to make it whiter). There was no restriction on this or any requirement to list ingredients.

Effects of the Act Local councils had to enforce a widespread ban on adulterating food. But they were not compelled to employ food analysts to find out the ingredients, so the law was not well applied.

1876 Rivers Pollution Act

Why? Since there was no restriction on what factory owners put into rivers, something might kill off fish or pollute drinking water. A Royal Commission recommended regulation.

Effects of the Act Polluting rivers was made illegal, but there were many exceptions to this which allowed factory owners and others to evade the law.

1875 Agricultural Holdings Act

Why? If tenant farmers improved the farms they rented and then left them they would lose what they had spent on their holdings. The government wanted to deal with this grievance without harming landlords.

Effect of the Act Landowners were to compensate tenants, if they left, for any improvements they had made to their holdings, unless the owners had put a statement in the tenancy agreements that they would not do this. Since the Act was permissive, it was left to the landowners to decide what to do and was therefore ineffective.

1875 Employers and Workmen Act

Why? Workers and employers were not treated in the same way if they broke contracts between each other. For employers it was a civil offence, but for workers it was a crime with harsher punishments.

Effect of the Act Breaking a contract would now be a civil offence for both employers and workers, so they were on equal terms.

1875 Conspiracy and Protection of Property Act

Why? Unions had campaigned for a change in the 1871 Criminal Law Amendment Act to allow peaceful picketing (see page 50).

Effects of the Act Peaceful picketing was allowed as long as it was only 'to obtain or communicate information'. Union leaders thought a major grievance had been removed. But most trade union leaders, with a few significant exceptions, still supported the Liberal Party, and trade unionists elected to Parliament went on the Liberal side.

1876 Merchant Shipping Act

Why? Shipowners sometimes overloaded ships so that they were in danger of sinking. The Radical Liberal MP Samuel Plimsoll mounted a high-profile campaign to get a 'load line' on ships which must remain above the surface of the water.

Effects of the Act The load line had to be painted on, but shipowners could decide where it was to go. Plimsoll wanted government inspectors to decide.

1876 Education Act

Why? Many school boards had not made education compulsory under the 1870 Act (see page 48). Conservatives also wanted to help Anglican schools by getting them more pupils and school fees.

Effects of the Act Children over ten could not work for a time unless they showed they had reached a certain basic standard at school or at least attended school for a few years. Anglican schools therefore got more pupils as they were the only ones available in many villages.

FOCUS ROUTE

1 Make your own copy of the table below. Complete it to show the similarities and differences between Disraeli and Gladstone. Refer to pages 69–71 including Chart 4C.

	Differences (policy or method)	Similarities (policy or method)
The economy		
Social reform		
Ireland		
Political beliefs		
Ways of campaigning		

2 In which policy areas is there
  a) the greatest difference
  b) the most similarity?

The economy

Both believed strongly in free trade (see page 41) and low taxes. Northcote, Disraeli's Chancellor of the Exchequer, who had once been Gladstone's private secretary, cut taxes at the start of the 1874–80 ministry. Yet the Conservatives were generally more concerned to reduce rates (local taxes), while Gladstone specially wanted to abolish income tax. He was much more concerned with finance and cutting government spending. The Liberals left a £5–6 million surplus on the annual budget in 1874. The Conservatives left an £8 million deficit in 1880.

Social reform

The Liberals introduced many reforms for institutions such as the army and the civil service. Conservatives avoided institutional change and emphasised social reform, but their measures often carried on from where the Liberals left off (see Chart 4C).

Ireland

The Conservatives strongly opposed the disestablishment of the Church of Ireland in 1869, and Disraeli condemned the idea of Home Rule for Ireland in his 1880 election address, although Gladstone was not at that stage converted to it.

Political beliefs and the Church

Both strongly defended the established Church of England and aristocratic landowners' role in government. While Disraeli remained elitist and old-fashioned in many ways, Gladstone saw more need for reform as a way of preserving traditional systems.

On Church affairs Disraeli readily accepted the 1874 Public Worship Regulation Bill which was intended to stop elaborate RITUAL in Anglican services. Gladstone opposed it because it meant too much government interference in church worship.

RITUAL
Religious ceremonies.

■ **4C Links between Conservative and Liberal social reform**

	DISRAELI'S CONSERVATIVE GOVERNMENT 1868	**GLADSTONE'S LIBERAL GOVERNMENT 1868–74**	**DISRAELI'S CONSERVATIVE GOVERNMENT 1874–80**
Artisans' dwellings	Torrens Act, 1868 (from a *Liberal* MP) allowed local councils to demolish individual slum houses, but it was weakened by amendments		Artisans Dwelling Act, 1875, allowed local councils to demolish whole areas of slums (p. 67)
Public health	Conservatives appointed Royal Commission on sanitation (draining and removing sewage) in 1868	Commission findings led to Liberals' Public Health Act, 1872, which ensured there were sanitary authorities in every part of the country (p. 49)	Conservatives' Public Health Act, 1875, gave a clear statement of what the sanitary authorities established in 1872 had to do (p. 67)
Education		Liberals' Education Act, 1870, set up schools boards to 'fill up the gaps' where there were no schools (pp. 47–48)	Conservatives' Education Act, 1876, effectively compelled children to attend schools (p. 68)
Farming			Conservatives' Agricultural Holdings Act, 1875, said landowners should compensate departing tenants for making improvements to their holdings, but landowners could opt out (p. 68)
Trade unions		Liberals' Criminal Law Amendment Act, 1871, **banned** peaceful picketing and was strengthened by Conservative amendments in the Lords (the Home Office later drafted a bill to alter it, which would probably have been introduced in 1874 if the Liberals had stayed in power)	Conservatives' Conspiracy and Protection of Property Act, 1875, **allowed** peaceful picketing. Liberal MPs amended and extended Conservative law on trade unions
Licensing		Liberals' Licensing Act, 1872, **restricted** pub opening hours	Conservatives' Intoxicating Liquors Act, 1874, **increased** pub opening house again and introduced procedure to compensate publicans who lost their licences

Key

→ indicates the reforms in an earlier law being extended by a later law

✗→ indicates reforms in an earlier law being partly reversed by a later law

Ways of campaigning

Both saw their role as educating the voters rather than following popular opinion. Gladstone spoke to massive audiences in halls and open spaces around the country. Disraeli did little of this for personal and political reasons. He disliked this kind of contact with the masses. He recorded how a 'great mob' cheered him at Carlisle station in 1868: 'It was an ordeal of ten minutes; I bowed to them and went on reading; but was glad when the train moved.' Gladstone spoke to thousands at railway stations when he travelled (see Source 5.7, page 85).

Conservatives believed in a more traditional kind of politics, and Disraeli condemned Gladstone in 1880 for 'spouting all over the country, like an irresponsible DEMAGOGUE' which was 'wholly inexcusable in a man who was a statesman'.

Approaches to governing

Gladstone himself worked on the details of his main Irish reforms. The most important social reforms in Disraeli's ministry were the work of Richard Cross, his Home Secretary, and civil servants. Disraeli decided priorities and generally took more interest in foreign policy where he was occasionally responsible for initiatives.

DEMAGOGUE
Leader of the people or mob. Generally used as a term of abuse for a political agitator.

FOCUS ROUTE

1 List Disraeli's aims in imperial policy.
2 How far did events help him achieve his aims?
3 In what ways did each event cause problems for his government?
4 How far was Disraeli responsible for the main decisions in imperial policy?

F What did Disraeli's second ministry achieve in the empire?

Historians often suggest that Disraeli followed a similar policy to Palmerston (Prime Minister 1855–58, 1859–65 and Foreign Secretary for long periods before). Like Palmerston, he had an 'active' foreign policy, using British naval power and defending the Turkish Empire against Russia (see page 53). Like Palmerston, Disraeli's foreign policy was wholly designed to strengthen British interests, but he responded to events rather than following a plan, as Paul Smith suggests in his biography (see Source 4.19).

SOURCE 4.19 Paul Smith in *Disraeli*, 1996

Entering office at an epoch when Britain's security was under no immediate threat and her empire not in an expansionist phase, he had no external policy and needed none, beyond a general intention to make British power influential and respected as the Liberals were accused of having failed to do.

How imperialist was Disraeli?

Disraeli stressed the importance of empire throughout his career. In 1849 he told the House of Commons that colonies were 'the surest sources of your wealth and the most certain support of your power'. He made some private remarks about the high cost of defending colonies when he was Chancellor of the Exchequer, but there was no doubt about his long-term commitment to empire.

He aimed to consolidate and strengthen the existing empire. He does not seem to have foreseen the big IMPERIAL expansion that came from the 1880s (see Chapter 6), but stressed connections with existing colonies in his speech at the Crystal Palace in 1872 (see page 63).

Colonial historians emphasise how officials on the spot around the empire often took key decisions. In this way, officials decided to take over the Fiji islands and extend British power in Malaya in Disraeli's second ministry. For some years Disraeli largely left colonial issues to his Colonial Secretary, Lord Caernarvon, but at the same time his grand statements about empire would encourage officials to be expansionist.

IMPERIAL
Relating to an empire.

Consolidating the Empire

The purchase of Suez Canal shares, 1875

Why? The bankrupt Egyptian ruler was selling his 44 per cent of the shares in the Suez Canal (see Map 3G, page 53). When it was completed in 1869 the canal, built by a French company, provided the quickest route to India. Disraeli therefore took a personal initiative as he did not want the French to get the shares.

What was achieved? Disraeli did the deal quickly and successfully. However, the 44 per cent of shares did not give control over the canal, and an international agreement already guaranteed free movement through it.

1876 Royal Titles Act proclaiming Queen Victoria to be Empress of India

Why? Queen Victoria proposed this but Disraeli thought having her as Empress would appeal to the Indians' imagination and he did not want to disappoint his sovereign.

What was achieved? Victoria was proclaimed empress at a gaudy and elaborate ceremony in Delhi in 1877. The effect in India is impossible to calculate. It probably boosted enthusiasm for empire in Britain later in the nineteenth century.

■ 4D Southern Africa, late 1800s

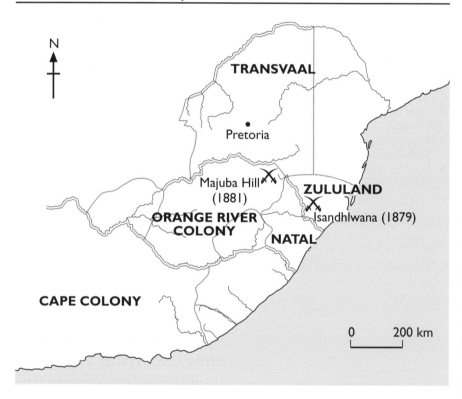

Southern Africa, 1877–79

The Colonial Secretary, Lord Caernarvon, wanted to join the Boer colonies of Transvaal and the Orange Free State with the British ones – Cape Colony and Natal – in a federation under British rule. The Boers did not want this, but Caernarvon got his opportunity when the Transvaal was bankrupt, threatened by Zulus and needed help. Disraeli left the decision to Caernarvon, and the Transvaal was duly added to the British Empire in 1877.

Trouble followed after Caernarvon's resignation when Hicks Beach was Colonial Secretary. The Governor of Cape Colony, Sir Bartle Frere, wanted to extend British control and act against the Zulus. Events moved rapidly towards a Zulu War in 1879 when a British force was defeated at Isandhlwana. Victory was eventually achieved, but at a considerable cost in money, lives and military prestige. Sources 4.20–4.26 give an indication of relations between Frere and British ministers.

ACTIVITY

1 What do sources 4.20–4.26 suggest were the main concerns of
  a) Sir Bartle Frere
  b) the government
  c) Gladstone in deciding what should and should not be done in southern Africa in 1878–79?

2 How far did Frere disobey government orders?

The matters in Eastern Europe and India referred to in Source 4.22 were the crises in the Turkish Empire and Afghanistan (see pages 73–74 and 75–78).

ULTIMATUM
Final demands which must be accepted, generally with a threat of serious consequences if they are not agreed.

MISSION
A group of British government representatives (diplomats) in a foreign country who would negotiate with the government there and look after British interests.

SOURCE 4.20   Sir Bartle Frere, governor of Cape Colony, explained his fears about the Zulus in a letter to Hicks Beach, Colonial Secretary, 30 September 1878

The Zulus are now quite out of hand ... I assure you that the peace of South Africa for many years to come seems to me to depend on your taking steps to put a final end to Zulu pretensions to dictate to Her Majesty's Government what they may or may not do to protect Her Majesty's Colonies in South Africa.

SOURCE 4.21   Hicks Beach wrote to Disraeli, 3 November 1878

I cannot really control [Frere] without a telegraph – (I don't know that I could with one) – I feel it is as likely as not that he is at war with the Zulus at the present moment; and if his forces should prove inadequate, or the Transvaal Boers should take the opportunity to rise, he will be in a great difficulty, and we shall be blamed for not supporting him.

SOURCE 4.22   Following Cabinet discussion, Hicks Beach wrote to Frere on 7 November 1878. Frere received the letter on 13 December, but a telegraphed summary had reached him on 30 November

*The fact is, that matters in Eastern Europe and India, of which you have by this time heard, wear so serious an aspect that **we cannot now have a Zulu war in addition to other greater and too possible troubles.***

SOURCE 4.23   On 8 December 1878 Frere sent the Zulu chief, Cetywayo, an ULTIMATUM demanding major changes in the Zulu military and social system. Frere wrote to Hicks Beach about the ultimatum, 23 December 1878

My own impression is that it is quite impossible for Cetywayo to submit ... he would find a large residuum of his soldiers who are fully convinced of their own superiority to us and will not give in without a trial of strength.

SOURCE 4.24   Following serious losses in the Zulu War, Hicks Beach gave Frere a government reprimand in a dispatch, sent 19 March 1879 and subsequently published

[HM Government] have been unable to find in the documents you have placed before them that evidence of urgent necessity for immediate action which alone could justify you in taking, without their full knowledge and sanction, a course almost certain to result in a war, which, as I had previously impressed upon you, every effort should have been used to avoid.

SOURCE 4.25   From a private letter Disraeli wrote to Lady Chesterfield, 28 June 1879

Sir Bartle Frere, who ought to be impeached [brought to trial by Parliament], writes always as if he were quite unconscious of having done anything wrong!

SOURCE 4.26   Gladstone condemned the Zulu War in a speech during his by-election campaign in Midlothian, November 1879

[A] nation whom we term savages have in defence of their own land offered their naked bodies to the terribly improved artillery and arms of modern European science, and have been mowed down by hundreds and by thousands, having committed no offence, but having ... done what were for them, and done faithfully and bravely what were for them ... the duties of patriotism.

Afghanistan, on the north-west frontier of India, 1878–79

Disraeli appointed Lord Lytton as Viceroy in India in 1876 because he wanted a more active person. As he put it, 'we wanted a man of ambition, imagination, some vanity and much will – and we have got him.'

Afghanistan was an important buffer state against the Russians (see Map 5C, page 89), and Lytton unsuccessfully tried to persuade its ruler to receive a British MISSION in his capital, Kabul. When Lytton got reports of a Russian mission there he wanted to act. The British government protested to the Russians and told Lytton to delay until it got a reply. Lytton sent a small force which was turned back, and the British government then responded to the snub with a full-scale military expedition. Disraeli's attitude to Lytton's actions is unclear (see Sources 4.27 and 4.28).

SOURCE 4.27 Disraeli wrote to Lord Cranbrook, the Secretary of State for India, on 17 September, 1878

With Lytton's general policy I entirely agree. I have always been opposed to, and deplored, 'masterly inactivity' ... there should be no delay in the mission.

SOURCE 4.28 On 26 September Disraeli wrote to Cranbrook about Lytton

He disobeyed us ... He was told to send the Mission by Candahar (Kandahar). He has sent it by the Khyber [Pass], and received a snub, which it may cost us much to wipe away.

When V-Roys [Viceroys] and Comms-in-chief disobey orders, they ought to be sure of success in their mutiny. Lytton, by disobeying orders, has only secured insult and failure.

In public, however, Disraeli defended the policy strongly and spoke of getting a more 'scientific' or defensible frontier for India. The military expedition succeeded and established a mission in Kabul. Unfortunately it was then massacred by disobedient Afghan soldiers, and the government had to go through the whole process again.

ACTIVITY

1 How consistent or inconsistent was Disraeli over events in Afghanistan?
2 Why might Disraeli's public view have been different from his private one?
3 Read Source 4.26 again. Write a short speech for Gladstone's Midlothian campaign about events in Afghanistan. (Note that he could not have seen the private letters quoted in Sources 4.27 and 4.28.)

How far was there a real difference between Disraeli and Gladstone on empire?

There were clear differences in thinking and language about empire between Disraeli and Gladstone (see Chart 4E) but not such obvious differences in action (see Chart 4F).

■ **4E Differences in thinking and language on empire**

DISRAELI

• Emphasised how empire strengthened England.

• Referred to 'moral and political considerations which make nations great' and 'distant sympathies which may become the source of incalculable strength' in his speech at the Crystal Palace.

• Usually looked at the overall gains rather than the cost of individual actions.

GLADSTONE

• Emphasised the rights of nations within the empire and thought of a loose association of self-governing states.

• Claimed that Liberals were most concerned with 'the welfare of these communities' and were happy to see their 'administrative emancipation'.

• Was interested in details about colonial administration, having been a minister at the Colonial Office in 1835 and 1845. Argued that the military expeditions in Disraeli's second ministry cost far too much.

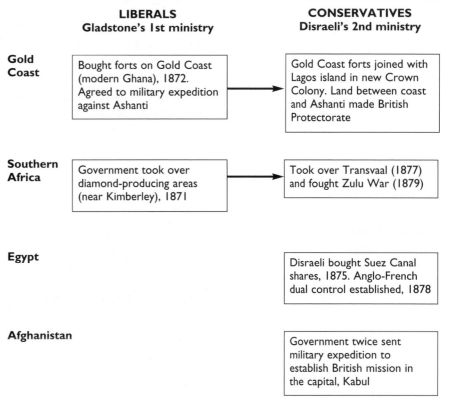

	LIBERALS Gladstone's 1st ministry	**CONSERVATIVES** Disraeli's 2nd ministry
Gold Coast	Bought forts on Gold Coast (modern Ghana), 1872. Agreed to military expedition against Ashanti	Gold Coast forts joined with Lagos island in new Crown Colony. Land between coast and Ashanti made British Protectorate
Southern Africa	Government took over diamond-producing areas (near Kimberley), 1871	Took over Transvaal (1877) and fought Zulu War (1879)
Egypt		Disraeli bought Suez Canal shares, 1875. Anglo-French dual control established, 1878
Afghanistan		Government twice sent military expedition to establish British mission in the capital, Kabul

■ **Learning trouble spot**

Beaconsfieldism

When Disraeli became Earl of Beaconsfield in 1876, Gladstone and other Liberals used this word when criticising Disraeli's imperial policy. It refers to the way Disraeli's government emphasised imperial greatness, relying on show rather than substance, while ignoring Parliament and wasting money.

G   How successfully did Disraeli's second ministry deal with the Eastern Question?

Gladstone and Disraeli had their bitterest clashes over the Eastern Question (what to do about the Turkish Empire – see page 53). Now it looks like a clash about principles, but at the time Disraeli faced big practical difficulties. He had to react to events, find the truth about rumours, handle powers with much bigger armies and cope with a government split. Derby, his Foreign Secretary, resigned in the middle of the crisis and was replaced by Disraeli's former opponent, Salisbury. To add to the problems it seems that Derby's wife, who knew the Russian ambassador well, passed Cabinet secrets to him and his government.

July 1875	Christian Slavs revolted against Turkish rule near the north-western edge of the Turkish Empire in Bosnia-Herzegovina.
December 1875	Austria produced the Andrassy Note (named after the Austrian Foreign Minister), recommending the Turkish government to make reforms. Disraeli reluctantly agreed to sign it.
April 1876	Revolt spread to Bulgaria.
May 1876	Austria, Germany and Russia sent Berlin Memorandum demanding Turkish reforms. The British government refused to sign it as the demand included a threat of force. Britain sent a fleet to Besika Bay (near Dardanelles), indicating it was prepared to support Turkey if Russia or other powers intervened. It effectively encouraged the Turks to resist demands.
May–June 1876	Turks used troops outside their regular army – the Bashi-Bazouks – against rebels in Bulgaria.
Late June 1876	News of Turkish atrocities in Bulgaria appeared in English newspapers (see Source 4.29).
July 1876	Elliot, the British ambassador in Turkey, suggested the reports had been exaggerated, and Disraeli took this line in the House of Commons (see Source 4.30).
September 1876	Gladstone took the lead in agitation against the atrocities.
December 1876–January 1877	Conference of representatives from great European powers at Constantinople (the Turkish capital) proposed reform in how the Turkish empire was run in south-east Europe (the Balkans), but the Turks refused to accept it. Salisbury, as British representative, wanted to use threats against the Turks, but the government did not agree.
April 1877	Russia went to war with Turkey. British public opinion was generally hostile to the Russians and became more sympathetic to the Turks, who now appeared as underdogs rather than persecutors.
January 1878	Russian troops approached Constantinople and threatened the straits between the Black Sea and the Mediterranean.
February 1878	British fleet moved near to Constantinople to protect British lives and property there, but also as a warning to the Russians not to advance further.
March 1878	Russians forced the Treaty of San Stefano on the Turks (see Map 4H). The British government decided to send troops from India to the Mediterranean; Derby resigned as Foreign Secretary because the policy was too warlike. Salisbury replaced him. The Russian government, under pressure from Austria and Germany as well as Britain, agreed that the main European powers should meet in a congress to change the San Stefano Treaty.
May–June 1878	Salisbury negotiated Anglo-Russian, Anglo-Austrian and Anglo-Turkish agreements which formed the basis of the settlement at the Congress of Berlin.
June–July 1878	Congress of Berlin, hosted by the German Chancellor, Bismarck. Disraeli and Salisbury were the British representatives (see Map 4I).

SOURCE 4.29 The first report of atrocities was in the *Daily News*, a newspaper which strongly supported the Liberals, 23 June 1876

Bulgarians speak of 30,000 [deaths] and of the destruction of upwards of a hundred villages ...

[In one village the Turkish commander] made an attack upon the church, and old men, women and children were indiscriminately slaughtered. Every house in the village was burnt ... a number of women were carried off as legitimate prizes by the Bashi-Bazouks.

SOURCE 4.30 Disraeli replied to a question on the atrocities in the Commons, 10 July 1876

I cannot doubt that atrocities have been committed in Bulgaria; but that girls were sold into slavery, or that more than 10,000 persons have been imprisoned, I doubt. In fact, I doubt whether there is prison accommodation for so many, or that torture has been practised on a great scale among an Oriental people who seldom, I believe, resort to torture, but generally terminate their connection with culprits in a more expeditious manner.

NEUTRALITY UNDER DIFFICULTIES.

SOURCE 4.31 A cartoon in *Punch*, 5 August 1876

■ 4H The Treaty of San Stefano

- Divided most of the Turkish Empire in south-eastern Europe among south-east European nations like Bulgaria and Serbia.
- Created a large Bulgaria which would have a Russian army of occupation for two years. It had a coastline on the Aegean which might give Russia access to the Mediterranean.
- Russia gained land to the west and east of the Black Sea.

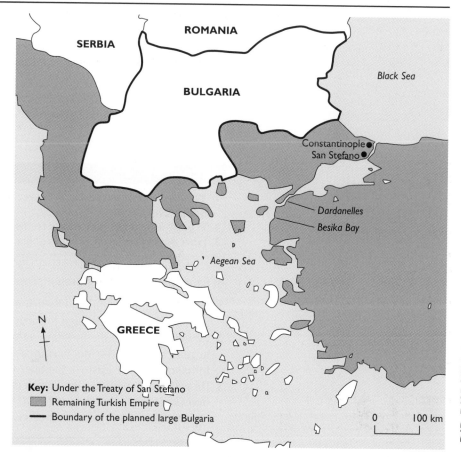

Key: Under the Treaty of San Stefano
  Remaining Turkish Empire
  ─── Boundary of the planned large Bulgaria

0   100 km

■ 4I The Congress of Berlin Settlement

- Much land from the Turkish Empire was still to form states for Balkan nations, but some was occupied by Austria-Hungary.
- Bulgaria was split, to create a small independent Bulgaria and Eastern Rumelia (in the Turkish Empire but with a Christian governor), and the Aegean coastline was restored to Turkey.
- Britain gained Cyprus in return for promising to defend the Turkish Empire.

Key: Under the Congress of Berlin Settlement
  Remaining Turkish Empire
  ++++ Boundaries of Bulgaria and Eastern Rumelia

0   100 km

SOURCE 4.32 Sir Henry Elliot, the British ambassador in Constantinople, gave this view of the Bulgarian atrocities in a dispatch to the Foreign Secretary, September 1876

We may and must feel indignant at the needless and monstrous severity with which the Bulgarian insurrection was put down, but the necessity which exists for England ... is not affected by the question whether it was 10,000 or 20,000 persons who perished ... We have been upholding what we know to be a semi-civilized nation, liable under certain circumstances to be carried into fearful excesses; but the fact of this having just now been strikingly brought home to us all cannot be a sufficient reason for abandoning a policy which is the only one that can be followed with a due regard to our own interests.

ACTIVITY

1 What aspects of the report in Source 4.29 on page 76 would particularly anger British Christians?
2 In what ways might they object to the tone of Disraeli's reply in Source 4.30?
3 How does Elliot justify Britain's policy over Turkey in Source 4.32?

In handling the Eastern Question, Disraeli's chief concerns were:

1 He followed the traditional British government policy of supporting Turkey to block Russian expansion towards the Mediterranean.
2 He believed that if the Russians gained Constantinople and got access to the Aegean and then the Mediterranean, they could endanger Britain's route to India and the Far East via the Suez Canal.
3 He wanted to maintain the British empire. Millman, in a key work on *Britain and the Eastern Question, 1875–1878*, concluded that Disraeli 'was prepared for any Ottoman (Turkish) sacrifice consistent with British prestige'.

ACTIVITY

1 Find evidence from the events of 1875–78 which illustrate Disraeli's concerns (listed above) in handling the Eastern Question.
2 Assess how far he achieved his aims at the Congress of Berlin, using the list of concerns and Charts 4H and 4I.
3 How far did Britain achieve Disraeli's wish for Britain to have a central role in European diplomacy during the crisis of 1875–78?

SOURCE 4.33 In a letter to his wife during the Congress of Berlin, the Foreign Secretary, Lord Salisbury, commented on Disraeli's part in it

What with deafness, ignorance of French, and Bismarck's extraordinary mode of speech, Beaconsfield [Disraeli] has the dimmest idea of what is going on – understands everything crossways – and imagines a perpetual conspiracy.

SOURCE 4.34 In his diary, Edward Hamilton, Gladstone's private secretary, recorded the judgement of Lord Odo Russell, the British ambassador in Berlin

[T]he impression which Lord Beaconsfield [Disraeli] made ... was extraordinarily great, and ... it was impossible to overrate the extreme ability with which he conducted much of the Congress business. The other representatives were evidently afraid of him ... no one was regarded with so much curiosity or treated with so much deference.

ACTIVITY

Judgements differ on Disraeli's role at the Congress of Berlin. Which of Sources 4.33 and 4.34 do you think gives a more reliable judgement? Explain your choice.

How did Gladstone and Disraeli differ over the Eastern Question?

Gladstone came out of retirement to launch an impassioned campaign against Disraeli's approach to the Bulgarian atrocities. He published a bestselling pamphlet and spoke to massive audiences condemning the Turks but both Gladstone and Disraeli thought the Turkish Empire served a useful purpose. Gladstone believed Turkish control prevented a 'wholesale scramble' for the area, though the Turkish government needed to mend its ways if it were to keep power. There were some similarities in policy, but Chart 4J suggests how their attitudes differed.

■ 4J How Disraeli and Gladstone differed in their attitudes over the Eastern Question

DISRAELI

Most important issue
- Strengthening the empire
  Said about the Bulgarian atrocities: 'What our duty is at this critical moment is to maintain the Empire of England.' Judged situation by political needs.

Ideas on morality
- Wrong to judge what happened in eastern Europe by standards and norms in western Europe.

Views on nationalism in the Balkans (south-east Europe)
- European peace and the balance of power were more important than national rights.

GLADSTONE

Most important issue
- Standards of right and wrong (morals)
  Condemned Elliot's dispatch (Source 4.32), saying 'What is to be the consequence to civilisation and humanity ... if British interests are to be the rule of British agents all over the world, and are to be for them the measure of right or wrong?'

Ideas on morality
- Thought Christian principles have a universal application.

Views on nationalism in the Balkans (south-east Europe)
- Believed in certain rights for all nations and thought Balkan peoples capable of governing themselves.

Jingoism

As Britain opposed Russia's advance towards Constantinople in early 1878, there was much public enthusiasm for showing national strength and taking military action. These feelings became known as 'jingoism' because they were well expressed in the chorus to a music hall song (see Source 4.35). They were widely held, but Source 4.36 was one reply.

SOURCE 4.35 The chorus of the famous jingo song performed by 'The Great MacDermott' and a wide range of imitators from early 1878. The Bear symbolised Russia

SOURCE 4.36 A reply to the jingo song

We don't want to fight, but by Jingo if we do,
We've got the ships, we've got the men, and got the money too.
We've fought the Bear before, and while we're Britons true,
The Russians shall not have Constantinople.

I don't want to fight, I'll be slaughtered if I do!
I'll change my togs and sell my kit and pop (pawn) my rifle too!
I don't like the war, I ain't no Briton true,
And I'd let the Russian have Constantinople.

PATRIOTISM
Love of one's own country.

SATIRE
A piece designed to criticise and make fun of (ridicule) people, ideas or organisations.

SOURCE 4.37 Disraeli got reports about popular feeling and the music hall songs. Salisbury commented to his wife in 1878

He [Disraeli] is of course much disgusted at the Jingo outbreak in England.

ACTIVITY

1 **a)** What are the main sentiments in Source 4.35?
  b) Why do you think it is frequently used to show what is bad about PATRIOTISM and imperialism?
2 How far should Source 4.36 be taken as a pacifist statement (against war) or a piece of SATIRE?
3 Refer to Source 4.37. Why might Disraeli be both pleased and disgusted by jingoism?

H Why were the Conservatives defeated in 1880?

The Conservatives lost the 1880 election. There were several reasons, including:

1 Economic depression. This was particularly severe in farming, with far more cheap food imports. Disraeli, who did not think protection was practical any longer, had no answer to this. Unemployment also appears to have increased by 1879 although we have no clear overall figures to show by how much.
2 Difficulties in the empire. Disraeli's foreign and imperial policies did produce clear successes for Britain but they were costly and sometimes unpopular.
3 Gladstone's Midlothian campaigns. Gladstone came out of retirement to campaign against Disraeli's policies and in particular his handling of the Eastern Question following the massacre of Bulgarian Christians. This culminated in his high-profile campaign in the Midlothian by-election in 1879, when he fiercely attacked Disraeli's imperial policies, which he labelled 'Beaconsfieldism'.
4 Party organisation. After the 1874 election the Conservatives lost their Principal Agent who had built up and co-ordinated local Conservative associations across the country. The Liberals improved their organisation with the National Liberal Federation.

DISCUSS

Which of the factors would have been the most important in deciding the way working-class electors voted in 1880?

Disraeli reborn!

Disraeli died in 1881. During Disraeli's life, Conservatives had very mixed views about him. After his death they created a myth about him as a Conservative hero. In 1883 the Primrose League was founded in his memory and named after his favourite flower (see page 168). Faced with the popular cult surrounding Gladstone and lacking CHARISMATIC leaders of their own in the early 1880s, the Conservatives invented a kind of mythical Disraeli, reborn as a Tory Democrat. Disraeli had written sympathetically about the poor in *Sybil* in the 1840s, given workers the vote in 1867 and then introduced reforms to help them in his second ministry. Lord Randolph Churchill (see page 165) referred to 'the great Tory democracy which Lord Beaconsfield constructed'.

CHARISMATIC
Having leadership qualities which inspire others.

CHAPTER 4 REVIEW ACTIVITY

Lord Randolph Churchill, who frequently used the phrase Tory Democrat, was not very consistent or specific about his policies. He kept saying he would 'trust the people'. Clearly he believed in preserving the empire and British traditions while delivering social reform.

1   You are a speech writer for Lord Randolph Churchill. Provide him with a dossier of evidence to support his claim that Disraeli was a Tory Democrat. Find at least one point under each of the following headings.

  a) His politics in the 1830s–50s (pages 58–59)
  b) Role over parliamentary reform (pages 13–14 and 62)
  c) Speeches in 1872 (pages 63–64)
  d) Position at the start of his second ministry (page 66)
  e) Social reforms in his second ministry (pages 67–68).

2   For each heading summarise for Lord Randolph what Disraeli's critics might say about each point.

3   Write two paragraphs summing up your view of Disraeli. Does he deserve to be seen as a Conservative hero or was he a self-seeking opportunist?

KEY POINTS FROM CHAPTER 4

Did Disraeli offer a practical alternative to Liberalism?

1   The split in the Conservative Party between Protectionists and Peelites in 1846 weakened the party for years afterwards.

2   Conservative MPs were suspicious of Disraeli, but he was by far their most able leader in the Commons and showed great parliamentary abilities, particularly in steering through the Second Reform Act in 1867.

3   By 1874 Disraeli established a clear set of Conservative beliefs to preserve the constitution, maintain empire and undertake social reform, though he lacked detailed policies.

4   His second ministry, from 1874–80, introduced significant social reforms and achieved successes abroad, but the financial costs and attempts at imperial grandeur were controversial.

5

Should Gladstone have stayed in retirement?

CHAPTER OVERVIEW Gladstone had retired as Liberal leader in 1875 when he was 65. His government had been unexpectedly defeated, and he wanted to spend his last years studying religion and Greek classics. Yet this was not exactly ordinary retirement. He remained an MP, and he had written in one memorandum that he was prepared to come back if there was 'some great evil' to fight or 'some great good' to be done for the nation. He did not have to wait long. In 1876 that 'great evil' appeared as British people learnt of Turkish troops massacring Bulgarian Christians. As news of the massacre appeared in English newspapers in June 1876, public agitation developed but Gladstone was not involved until late August. Then he wrote a pamphlet called *The Bulgarian Horrors and the Question of the East*, which was published on 6 September and sold 200,000 copies in a month. Gladstone told Granville, the Whig leader in the Lords: 'Good ends can rarely be obtained in politics without passion: and there is now, the first time for a good many years, a virtuous passion.'

Gladstone's return to politics in 1876 was one of the big decisions of his career. And it raises again the intriguing question about Gladstone. How far was he motivated by idealism? How far by political opportunism – the opportunity to get back at Disraeli?

1 Gladstone himself said twenty years later that he had 'postponed' doing anything about the Bulgarian Atrocities until he heard of a working man's meeting in Hyde Park about them. Then he saw 'that the iron was hot and that the time to strike had arrived'.
2 Historian H.C.G. Matthew states, 'Gladstone experienced a conversion of Evangelical intensity' over the Bulgarian Atrocities.
3 Richard Shannon declares, 'It was far less a case of Gladstone exciting popular passion than of popular passion exciting Gladstone'.
4 Ann Pottinger Saab suggests he was balancing the case for maintaining the Turkish Empire and keeping up British influence against what was wrong with Turkish rule. In short, he was balancing the rights and wrongs of the matter.

Whatever his motives it was a triumphant return.

Gladstone achieved his greatest popular reputation in the years from 1876. In their homes, increasing numbers of people had Gladstone tiles, plates, mugs, tea caddies and pottery figures (Tories would sometimes excrete in Gladstone chamber pots). When Gladstone gave a series of speeches near Edinburgh, people came from as far away as the Hebrides islands to see him. When he travelled, crowds would gather at the railway stations and people even stood by the railway lines in open country hoping to catch a glimpse of him.

SOURCE 5.1 Verse sung in a Midlands pub in the 1880s using affectionate and common nicknames for Gladstone

God bless the People's William,
Long may he lead the van,
Of liberty and freedom,
God bless the Grand Old Man

To cap it all, in 1880 he once again became leader of a Liberal government, at the age of 70. It was a triumphant return but it was eventually to lead to failure for both Gladstone and his party. Gladstone became increasingly difficult to work with. When he took up the cause of Irish Home Rule in 1886 he split the Liberal Party which, as a direct result, was largely confined to opposition for the next twenty years. It would be easy to conclude that it would have been better for the Liberals if Gladstone had stayed in retirement. So in this chapter you will investigate the successes and failures of this final phase of Gladstone's career. Did Gladstone make the right decision?

This chapter asks:

A How effective and influential was Gladstone's speaking? (pp. 83–86)

B Did Gladstone continue or reverse Disraeli's policy abroad? (pp. 87–90)

C What did Gladstone's second ministry achieve at home, 1880–85? (p. 90)

D Did Gladstone split the Liberal Party? (pp. 91–93)

E The final years (p. 94)

F Review: Should Gladstone have stayed in retirement? (p. 94)

FOCUS ROUTE

List the different methods Gladstone used to win popular support. For each, make notes on how it helped him.

A How effective and influential was Gladstone's speaking?

Gladstone went back to political campaigning over the Bulgarian atrocities in 1876. After publishing his best-selling pamphlet on the atrocities he began a series of speeches across the country. His attacks on the Disraeli government's policy abroad came to a climax when he contested the Scottish constituency of Midlothian near Edinburgh in late 1879. This was his first 'Midlothian campaign', and a second followed for a general election in early 1880.

There had been a Christian religious revival in 1873–75 when millions of Britons attended meetings led by the American evangelist Moody and his hymn-writer Sankey. Gladstone seems to have captured the spirit of this revival. His speeches had a religious intensity, and he became a kind of cult figure, popularly known as the 'Grand Old Man' from the early 1880s.

What was it like to hear a great speech by Gladstone?

There are no films with a sound track of Gladstone and recordings of his voice give little idea of his impact. The best evidence comes from those who heard him (see Sources 5.3–5.6).

SOURCE 5.3 Gladstone's private secretary, Edward Hamilton, described his voice and manner

There was great animation and energy in his manner. But most impressive of all was his voice. It was pitched in a middle key. There was a melodiousness about it which hardly could be excelled, if indeed it was ever equalled; and it was used with great dramatic effect. He had an extraordinary power of modulating it. It was always clear when it was subdued; it was never harsh or grating when it was raised to its full power. He could regulate it with as much ease as the organist, skilled in the manipulation of keyboards and stops, can regulate the instrument at which he is sitting.

SOURCE 5.4 The Liberal journalist, W.T. Stead, described the religious impact Gladstone could make, referring to his speech at Blackheath in September 1876

Mr Gladstone seems to deliver himself of the conclusion of some of his periods as the hunter hurls the spear at his victim, with muscles quivering and the whole energy of the man concentrated into the single act ...

The address was throughout PERMEATED by a religious spirit. In its lofty appeal to man's better nature, in its earnest pleading of the cause of the oppressed, in its constant recognition of the superintendence and government of the Almighty, it was much more a religious address than many a score of sermons that were preached on the following Sunday.

PERMEATED
Mixed with and influenced by.

SOURCE 5.5 W.L. Watson recounted what it was like to be an ordinary member of the audience, describing a meeting in London at the 1880 general election

Surrendering myself to the prevalent sentiment [general feeling], it seemed to me as if someone had touched the stops of a mysterious organ, that searched us through and through. Two more sentences, and we were fairly launched upon a sea of passion ... In that torrent of emotion, the petty politics of the hour figured as huge first principles, and the opinions of the people became as the edicts of eternity ...

All through a speech of long tortuous sentences he endowed us with a faculty of apprehension [ability to understand] we did not know we possessed. And then the peroration [conclusion]: 'You are shortly to pronounce your verdict, you and the people of these isles; and, whatever that verdict may be, as I hope it will be the true one, I trust it will be clear.' ... We leaped to our feet and cheered ... When I stood in the free air outside once more, it seemed somewhat unreasoning, all this ecstasy; clearly I had been Gladstonised; and I voted for him at that election.

SOURCE 5.6 On 29 November 1879 *The Times* gave a more reflective and analytical comment on Gladstone's speaking after the first Midlothian campaign, but from a hostile viewpoint

In a statesman who ... aspires to the direction of public affairs, that which is expected is a certain calmness of judgement, exhibiting itself in some reserve of language and deliberateness in argument. A more passionate temper may, indeed, for a while command some popular enthusiasm. But it sacrifices the confidence of the more thoughtful classes; and without the support of those classes it is, happily, impracticable at present for any government to maintain itself in England.

ACTIVITY

Study Sources 5.3–5.7.

1 What characteristics of a good political public speaker are evident in Sources 5.3 to 5.5?

2 What impact did Gladstone have on his audiences?

3 **a)** How different are Sources 5.5 and 5.6 in their interpretations of Gladstone's effect as a public speaker?

   b) In what ways might parts of Source 5.5 be used to support the argument in Source 5.6?

SOURCE 5.7 Gladstone shown leaving West Calder railway station during the first Midlothian campaign and the kind of enthusiasm many people felt for him

TALKING POINT

What are the advantages and dangers of an emotional style for politicians in public speaking?

How did the impact of Gladstone's speaking vary?

Gladstone spoke to thousands both indoors and outdoors. When he spoke at Bingley Hall, Birmingham in 1877, for instance, the audience was estimated at 25,000. There were no microphones then, and the *Daily Telegraph* estimated that no more than 1500 could hear properly in an open-air meeting. Most of his large audience would not actually have heard the speeches. They were attending a kind of demonstration or perhaps something like a large religious service. When he spoke to 10,000–15,000 people in the pouring rain at Blackheath in September 1876 there were shouts of 'We want you!' and 'Lead us! Lead us!' at the end. Those who could not hear the speech took in the atmosphere and read it in the newspaper afterwards. Journalists and news agencies recorded the speeches for the press, where they would look far less emotional and much more reasoned.

Nonconformists gave Gladstone particularly strong support. They generally thought it important to act against evil in the world, and Gladstone based his arguments on Christian moral principles. By the 1880s Nonconformist papers were making strong statements of support for the Liberal Party (see Source 5.8).

SOURCE 5.8 The *Nonconformist* supports the Liberals in 1880

The Liberal Party has striven to follow the fiery pillar of conscience into this promised land. It has striven to be the party of moral principle as against that of selfish and corrupt interests, the party of peace as against that of violence, the party of popular improvement and reform as against that of resistance to progress, the party of justice as against that of despotic force or social disorder. The backbone of this party has been the religious Protestantism and Puritanism of England.

ACTIVITY

1 What claims does the *Nonconformist* make for the Liberal Party in Source 5.8?
2 If you have studied Disraeli's second ministry, suggest what policies and actions of the Liberals and Conservatives would explain the views expressed in Source 5.8.

SOURCE 5.9 One of several cartoons showing Gladstone as an axeman. This is from *Punch* in May 1877 when Gladstone was criticising the Turkish Empire

DISCUSS

1 How could the descriptions of tree-felling help Gladstone in getting political support?
2 How far did a 'personality cult' develop around Gladstone and how far did he encourage it?
3 How different was he from Disraeli in this? (See page 71.)
4 What comparisons could you make between Gladstone's tree felling and a modern politician's photo opportunity?

The full effect of Gladstone's speaking and its impact on the 1880 election are difficult to assess but Gladstone's campaigns from November 1879 to April 1880 did get great attention and, whether by coincidence or not, the Liberals gained a parliamentary seat at every stop where Gladstone had spoken.

Gladstone was becoming something of a cult figure. Many of his admirers travelled to his home at Hawarden in North Wales. In 1877 the Salford Liberal Association chartered three trains and took 1600 members to his home to hear him speak. They were not the only ones. The greatest excitement was to see Gladstone enjoying his favourite hobby – chopping down trees.

SOURCE 5.10 A writer who admired Gladstone recorded the response of a party of Bolton Liberals to his tree felling, in a biography published in 1882.

As the chips flew at the strokes of their axes, the admiring excursionists picked up some of the fragments, and carefully treasured them as mementos of their visit.

SOURCE 5.11 A journalist described the same incident for *Lloyd's Weekly* soon after it happened in August 1877

It would be impossible to conceive a more theatrical exhibition than that which took place the other day at Hawarden ...

[Gladstone and his son], in proper workmen's garb, moved in a body towards the doomed tree, and an extraordinary scene, worthy of the Adelphi Theatre in its palmy days, was set.

In the front stood the two woodmen, their axes gleaming in the sun; and, at a respectful distance around, the excursionists ... massed themselves ... The woodmen, intently watched by the crowd, threw off coat and waistcoat ... and made the air ring with their lusty blows.

ACTIVITY

1 **a)** How do Sources 5.10 and 5.11 give a different impression of the scene at Hawarden?
  b) Why are they so different?

SOURCE 5.12 Lord Randolph Churchill, a Conservative opponent, commented in 1884

Gentlemen, we live in an age of advertisement ... The Prime Minister [Gladstone] is the greatest living master of the art of personal political advertisement ... Every act of his, whether it be for the purposes of health, or of recreation, or of religious devotion, is spread before the eyes of every man, woman and child in the United Kingdom on large and glaring placards ... For the purposes of recreation he has selected the felling of trees ... Every afternoon the whole world is invited to assist at the crashing fall of some beech or elm or oak.

Gladstone becomes leader of the Liberals

When the Liberals won the 1880 election Hartington was their leader in the Commons and Granville their leader in the Lords. The Queen, who hated Gladstone, might have been expected to ask either of them to form a government, but they were not confident enough to do so without Gladstone's support.

Gladstone sent a message to them through Lord Wolverton that he would not serve as a minister in somebody else's government. He believed that circumstances demanded his return as prime minister. The Liberals agreed and on 23 April 1880 Queen Victoria reluctantly asked him to form his second ministry.

DISCUSS

Does what you have read in Sources 5.3–5.12 indicate Gladstone had good reasons for believing he was the best choice for Liberal prime minister?

FOCUS ROUTE

1 Summarise in notes the main problems Gladstone's government faced in southern Africa, Egypt, the Sudan and Afghanistan.
2 Identify
   a) what action the government took
   b) any motives it appears to have had
   c) any mistakes it made
   d) any successes it gained.

B Did Gladstone continue or reverse Disraeli's policy abroad?

In the 1880 election campaign Gladstone had furiously condemned Disraeli's government for wasting money on colonial expeditions and ignoring the rights of native peoples. Yet after the election, with a majority of over 70, Gladstone's second government launched more expensive expeditions than Disraeli's and conquered Egypt. He wanted to solve problems through a Concert of Europe, but Europe's most powerful minister, Bismarck, described him as a 'mad' professor. He wanted to limit defence spending to keep down taxes. Yet from 1880 to 1886 defence spending rose by £4.5 million. Income tax, which averaged 3.3d in the £ in 1874–80, averaged 5.7d during Gladstone's ministry in 1880–85.

Gladstone was not as inconsistent or hypocritical as this sounds. He had never opposed having an empire. He accepted that military expeditions were sometimes necessary and thought European empires had some value in spreading Christian civilisation. In 1874 he had left a surplus in the budget for Disraeli's government but then he inherited a far worse financial position in 1880.

Yet even allowing for all this, Gladstone's government seems to have done roughly the opposite of what he had preached.

Any government had to react to crises around the empire. Was Gladstone powerless to stop his ministers, commanders and colonial governors from taking action? Did he follow, or at least attempt, a different policy or did he do just the sort of thing he had condemned? This section examines the crises he faced and why he acted as he did.

Southern Africa

Britain had taken over the Transvaal from Boer rule during Disraeli's ministry. Gladstone proposed that the Transvaal should govern itself within a federation of southern African states under the sovereignty of Queen Victoria. The Boers of the Transvaal refused to accept this, assembled an armed force and fought the Battle of Majuba Hill in 1881, where they killed a British general and killed or captured all his troops. Gladstone decided against the normal government policy of assembling a large enough army to defeat the Boers and show British supremacy. Instead, in the 1881 Pretoria Convention, he agreed that the Transvaal should be self-governing under British sovereignty (overall control). Later, the London Convention in 1884 did not mention the claims to sovereignty.

■ 5A Southern Africa, late 1800s

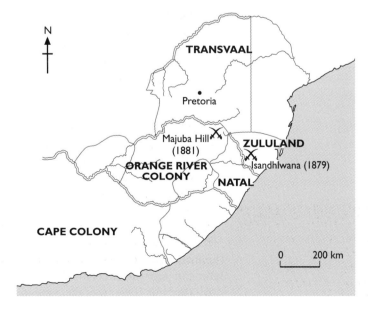

■ 5B Egypt and Sudan

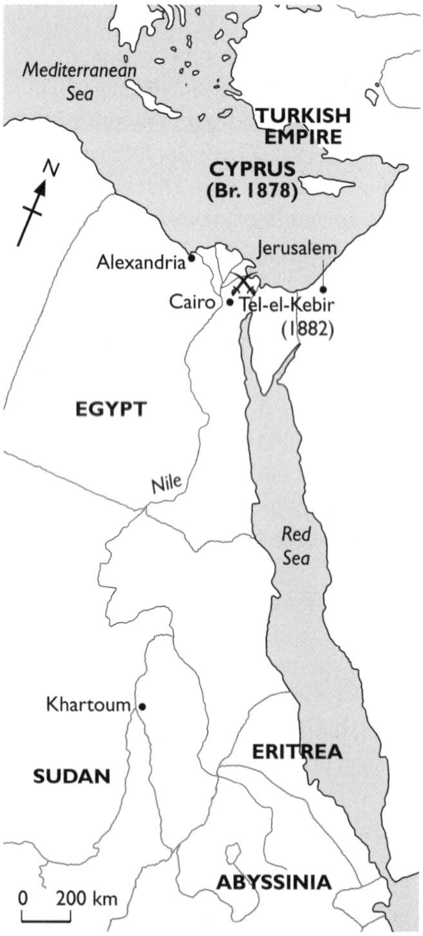

Map showing the Eastern Mediterranean and north-east Africa, with labels: Mediterranean Sea, TURKISH EMPIRE, CYPRUS (Br. 1878), Alexandria, Jerusalem, Cairo, Tel-el-Kebir (1882), EGYPT, Nile, Red Sea, Khartoum, ERITREA, SUDAN, ABYSSINIA. Scale 0 200 km.

TALKING POINT

In general Gladstone was concerned about how people's self-interest could interfere with their judgement, but he seems to have had no worries about his Egyptian investments which were quite unknown to the public.

Think about the normal practice at the time and Gladstone's views on the intervention. Did he act rightly?

Egypt

Although in theory Egypt was part of the Turkish Empire, in practice it was governed by a native ruler, the Khedive. When he fell seriously into debt in the 1870s, the Egyptian government borrowed extensively from British and French citizens and their governments then supervised how the Egyptians spent the money. This Anglo-French intervention led to an Egyptian nationalist revolt led by Arabi Pasha who largely took over the country. In 1882 there was a riot against westerners in Alexandria and about 50 were killed.

The chaos raised wider issues. The Suez Canal ran through Egypt. Disraeli had bought 44 per cent of the canal shares for the British government in 1875, and it was vital for communications with India. Industrialists and merchants, who worried about economic depression, wanted to maintain and expand trade with India and Africa. The government, which had looked weak in dealing with the Boers in southern Africa (see page 87) and terrorists in Ireland (see Chapter 14), needed to look strong in dealing with British interests elsewhere. It tried diplomatically to get agreement between the major European powers about how to deal with Egypt, but when that failed it acted militarily.

Government action

The British and French fleets were already off the Egyptian coast, and most of Gladstone's Cabinet wanted to act. Gladstone did not, but he gave way to pressure from the Cabinet. Admiral Seymour, in charge of the fleet, was ordered to prevent the Egyptians from improving Alexandria's defences. He took this to mean bombarding the place. The French did not act. The British continued, sent a military force under Sir Garnet Wolseley, which won the Battle of Tel-el-Kebir, and took over Egypt in 1882.

Gladstone had always opposed taking new places such as Egypt to defend the route to India, but an emergency arose in 1882 and Gladstone saw the campaign as 'an upright war, a Christian war'. Had he really acted in line with his own principles?

Gladstone's personal financial interests in Egypt

When he became prime minister Gladstone was not expected to dispose of his investments or hand them over to others as government ministers do today. His largest single investment was in Egyptian bonds (loans to the Egyptian government). Gladstone told the House of Commons that Britain was fighting in Egypt for 'established rights'. He did not tell Parliament that he was one of the foreign bondholders. Before the British invasion there was doubt about the safety of the investment, and Gladstone's bonds were worth £17,100; afterwards, as a result of government action, they were worth about £24,600 and amounted to around a third of his investments. He was about £7,500 better off, which in today's money is around £400,000.

Sudan

The Sudan was traditionally governed by Egypt, but it was taken over by a Muslim fanatic known as the Mahdi. In 1883 his troops massacred an Egyptian force led by a British officer. Early next year Gladstone's government sent a Christian fanatic, General Gordon, to the Sudan with a small force and unclear instructions.

His orders from the Foreign Secretary were to:

- 'report' to the government 'on the military situation'
- 'consider and report' on the best way of evacuating troops from the Sudan (or 'Soudan' as it was then)
- 'pay especial consideration' to discouraging the slave trade
- 'perform such other duties as the Egyptian government may desire to intrust to you'.

The British government's man in Egypt, Sir Evelyn Baring, told Gordon the main aim was 'the Evacuation of the Soudan'. The Khedive of Egypt appointed him 'Governor General of the Soudan'.

Gordon tried to gain power in the Sudan, but the Mahdi's forces beseiged him in the capital, Khartoum. Gladstone resisted pressure to send a relief force for some months. Gordon sent contradictory messages from Khartoum, so the prime minister thought he was 'not wholly sane' and had 'disobeyed his instructions', but the government sent a relief force eventually. There was a telegraph link part way up the Nile so the newspapers had frequent reports. In the end, Gordon and his troops were killed two days before the relief force reached Khartoum. The news brought a tremendous reaction in Britain and harmed Gladstone's reputation greatly.

SOURCE 5.13 The *Morning Post*, a strongly Conservative newspaper, reports the fall of Khartoum, 6 February 1885

Khartoum has fallen, and Gordon is either a prisoner or slain. Such was the terrible message from the Soudan which fell yesterday like an avalanche upon the country, and spread consternation in every British home. At the very moment when a personal heroism unsurpassed in the annals of history was confidently believed to have been crowned with its fitting reward, at the very instant when unexampled courage, intelligence, and endurance were about to be sealed by the vulgar stamp of success, the crown was torn from the victor's brows by the treachery of those for whom he had unselfishly sacrificed himself.

> **ACTIVITY**
>
> Gladstone's nickname was the Grand Old Man (often shortened to GOM). Opponents now called him the MOG – Murderer of Gordon. How justified was this?

Afghanistan

■ 5C Afghanistan – the border region between Russia and India

The British army was heavily involved in Afghanistan when Gladstone became prime minister in 1880 (see pages 73–74). His government withdrew the British force there by spring 1881, but had an agreement with the Afghan ruler that he would do what Britain wanted in foreign policy. Here, at least, the Liberals managed to keep up British influence, act peacefully and keep down spending.

Problems arose again in early 1885 when the Russians encroached on Afghanistan's northern border with fighting around Penjdeh. With much criticism aimed at the government over Gordon's death, Gladstone took a strong line. He got permission from Parliament to spend an extra £11 million in the Afghanistan and Sudan areas. The threat of action helped achieve a peaceful agreement with Russia, and the disputed border area was divided up, but the government still spent around £9 million, even though it sent no major force to Afghanistan or the Sudan.

At the end of Gladstone's second ministry, Britain gained rights to more territory at the Berlin conference which divided up Africa among European powers (see page 112).

RUSSIA

Caspian Sea

Border uncertain until 1885

Penjdeh

PERSIA

Kabul

AFGHANISTAN

Khyber Pass

Kandahar

Delhi

Persian Gulf

INDIA

N

Arabian Sea

0   200 km

ACTIVITY

Here is the chart that you first encountered on page 75. Now it has a final column summarising Gladstone's policies in his second ministry.

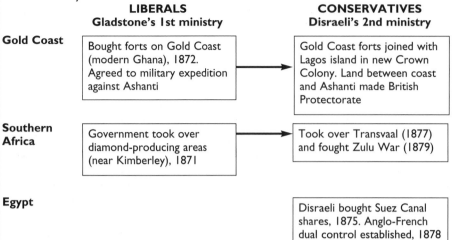

	LIBERALS Gladstone's 1st ministry	CONSERVATIVES Disraeli's 2nd ministry	LIBERALS Gladstone's 2nd ministry
Gold Coast	Bought forts on Gold Coast (modern Ghana), 1872. Agreed to military expedition against Ashanti	Gold Coast forts joined with Lagos island in new Crown Colony. Land between coast and Ashanti made British Protectorate	
Southern Africa	Government took over diamond-producing areas (near Kimberley), 1871	Took over Transvaal (1877) and fought Zulu War (1879)	Accepted Transvaal's substantial independence after Boers had beaten British (p. 87)
Egypt		Disraeli bought Suez Canal shares, 1875. Anglo-French dual control established, 1878	British conquered Egypt, 1882, and took over administration (p. 88)
Afghanistan		Government twice sent military expedition to establish British mission in the capital, Kabul	Threatened action against Russia when it encroached near Penjdeh on Afghan border (p. 89)

1 For each of the new boxes explain whether you see these as continuations of earlier Conservative policies or discontinuities, or reversals. For each one explain your answer.
2 In Section 3 you will explore these issues in greater depth. For now make your own overview judgement: to what extent did Gladstone's government continue or reverse Disraeli's policies abroad?

FOCUS ROUTE

Which reforms in Gladstone's second ministry were most important and why?

ATHEIST
One who does not believe in the existence of God.

HOME RULE PARTY
Party with MPs in the Westminster Parliament which worked to get self-government for Ireland.

C What did Gladstone's second ministry achieve at home, 1880–85?

Gladstone himself concentrated on how to deal with the crisis in Ireland in the early part of his second ministry (see Chapter 14). Domestic reforms were largely the work of his ministers, and the reforms in 1880–85 were undoubtedly less significant than those in the first ministry. The ministers faced difficulties in the House of Commons because some Irish MPs were making full use of opportunities to obstruct business. A lot of time was also spent discussing whether an ATHEIST Liberal MP, Charles Bradlaugh, should swear the oath referring to God which other MPs took. Four young Conservative MPs, eager to make their reputations and embarrass the government, spent ages talking about this issue. The MPs became known as the Fourth Party – the Liberals, Conservatives and HOME RULERS were the first three parties.

■ 5D Laws passed during Gladstone's second ministry

1880 Education Act	Made school attendance compulsory for all children aged from five to ten.
1880 Burials Act	Allowed Nonconformists to have consecrated graveyards beside their own chapels.
1880 Ground Game Act	Let tenant farmers shoot rabbits and hares which might be eating their crops, whatever their landlords said about it.
1880 Employers' Liability Act	Extended a workman's right to get compensation for accidents at work.
1883 Agricultural Holdings Act	Forced landowners to compensate tenants, if they left, for any improvements they had made on the owners' land.
1881 Second Irish Land Act	Gave far more rights to Irish tenants (see Chapter 14).
1884 Third Reform Act	Extended the vote to householders in the counties (see Chapter 1).

ACTIVITY

Look back to the chart on page 70. How far do the measures outlined in Chart 5D reverse or continue the policies of Disraeli's Conservative government?

FOCUS ROUTE

1 What were the difficulties in managing the Liberal Party and how did Gladstone's leadership help resolve or worsen these?
2 Make notes on why each of the following was important in breaking up the Liberal Party:
  a) Existing splits between Whigs and Radicals
  b) Chamberlain's programme in 1885
  c) The Home Rule for Ireland issue and Gladstone's lack of consultation?
(See Chapter 14 on Irish Home Rule and Source 10.7 on page 171 for 1886 election result.)

D   Did Gladstone split the Liberal Party?

It will be clear from all that you have so far studied that the Liberal Party contained different groups with very varied views. Gladstone had once helped to unite the different groups in the 1860s, but splits were always possible, even likely.

In 1886 the Liberal Party suffered a decisive split. Gladstone wanted Parliament to grant Home Rule (self-government) to Ireland. He put forward a bill to achieve this. Ninety-three of his own MPs opposed it. As they wanted to keep the union between Britain and Ireland, they were known as Liberal Unionists, and they broke away from the main part of the Liberal Party, which Gladstone still led.

After the defeat of the Home Rule Bill Gladstone's government resigned, and a general election followed in late 1886. The Conservatives and Liberal Unionists made a pact not to oppose each other and Gladstone's Liberals lost support and seats in many English counties. Although the Conservatives did not have an overall majority in the House of Commons, they could govern as long as the Liberal Unionists supported them.

Many expected the Liberals to reunite but the split remained permanent, and the Conservatives dominated politics for the next twenty years to 1905.

The Liberals were severely weakened for the next twenty years so naturally much of the blame for this split has been attached to Gladstone's decision to propose Home Rule against the will of so many of his MPs. How far you agree that Gladstone was to blame depends heavily on your view of a number of other issues:

1 Whether the Liberal Party was so disunited it was bound to split over **something** at **some** point anyway.
2 What **Gladstone's real motives** were in pursuing Home Rule for Ireland. Was he committed to it out of principle? Or could he, once again, be accused of opportunism?
3 **How well Gladstone managed** his party. His leadership had always depended on the strength of his personality. Was Gladstone's leadership style a strength or a weakness?

We will now examine these issues one by one.

Issue 1: Was the Liberal Party likely to split anyway?

From the beginning the Liberal Party was a combination of different groups. Despite success under Gladstone they never fused together in some new coherent Gladstonian Liberal Party. Gladstone was very different from the earlier Whig leaders of the party. Reforms in his first ministry had upset many Liberal supporters. Historians have often suggested that the Liberals became further divided in two major ways in the 1880s.

■ 5E Divisions in the Liberal Party, 1880s

1 There were big divisions between left-wing Radicals and right-wing Whigs, though they did not form coherent groups.

The Radicals are sometimes estimated at around a third of the Liberal MPs, but they had very varied ideas. In a few cases, Whigs left to join the Conservatives.

2 The Liberals were split into too many different sections, and lots of Liberals had their own fads (personal ideas). This argument was strongly developed by D.A. Hamer in the 1970s. He stressed how Nonconformist groups, especially, in the Liberal Party were obsessed with single aims. It was difficult to get them to work together, but Liberal leaders in the 1880s developed their own policies without much reference to the fads.

The National Liberal Federation

Today political parties have national organisations linked with local parties in each constituency. Parties advertise for members and anyone can join. The nineteenth-century Liberal Party was not like this. To improve Liberal organisation around the country and provide some sort of national party, Joseph Chamberlain started the National Liberal Federation at Birmingham in 1877, and Gladstone addressed a great meeting at its launch. It probably helped the Liberals win more MPs in the 1880 election and seems a big advantage for any Liberal leader. However, the Federation caused two major problems:

- It was intended not only to provide willing helpers to support MPs and leaders but also to suggest policies. At its national meetings, party activists indicated what reforms they wanted most. In this way it could be seen as a threat to the leaders as well as a support. Chamberlain privately saw it becoming 'a very powerful organisation' which the Whigs and parliamentary WHIPS would detest.
- It developed from the Birmingham Liberal Association and was run on the model of the Birmingham party. This encouraged lots of ordinary Liberals to participate but ensured that the whole organisation was run by committees which were indirectly elected and to which members could be co-opted (not elected). It was soon nicknamed the 'CAUCUS' after American organisations run by a few party bosses who were seen as wire-pullers controlling others, not genuine popular representatives.

Chamberlain's Unauthorised Programme

Chamberlain toured the country for several months in 1885, putting forward a programme of radical reforms.

1 Free education paid for from rates
2 PROGRESSIVE TAXATION
3 Elected local councils
4 Land reform – allowing local councils to buy land which could provide allotments and smallholdings

These were intended to influence voters in the general election that would follow parliamentary reform at the end of 1885. His main ideas were generally called the 'Unauthorised Programme' because they were not agreed by other Liberal leaders, including Gladstone. Although Chamberlain thought they would appeal to masses of new working-class voters, many Liberals thought they did more harm than good. The Liberals won most county constituencies, but the Conservatives got more seats in boroughs where Chamberlain had hoped to do well. Some of the reforms probably appealed to many wage-earners, but all kinds of people worried about the extra rates (local taxes) they would have to pay as a result.

All this suggests the Liberal Party was bound to disintegrate. It might sound like chaos to you. However, more recent work, particularly by Jonathan Parry (1993) and Terry Jenkins (1994), suggests the Liberal Party could well have held together, and there are many reasons for thinking this:

- The Whigs were strong in Gladstone's second ministry and Hartington, their leading figure, looked likely to take over as prime minister. Almost everyone thought Gladstone was about to retire. The Whigs did not feel threatened by the rest of the party. They might soon take control of it.
- Very few Whigs did break away before 1886.
- Whigs supported the Third Reform Act because they believed in this kind of constitutional reform. Like other Liberals, they wanted more elected councils in England and Ireland.
- At the left-wing end of the party, the Radicals disagreed among themselves over many aspects of domestic policy. It would have been difficult for them to break away from the Liberal Party as a group.
- Hartington, the most prominent Whig, and Chamberlain, the most prominent Radical, had significant common ground over the issue of Britain's empire.

WHIPS
MPs appointed by the party leaders to persuade other MPs to support the leadership and its policies.

CAUCUS
Word for organisers who tried to manage elections or control a political party.

TALKING POINT

At the time, Chamberlain's reforms were described by some as radical and by others as socialist.

Which description would you give to them? (See page 149 on socialism and note that Chamberlain was a wealthy manufacturer who believed in maintaining private property.)

PROGRESSIVE TAXATION
Taxation which falls more heavily on the wealthy, so that they pay a higher proportion of their wealth in tax than people who are less well off.

Issue 2: What were Gladstone's motives?

Why did Gladstone propose Home Rule? Was it because he thought it was the only way of governing Ireland satisfactorily?

Gladstone believed in nations in the empire running their own affairs if they could; he saw that his Irish reforms had so far failed and Irish MPs were having a bad influence on the House of Commons. Some historians including Matthew (1995) and Shannon (1999) emphasise how he gradually accepted Home Rule. Shannon reckons Gladstone saw the need for Home Rule during troubles in 1882, and that the idea crystallised in the spring of 1885. Gladstone denied that taking up Home Rule involved a change of mind, and from his diaries, Matthew (1995) sees it as 'the product of experience'. Terry Jenkins (1994) accepts that Gladstone was converted to Home Rule but also thinks he was influenced by personal ambition. Home Rule was one of the issues Gladstone called his 'specialities' – matters which he thought he could tackle better than anyone else.

Was it because he thought it was the best way of keeping control of the Liberal Party?

Several historians have seen Home Rule as a way of dealing with Liberal Party problems. Cooke and Vincent (1974) explain politicians' actions in 1885–86 largely as tactics to gain power and see Gladstone taking up Home Rule to outmanoeuvre his rivals. Chamberlain saw it that way: 'There was nothing else for him except my [Unauthorised] Programme [and] to have adopted that would have been humiliating.' Hamer (1972) thinks Gladstone needed a great issue to draw the party together under his leadership.

Was it because he thought it was a way of getting a majority in the House of Commons and getting back into government?

After the 1885 general election the number of Liberal MPs just equalled the total of Conservative and Irish Home Rule Party MPs in the House of Commons, so Gladstone could clearly become prime minister with Irish support if he were willing to introduce Home Rule. The first public statement suggesting Gladstone wanted Home Rule came from his son, Herbert Gladstone, to journalists in December 1885. Parnell's Irish Home Rule Party had just done very well in the election, and Herbert suggested this had had an 'inevitable effect' on Gladstone. People took this to mean that he now wanted Home Rule.

Issue 3: How well did Gladstone manage his party?

Any leader would have found difficulty in managing the Liberal Party. Gladstone's own personal style arguably made it a bigger problem. When he came back as prime minister in 1880, aged 70, he said it was only temporary, to tackle the evil legacy of Disraeli, and always seemed about to retire again. He often pursued his own ideas without consulting colleagues very much.

When Gladstone formed a government in 1886 to examine the possibilities of Home Rule, Hartington and other Whigs would not join. Gladstone did not consult his Cabinet or his Liberal MPs about his scheme but just presented them with a package (see page 237). Chamberlain, who had argued for local government in Ireland, resigned because he did not agree with Gladstone's proposals. Both wings of the party, the Whigs and the Radicals, had worries about how much power the Irish Parliament would have and its impact on the empire. Both groups resented the way Gladstone seemed to be using his popularity outside Parliament to ignore colleagues inside. As Hartington put it, 'Did any leader ever treat a party in such a way as he has done?'

Who split from the Liberal Party over Home Rule?

Gladstone's first Home Rule bill was defeated in the House of Commons – 93 Liberal MPs voted against it. They were a mixed bunch. Over half of them were from aristocratic families, and they also included a small number of Radical MPs. Yet, the National Liberal Federation, which Chamberlain had started, overwhelmingly supported Gladstone and, in the end, fewer than 10 per cent of the Liberal activists seem to have left the party over Home Rule.

ACTIVITY

Here are three suspects on trial for their role in the Liberal Party split in 1886.

WILLIAM GLADSTONE
Leader of the Liberal Party

JOSEPH CHAMBERLAIN
Leader of the Radicals

LORD HARTINGTON
Leader of the Whigs

1 What evidence can you gather against each one?
2 Do you think Gladstone was
   a) mostly
   b) partly
   c) not at all
   to blame for the split in the Liberal Party in 1886?

E The final years

Despite the split in the Liberal Party, Gladstone remained its leader until 1894. He still had a unique popular reputation and occasionally spoke to large audiences, but he was not expected to lead the Liberal Party regularly in the House of Commons.

In some ways Gladstone became more radical after 1886. He wanted measures to get more working men into Parliament and accepted many reforms approved by the National Liberal Federation Conference at Newcastle in 1891.

Above all, though, he led the Liberal Party in order to acheive Irish Home Rule. As he told Parliament in 1892, the Irish question was his 'primary and absorbing interest' and had been for the last seven years. The problem was that Irish Home Rule does not seem to have been popular in England, and when he did get a majority for it in the House of Commons in 1892, the Lords predictably turned it down in the next year.

He did become prime minister again for the period 1892–94. His fourth ministry introduced a few reforms, including some which restricted working hours for railway workers and employees in government factories, but disappointed some trade union leaders. After the House of Lords stopped Irish Home Rule Gladstone wanted a new campaign to reform the Lords, but his colleagues would not agree.

In 1894, with his eyesight fading, he retired because he did not agree with the rest of the Cabinet over naval spending. He also disliked the kind of IMPERIALISM that became increasingly popular (see Chapter 6) as it cost too much and stretched the military too far.

> **IMPERIALISM**
> Policy of extending a nation's power or influence over other territories – building an empire.

> **DISCUSS**
> In 1886, was a successful future for the Liberals more likely with Gladstone as leader or with Chamberlain? Give reasons for your choice.

F Review: Should Gladstone have stayed in retirement?

When he returned to politics in opposition in 1876, Gladstone became a more popular and charismatic figure than he had ever been before. His public-speaking contributions made the 1880 election campaign a far more national affair than any previous general election and contributed to the Liberals' victory.

On the other hand, few would claim that the achievements of his later ministries matched those of his first. He concentrated on the government of Ireland more than any other issue but failed to bring it peace or give it Home Rule. He played a crucial role in splitting and weakening his party in 1886.

Gladstone's approach to Home Rule led to a break with both the Whigs and some Radicals such as Joseph Chamberlain. Chamberlain wanted the state to tax the rich and use the money for land and welfare reform – a policy more like that of the Liberal and Labour parties in the twentieth century. Chamberlain was an enthusiastic supporter of the imperialist expansion in which all British governments participated and which appealed to the popular imagination. Gladstone wanted to cut state spending and was suspicious of imperialism. He concentrated on constitutional reform, preached Christian morality and radiated charisma. Gladstone's politics therefore looked old-fashioned in the last quarter of the nineteenth century while Chamberlain's seemed modern.

KEY POINTS FROM CHAPTER 5

Should Gladstone have stayed in retirement?

1 Gladstone had an unprecedented impact as a public speaker.
2 This led to his return as Liberal prime minister in 1880, but he had great difficulties in getting the sort of changes he wanted in British policy abroad in his second ministry.
3 The ministry introduced less significant reforms than his first, but the Third Reform Act (see Chapter 1) was important.
4 There were difficulties in managing the Liberal Party, and it split over Irish Home Rule in 1886.

Section 2 Review: Gladstone and Disraeli – how great were the differences between them?

There was fierce rivalry between Gladstone and Disraeli in 1876–80. Gladstone's attacks on Beaconsfieldism were aimed against his rival's personal morality and whole approach to government. Yet analysis of their policies shows marked similarities between the two leaders. Both wanted to help the monarchy, though they set about it in very different ways – Gladstone by lecturing Queen Victoria and Disraeli by flattering her. Both were strong supporters of the Church of England. Both thought the Turkish empire had a useful function. They certainly had very different views on empire, but when they faced similar problems in Africa and Afghanistan it is easy to argue that they gave similar responses (see Chart 4F and Activity on page 90).

Many of their differences came from their very different personal backgrounds and political needs. They were contrasting personalities. Recent historical writing on Gladstone emphasises his complex motivation, anguished Christian morality and how he became near impossible to work with in the 1880s. The most interesting work on Disraeli stresses his complex visionary ideas and Jewishness.

SECTION 2 REVIEW ACTIVITY

Gladstone and Disraeli – how great were the differences between them?

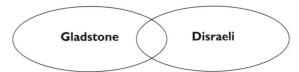

1 Make your own large copy of this diagram.
2 Look back through your work on Chapters 3–5 and in the different sectors of the diagram note information that is true of just Gladstone, just Disraeli or both of them. You can get some help from the information in the text above but make sure you also consider these pages as well:
   a) comparing what they did – see pages 69–70 and 79, and Activity on page 90
   b) comparing their characters – see page 62
   c) comparing their leadership styles – see page 71.
3 Once you have completed your diagram, use it to prepare a short PowerPoint presentation summarising your view on how deep the differences really were between the two men.

How successfully did Britain maintain and defend its empire?

■ A British Empire, early twentieth century

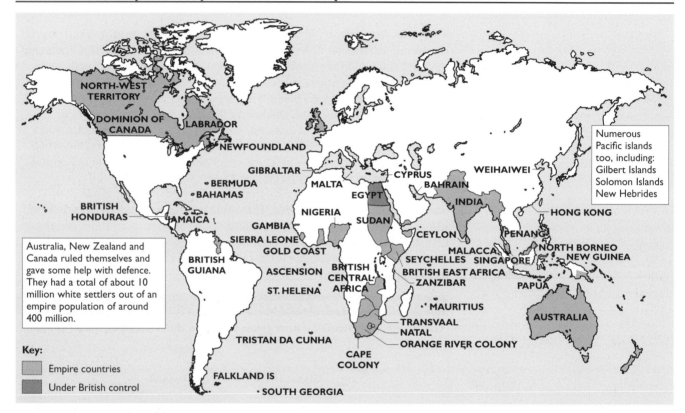

NORTH-WEST TERRITORY

DOMINION OF CANADA — LABRADOR

NEWFOUNDLAND

GIBRALTAR

BERMUDA
BAHAMAS

BRITISH HONDURAS

JAMAICA

MALTA

CYPRUS

EGYPT

NIGERIA

GAMBIA

SIERRA LEONE
GOLD COAST

BRITISH GUIANA

ASCENSION

ST. HELENA

BRITISH CENTRAL AFRICA

SUDAN

CEYLON

BRITISH EAST AFRICA
ZANZIBAR

WEIHAIWEI

BAHRAIN

INDIA

HONG KONG

PENANG

MALACCA
SEYCHELLES SINGAPORE

NORTH BORNEO
NEW GUINEA

PAPUA

MAURITIUS

AUSTRALIA

TRANSVAAL
NATAL
ORANGE RIVER COLONY

CAPE COLONY

TRISTAN DA CUNHA

FALKLAND IS

SOUTH GEORGIA

Numerous Pacific islands too, including:
Gilbert Islands
Solomon Islands
New Hebrides

Australia, New Zealand and Canada ruled themselves and gave some help with defence. They had a total of about 10 million white settlers out of an empire population of around 400 million.

Key:

Empire countries

Under British control

At the end of the nineteenth century Britain had a population of about 40 million but ruled a worldwide empire with a population of around 400 million. The scale of it was immense. This medium-sized European power controlled almost one quarter of the Earth's land surface. It was simply the largest empire the world had ever known, and most British people were apparently very proud of it.

India was Britain's prize possession. Nearly 300 million of the empire's 400 million people were in India. One Indian VICEROY, Lord Curzon, claimed: 'As long as we rule India we are the greatest power in the world. If we lose it, we shall drop straightaway to a third-rate power.'

It is no surprise therefore that the major foreign policy concern for successive governments was how to maintain and defend this empire. In many ways it was run on a very thin thread of power. Yet, while the greatest European powers had armies half a million to a million strong, Britain had about 200,000 men in the army and 100,000 in the navy.

Moreover it was not enough simply to defend the empire. Governments saw a fiercely competitive world where empires were either on the way up or on the way down. Other European countries were enlarging their empires and most British people believed that Britain needed to do the same.

This section examines how Britain did it.

Chapter 6 investigates the period up to 1902 – the end of the Boer War. This period has often been presented as one of 'splendid isolation' when Britain's navy ruled the seas and the British government felt little need of alliances. Throughout this time the main concern for the British was how to defend India against possible attack from Russia.

Chapter 7 investigates the period after 1900 when attention shifted from Russia to Germany. This chapter examines why Britain eventually went to war with Germany – and how far concerns about the empire were responsible.

Who managed foreign policy 1885–1914?

Lord Salisbury
Conservative Prime Minister 1885–86, 1886–92, 1895–1902
Foreign Secretary 1887–92, 1895–1900
He was Foreign Secretary for most of his time as Prime Minister. He gained an extraordinary mastery of foreign policy issues and effectively decided what should be done until the last years of his premiership. He was very sceptical about experts and tended to work out decisions for himself rather than relying on Foreign Office advisers

Lord Rosebery
Liberal Foreign Secretary 1886, 1892–94
Prime Minister 1894–95
Rosebery had considerable control over foreign affairs. He was an imperialist and although a Liberal openly followed a similar policy to the Conservatives

Joseph Chamberlain
UNIONIST Colonial Secretary 1895–1903
Chamberlain was the most enthusiastic imperialist among top British politicians. He tried to develop the colonies Britain had by improving transport and administration, and he wanted closer contacts between Britain and countries with British settlers, such as Australia. He influenced British foreign policy a lot, although he did not manage it directly

Lord Lansdowne
Unionist Foreign Secretary 1900–05
Lansdowne paid more attention to experts in the Foreign Office than Salisbury. He was readier to make agreements with other countries and was responsible for the Anglo-Japanese Alliance in 1902 and the Entente Cordiale with France in 1904

Sir Edward Grey
Liberal Foreign Secretary 1905–14
Grey worked closely with Foreign Office professionals. He was responsible for closer contacts with France as worries increased about Germany

UNIONIST
Person in the grouping of Conservatives and former Liberal Party members who opposed Home Rule for Ireland and wanted to keep it in a full union with Great Britain.

Committee of Imperial Defence (CID)
From 1902 defence was managed by this committee connected with the Cabinet and made up of ministers, army and navy chiefs, and expert advisers. It planned the defence of the empire, but differences between army and navy commanders reduced its effectiveness

How was British policy changing 1885–1902?

CHAPTER OVERVIEW

DOMINIONS
Countries outside the UK under the sovereignty (supreme power) of the British monarch but effectively having full powers to govern themselves and decide how far they will associate with the UK.

The British Empire was not only large but exceptionally varied. Whereas DOMINIONS like Canada and Australia governed themselves, other parts of the empire were under more direct British control. British trading companies took over large parts of Africa and British armies conquered areas like the Sudan. In India, the British ruled most of the country directly but Indian princes administered large parts as well.

By general consent India was the prize possession, so Russia, the country that most threatened India, was the state that Britain feared most. India was defended by an army of 225,000. About two thirds of these were Indian troops and there had been a serious mutiny against the British in 1857. Russia, on the other hand, had over one million troops who could threaten Indian frontiers and communications. Much of Britain's foreign and defence policy was designed to deal with this danger.

Meanwhile in Africa a different kind of imperial struggle was unfolding – as the European countries divided up the continent between them in the so-called 'Scramble for Africa'. By 1900 it was a war in South Africa that caused Britain the biggest military problems and raised doubts about British imperial strength.

This chapter examines this complex period through a range of themes. The key question is, **How was British policy changing in the period 1885–1902?**

A What was imperialism? (pp. 99–101)

B How was the empire presented to the British population and how popular was it? (pp. 102–107)

C What problems did Britain face defending its empire? (pp. 108–112)

D How did the Boer War change attitudes to empire? (pp. 113–115)

A What was imperialism?

Imperialism involves a stronger society controlling a weaker one. It therefore involves power, but different kinds of power.

Economic imperialism (informal empire)

A more wealthy or advanced group takes control of trade in an area, so that it can sell its goods to the inhabitants or get food or raw materials from them. It uses its power, often based on better weapons and transport, to manage the trade, and investors in the enterprise then hope for good profits.

Political imperialism (formal empire)

A state takes over another people's land and governs it, using soldiers and officials.

Social and cultural imperialism

The stronger society taking over another may think its beliefs and way of life – its general culture and civilisation – are superior to those of the weaker one. (The enthusiasm for empire in Britain and the way missionaries and empire builders spread Christianity illustrate this.)

'New imperialism'

This describes the attitude that predominated in the 1870s–90s. It was characterised by

a) growing competition between European countries to acquire colonies – a competitive struggle

b) greater popular enthusiasm for empire at home – empire as an object of national pride.

■ Learning trouble spot

Imperialism: a dirty word?

'Imperialism' is a good example of how the associations with a word can change over time. It seems to have begun its life as a term of abuse when opponents were criticising the aggressive, expensive aspects of Disraeli's approach to empire. In the late nineteenth century it was used more approvingly to refer to strengthening and making the best use of empire.

Most twentieth- and twenty-first-century commentators use the word 'imperialism' disapprovingly. They tend to stress the force and selfishness involved and how weaker societies had little or no choice in the matter. It is often used as a term of abuse for wealthy states and business companies gaining power for their own advantage.

ACTIVITY

Work individually or in pairs to write two definitions of imperialism – one supporting it and one hostile. Use 25–50 words for each.

■ 6A Government arguments for and against imperialism in the 1880s and 1890s

	For expanding the empire	Against expanding the empire
ECONOMIC	Many foreign states have introduced high taxes on British imports. If these states take over new areas they may levy import duties there too and shut Britain out of these markets. We need new colonies to boost our trade, to reverse the decline in industry and to safeguard jobs.	Only a minority of trade and investment is going to the colonies. Investors may be excited about the colonies, but many of the companies trading there do not pay any dividends. Once we get involved in taking over new colonies nobody knows what it will cost. Look at Egypt. We paid for one campaign to take over the country, and then people argued for another to secure the Sudan.
BRITAIN'S STATUS AS A GREAT POWER	It is more difficult to get joint action among European powers now. Competition with other countries means we cannot stand still. The Germans believe in *REALPOLITIK* in world affairs where force counts. Britain needs to be as powerful as possible, and we must back up our generals and traders when they are threatened.	Getting new colonies can upset other powers. Taking over Egypt ruined our relations with France. Colonial rivalries could lead to a war between European powers.
PUBLIC POPULARITY	With a larger electorate we need to bind everybody together more. If democracy is to work we have to get people thinking of common national interests. Imperialism does this brilliantly, and many workers are excited about emigrating to the new colonies.	There are dangers. If colonial wars go wrong or become too expensive, people might turn against the whole idea of empire. Gladstone used colonial failures very effectively to attack Disraeli in 1880.

REALPOLITIK

An approach to politics based on realities and a state's practical needs rather than a system of beliefs or ideas of right and wrong.

DISCUSS

Study Chart 6A. In the 1880s and 1890s the arguments in favour of imperialism generally outweighed the objections for both Liberal and Conservative ministers. Why do you think this was?

Pictures of imperialism

SOURCE 6.1 An illustration in a mid-nineteenth-century newspaper shows a British pioneer 'clearing his way up the Congo'

SOURCE 6.2 A garden party, on a croquet lawn at the front of the picture at Government House in one of the African colonies. The original caption is lost but this photo probably shows the assembled staff of Government House

SOURCE 6.3 Railways opened up large areas. This picture shows Joseph Chamberlain, the Colonial Secretary, travelling on the front of an engine in Uganda, January 1903

TALKING POINT

Which of Sources 6.1–6.3 would you select if you wished to portray the British empire

a) favourably
b) unfavourably?

ACTIVITY

1 **a)** What does Source 6.1 suggest about the nature of British imperialism?
   b) How accurate and reliable would you judge it to be?
2 **a)** How does Source 6.2 differ from Source 6.1 in its representation of the relationship between black and white in the British Empire?
   b) Is it more or less reliable than Source 6.1? Give reasons.
3 What does Source 6.3 suggest about the importance of railways in the British Empire?

FOCUS ROUTE

Draw a table to summarise how each of the following helped to popularise the empire:
• newspapers and magazines
• advertisements
• schools
• boys' magazines and stories
• youth movements
• theatre and music hall.

B How was the empire presented to the British population and how popular was it?

Newspapers and magazines

Photographers were travelling the world from the 1850s. At first their pictures were just published in expensive illustrated magazines, but then it got cheaper to develop photographs in the 1890s, and they were printed regularly in popular papers from 1904.

The most popular papers were imperialist ones. The *Daily Mail*, calling itself 'the voice of Empire', sold nearly a million copies a day at times during the Boer War in 1899–1902 and averaged over 750,000 in the early 1900s. By the 1890s there were enough telegraph lines to bring people news of frontier wars around the empire. In 1896 details of a campaign in Rhodesia, well inland in southern Africa, were getting to London within 24 hours. People could now follow imperial adventures day by day.

Advertisements

There were plenty of pictures too. The little 'cigarette cards' collected and exchanged by most British schoolchildren were issued by tea and sweet companies as well as tobacco manufacturers. Empire heroes and scenes made good sets of pictures. There were also eye-catching advertisements (see Sources 6.4–6.6). Children grew up with empire scenes all around them, and schools played their part as well.

SOURCE 6.4

SOURCES 6.4, 6.5 and **6.6**   Advertisements used to sell goods in Britain by associating them with the empire

SOURCE 6.5

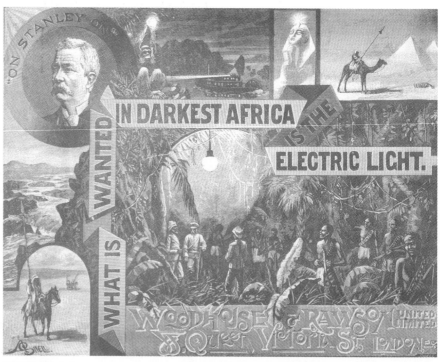

SOURCE 6.6

TALKING POINT

What comparisons could you make with modern advertisements which aim to sell products by associating them with fashionable people or situations?

ACTIVITY

In what ways do the advertisements in Sources 6.4–6.6 suggest that the empire was popular?

Schools

Public schools, which taught upper- and middle-class boys, emphasised how good team games were for physical fitness and character training – just the qualities needed to build the empire. Cadet corps and rifle clubs gave pupils military training, and there were plenty of school visits by explorers and old boys who had distinguished themselves in the empire. Sir Henry Newbolt's poem *Vitaï Lampada* (see Source 6.7) draws a direct link between school training and imperial duties and Newbolt's poetry sold well.

ACTIVITY

1 Which game is being described in verse 1 of Source 6.7?
2 What reason for winning is implied in the last four lines of verse 1?
3 Explain the message of verse 2.

SOURCE 6.7 Two verses from *Vitaï Lampada* (The torch of life) by Sir Henry Newbolt, *Selected Poems of Henry Newbolt*, Hodder and Stoughton

There's a breathless hush in the Close to-night –
Ten to make and the match to win –
A bumping pitch and a blinding light,
An hour to play and the last man in.
And it's not for the sake of a ribboned coat,
Or the selfish hope of a season's fame,
But his Captain's hand on his shoulder smote –
'Play up! play up! And play the game!'

The sand of the desert is sodden red, –
Red with the wreck of a square that broke; –
The Gatling's jammed and the Colonel dead,
And the regiment blind with dust and smoke.
The river of death has brimmed his banks,
And England's far, and Honour a name,
But the voice of a schoolboy rallies the ranks:
'Play up! play up! And play the game!'

Public school practices were often taken as some sort of models in the elementary schools attended by working-class and lower middle-class children.

SOURCE 6.8 Robert Roberts, born in 1905, went to a Church of England elementary school in Salford, Lancashire before and during the First World War. He remembered the teaching on empire when he wrote about his childhood in *The Classic Slum*, 1971

Teachers, fed on Seeley's imperialistic work The Expansion of England, *and often great readers of Kipling, spelled out patriotism among us with a fervour that with some edged on the religious. Empire Day of course had special significance. We drew union jacks, hung classrooms with flags of the dominions and gazed with pride as they pointed out those massed areas of red on the world map. 'This and this, and this', they said, 'belong to us!'*

SOURCE 6.9 Fred Willis recalled his lessons at a London elementary school around 1900

Geography was confined to the British Empire and countries were assessed not by their peoples but by the magnitude and wealth of their products. The only reference to people that I remember was 'The Indian can live on a handful of rice a day', which made us feel a particularly opulent race when we were enjoying our Sunday dinners.

Boys' magazines and stories

Many boys read magazines such as *Chums* or *Union Jack*, brimming with adventures from far-flung colonies. An increasing number of story books appealed to lads with a bit more pocket money but none of the radio, TV or music systems we have today. The author G.A. Henty, for example, turned out about three books a year and published a total of 82. Some were based on history, and most concerned the empire. Henty had been a war correspondent in different parts of the empire and he put his knowledge of India and Africa together with his feeling for 'tall' stories and schoolboy games. His middle-class heroes had the most gripping adventures which appealed to all classes.

SOURCE 6.10 *By Sheer Pluck*, 1884, was one of Henty's stories about conquering West Africa. At the start the hero, Frank, was playing well in a cricket match. Later he went to Africa and took part in the Ashanti Wars. After rescuing a British soldier from the mouth of an alligator, Frank got involved in a major battle with the Africans

The Ashantis were supposed to have had from fifteen to twenty thousand men in the field … they must have lost over two thousand … The body of the king's chief executioner was also pointed out by some of the prisoners. They fought with extraordinary pluck and resolution … upon our side the loss in killed was very slight, not exceeding eight or ten …

Our troops were in high spirits that night. They had won a battle fought under extreme difficulty, and that with a minimum of loss in killed. There were therefore no sad recollections to damp the pleasures of victory. Frank had been twice struck with slugs [rough bullets], but in neither case had these penetrated deeply, and he was able to sit round the camp fire and to enjoy his glass of rum and water.

Youth movements

The best way of entering into the spirit of adventure, while still at home, was probably to join one of the youth movements which generally had a patriotic feel to them. In the long run the most successful of these was the Boy Scouts, which began in 1908 and gained over 100,000 members in its first couple of years. Its founder, Baden-Powell, had made his reputation in the Boer War commanding the troops who held out at the siege of Mafeking.

SOURCE 6.11 Baden-Powell explained his thinking in *Scouting for Boys*, 1908

Every boy ought to learn how to shoot and to obey orders, else he is no more good when war breaks out than an old woman … I suppose every British boy wants to help his country in some way or other … There is a way … he can do so easily, and that is by becoming a scout.

A scout … is generally a soldier who is chosen, for his cleverness and pluck, to go out in front of an army in war to find out where the enemy are, and report to the commander all about them. But … there are also peace scouts, i.e., men who in peace time carry out work which requires the same kind of abilities … The History of the Empire has been made by British adventurers and explorers, the scouts of the nation, for hundreds of years past up to the present time.

Theatre and music hall

Imperial stories and songs were found in theatres. For example, the play *The Fall of Khartoum* (see pages 88–89), was popular, but seen by predominantly middle-class audiences.

Music halls were often larger than theatres, with a variety of seat prices attracting different classes of customers. They had their biggest following in London. The more imperialist acts generally appeared in halls with more middle-class customers, but they had an impact on the working class as well.

Artists had distinctive songs and took these from one hall to another. Some appear almost as travelling propaganda pieces, such as Charles Godfrey's song 'It's the English-speaking race against the world'. The songs were popular and widely performed by local amateurs or people who got the sheet music to play on the piano at home.

It is difficult to know how seriously to take all this, and there was sometimes a jokey side to it. Yet the songs and the memories of people who heard them suggest that music hall could create a very powerful patriotic and imperialist feeling. The Radical J.A. Hobson, who hated popular imperialism, claimed music halls had more influence on many of the middle and labouring classes than churches, schools or newspapers.

Assessing the popularity of the empire

So far we have been amassing examples of imperialist thinking. There is plenty more we could include. The examples give the strong impression that the British population wholeheartedly supported the empire. But did they? And in particular, did the working classes support it? What did they really think?

Did the working class support the empire?

It is very hard for a historian to work out a clear answer to this question. Today we can find answers to questions like this from public opinion polls. In the twenty-first century, polls find out what people think about key issues but they were not used in the nineteenth century. We do know that almost every Briton saw and heard facts, pictures and stories about empire and that lots of these were propaganda in favour of it. It is difficult to assess their impact because of the kind of knowledge we have and the way historians are biased.

1 We know what people see but not what they think

People were told about the British Empire. Many knew that they could gain advantages from it, and they were encouraged to support it and take pride in it.

Now, as then, schools teach children values. Today these tend to be ideas such as citizenship, tolerance and Christian morals. A hundred years or more ago they were generally patriotism (love of one's country) and national superiority as well as Christianity.

People are influenced by the beliefs and images around them, and they often come to accept these unconsciously. Think of the way advertising works. It is also often hard to interpret people's behaviour. They might have celebrated a British victory in some part of the empire just because Britain won or because it was a good excuse for a party, rather than because they were strong imperialists.

2 It is hard to distinguish between imperialism and patriotism

Enthusiasm for British victories, particularly successes over the French or Russians, did not necessarily mean enthusiasm for empire itself.

3 Empire was used in party politics

Conservatives presented themselves as the party of empire. They encouraged entertainers to present imperial themes and set out to create an atmosphere of imperial and national pride which they could use against their apparently less patriotic opponents in the Liberal Party.

Conservative success in elections might therefore be a way of measuring imperialist feeling except that there were many other reasons for voting Conservative and some Liberals were strong imperialists too.

4 Ideas were changing

A new enthusiasm for empire seems to have developed in the 1880s. The jingo song produced in 1878 (see page 79) is the most famous bit of showbusiness imperialism, but Gladstone still seems to have got much support in the 1880 election by attacking imperial adventures that went wrong.

The so-called 'new imperialism' then grew, reaching a popular climax in the Queen's Diamond Jubilee in 1897 and the excitements of the Boer War in 1899–1902 (see page 114). Problems in the war may have put people off empire, but many signs of support developed later, such as celebrating Empire Day. Overall support for empire probably fluctuated.

5 Historians' bias

British imperialism is still a live issue today in many parts of Africa and Asia and in Britain itself. British historians cannot be neutral about it. It arouses pride, shame, anxieties about racism or nostalgia for past greatness depending on a person's viewpoint. Left- and right-wing approaches differ markedly, and we view popular imperialism more emotionally than most history topics.

Case study: Who went 'mafficking' on Mafeking Night?

Mafeking was a small town on the edge of the Transvaal in South Africa (see Map 6G, page 113). Nobody would have bothered much about it, except that a British colonel, Baden-Powell, and his troops got cut off there in the early stages of the Boer War (see page 114). When a British force finally relieved the town in May 1900, people in British cities went wild. A new word, 'mafficking', was even used to describe how they joined in the patriotic demonstrations. Who took part in the celebrations and what do they tell us about popular imperialism?

SOURCE 6.12 R. Price, in his book *An Imperial War and the British Working Class* (1972), argues that the ethos (idea) of imperialism surrounding the Boer War had little impact on the working class. He sees the Mafeking Night celebrations as merely a one-off event, a big party which did not necessarily show much about people's long-term views on empire

It was a time for rejoicing; England had regained her honour. And this is what the crowds were about.

SOURCE 6.13 Fred Willis, a boy in London in 1900, described the scene in his memoirs, 1948

Gilded youth and the proletariat [wage-earning workers] united in celebrating this minor triumph in British history.

SOURCE 6.14 *The Times* reported celebrations in London and other cities

A remarkable demonstration of popular enthusiasm was witnessed in the streets of London last night when the report of the relief of Mafeking became known ...

At every step down Regent-street the excitement increased, and at Oxford-circus the people were running in all directions and shouting ...

Perhaps the most remarkable feature of the night's demonstration, which spread through the heart of London and into the suburbs, was the entire absence of unseemly or objectionable behaviour.

SOURCE 6.15 The *Liverpool Echo* emphasised the scale of the celebrations in Liverpool

As an indication of the public interest and enthusiasm it may be stated that on no previous occasion ... has such a multitude of people evinced so uncontrollable a desire to get into the heart of the city ... Had the electric car system supplied thrice or quadruple the extent of the facilities, which it gave, this would have been all insufficient to meet the public demands.

SOURCE 6.16 Bradford, in West Yorkshire, was a woollen manufacturing town. *The Times* reported how buzzers sounded at many factories in the district and crowds assembled. The Bradford *Daily Argus* gave detailed and enthusiastic reports including the following

Not a street in the city was without its enlivening features of colour and loyalty ... At noon to-day at Wyke Mills the workpeople gathered in the mill yard, and held an enthusiastic meeting, singing patriotic songs and cheering for Baden-Powell.

SOURCE 6.17
Part of a drawing from the *Graphic* showing the crowd when the good news from Mafeking was announced at London's Mansion House

ACTIVITY

1 Source 6.17 is an artist's portrayal of one part of London on Mafeking Night. In 1900 the upper and middle classes usually wore top hats and bowlers and working men generally wore cloth caps but also occasionally bowlers. Which classes appear to have made up the crowd?

2 a) How far do Sources 6.13–6.17 suggest working-class participation in the celebrations? Think of how large the demonstrations were and who appears to have taken part.

   b) What problems are there in assessing this working-class participation?

3 To what extent do the sources suggest real working-class enthusiasm for empire or just a wish to party and celebrate a national triumph, as Price suggests in Source 6.12?

Why emigrate?

One of the reasons why British people were enthusiastic about the empire was that they saw opportunities for emigrating. For some it was a permanent move, for others it was temporary. The people had a range of motives, which historians have studied. Chart 6B shows some of what they have found.

1 Study the thought bubbles. Classify them into groups as follows:
   a) adventure and excitement
   b) idealism and duty
   c) quality of life
   d) economic opportunity.

2 Which motives do you think would most apply to:
   a) a middle-class boy thinking of becoming a colonial administrator
   b) a working-class boy wanting to make a new life
   c) both boys?

3 Which of the motives are push factors (things that are wrong with Britain) and which are pull factors (things that are good about the destination)?

■ 6B Thoughts which made men emigrate to the empire

Am I a wimp or am I an adventurer like the ones I read about in my school prize book?

There's big game hunting! Tigers, leopards, lions … and they say the polo is good in India too.

Do I want to work at a desk in the City? There's plenty of money as a lawyer or a bank clerk. Pay's not so much in the colonial service, but it's easy to find servants and get a good holiday. Is it to be a solicitor's office, the bush or the Himalayan foothills?

I'm a good Christian. I've been confirmed. The school chaplain said we had a duty to teach unbelievers about our Lord.

I fancy men. But the laws here against homosexuality have got harsher and harsher. I'm told it just doesn't matter in the same way in the empire.

I could get a wife in a respectable villa in Putney, but what about a harem in Poona? I wonder what Indian women are like?

White people have a duty in Africa. The natives can benefit from all our know-how.

I might lose my job here when there's less work around. It's happened to lots of people, even some of the skilled workmen. But they say they're crying out for workers in Canada or Australia. Not the same fear of going to the workhouse out there. They say the bosses treat you better, and give you a bit more respect. Well, they can't just sack you and find lots of others looking to get taken on like there are back here.

It would be strange abroad, and it's a big risk. Yet people talk about Little Britains out in the empire. Australia sounds good; they're almost all British out there.

I thought my 12 shillings a week was good pay at first. Of course, I'll get over £1 in a few years, but that's not much if I have a wife and children. Now, out in Canada and Australia they say they'd just laugh at money like that. We'd live well there, not having to worry about whether we could afford a bit of meat.

I want promotion but will I get it here? There are lots of stories about how men get on in the empire.

C What problems did Britain face defending its empire?

FOCUS ROUTE

Make a copy of this table and fill it in as you work through this section.

Issue	Problem	Government action	How effective was the action?
India Routes to India China Indo-China Naval strength European alliances Relations with the USA			

The biggest problem of all – India

■ 6C Problems in defending the frontiers of India and keeping power there

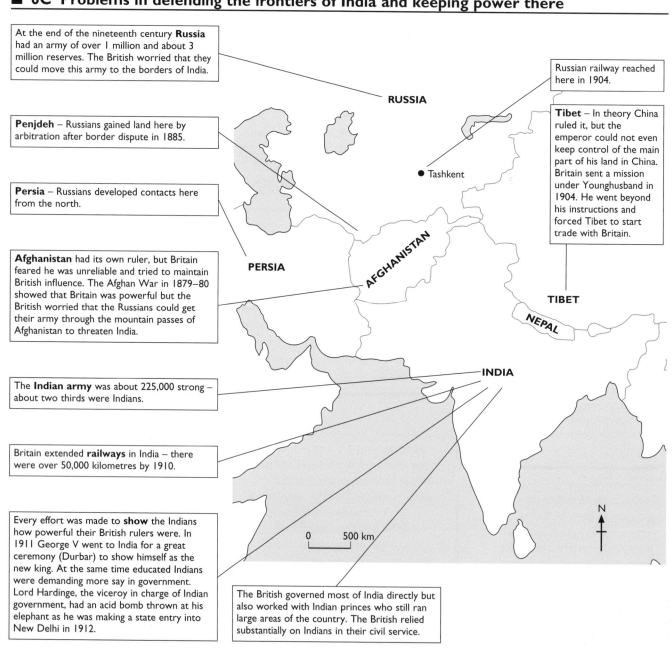

At the end of the nineteenth century **Russia** had an army of over 1 million and about 3 million reserves. The British worried that they could move this army to the borders of India.

Penjdeh – Russians gained land here by arbitration after border dispute in 1885.

Persia – Russians developed contacts here from the north.

Afghanistan had its own ruler, but Britain feared he was unreliable and tried to maintain British influence. The Afghan War in 1879–80 showed that Britain was powerful but the British worried that the Russians could get their army through the mountain passes of Afghanistan to threaten India.

The **Indian army** was about 225,000 strong – about two thirds were Indians.

Britain extended **railways** in India – there were over 50,000 kilometres by 1910.

Every effort was made to **show** the Indians how powerful their British rulers were. In 1911 George V went to India for a great ceremony (Durbar) to show himself as the new king. At the same time educated Indians were demanding more say in government. Lord Hardinge, the viceroy in charge of Indian government, had an acid bomb thrown at his elephant as he was making a state entry into New Delhi in 1912.

Russian railway reached here in 1904.

Tibet – In theory China ruled it, but the emperor could not even keep control of the main part of his land in China. Britain sent a mission under Younghusband in 1904. He went beyond his instructions and forced Tibet to start trade with Britain.

The British governed most of India directly but also worked with Indian princes who still ran large areas of the country. The British relied substantially on Indians in their civil service.

RUSSIA

• Tashkent

PERSIA

AFGHANISTAN

TIBET

NEPAL

INDIA

0   500 km

N

SOURCE 6.18   Members of Indian royalty entertaining British officials, 1907

Defending the routes to India

Once the Suez Canal was opened in 1869, the quickest route to India ran through the eastern Mediterranean. This was only good for steamships as there was not enough wind to power sailing ships through the canal, but steam gave the fastest, most reliable journey. The Suez Canal made the Eastern Mediterranean a much more strategically important area for Britain.

Map 6D shows what problems arose in the eastern Mediterranean in 1886–1900.

■ 6D Problems in the eastern Mediterranean 1886–1900

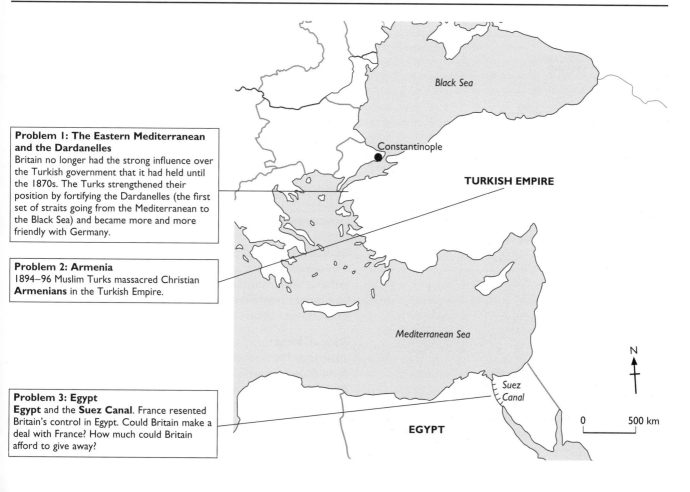

Problem 1: The Eastern Mediterranean and the Dardanelles
Britain no longer had the strong influence over the Turkish government that it had held until the 1870s. The Turks strengthened their position by fortifying the Dardanelles (the first set of straits going from the Mediterranean to the Black Sea) and became more and more friendly with Germany.

Problem 2: Armenia
1894–96 Muslim Turks massacred Christian **Armenians** in the Turkish Empire.

Problem 3: Egypt
Egypt and the **Suez Canal**. France resented Britain's control in Egypt. Could Britain make a deal with France? How much could Britain afford to give away?

Black Sea

Constantinople

TURKISH EMPIRE

Mediterranean Sea

Suez Canal

EGYPT

N

0   500 km

Problem 1: The Eastern Mediterranean and the Dardanelles How to keep the eastern Mediterranean safe for British shipping and stop the Russians getting there.

Government action Made the **Mediterranean Agreements** in 1887 – notes exchanged between the governments of Britain, Italy and Austria-Hungary. They agreed to keep the status quo (existing arrangements) in the eastern Mediterranean and south east Europe, particularly around the waters between the Black Sea and the Mediterranean near the Turkish capital, Constantinople. The Agreements were largely secret but lapsed in 1897 because Britain would not promise to defend the straits near Constantinople as the Austrian government demanded. The British army and navy commanders had told Salisbury in 1892 that they could not fight a campaign there against French opposition because they would not be able to safeguard supply routes through the Mediterranean.

Problem 2: Turkish massacre of Armenian Christians, 1894–96 There were about one million Christian Armenians in different parts of the Turkish empire. After Armenian rebellions against Turkish rule from 1894, numbers were killed, including some beaten to death on the streets of Constantinople in 1896. Public protests followed in Britain.

Government action The British government no longer supported Turkey and pressed it to reform. Salisbury wanted to send a British fleet, but naval commanders opposed this because of the difficulties. He tried to get European governments to take joint action as they had done earlier in the nineteenth century, but with no success. The British government wanted to act but could not.

Problem 3: Egypt Britain's occupation of Egypt ruined relations with France and therefore weakened her diplomatic position in Europe as a whole.

Government action Negotiated an agreement with Turkey in 1887: Britain would leave Egypt in three years' time as long as it could take over again if there were any threat to the Suez Canal. France did not agree to this as it was worried about Britain's retaking Egypt. By the end of the 1880s Salisbury had decided no compromise was possible. Britain would keep control permanently.

> **SPHERES OF INFLUENCE**
> Areas where a more advanced industrial country controls much of the trade and might have mining rights, railways and significant influence in government.

Competing for China and Indo-China

■ 6E Rivalry in the Far East

China

China still had its own government under Manchu emperors, but European states used force to create SPHERES OF INFLUENCE where they controlled trade with ports and railways. Britain had got in first, pounding the Chinese into submission with its guns and warships and developing trade in central China.

Problem There was fierce competition in northern China as European states bullied the Chinese government for concessions. The Germans gained Kiaochow Bay in 1897; then the Russians got Port Arthur in 1898.

Government action Salisbury's government took the trading port of Weihaiwei in compensation for Britain. He did not think it mattered much but believed the public expected some sort of gain to keep up with other countries. Britain was without support from other European states, and Germany and Russia soon found more ways of increasing their power in northern China.

Indo-China

Problem The French were developing their empire from Indo-China towards India.

Government action In 1895–97 Britain made agreements with France to keep Siam independent while accepting French control of other lands in Indo-China. In this way the French would be less of a threat to Burma into which the British had moved from India.

ACTIVITY

Eight problems are mentioned on pages 109–111.
Draw a diagram like this:

Write one problem in each circle then add lines and notes to explain how the problems, and Britain's solutions to them, are connected with each other.

Maintaining naval strength

Problem Britain had to have the naval strength to safeguard her trade and the empire. The government was most concerned that its fleet should be as strong as the total of ships France and Russia together had in the Mediterranean. This meant a big shipbuilding programme.

Government action The **1889 Naval Defence Act** stated that the British navy would be as strong as the next two greatest navies in the world combined – the so-called Two Power Standard. Once the standard was stated, the government could not easily give it up, and widespread public demands for more ships continued in the 1890s. As a result much more was spent on the navy – £18.7 million in 1896 compared with £11 million in 1883 – despite generally falling prices. Yet Britain still could not keep up with the rest of the world put together. Besides France and Russia, other nations, such as the USA and Japan, were expanding their fleets. In 1883 Britain had 38 battleships compared with 40 for other countries combined; by 1897 it was 62 against 96.

European alliances

Problem In 1894 the **Dual Alliance** between France and Russia was signed. This was bad news for Britain. The two powers that most threatened different parts of the empire had come together.

Government action Not much. Britain might have joined the **Triple Alliance** (Germany, Austria-Hungary and Italy). It already had the Mediterranean Agreements with Austria-Hungary and Italy. Joseph Chamberlain, the Colonial Secretary, suggested an alliance with Germany from 1897, and there were attempts from 1898 to 1901, which all failed.

Britain wanted Germany to promise that it might fight against Britain's main enemy, Russia, if there were an Anglo-Russian war in the east. (Remember how Germany, Russia and Britain were all trying to gain some control in northern China.) Germany wanted Britain to promise that it might fight against Germany's main enemy, France, if there were a Franco-German war in the west. Neither side was prepared to make the necessary promise, which could involve a great war that benefited the other side more. Furthermore, Germany was just beginning to create a navy and wanted big changes in the world. Britain, with the world's greatest empire, had a very different view.

Relations with the USA

Problem The USA was developing a strong navy. The British navy, with so much to do around the world, could not challenge it in the Caribbean or near North America. Britain needed good relations with the USA to safeguard British colonies in North America and strengthen it in the world. In 1895 the American president threatened Britain over a border dispute between Venezuela and British Guiana. The USA was also keen to build and control a canal through Panama, linking the Atlantic and the Pacific.

Government action Britain agreed to settle the Venezuelan border dispute by the ARBITRATION procedure the USA wanted, which actually led to a decision largely in Britain's favour. There had been an agreement in 1850 for Britain and the USA to join in building any future canal in Panama but by the Hay–Pauncefote Treaty in 1901, Britain agreed that the USA alone should make a canal there and fortify it. British ministers got friendship with the USA by accepting its predominance around the American continent.

ARBITRATION
Procedure for judging and making a decision in a dispute by a person or group not directly involved.

France used **Senegal** as a base for going east, taking over French West Africa in 1876 and moving towards the Sudan.

From 1875 the British owned a minority of shares in the **Suez Canal**, which was essential for communications to India

In 1882 Britain occupied **Egypt** and then established control.

The ruler of Egypt had traditionally ruled the **Sudan**. General Gordon was killed there in 1885. Britain reconquered it in 1898, after winning the **Battle of Omdurman.** A French expedition reached the area at the same time and the British met them at **Fashoda** three days after the battle. The French group was much smaller and had no communications with their base. The British, with nearby telegraph, rail and river links, were clearly in control and so the French had to accept British occupation of the Sudan.

East Africa
Britain had two strategic worries about this area:
1 British-controlled Egypt relied on **Nile** river waters for its survival. Any state controlling this area could threaten Egypt by damming or cutting off the flow.
2 This area was important for **sea routes to India** and other parts of Asia, whether via the Red Sea or via South Africa.

In 1886 an agreement between Britain and Germany divided **east Africa** between themselves and the Sultan of Zanzibar, who looked to Britain for support. In 1890 an Anglo-German agreement confirmed British control of the region.

West Africa
A very competitive scene where Britain, France and Germany all tried to get territory. British representatives went to a conference at Berlin in 1884–85 to get agreement on how to divide west Africa. They agreed that European powers already holding a coastline could take inland territory behind, but they must get effective control of it. The British mainly worked with African kings and chiefs but were ready to use force like other European countries.

Britain concentrated on the **Niger** area. In 1885 it established a protectorate in the Niger delta to keep others out. A protectorate is an area where the people still have their own kind of government but are under the power and protection of a stronger country.

British representatives made treaties with local rulers in the **Cameroons** from late 1883, but Germany took over the area in 1884.

In 1885 the British took south **Bechuanaland** as a colony and north Bechuanaland as a protectorate.

Most of modern **South Africa** was divided between the British colonies of the Cape and Natal and the republics of Transvaal and the Orange Free State run by the Boers (descendants of Dutch settlers). The British government was anxious to get overall control, and tensions eventually led to the Boer War (1899–1902).

The British government was worried that the Germans, Portuguese or Boers might take the lands which became **Rhodesia**. As they wanted to avoid too much public expenditure or risk, in 1889 they gave Cecil Rhodes' **British South Africa Company** a charter to take over the land.

In 1890 an Anglo-French Convention confirmed that France had **Madagascar** and Britain **Zanzibar**.

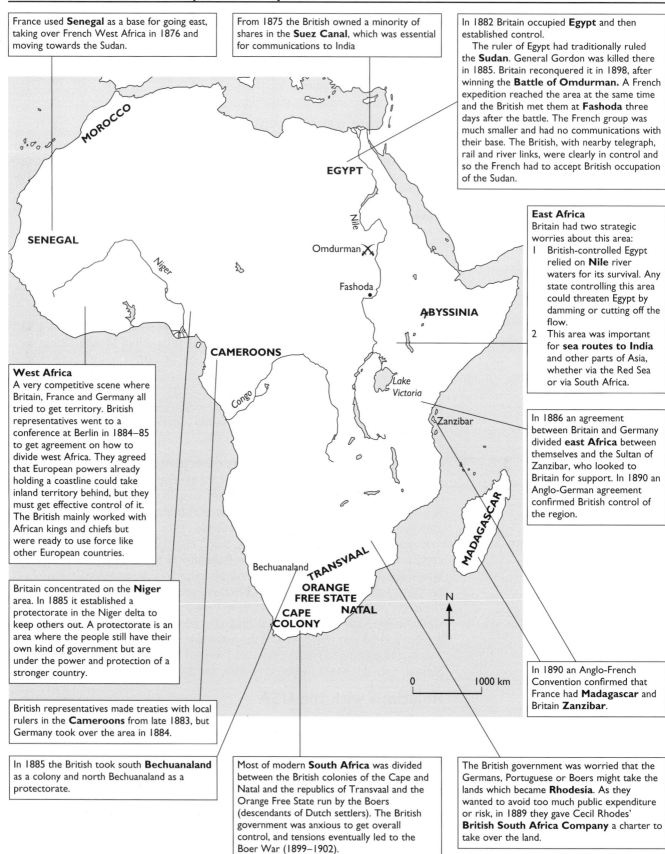

MOROCCO

SENEGAL

EGYPT

Nile

Omdurman ✕

Fashoda

ABYSSINIA

Niger

CAMEROONS

Congo

Lake Victoria

Zanzibar

MADAGASCAR

Bechuanaland

TRANSVAAL

ORANGE FREE STATE

CAPE COLONY

NATAL

N

0   1000 km

FOCUS ROUTE

Draw a diagram, of three concentric circles, to show the causes of the Boer War:

a) in the inner circle put short-term causes triggering war
b) in the central circle put intermediate causes
c) in the outer circle put long-term causes.

D How did the Boer War change attitudes to empire?

Why did Britain go to war with the Boer republics in 1899?

Charts 6G–6L tell the story of the Boer War and its effects.

■ 6G The battle to control Southern Africa in the Boer War

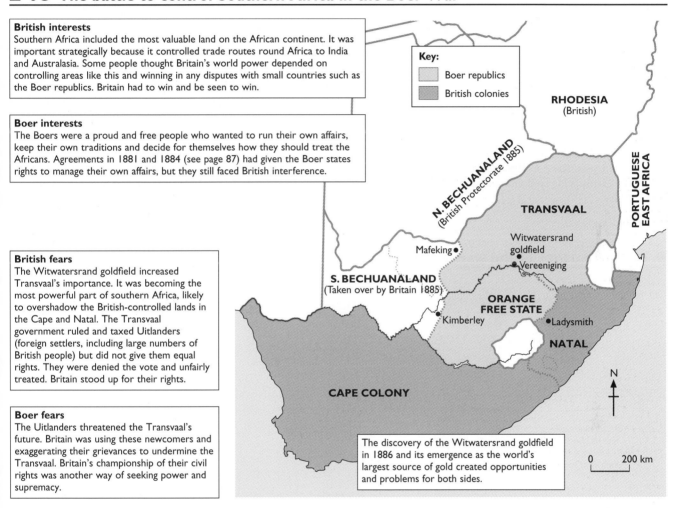

British interests
Southern Africa included the most valuable land on the African continent. It was important strategically because it controlled trade routes round Africa to India and Australasia. Some people thought Britain's world power depended on controlling areas like this and winning in any disputes with small countries such as the Boer republics. Britain had to win and be seen to win.

Boer interests
The Boers were a proud and free people who wanted to run their own affairs, keep their own traditions and decide for themselves how they should treat the Africans. Agreements in 1881 and 1884 (see page 87) had given the Boer states rights to manage their own affairs, but they still faced British interference.

British fears
The Witwatersrand goldfield increased Transvaal's importance. It was becoming the most powerful part of southern Africa, likely to overshadow the British-controlled lands in the Cape and Natal. The Transvaal government ruled and taxed Uitlanders (foreign settlers, including large numbers of British people) but did not give them equal rights. They were denied the vote and unfairly treated. Britain stood up for their rights.

Boer fears
The Uitlanders threatened the Transvaal's future. Britain was using these newcomers and exaggerating their grievances to undermine the Transvaal. Britain's championship of their civil rights was another way of seeking power and supremacy.

Key:
- Boer republics
- British colonies

RHODESIA (British)

N. BECHUANALAND (British Protectorate 1885)

S. BECHUANALAND (Taken over by Britain 1885)

TRANSVAAL

PORTUGUESE EAST AFRICA

Mafeking●

Witwatersrand goldfield
●Vereeniging

●Kimberley

ORANGE FREE STATE

●Ladysmith

NATAL

CAPE COLONY

The discovery of the Witwatersrand goldfield in 1886 and its emergence as the world's largest source of gold created opportunities and problems for both sides.

N

0   200 km

■ 6H Increasing distrust and tensions on both sides

1895	Joseph Chamberlain, the new Colonial Secretary, was dedicated to strengthening the British empire, and southern Africa was important in this.
End of 1895	In the Jameson Raid a force assembled from Cecil Rhodes' British South Africa Company invaded the Transvaal in an unsuccessful attempt to overthrow the government. When the raid failed the German Kaiser, Wilhelm II, sent a telegram of support to the Boers' leader, Kruger.
1897	Chamberlain appointed an enthusiastic imperialist, Sir Alfred Milner, as British High Commissioner in southern Africa and Governor of Cape Colony. Milner clearly wanted to establish British power over the whole of southern Africa.
March 1899	In the Transvaal, a Boer policeman shot a drunken British worker called Tom Edgar and was not punished for his action.
May–June 1899	Negotiations failed between Milner and Kruger, President of the Transvaal.
Summer 1899	The British government sent a further 10,000 troops to southern Africa.
October 1899	Some British troops appeared to be grouping near the Transvaal border, and so Kruger declared war.

■ 6I The main phases of the Boer War and its results

October 1899–January 1900	The Boers made early gains. They besieged British troops in Ladysmith, Kimberley and Mafeking. Boer skill and bad British generalship led to striking British defeats.
March–September 1900	The British struck back, defeated the Boers in open battle and relieved the besieged towns. They appeared to conquer the Boer lands and take over.
October 1900–March 1902	The Boers used guerrilla warfare against the British. Britain replied by burning farms and putting Boer women and children in concentration camps.
March–May 1902	Negotiations led to the Treaty of Vereeniging which ended the war.
May 1902	The **Treaty of Vereeniging** ended the war when the Boers submitted. Boer republics in southern Africa were able to elect their own governments. They kept full control over the Black Africans and generally treated them more harshly than the British did.
1910	A Liberal government created the Union of South Africa, bringing the Boer republics together with earlier British colonies. It was a dominion which governed itself. The Liberals believed in the white settler colonies running their own affairs. They were uneasy about the lack of voting rights for Black Africans but agreed that the Boers should decide this.

GUERRILLA WARFARE

Involves fighters who are not always part of an organised or regular army. They generally fight in small groups using whatever cover they can find and launching surprise attacks on the enemy. Once the Boers' regular armies were beaten, they used these tactics. Many were farmers who knew the countryside well and could use farms as shelter.

CONCENTRATION CAMPS

The British decided that moving Boer families into these camps was the only way to stop them helping the guerrillas. The camps were intended to confine rather than punish the Boers, but the people were housed in tents, badly fed and overcrowded, so many Boer women and children died. Thus the British invented the concentration camp, though they did not develop the refined cruelty of the later Nazi ones.

■ 6J The balance of the war for Britain

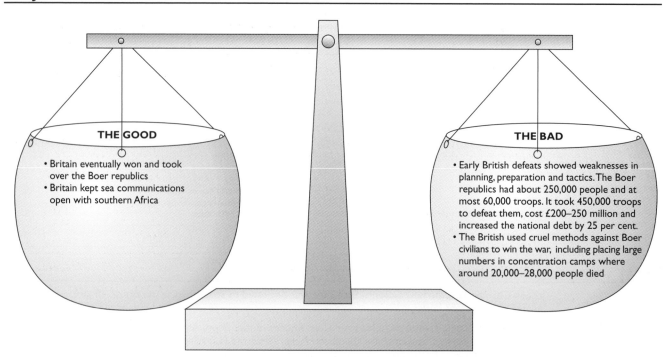

THE GOOD
- Britain eventually won and took over the Boer republics
- Britain kept sea communications open with southern Africa

THE BAD
- Early British defeats showed weaknesses in planning, preparation and tactics. The Boer republics had about 250,000 people and at most 60,000 troops. It took 450,000 troops to defeat them, cost £200–250 million and increased the national debt by 25 per cent.
- The British used cruel methods against Boer civilians to win the war, including placing large numbers in concentration camps where around 20,000–28,000 people died

DISCUSS

Chart 6J shows the balance as equal. Which way do you think it fell for each of the groups of people listed in Chart 6L?

The war and British expansion in Africa aroused strong enthusiasm

… BUT … **Opposition grew to the war, which was strongly associated with the Colonial Secretary, Joseph Chamberlain**

■ 6L Different viewpoints on the Boer War

Who	How they might view the war	How opinions changed after the war	Changes linked with the war in different ways
Liberals already doubtful about the empire	They read reports from critical journalists in southern Africa describing what cruel methods the British used. These increased their doubts about whether it was right to expand the empire as before.	Most Liberals accepted that Britain should keep its empire, but colonists should govern themselves so that the empire developed as a 'Commonwealth of free nations'. A few Liberals opposed empire.	Liberal governments gave the southern African republics self-government. Growing intellectual opposition to empire.
Imperialists believing strongly in the empire	They enjoyed celebrating the victories, but they were shocked that it took so many men and cost so much. They questioned what would have happened if there had been a big threat in some other part of the empire when the war was on.	Imperialists believed Britain must improve its 'national efficiency'. It needed a better organised army, a fitter population to serve in it and a stronger defence overall.	Army reforms by Liberal Secretary for War, Haldane. Welfare reforms by Liberal governments from 1906. Scares about Britain's naval strength, leading to more shipbuilding.
Conservative government believing strongly in the empire but worried about maintaining it.	Although Britain did win the war they worried that the early defeats showed military weakness. The Conservatives won a big victory in the 1900 General Election, but they worried that the costly guerrilla campaign by the Boers that followed lost them support.	Some ministers saw a strong case for making alliances with other states. The Conservative Party lost support over 'Chinese slavery' in southern Africa (the way Chinese people were brought to work in the gold mines). When Chamberlain proposed tariff reform (charging taxes on imports – see page 178) to strengthen the empire there was little support for it.	1902 Anglo-Japanese Alliance 1904 Entente Cordiale with France 1906 General Election – overwhelming victory for the Liberals and Conservative defeat.

CHAPTER 6 REVIEW ACTIVITY

Many writers have described British foreign policy in the 1890s as one of 'splendid isolation', implying that Britain was so strong it did not need allies.

From the information below and from what you have read in this chapter decide whether 'splendid isolation' is an accurate description of Britain's imperial and foreign policy between 1886 and 1900. Give reasons for your answer.

Some arguments to say YES
- Joseph Chamberlain, the Colonial Secretary, used the phrase in 1902, emphasising how Britain was not alone, but 'surrounded and supported' by her kinsfolk in white settler colonies.
- The Unionist minister Goschen, First Lord of the Admiralty, said in 1896 that isolation was 'deliberately chosen' so that Britain was free to act 'in any circumstances that may arise'.
- Lord Salisbury argued to the Queen that the government could not make alliances promising other countries military help 'because it cannot be sure that parliament would make such a promise good'. He wanted to avoid commitments which might be difficult or impossible to fulfil, and so let the Mediterranean Agreements lapse in 1897.
- When disputes arose over Britain's position in the Sudan (see page 112) and north China (see page 110) in 1897–98 the British government was very aware that it had no obvious friends among European states.

Some arguments to say NO
- Whatever British ministers said, the government did make agreements promising military help to other states, but they were often secret.
- While they lasted between 1887 and 1897, the Mediterranean Agreements committed Britain to act jointly with Austria-Hungary and Italy.
- There were treaties from the past which still appeared to commit Britain to support Turkey, Portugal and possibly Belgium.
- Britain made new agreements with Siam and Spain which brought commitments in 1897 and 1899.
- Britain promised to defend Portugal's colonies in 1899 as part of a deal to cut off supply lines for the Boer republics which needed a route to the sea through Portuguese land.
- The British government made several attempts to get an alliance with Germany in 1898–1901.

KEY POINTS FROM CHAPTER 6

How was British policy changing 1885–1902?

1 Imperialism may be both political and economic as advanced industrial states take power and trade in less developed parts of the world.

2 Britain expanded its empire both to increase trade and to keep up with other countries.

3 There was much publicity and propaganda about the empire and it seemed popular, although it is difficult to assess people's feelings accurately.

4 British governments were worried about their naval strength and about threats to their empire in Asia, Africa and the Americas.

5 There was much early enthusiasm for the Boer War, but the British government had more difficulty than it expected fighting in southern Africa, and the war quickly became unpopular

7

How did Britain's foreign policy change after 1900?

CHAPTER OVERVIEW

Some historians see a turning point in Britain's foreign policy soon after 1900. The Boer War altered many people's views. Salisbury retired as prime minister in 1902 and new people took charge. Britain made new alliances and agreements with foreign powers. Defending the empire was still Britain's overriding concern but its view of where the main threat lay was gradually shifting. The old worry, Russia, was replaced by the new worry – Germany.

This chapter explores how this happened:

A How did Britain deal with its defence problems after 1900? (pp. 117–120)

B Why did Britain make agreements with France and Russia? (pp. 120–123)

C Why and how did disputes develop between Britain and Germany? (pp. 124–128)

D Why did Britain become involved in the First World War? (pp. 129–133)

FOCUS ROUTE

As you work through Section A make brief notes about how Britain strengthened its navy, 1900–14.

A How did Britain deal with its defence problems after 1900?

Since 1889 Britain had tried to maintain the Two Power Standard, meaning that it aimed to ensure its navy was as strong as the next two greatest naval powers combined. After 1900, it became clear it was impossible to maintain this in Far Eastern waters. Britain had four large warships there; France and Russia together had six, and the Russians were building three more.

The Russian threat to India seemed to be increasing, with activity in Persia and a railway being built to Tashkent (see Map 6C, page 108). Russia was also making gains in northern China and threatened British interests there. It took substantial control of Manchuria in 1901 and Britain feared it might move into Korea. A new strategy was required.

The Anglo-Japanese Alliance of 1902

Britain couldn't maintain enough ships to stay ahead in the Far East, and feared Russian power, so it entered an alliance with Japan. It was agreed that if Britain or Japan were at war with **only one** country the other would remain neutral. If either Britain or Japan were at war with two countries at once the other partner in the alliance would help in the war. Japan, like Britain, wanted to resist Russia in northern China and was ambitious to gain land there. Japan had six large warships which, together with Britain's four, would more than match the French and Russian navies in the east. In 1904 the Japanese navy actually destroyed much of the Russian navy in the Russo-Japanese war.

The Alliance was **renewed in 1905**. This time, however, they agreed that if only one other country attacked their territories on the Asian mainland they would help each other in war. It was a warning to the Russians not to attack Britain in India or Japan in Manchuria or Korea.

The Blue Water policy

In the early 1900s many of Britain's rivals had very large armies. Both the Committee of Imperial Defence, which was in charge of defence planning from 1902, and most of those in government thought that a strong navy was vastly more important than building up a large army. Chart 7A explains why. They evolved the so-called Blue Water policy, which held that the navy was all-important for defence and the army much less significant.

■ 7A The thinking behind the Blue Water policy

Britain is an island which feeds itself and supplies its industry from overseas

Britain gains an increasing proportion of its wealth from trade and shipping

States with the strongest navies are always the greatest powers

Nearly 50% of Britain's meat, 80% of its wheat and 90% of its raw materials came from abroad.
Any enemy which got control of the seas around Britain could starve it out. It would not need to invade to bring down the country.

The navy was therefore far more important than the army for **home defence**.

Over 50% of the world's merchant ships were British and the navy had to ensure they could do business around the world. Britain depended on the navy to defend and trade with its **empire**. If Britain lost control of the seas it could not transport troops to fight in the colonies.

The navy was therefore far more important than the army for **empire defence**.

In 1890 an American, A.T. Mahan, published his book *The Influence of Sea Power upon History 1660–1783*. In this and later books he argued that states with the best navies had risen to be the greatest powers. To get power and wealth they needed large battle fleets, the right naval bases, trade, colonies and a capacity to blockade enemies at sea. This theory, which explained Britain's strength in the world, was naturally popular and confirmed traditional thinking in Britain. Most strategic thinkers agreed with this policy.

The navy was far more important than the army for **overall strength**.

ACTIVITY

You are a member of the British Cabinet in 1904. You have to decide whether to build a new type of battleship – later called a Dreadnought. Your civil servants have provided some information and arguments for and against to guide you.

1 The new ship would be superior to present ones – both yours and your enemies' – in almost every way, especially in fire-power. Its fire power would be worth more than three current battleships. It would be faster than any other ship – with a top speed of 21 knots.

2 Britain already has naval supremacy. It has a stronger and better navy than its European competitors. This new ship would outclass your current ships and make most of your current fleet look old-fashioned and obsolete.

3 The government still claims to maintain the Two Power Standard and the British public expects to keep ahead of other countries in sea power. We know how the press can whip up scares about our naval strength and how governments then have to respond.

4 Several countries are said to have the idea of this super battleship already. Some other country may build one even if you did not. However if Britain builds one others would certainly do the same which would increase the arms race with all the expense and risk that involves.

5 The new ships would be very expensive. Each new ship will cost nearly £1.8 million on top of existing spending. Britain spent £34.5 million on its navy in 1903 – that is nearly £1 (an unskilled working man's weekly wage) for every man, woman and child. The new ships will mean higher taxes or increased borrowing or both.

6 If Germany built such a ship it would be too big to move through their Kiel canal from the Baltic to the North Sea. It would not be as useful or as flexible as Britain's.

7 Building a super-ship will be much less expensive than building up a land army to match other European powers.

8 Germany is your number one concern. Germany has a superior steel industry to Britain and is a larger, wealthier nation. They have the money and the steel to build more ships than Britain. It will be hard to stay ahead of Germany.

9 Army leaders are adamant that Britain needs to invest in its land forces as well as its navy to be able to compete with the growing armies of the other European powers.

10 The most prominent strategic thinkers accept the Blue Water policy. It is Britain's naval strength that really matters.

On your own
1 Sort the arguments into arguments for and arguments against building the new ship.
2 Decide which two arguments you think are strongest or most important in the context of 1904.
Working in groups
3 As a group decide whether Britain should or should not build these ships. You have to consider three issues:
a) Will it help Britain maintain naval supremacy?
b) Will it fuel an arms race – and if it does, is that wise?

c) Is it the best use of government defence spending?
If you can answer yes to more questions than no then probably you should go ahead and build the ships.
4 Finally, whatever your decision you now have to decide whether
a) to keep your decision a secret for the time being or
b) to make it public immediately.
If you decide a) write a 200-word confidential memo explaining your decision, to be filed with secret government papers.
If you decide b) write a 200-word press release explaining your decision to the eager public.

In 1904 the Conservative government decided to build the first Dreadnought. It was completed when the Liberals were in power in 1906. More soon followed (see Chart 7H, page 126).

SOURCE 7.1 Britain's first 'ironclad' warship – the *Warrior*, launched 1860

SOURCE 7.2 A steam-powered warship – the *Devastation*, launched 1871

SOURCE 7.3 The first *Dreadnought*, 1906

ACTIVITY

Using just the picture evidence work out how each of the ships 7.2 and 7.3 was an improvement on the last.

Improving the armed forces

Modernising the navy

Introducing Dreadnoughts was just one way in which Fisher, the First Sea Lord (top naval commander), changed the navy from 1904.

There were other changes too. In a gigantic slimming-down operation Fisher scrapped many old ships, which he reckoned were not up to modern warfare, and replaced them with a smaller number of larger, more effective ones.

Focus on Germany

Although in public the British government claimed to maintain the Two Power Standard well into the twentieth century, in practice it became irrelevant and was abandoned. In the late nineteenth century it had involved combating the threat of France and Russia. In 1904 Japan had smashed the Russian navy in the Russo-Japanese War and Britain made an entente with France (see page 121).

Soon the German and American navies emerged as the second and third strongest in the world. Nobody in government seriously thought Britain would fight the Americans, so that left Germany. By 1909 ministers secretly decided that their priority should be a 60 per cent superiority in big warships over Germany.

Britain focused on defending itself against Germany and relied more on friends around the world.

Work with friends

As the old ships were scrapped, so Britain stopped showing off so many gunboats in the colonies. It largely withdrew its navy from around America and the Far East, relying instead on the USA and Japan as friendly powers. It concentrated its naval power on the Channel, the Atlantic and the routes to India, though it also relied increasingly on the support of French ships in the Mediterranean.

Reforming the army

Haldane, the Liberal Secretary for War from 1905, supervised some army reforms.

- He established a **General Staff** for military planning in 1909.
- An **Expeditionary Force** was organised to go abroad quickly – possibly to defend India or to fight the Germans in France.
- A reserve force – **Territorial Army** – was to defend Britain if necessary.

As a result the army looked more efficient but it was smaller than those in large European countries and the army and navy did little to work together in planning for war.

FOCUS ROUTE

Create a timeline on which you place the key events that led to closer links between Britain, France and Russia, 1904–14. Place events to do with France on the left and events to do with Russia on the right.

B Why did Britain make agreements with France and Russia?

The Entente Cordiale, 1904

Britain made this agreement with France in 1904 and it was mainly about settling past differences over colonies, particularly in Africa. Since the agreement later led to Britain and France fighting together against Germany in the First World War, historians often classify it as a step towards war. People at the time saw it as another way of preserving an empire. It helped to solve at least three different problems for Britain, only one of which was to do with Germany (see Chart 7B).

SOURCE 7.4 A French view of British control in Egypt in the late nineteenth century – a drawing in *Le Petit Journal* with the title 'A Protector'

■ 7B Why the Entente Cordiale was useful for Britain

A Britain needed to improve relations with France

- Britain and France had parliamentary systems and governments elected by a large part of their population. They therefore had much in common against the empires of eastern Europe, but ever since Britain took Egypt in 1882 they had been hostile towards each other.

- Other European powers saw that Britain's bad relations with France weakened its position. The threat from France could stop Britain acting in the Mediterranean, for example.

- They were rivals in Africa and Asia. The British had gained satisfactory compromises over disputes in West Africa, Sudan and south-east Asia in the 1880s and 1890s, but tensions continued.

- Getting agreement with France could not only give Britain greater freedom of action but also keep defence costs down.

B An understanding with France could lead to an agreement with Russia, France's partner in the Dual Alliance

- In 1904 the British government was still more worried about threats from Russia than any other country. Russia endangered India, the most important part of the empire.

- Lord Lansdowne, the Foreign Secretary who made the Entente, wrote that 'a good understanding with France would not improbably be the precursor of a better understanding with Russia'.

- Historian Keith Wilson (1985) argues that the hope of improving relations with Russia was the main reason for the Entente.

C Britain was worried about German naval power

- In 1902 Lord Selborne, First Lord of the Admiralty, argued in a memo for the Cabinet that the German fleet was 'designed for a possible conflict with the British fleet'.

- France was strongly opposed to the German empire because, when it was established in 1871, it had taken France's eastern provinces, Alsace–Lorraine. If Britain were worried about Germany, it would be wise to have at least friendly relations with France.

The Entente Cordiale was useful to France as well, but for different reasons. France was allied with Russia; Britain was allied with Japan and had pledged to support it if Japan were at war with two other countries (see Chart 7C). France was increasingly worried that a war between Russia and Japan in the Far East might lead to France fighting a war with Britain. When the Russo-Japanese War broke out and the Japanese attacked the Russian fleet at Port Arthur in February 1904, Britain and France speeded up negotiations for an agreement between themselves.

■ 7C France's worries

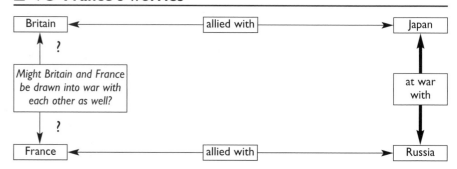

The effects of the Entente

The Entente Cordiale settled disagreements between Britain and France about colonies, and the most important were in Africa.

* France now accepted the British occupation of Egypt.
* In return, Britain agreed to support France in gaining more power in Morocco. There were secret clauses about France gaining a PROTECTORATE in Morocco if the sultan who ruled it were overthrown.

It also raised some difficult questions.

* There was nothing in the Entente against Germany, but how might the Germans see it?
* How might it affect Britain's relations with Germany?
* Britain already had secure control of Egypt. Was it wise to promise the French support in extending their power in Morocco where the sultan was still in charge and Germany had some claims?

How did Britain and France become more closely linked after 1904?

The Entente Cordiale in 1904 was just a friendly understanding between Britain and France by which they settled some disagreements over colonies. Over the next ten years they went on to establish much closer links.

The First Moroccan crisis, 1905–06

In 1905 the German ruler, Kaiser Wilhelm II, went to Tangier in Morocco where he made a speech emphasising the sultan of Morocco's independence and German interests in the country. Since Britain had agreed in the Entente Cordiale to support France in Morocco, it seemed to many people that Germany was testing whether Britain would do so. Britain did give support, and in 1906 France got a satisfactory agreement at a conference of European government representatives in Algeciras.

SOURCE 7.5 The Senior Clerk in the Foreign Office, Eyre Crowe, explained his view of what had happened in a memo, 1907

[In the Entente Cordiale] there had been but a friendly settlement of particular outstanding differences ... now there had emerged an element of common resistance to outside dictation and aggression, a unity of special interests tending to develop into active co-operation against a third Power [clearly, Germany].

> **PROTECTORATE**
> An area where the people still have their own kind of government but are under the power and protection of a stronger country.

■ 7D The Moroccan crises, 1905–06 and 1911

Discussions between British and French military commanders

During the Moroccan crisis British and French naval and army commanders started discussions about how they could work together against Germany if necessary. While the crisis was developing in 1905, the Conservative Foreign Secretary, Lord Lansdowne, was replaced by the Liberal, Sir Edward Grey. Grey was already suspicious of Germany. He had said privately in 1903 that 'Germany is our worst enemy and our greatest danger' and he agreed that talks should continue. They then developed much further over the following years. Although Grey spoke about them with the prime ministers, Campbell-Bannerman and Asquith, he did not tell the Cabinet until 1911. The Cabinet allowed them to continue as long as Britain were not committed to support France in any war.

The Anglo-Russian Agreement, 1907

Why was it made?

For years British governments and defence chiefs had been worried about the Russian threat to India. The Entente Cordiale was made partly in the hope of getting a later agreement with Russia. Although the Russians had been defeated in the 1904–05 Russo-Japanese War, Grey and many others still believed they could be dangerous in the future.

The details of the Anglo-Russian Agreement are in Chart 7E. You can see the main focus is on Asia. The Agreement was about **empire defence**. However, it also affected the **balance of power in Europe**. Grey had indicated in February 1906 that if Russia, France and Britain all came to a friendly understanding they would be really strong and could successfully take action against Germany if it were necessary.

The Agreement concerned areas to the north of India, where there had long been rivalry between Britain and Russia, but it did not end disputes about these areas. Britain was still worried about Russian activity in several regions, especially when Russian troops went into northern Persia to deal with unrest.

■ 7E The main terms of the Anglo-Russian Agreement 1907

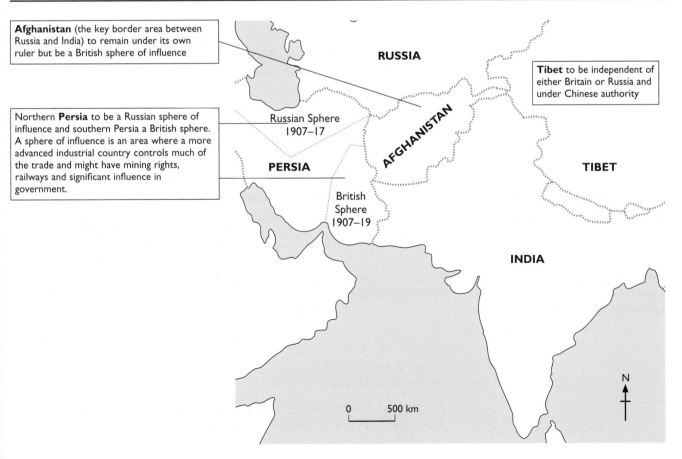

Afghanistan (the key border area between Russia and India) to remain under its own ruler but be a British sphere of influence

Northern **Persia** to be a Russian sphere of influence and southern Persia a British sphere. A sphere of influence is an area where a more advanced industrial country controls much of the trade and might have mining rights, railways and significant influence in government.

Tibet to be independent of either Britain or Russia and under Chinese authority

RUSSIA

Russian Sphere 1907–17

PERSIA

AFGHANISTAN

TIBET

British Sphere 1907–19

INDIA

N

0   500 km

FOCUS ROUTE

1 List the main fears that Britain had about Germany. For each give at least one piece of evidence that would back it up.
2 Make brief notes on what the government did or tried to do about each fear.
3 In your opinion which, if any, of these problems between Britain and Germany could have been settled by discussion?

C Why and how did disputes develop between Britain and Germany?

In the late nineteenth century the British government and the public had seen Russia as the main threat to their empire. In the early twentieth century they came to see Germany as the main danger, both to the empire and to Britain itself. Why was this?

Fears about Germany's economic strength

SOURCE 7.6   Population of Britain and Germany, 1890–1911

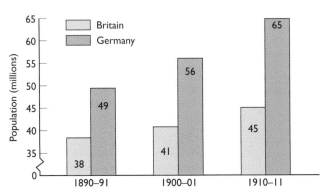

SOURCE 7.7   Percentage of world manufacturing capacity, Britain and Germany, 1870 and 1906–10

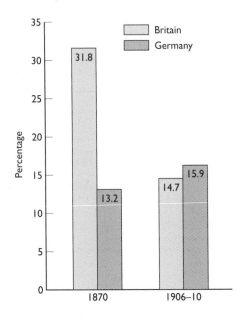

In steel, the most important basic industry for war, Britain's comparative decline was more dramatic: in 1860 it produced more than twice as much as Germany, in 1914 under half as much.

SOURCE 7.8   Percentage of world trade, Britain and Germany, 1880–1913

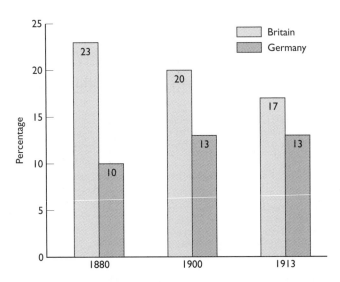

Many people in the 1890s were worried about how Germany was outselling Britain abroad and how much Britain bought from Germany. In 1896 E.E. Williams' book, *Made in Germany*, listed page after page of German imports. Britain depended on Germany for many specialised goods, such as certain chemicals and scientific instruments. Yet both sides benefited from the trade, and Britain sold many textiles to Germany.

SOURCE 7.9   The newspaper owner, Lord Northcliffe, motoring round Germany in 1909, wrote back home

Every one of these new factory chimneys is a gun pointed at England, and in many cases a very powerful one.

■ 7F Berlin–Baghdad railway

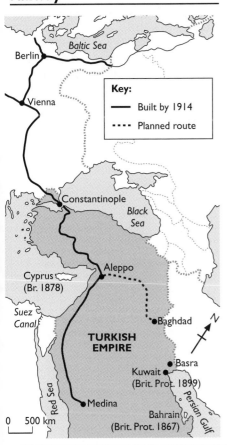

Key:
— Built by 1914
····· Planned route

Berlin
Baltic Sea
Vienna
Constantinople
Black Sea
Cyprus (Br. 1878)
Aleppo
Suez Canal
TURKISH EMPIRE
Baghdad
Red Sea
Medina
Kuwait (Brit. Prot. 1899)
Basra
Bahrain (Brit. Prot. 1867)
Persian Gulf

0   500 km

Fears about German colonisation and expansion

Relations became more difficult after 1897 when the German government decided to become more of a world power. British representatives actually tried several times to get an alliance with Germany between 1898 and 1901, but each effort failed and disagreements increased:

- In 1898 Germany started a naval building programme masterminded by Admiral Tirpitz. Over the following years this turned into an arms race with Britain as each side apparently tried to outdo the other in building more battleships (see Chart 7H on page 126).
- Germany began to extend the Berlin to Constantinople railway into the Turkish Empire (see Chart 7F). This was seen by Britain as an attempt to extend German trade and influence in the area.
- Germany challenged French influence in Morocco leading to the first Moroccan crisis of 1905 (see page 122) and then to a second crisis in 1911 (see page 128).

Underlying these specific issues were more general disagreements, misunderstandings and mistrust. Britain feared German militarism and felt threatened by Germany's naval ambitions. Germany resented British arrogance. It felt it had as much right as Britain to become a world power. These attitudes are summarised in Chart 7G and in Sources 7.10–7.12 on page 127.

■ 7G Germany and Britain: mutual mistrust

Being cut off by the sea, Britain does not understand the threats Germany faces from other European powers.

The Prussians created Germany by war in their own militaristic image. They beat up the French and seized their provinces of Alsace and Lorraine in 1870.

The British think they have some God-given right to the greatest empire on earth. They believe that they, rather than any other nation, are spreading civilisation to backward people and that their empire will further the interests of all humanity. This is monstrous arrogance. Underneath the high-flown language the British are just as concerned with power and wealth as anybody else and think they should maintain their economic advantages for ever.

Germany may have a Parliament, but it is the Kaiser, his chosen ministers and his generals who really decide. Bismarck, the German Chancellor before 1890, said the big issues were decided by 'blood and iron', and that is the German way of doing things.

Germany needs a bigger navy to defend its growing overseas trade. Britain has been in the habit of just throwing its weight around.

In the Boer War, for example, the British just seized some German steamers because they suspected they were carrying goods for the Boers. How long is Germany going to put up with humiliations like this?

We must get a battle fleet in the North Sea so that the British have no inclination to attack us. They must know that if they do attack they will risk losing.

Germany might face a battle in the North Sea on near equal terms quite calmly. A defeat would not ruin the German nation, which would remain the greatest land and industrial power in Europe.

No other country runs the same risks as Britain in a naval war. If we lost at sea our industry would stop for lack of raw materials, we'd face a food shortage and a possible invasion, and we wouldn't be able to keep contact with our colonies. It would be a disaster almost unparalleled in British history.

■ **7H Naval arms race between Britain and Germany**

Position in 1898

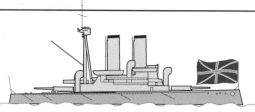

Britain well ahead of Germany. German naval building programme started.

Main events		Other relevant developments

1902 Memorandum from Selborne (First Lord of the Admiralty) argued that the German fleet was designed for operations in the North Sea and threatened Britain. Germany might move against Britain when its navy was involved elsewhere, and so this limited Britain's ability to act around the world.

1902

1904 Britain decided to build the first Dreadnought.

1904

1904 Entente Cordiale with France

1905–06 First Moroccan crisis – Britain sided with France against Germany

1906 Britain launched first Dreadnought.
Germany built a similar ship.

1906

1907 Negotiations at an international conference failed to get an agreement about limiting or slowing down German shipbuilding.
Germany announced new increases in naval shipbuilding.

1908 Scare in Britain about German shipbuilding. Campaign in Britain used the slogan 'We want eight and we won't wait', calling for more Dreadnoughts.
Liberal government decided to build four more and then another four if necessary

1908

1909–12 Intermittent negotiations between Britain and Germany about limiting the German navy.

1910

In **1911–12** Germany indicated it would agree to limit its navy only if Britain promised to stay neutral in any war Germany fought. This would mean Britain taking no part in a war between Germany and France. Britain thought this would be too dangerous and would isolate it from France and Russia.

1911 Second Moroccan crisis – Britain again supported France against Germany

1912 Although there was no agreement, Germany reduced rate of shipbuilding to concentrate on the army.

1912

1912 Anglo-French naval agreement about positioning British and French navies (see page 128).

Position in 1912

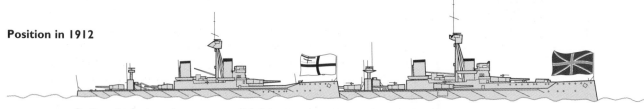

Both navies had much more powerful ships than in 1898. Britain was still ahead but Germany was much closer.

ACTIVITY

Draw a graph like this:

and complete to show when the arms race was at its height and when it slowed down.

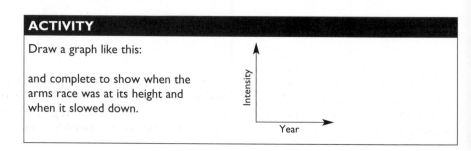

How did people in Britain respond to 'the German threat'?

It is clear from Chart 7H that the arms race was supported by public opinion in Britain – indeed the campaign to build more Dreadnoughts was very popular.

Between 1900 and 1914 many books and newspapers encouraged British people to think of Germany as an enemy. One of the bestselling books of 1903 was Erskine Childers' *Riddle of the Sands*, about a British sailor who discovers that German ships are preparing to attack England. Sources 7.10–7.12 are other examples from a novel, a popular newspaper and two magazines.

SOURCE 7.10 William Le Queux published *The Invasion of 1910* in 1906. His imaginary attack took place while the Kaiser was staying anonymously in a Scarborough hotel. The first signs of trouble were mysterious men working on telegraph poles in East Anglia who turned out to be Germans sawing them down and cutting the lines. Hundreds of German soldiers soon poured into Suffolk and went on to besiege London. Le Queux warns at the end of his book:

The British nation had been warned against the danger; it disregarded the warning. In the two great struggles of the early twentieth century, in South Africa and the Far East, it had before its eyes examples of the peril which comes from unpreparedness and from haphazard government. It shut its eyes to the lessons.

SOURCE 7.11 The *Daily Mail*, one of Britain's best-selling newspapers, had much to say about war dangers, as in these extracts from articles about Germany by Bart Kennedy, June 1906

For the last generation they [the German people] have been cowed and coerced by a gang of Prussian Huns – madmen, whose chief ambition was to disturb the world's peace so that they could show off the effect of a big conscript army ... there is the danger of a small knot of Prussians forcing on one of the most horrible and desolating wars to be known in the history of mankind. And absolutely the only thing to influence this knot of Huns is force. They are amenable to no moral or intellectual influence.

SOURCE 7.12 Two examples of anti-German sentiment in magazines.

A Frame from a picture sequence by John F. Campbell in the popular Pearson's Magazine, 1910. The sequence describes how a German invasion might progress. The original caption for this frame was 'When the Germans invade England, the first thing they will do after landing is to make for the stations and seize control of the railways'

B G.L. Garvin's article on 'The German Peril' in the *Quarterly Review* (an intellectual right-wing periodical) in 1908 was intended as serious factual argument

Nothing can be much more certain than that, if we are locked in a life-and-death struggle with Germany, she will attempt invasion. Her naval officers have sounded and sketched our harbours and studied every detail of our coasts. Her military officers have carried out staff-rides in this country. They have examined, as it were, every inch of our surface through a military microscope ...

There are, in this country, some 50,000 German waiters; and a large number of these are employed in connexion with the hotels at railway stations ... The nakedness of our land is spied out ... A force may be thrown upon our shores before war has been declared.

Governments make the key decisions on foreign policy but in a democratic system they are strongly influenced by public opinion. Governments need to win votes, and they need public support behind them to fight a war. Strong suspicion of German intentions had its effect on politicans' policies.

Meanwhile specialist pressure groups sprang up to push the government to respond to the German threat. The Navy League agitated for a stronger navy and the National Service League pressed for conscription to produce a stronger army. Both groups gained around 100,000 members in the years up to 1914. Over 150 schools had Officers' Training Corps by 1910 which taught young men the skills of warfare and military leadership.

At the government level there were also influential civil servants in the Foreign Office who were agitating for stronger defence against the German threat and were pushing the government towards closer relations with France.

These ingredients combined into a powerful war-flavoured cocktail. Indeed the historian Norman Stone said that, well before the outbreak of the Great War in 1914, war with Germany 'had already broken out in people's minds.'

There was popular enthusiasm for war and people began to assume it was necessary.

TALKING POINT

Discuss any examples that you are aware of where government foreign policy has either been influenced by or ignored popular opinion. What happened and why?

ACTIVITY

How far do Sources 7.10–7.12 support the comment by Norman Stone that 'war had already broken out in people's minds'?

Second Moroccan crisis, 1911

In 1911 the French were helping the Sultan of Morocco put down a rebellion in his country when a German gunboat turned up off the Moroccan coast at Agadir (see Map 7D). What was it doing there? Obviously it was some kind of threat and the German government demanded that the French give Germany their African land near the Congo river if France took control in Morocco.

This might have remained a dispute between Germany and France over African land, but the British government saw it as part of a struggle between the great powers. Furthermore, under the Entente Cordiale, Britain had agreed to support France in Morocco, so British national honour was also in question. Following discussions with Grey and the Prime Minister, Lloyd George, the Chancellor of the Exchequer, used a speech at the Lord Mayor of London's banquet to warn Germany that Britain would not stand by and be ignored. In this way Britain became a major player in a Franco-German dispute.

The Germans got some land from the French Congo in compensation, but the crisis had strengthened Britain's relations with France and increased tension with Germany.

Anglo-French Naval Agreements, 1912

Britain was intending to reduce her warships in the Mediterranean to concentrate more on the English Channel and North Sea, while France was intending to do the reverse, concentrating on the Mediterranean while withdrawing some ships from Channel ports. The two states therefore agreed to do this together and made further plans for possible joint action and defence. They now relied on each other to defend their vital interests. Ministers and representatives on both sides later interpreted these arrangements as implying a promise that Britain would defend France's northern coasts and France would defend British interests in the Mediterranean.

Anglo-German relations from 1912

In several ways Anglo-German relations seemed to improve between 1912 and 1914:

- Germany was building naval ships less rapidly. The British navy was estimated to be about 60 per cent stronger than the German in 1914.
- There was a Balkan war in 1912 when small countries bordering the Turkish Empire attacked it. After the war Grey organised a peace conference in London (December 1912–May 1913), getting useful co-operation from Germany as well as other powers.
- Britain and Germany negotiated agreements over colonial disputes in 1914. They agreed that a future extension of Germany's Berlin–Baghdad railway should be divided between them. Britain would control the last part down to Kuwait to safeguard its interests around the Gulf (see Map 7F). They also settled disputes about their interests in Portuguese colonies.

Kennedy and Steiner, who wrote important books in the 1970s and early 1980s, both contrast the easy settlement of colonial disputes between Britain and Germany with the continuing bitter rivalry over naval power. Germany wanted to be powerful in the North Sea and Britain believed it must have control there. No compromise was possible.

ACTIVITY

Bearing in mind all that you have read over the past five pages would you say that in mid-1914 war between Britain and Germany was:
a) unlikely
b) possible
c) likely
d) inevitable.
Choose one option and write a paragraph to justify your decision. Refer to evidence from the past five pages.

Archduke Franz Ferdinand, heir to the throne of Austria-Hungary, was murdered by a Serb terrorist at Sarajevo in the Balkans on 28 **June** 1914.

In late **July** Austria sent Serbia an ultimatum (a set of final demands). Serbia could not agree to all of the demands and rejected the ultimatum.

Austria-Hungary declared war. It had already discussed this with Germany, its main partner in the TRIPLE ALLIANCE.

Russia predictably supported the Serbs who, like Russians, were Slav by race and Orthodox Christians in religion.

France supported Russia because they were partners in the Dual Alliance.

Germany had long planned how it would attack France through Belgium before launching a major assault on the Russians. Germany declared war on France on 3 **August** and their army then invaded Belgium on 4 August.

Britain, which had signed the 1839 Treaty of London about keeping Belgium neutral (free from foreign armies), declared war on the same day.

D Why did Britain become involved in the First World War?

In June 1914 the heir to the throne of Austria-Hungary was assassinated by Serb terrorists in Sarajevo. Chart 7I summarises the now familiar chain of events that followed and which triggered the start of the First World War. But this does not explain exactly why Britain got involved.

ACTIVITY

Anglo-German relations 1898–1914

Draw your own copy of this diagram. Add brief explanations of how each development affected Anglo-German relations. Then place them on the graph. Discuss this with a partner and redraw the line if necessary.

BETTER RELATIONS

1898–1901
Attempts to make Anglo-German alliance

1902
Selborne Memorandum

TIME

WORSE RELATIONS

1904
Entente Cordiale

1905–06
First Moroccan crisis
1906
Britain builds first Dreadnought

1908–09
Naval scares

1909–10
Failure to negotiate naval limitations

1911–12
Second Moroccan crisis

1912
Negotiations on naval limitations fail

1912–14
Germany builds warships less rapidly. Britain and Germany work together over Balkans and colonial interests

---

TRIPLE ALLIANCE
In 1879 Germany had formed an alliance with Austria-Hungary to support each other in the event of one member going to war. In 1882 Italy joined too and so it became known as the Triple Alliance.

Factor 1: the Entente with France

The Liberal Cabinet made the final decision to go to war only after long discussions. The Foreign Secretary Edward Grey argued strongly for supporting France and seems to have threatened to resign if Britain did not (see Source 7.17). It was a hard decision for Liberals who disliked using war to settle international disputes but they knew that if they did not agree on war their government would fall and be replaced by a coalition or a Conservative alternative, which would almost certainly go to war. In the end, Britain's decision was based on a range of factors

There had been discussions between army and naval officers in Britain and France since 1905–06. There were further agreements in 1912 about how they would arrange their navies. There were no formal commitments to fight together, but how far did the understandings draw Britain into war?

SOURCE 7.13   Winston Churchill, First Lord of the Admiralty in 1914, later described the situation in *The World Crisis 1911–14*, 1923

It is true to say that our Entente with France and the military and naval conversations that had taken place since 1906 had led us into a position where we had the obligations of an alliance without its advantages.

SOURCE 7.14   Churchill recorded in 1923 how Grey, the Foreign Secretary, promised help to France before the Cabinet had decided what to do

[H]e said to me, 'You should know I have just … told Cambon [the French ambassador] that we shall not allow the German fleet to come into the Channel.'

SOURCE 7.15   Grey explained his thinking in his MEMOIRS, 1926

[T]he French Fleet was in the Mediterranean; the main British Fleet in the waters of Great Britain. The French north and west coasts were therefore left entirely without naval defence. Had not the naval conversations then placed France (if we stood aside) at a positive disadvantage? Had they not, in fact, created an obligation, in spite of express stipulations that they were not to do so? This consideration did not originate the suggestion of guaranteeing the French north and west coasts, but it clinched it.

> **MEMOIRS**
> Someone's written account of incidents in their life which they write up later.

SOURCE 7.16   Grey explained his view to the House of Commons, 3 August 1914

My own feeling is that if a foreign fleet engaged in a war which France had not sought, and in which she had not been the aggressor, came down the English Channel and bombarded and battered the undefended coasts of France, we could not stand aside and see this going on practically within sight of our eyes, with our arms folded, looking on dispassionately, doing nothing! I believe that would be the feeling of this country.

SOURCE 7.17   Grey's role in Cabinet was recorded in a very indirect way. Lord Riddell noted the comment of another Cabinet minister, C.F.G. Masterman, describing Grey's position at a Cabinet meeting before the declaration of war.

Grey made it absolutely plain that unless France was supported, he would resign. On one occasion he remarked with great emotion, 'We have led France to rely upon us, and unless we support her in her agony, I cannot continue at the Foreign Office.'

ACTIVITY

1   In what ways do Sources 7.13–7.17 indicate that the British government was morally committed to support France?
2   How important do Sources 7.13–7.18 suggest the commitment was in taking Britain into war?
3   In what ways does Source 7.18 indicate it was in Britain's interests to support France?

SOURCE 7.18   Haldane, the Secretary for War, later recorded his thinking at the time

I knew that if we kept out and allowed Germany to get possession even for a time of the north eastern shores of France, our turn would come later and that we should be in the greatest peril, our Navy notwithstanding, and that we might go down without a friend in the world, under a tremendous combination against us.

Factor 2: Commitments to Belgian neutrality

There was some legal dispute about whether Britain had promised to protect Belgium in the Treaty of London which it signed in 1839. Most of the Cabinet thought Britain had the right, but not the duty, to take action if Belgium were invaded.

■ 7J Location of Belgium

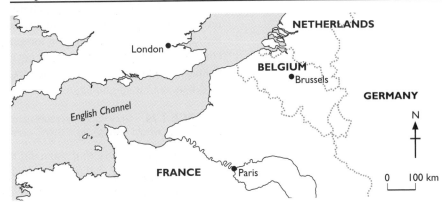

SOURCE 7.19 Article 7 of the Treaty of London, 1839, stated that Belgium should be a neutral country without troops from other states. The original treaty is in French.

La Belgique ... formera un Etat indépendant et perpétuellement neutre. Elle sera tenue d'observer cette même neutralité envers tous les autres Etats.

Belgium ... shall form an independent and permanently neutral state. It will be obliged to observe this same neutrality towards all the other states.

(Historians may debate how to translate 'tenue' in the treaty. It is taken here to mean that Belgium was obliged to observe neutrality.)

SOURCE 7.20 Grey described his thinking about the situation in Belgium in his memoirs, 1926

If she [Belgium] were to acquiesce voluntarily, or even under duress [wrongful pressure], in the passage of German troops, we should be entitled to send troops to vindicate [defend] the neutrality and resist the violation of it; but it was clear that an appeal from her for help, when she was herself fighting for what we were pledged to defend, would be particularly strong and moving. How could we possibly resist it?

SOURCE 7.21 Grey explained the options in a statement to the House of Commons, 3 August 1914

It may be said, I suppose, that we might stand aside, husband [save] our strength, and that whatever happened in the course of this war at the end of it intervene with effect to put things right, and to adjust them to our point of view. If, in a crisis like this, we run away from those obligations of honour and interest as regards the Belgian Treaty, I doubt whether, whatever material force we might have at the end, it would be of very much value in face of the respect we should have lost.

SOURCE 7.22 On 29 July 1914 Asquith told the King

[Supporting Belgium is a matter of] policy rather than legal obligation.

SOURCE 7.23 Churchill later wrote in *The World Crisis 1911–14*, 1923

Belgium and the Treaties were indisputably an obligation of honour binding upon the British State such as British Governments have always accepted; and it was on that ground that I personally, with others, took my stand.

ACTIVITY

1 What alternative to war does Grey put forward in Source 7.21, and why does he think it would not work?
2 Did the statement in the Treaty of London (Source 7.19) provide good reason for Britain declaring war on Germany when the German army invaded Belgium?
3 What different reasons do Sources 7.19–7.23 give for supporting Belgium?
4 What do you think Asquith meant by support for Belgium being a matter of 'policy rather than legal obligation' (Source 7.22)?

Factor 3: Concern about the Balance of Power

All through the nineteenth century British governments had been concerned about the Balance of Power. The aim of this policy was that no state should be allowed to get in such a strong position that it threatened all the others. Napoleon's France had successfully dominated the rest of Europe in the early nineteenth century; British statesmen had since been concerned that there should never be a repeat performance. On 3 August 1914 Sir Edward Grey stated in the House of Commons that there was 'a common interest against the unmeasured AGGRANDISEMENT of any Power'. Many historians emphasise this as the strongest underlying reason for going to war. If Germany dominated the continent of Europe Britain could never feel secure. Germany wanted to change the balance of power in the world. Britain wanted to keep it essentially as it was.

> **AGGRANDISEMENT**
> Process of gaining greater strength and superiority.

SOURCE 7.24 Grey spoke to representatives from Empire Dominions in 1912 about what Britain would have to do if there were a European war

[O]ur concern in seeing that there did not arise a supremacy in Europe which entailed a combination that would deprive us of the command of the sea would be such that we might have to take part in that European war. That is why the naval position underlies our European policy.

ACTIVITY

1 In Source 7.24 what is Grey's explanation of why Britain would have to take part in a European war?
2 How could a German takeover of Belgium and the north coast of France create the situation he describes? Refer to Map 7J.
3 From what you have read about the Entente with France, the German invasion of Belgium and concerns over the Balance of Power, how likely was it that Britain would have gone to war if Germany had invaded France without going through Belgium?

Factor 4: Concerns about Russia

In *The Policy of the Entente 1904–14* Keith Wilson (1985) argues that throughout this period Britain's foreign policy makers were more interested in the empire than Europe and so saw themselves less threatened by Germany than by Russia. He claims that good relations with Russia were the main objective of British policy throughout these years. This continues into the atmosphere of 1914. The view was that if France and Russia were to defeat Germany in war without British support, a confident Russia would be a serious threat to India and many other British possessions.

Why did Britain go to war in 1914?
Through this chapter you have examined a number of aspects of Britain's foreign policy that helped lead Britain into war in 1914. Here is a summary:

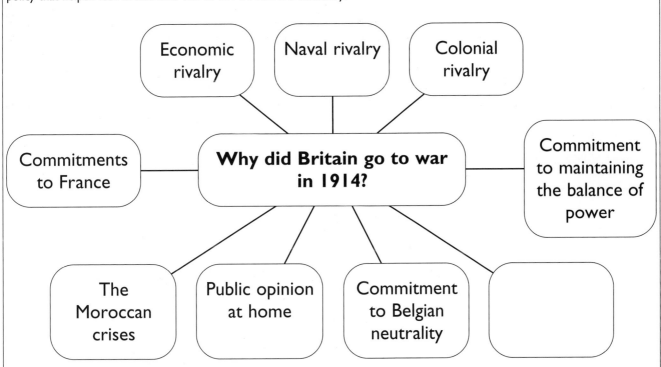

Stage 1 – explain each factor
a) Make your own copy of this chart. For each factor note your own explanation for how this helped lead Britain into war. Include examples or evidence where possible.
b) Add other factors that you think are important.

Stage 2 – link the factors
Many of these factors are linked with each other. For example: the Moroccan crises helped strengthen Britain's commitments to France. On your own diagram add lines and explanations to show some of the other links that you are aware of.

Stage 3 – rank the factors
At different times historians have chosen one factor as more important than others. There are examples on pages 130–132. Now it is your turn. Which of these factors do you think is most important in causing Britain to join the war and which is least important?

Stage 4 – long or short term
Place the factors in a grid like this.

	Long term	Short term (1911–14)
More important		
Less important		

Stage 5 – Write an essay
Use your completed charts to write an essay answering: Why did Britain go to war in 1914?

CHAPTER 7 REVIEW ACTIVITY

At some point Germany replaced Russia as the greatest danger in the minds of British foreign policy makers. A number of possible turning points are given in the chart below.

1 Either individually or in pairs work out which seems the most decisive moment in shifting the focus from Russia to Germany.

2 Write an explanation of your choice.

1902	1905–06	1907	1908–09	1911	1912
Selborne's memorandum on German naval power. In 1901 Selborne calculated British naval strength mainly in comparison with France and Russia combined. In 1902 he identified the threat from Germany	Russia was defeated in the 1904–05 Russo-Japanese War. Germany's navy replaced Russia's as the world's third strongest. Britain then calculated the Two Power Standard by comparison with France and Germany instead of France and Russia. The First Moroccan crisis worsened relations with Germany	ANGLO-RUSSIAN AGREEMENT Until then the Committee of Imperial Defence regarded Russia as Britain's main enemy when making war plans	Scare over German naval building. Britain decided to build more Dreadnoughts. Russia backed down in a dispute, when Austria-Hungary took permanent control of the Balkan province of Bosnia, and so looked weaker	The Second Moroccan crises worsened Anglo-German relations	The Anglo-French Naval Agreements meant Britain relied on France to maintain its interests in the Mediterranean, and France was Russia's ally

KEY POINTS FROM CHAPTER 7

How did Britain's foreign policy change after 1900?

1 Britain faced similar problems in defending the empire in the early twentieth century as it had done before 1900, but the danger from Russia declined and the danger from Germany increased.

2 Britain concentrated even more than it had done before on having a strong navy and built more advanced warships known as Dreadnoughts.

3 Britain made an alliance with Japan in 1902 and agreements with France and Russia in 1904 and 1907.

4 There was growing concern about German power, which led to a naval arms race.

5 There is debate about how far it was commitment to France, the defence of Belgium or concern over the Balance of Power that led Britain to fight in the First World War.

Who should the working classes vote for?

SOURCE I Detail from a cartoon in *Punch*, ridiculing the idea of agricultural workers being given the vote in 1873. Twleve years later it became reality

This is Jack Hodge, a farm labourer. To be exact, it is a middle-class cartoonist's view of Hodge. In 1885 he could vote for the first time in his life.

He was one of about two million working men in the countryside who got the vote under the 1884 Reform Act. The workers in big towns had voted for nearly twenty years and there was now a working class majority in the electorate. But who would Jack Hodge vote for? How would he decide? And would his decision really change politicians' policies or help Hodge himself?

Politicians had to find a way of appealing to Hodge, but Hodge and his brother workers had to decide whether they were best represented by the old parties or needed a new one of their own.

The greatest working-class heroes of 1867–1918 were probably the Liberal leaders Gladstone and Lloyd George. The most successful political party from 1885 to the end of the twentieth century was the Conservative Party. Was there room for and a need for a new third party – a Labour Party?

In this section you will examine the changing fortunes of the new and old parties through this period.

- Chapters 8 and 9 look at the growth of trade unions and the rise of the Labour Party.
- Chapter 10 focuses on the Conservatives.
- Chapters 11–13 chart the phenomenal success followed by the sudden decline of the Liberal Party.

It is a complex period with many overlapping threads. At the end you will be in a position to investigate the key question:
How successfully did political parties respond to the development of democracy and changes in the working class?

What was the working class?

There are different ways of defining the working class but in the nineteenth century the term was mostly used of workers and their families who earned their living by physical labour and earned wages from others. By this definition about 75–80 per cent of the population of Britain were working class between 1850 and 1918.

Many were working in manufacturing industries but, as you can see from Sources 2–9, members of the so-called working class had a massive range of jobs

SOURCE 2 Print of navvies in London working on the South-Western Railway in 1848. Navvies were labourers who dug out and made new earth-works, such as canals (navigations) and railways. Railway building was at its peak in the late 1840s. The navvies were hired and dismissed as they were needed, and the work was often dangerous. They frequently came from country areas where it was difficult to find jobs, and many came over from Ireland. They generally earned high wages and had a reputation for hard work and heavy drinking

SOURCE 3 Engraving of a London scavenger (street cleaner) used to illustrate Henry Mayhew's *London Labour and the London Poor*, 1851. Large numbers of scavengers and street sweepers were employed on a weekly basis to clean London streets, while nightsoilmen emptied cesspits of excrement and carted it away

SOURCE 4 Engraving of a London chimney sweep used to illustrate a report by Mayhew in the *Morning Chronicle*, 1849 and then in *London Labour and the London Poor*, 1851. Sweeps were not allowed to employ boys to climb chimneys after 1842, and they generally went from door to door looking for work. They were paid for each chimney they swept

SOURCE 5 Picture of a railway engine driver in 1852. Driving steam engines was a highly skilled job, and the drivers were generally trained and employed by the railway companies on a long-term contract

SOURCE 6 Photograph of workmen employed on reconstructing the Crystal Palace (used for the Great Exhibition in 1851) when it was re-erected in the London suburb of Sydenham in 1853. They would be employed by the week

SOURCE 7 Engraving of a group of Yorkshire factory girls drawn from a photograph in 1856. They would be in regular employment in woollen or linen mills, and women factory workers generally earned considerably more than the women making goods in their own homes or working as servants. By the mid-1850s their working day was restricted to 10½ hours, but they were under strict factory discipline

SOURCE 8 Engraving of a tailor and his family sewing clothes for the army in an attic in London's East End in 1863. These workers generally earned far less than those in factories, but they did not have to follow the factory owner's rules or overseer's instructions. They were paid on a piece-rate basis (according to how much work they did) and often worked very long hours just to get enough to live

SOURCE 9 Picture of a metal worker making a machine part in his workshop in 1867. He was paid according to how much he manufactured and rented his own workshop. The picture is from *The Child's Book of Trades* to show different occupations

■ A Class divisions used by historians

UPPER CLASS

Generally large landowners. Very successful factory owners, merchants and bankers bought estates to make themselves into country gentlemen when they got enough money.

MIDDLE CLASS

Upper middle class
• Factory owners and merchants who made wealth as 'entrepreneurs' (by taking risks with their money).
• 'Professional' men who got large incomes by using their skills, such as doctors and lawyers. Many other professions organised themselves in associations during the nineteenth century, such as architects in 1837.

Lower middle class
A great range of shopkeepers, clerks writing in offices, and others who worked with their brains and pens rather than physically.

WORKING CLASS

Generally used for those who did physical work and earned wages from others. Included about 75–80 per cent of the labour force from 1850 to the First World War. This is often subdivided into skilled craftsmen, such as carpenters and railway engine drivers, and unskilled workers, such as building labourers.

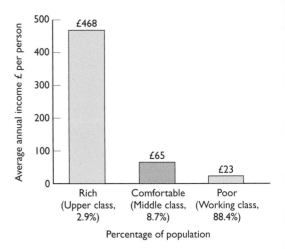

SOURCE 10 Sir Leo Chiozza Money, a Liberal MP who wrote a number of books on economic issues, estimated UK incomes, 1904

In 1904 Liberal MP Sir Leo Chiozza Money estimated the number of people in each class and their approximate income (Source 10). The working class earned a lot less than the upper and middle classes but there was also a lot of variation among the earnings of working-class people.

Some of the working class were casual labourers who did not know from day to day if they would have a job to go to. During periods of depression when the British economy was growing slowly or declining, such workers might have no job at all for long periods. Henry Mayhew, writing about the London poor in 1850, described how there were normally large numbers of people looking for work each day. At the other extreme there were skilled craftsmen or tradesmen who had secure employment and a good wage, and who were much in demand at all times.

These differences led Marxists (see page 151) to refer to the most skilled and best-paid workers as a 'labour aristocracy'. Some were craftsmen in traditional industries such as coach-making or cabinet-making; others were skilled engineers, ship-builders or engine drivers. These workers could easily earn twice as much as unskilled labourers. They wanted to emphasise how different they were from the labourers, not what they had in common.

The term labour aristocracy has fallen out of fashion among today's historians but it is difficult to write about a single 'working class'. There was a complicated hierarchy, not a clear divide between employers and workers.

Working-class identity

One theme of this period is the emergence of a powerful working-class identity or consciousness and attempts by left-wing politicians to build on this for political ends. Being working class was not just a matter of what people did or earned, but how they thought. Working-class 'consciousness' involved **solidarity with other working-class people**:

• They had to be conscious of what they had in common with **everybody else who earned wages by doing manual work**, not just people in their own occupation. A sense of solidarity just with others who were, say, carpenters or butchers' boys was not enough.

- They had to identify with workers **nationwide**, not just with those in their own town or region.
- They had to have a **sense of class conflict** – that they were exploited by their employers and that their employers were opponents. They therefore had shared interests with other members of the working class and should act together against their employers. Class consciousness therefore means some hostility between classes.

The most important historian to put forward these ideas was Karl Marx, whose beliefs are summarised on page 151. Chapters 8 and 9 examine the impact of these ideas.

SOURCE 11 A: Real wages 1851–1913

Real wages = buying power. They show what people can buy with the money they earn. We calculate real wages by estimating what items an average family buys and working out the price of these items – the so-called cost of a family shopping basket. If wages were increasing at the same speed as prices, the graph would be flat. This graph shows the best recent estimates for the nineteenth century

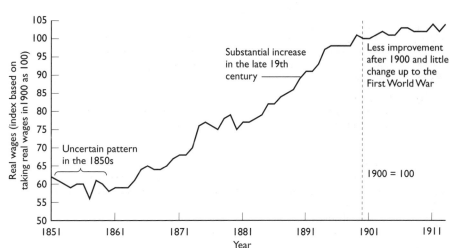

The trend of graph A may be upward (in 1900 real wages were almost double what they had been in the mid-1850s) but you can also clearly see that within this overall picture there were fluctuations both in real wages and in the economy as a whole. There were booms when manufacturers and traders believed there was high demand for their goods so they produced more and employed more people. There were also slumps when demand fell or had been over-estimated and there was a decline in world trade. Fewer goods were made and fewer people were employed. These look like little blips on a graph but they made a big difference to the workers. If there was no work casual labourers found it hard to pay the rent or feed their families.

SOURCE 11 B: Total wealth produced in Britain 1855–1913

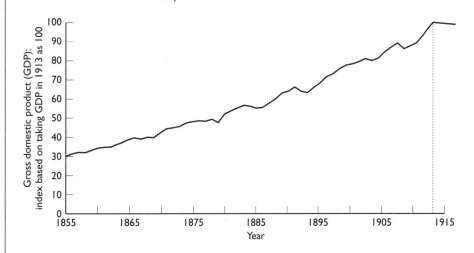

ACTIVITY

Part B of Source 11 shows substantial economic growth but how far did British workers benefit? It is hard to get agreed statistics as researchers have collected information in different ways but the two graphs in Source 11 compare real wages and overall economic output in the period.

1 Study Source 11 carefully. Explain in your own words
   a) what really happened to real wages between 1851 and 1911
   b) which decades saw the biggest change and what the changes were
   c) whether real wages increased in line with overall economic growth and, if not, what the differences were.

2 When might a worker have been most likely to
   a) ask his employer for higher wages
   b) lose his job
   c) feel 'I've never had it so good'?

How did trade unions try to get a better deal for workers?

CHAPTER OVERVIEW

Trade unions are formed by workers to get a better deal from their employers. This obviously means better pay and shorter hours but nineteenth-century unions were often just as concerned about working conditions and controlling who could or could not do the work.

Before 1850 most trade unions were small societies of skilled workers who just existed to help their own members and run savings schemes. By the First World War they represented four million workers, organised massive strikes and were among the most powerful organisations in the country, commanding the attention of employers, newspapers and government ministers. Chart 8A summarises the main developments.

■ 8A Development of trade unionism from the early 1800s

Early 1800s	Many **small trade societies** of skilled workers and a few larger unions
1851 onwards	**New Model Unions** – nationally organised unions of skilled working men, starting with the Amalgamated Society of Engineers, 1851
1866–68	**Crisis** over the **legal position** of unions. Trade unions group together to form the Trades Union Congress (TUC)
1871 and 1875	New laws define unions' legal position
Early 1870s	Economic boom leads to formation of unions among unskilled workers. These decline in late 1870s because of economic slump
1888–90	Growth of **New Unionism** – larger unions which include many unskilled and semi-skilled workers
1890s	**Conflict** as some employers try to resist union power, fight and gain legal decisions against unions
1900–01	**Taff Vale** decision limits unions' power to strike and picket (standing outside a workplace where there is a strike to show others that the strike is taking place and to discourage them from working)
1906	**Trade Disputes Act** protects unions from legal action over strikes
1910–14	**Union growth** and greater militancy (being prepared to fight and take strong action) with large-scale strikes

In this chapter you will be examining how these changes took place:

A How did trade unions grow 1850–1900? (pp. 141–145)

B Why did trade unions become more militant 1900–14? (pp. 146–148)

This chapter is closely linked to Chapter 9. In Chapter 9 you will examine the parallel story of the development of the Labour Party over the same period.

FOCUS ROUTE

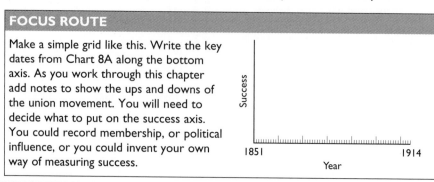

Make a simple grid like this. Write the key dates from Chart 8A along the bottom axis. As you work through this chapter add notes to show the ups and downs of the union movement. You will need to decide what to put on the success axis. You could record membership, or political influence, or you could invent your own way of measuring success.

FOCUS ROUTE

1 **a)** Draw a timeline from 1870 to 1890 on the left of a page. As you read pages 141–144, list laws, strikes and other trade union developments on the right.

   b) Rate each event from +5 (great success) to −5 (serious failure) for the trade unions.

2 Decide which two or three events were most important in trade union growth.

A How did trade unions grow 1850–1900?

The first workers to form trade unions were not the ones who suffered most hardship. They were the skilled ones who could pressure employers and bargain with them successfully. They were moderate. They encouraged their members to help themselves by getting educated and saving for hard times. They acted as 'friendly societies', using their members' weekly subscriptions to provide benefits when they were ill or could not find work. They generally avoided conflict with their employers, using persuasion rather than strikes to win improved conditions.

As railways and postal services allowed workers to keep in touch with others across the country, they formed truly national organisations like the Amalgamated Society of Engineers founded in 1851. Twentieth-century historians called them 'new model unions'.

Despite setbacks the unions grew. By 1870 it is estimated that they had around half a million members – roughly double the figure for 1850. All the same this remained only a small proportion of Britain's 12 million workers. Unions expanded and were generally more active in economic booms. They had more bargaining power then. Strikes were more of a threat to employers when their order books were full and they needed workers the most.

Union leaders wanted to look respectable and generally tried to avoid strikes. As one trade union leader, George Odger, put it, strikes were 'to the social world what wars are to the political world'. Unfortunately, as the *Flint Glass Makers' Magazine* suggested, they could not be avoided in all cases, and there were some bitter disputes.

Crisis 1: the Sheffield Outrages

One way a union could protect itself and its members was by ensuring that anyone who wanted to work in their industry had to be a member of their union. In Sheffield in 1866 this led to extreme violence. Members of the cutlers' union dropped a barrel of gunpowder down a saw-grinder's chimney and blew up his house because he had not paid his union dues. Following this incident other examples of local union intimidation came to light and there was a national scandal.

Crisis 2: Hornby v Close – a legal battle

When the treasurer of the Bradford branch of the Boilermakers' Society embezzled £24 of the union's funds, a judge ruled that the union could not get the money back because it had no status in the law courts. Other judges would have to make the same decision if a similar case came to court again. The implication was that, in future, officials could take union money for themselves without their members being able to take legal action against them.

TRADES UNION CONGRESS

A conference called by trade unionists in Manchester in 1868 is generally seen as the first TUC. It aimed to meet annually and started the conferences which continue today. It became a national institution. Leaders of skilled unions in London also joined together to influence politicians and public but did not create any similarly long-lasting organisation.

How did the unions organise to deal with the crisis?

The government set up a Royal Commission to investigate and report on trade unions; the unions organised themselves to put their case and started the Trades Union Congress (TUC). The outcome was new laws affecting trade unions.

In 1871 the Trade Union Act gave the unions legal recognition (status in the law courts) but the Criminal Law Amendment Act banned picketing. After much campaigning, the 1875 Conspiracy and Protection of Property Act allowed it as long as the pickets were present only 'to obtain and communicate information'. Over the next thirty years there was fierce debate about what pickets should or should not be able to do, and it led to some of the biggest battles in trade union history.

■ 8B The debate about the role of unions at the end of the 1860s

TRADE UNIONIST

Workmen must combine just to get a fair day's wage for a fair day's work. A skilled workman has no property to bargain with, only his skills and labour. The towns seem full of labourers, often looking for casual work. Unless there are restrictions employers can hire them to do less demanding parts of a craftsman's job or to make cheap, shoddy goods, and then the skilled worker is helpless.

EMPLOYER

The price of goods and services is fixed by the laws of supply and demand, and the price of labour is no exception. Union members often intimidate employers and other workers, as we saw at Sheffield. No group of workmen has a right to stop others working or to tell an employer that he cannot hire another man. What about the rights of workers outside unions?

How did trade unions grow in the 1870s?

Trade unions grow in economic booms, and there was a very marked boom from about 1867 to 1873. The high demand for labour encouraged workers to form unions. Gas stokers, building labourers, farm workers, railway workers and dockers all organised. Many unions attempted strikes and some won shorter hours, but their success was generally short lived. During an economic slump in the later 1870s they lost members and sometimes collapsed. Yet many survived, including the Amalgamated Society of Railway Servants, and they showed how large numbers of workers would organise if the economic conditions were right.

Some fought for better wages and working hours, but they were usually more concerned about the effects of new machinery and changed working arrangements. Industrial disputes are often described in terms of militant trade unions, employer fight-backs and political conflict. These were all important after 1870, but disputes were also about a lot of worried men trying to cope with new technology and fierce competition. Britain no longer had the same industrial lead as in the 1850s and 1860s, prices went down sharply between 1873 and 1896, and there was great worry about German imports by the 1890s. If prices and profits fell, employers might reasonably reduce wages as well, but that would bring obvious problems.

THE SWEATER'S FURNACE: OR. THE REAL "CURSE" OF LABOUR.

SOURCE 8.1 Etching, with the caption 'The Sweater's Furnace or the Real "Curse" of Labour', in *Punch*, 1888

ACTIVITY

1 Trade unions developed early in coal mining and grew stronger in the late 1800s. What aspects of miners' work would encourage trade union growth?
2 How might a worker use Source 8.1 to argue that trade unions were necessary?
3 How might an employer use Source 8.3 to argue that stricter workshop discipline was often necessary?

SOURCE 8.2 Miners cutting and moving coal in north-east England, 1871

SOURCE 8.3 Print showing men in a small workshop handing over money for beer, which the lad is about to fetch, *c.* 1890

FOCUS ROUTE

Make brief notes on the following:

a) Why new unions evolved
b) What was different about New Unionism
c) The employers' response to New Unionism
d) The Taff Vale Case.

New Unionism

From the mid-1880s there were various initiatives among workers, such as the National Labour Federation started around Newcastle-on-Tyne in 1886, but three strikes in London have generally been seen as the start of New Unionism. They came during a trade boom. All three groups of workers had limited skills, looked in a bad bargaining position and yet won their strike. All were connected with the start of new trade unions, and all had leaders with a flair for publicity.

1888 Matchgirls at Bryant and May's who dipped matches in phosphorus
Won with help from London socialists

1889 Gasworkers who stoked ovens with coal
Won eight-hour day instead of twelve

1889 Dockers who got work loading and unloading ships on a casual day-by-day basis
Won wage increase

The successs of these strikes led to a recognisably different type of union, characterised as New Unionism.

Key features of New Unionism
- Unskilled and semi-skilled workers organising in larger unions
- General unions of workers in different trades, not just one occupation
- Socialist leaders in many unions
- Emphasis on fighting employers rather than providing welfare benefits
- More ambitious demands, such as the eight-hour day.

By 1890 there were some big new unions. The seven largest claimed 320,000 members altogether. The best calculations suggest that in total unions had over 1.5 million members in the early 1890s, which was probably about double the number at the start of 1888. Most trade unionists were men and made up about 15 per cent of an overall male workforce of around 10 million.

Then union numbers started to fall with a trade slump around 1890 and just over 10 per cent of all workers were apparently in unions by 1895. Under a tenth of those would have been in new unions. Long-established coal and cotton unions were much larger than the general and unskilled ones.

Historians agree that the successes in 1888–90 gave encouragement to all unions. As new unions introduced welfare benefits and old unions opened themselves up to new members, they often became more like each other. They put forward many similar demands in the 1890s and often faced common problems.

How did employers respond to New Unionism?

Employers frequently worked with the unions. There was more COLLECTIVE BARGAINING, where groups of employers negotiated with unions. Clegg, Fox and Thompson, in their great trade union history (1964), argued that this was the 'outstanding feature' of the period.

Some developed their own **organisations to break strikes**. For example, the National Free Labour Association was established in 1893 to provide workers when others were on strike.

Bitter strikes raised issues over how far **picketing** could go. The 1875 Conspiracy and Protection of Property Act allowed picketing only if it was 'to obtain or communicate information'. When the Amalgamated Trade Society of Fancy Leather Workers organised a strike against a manufacturer of fancy leather goods called Lyons, they had large numbers of people around Lyons'

DISCUSS

In what ways did employers

a) co-operate with
b) oppose

trade unions?

COLLECTIVE BARGAINING
Negotiating and bargaining between unions, representing workers who work for different employers, and a group of employers or their representatives.

premises holding out cards which urged men not to work. The court ruled in the case of Lyons v. Wilkins that this was not just giving information but putting pressure on people to strike and therefore against the law. The 1875 Act was being interpreted more strictly in the courts than it had been before.

The Taff Vale case

The crisis for the unions came with a strike in 1900 on the Taff Vale Railway which transported coal in South Wales. The strike was called when the company dismissed a signalman who refused to move to a new signal box. Bell, the moderate secretary of the Amalgamated Society of Railway Servants (ASRS), was against strike action, but his men wanted to come out, and the union's executive backed them. The management got workers from the National Free Labour Association to keep their railway running, and the union organised mass picketing to prevent them.

After the strike, the railway company took the union to court to get DAMAGES for what it had lost because of interrupted services and extra costs during the strike. The case went right through the legal system to the judges in the House of Lords, the country's top court, who decided the union should pay £23,000 to the railway company. The court said that trade unions had to answer in court for what their officials or representatives had done – the so-called doctrine of 'representative action'. Decisions in court cases create what is called legal precedent, meaning that courts must make a similar judgement if a similar case arises in the future. If workers broke their contracts in a strike or used mass picketing and the unions backed them, then the unions might have to cover employers' losses.

> **DAMAGES**
> In civil law, payment to compensate for losses suffered.

SOURCE 8.4   The union's case, after the strike, from its paper, the *Railway Review*

The present state of the law, or, at any rate, its interpretation by learned judges, is a monstrous injustice to working men. It is obviously one-sided and unfair. A Trade Unionist may not persuade – he can only communicate information; he may not distribute a handbill telling a man he will be a blackleg if he takes up work in a strike – that is a libel. But an employer may hire a gang of ruffians who will capture all the riff-raff they can get hold of, this gang may lock men in waiting rooms and railway carriages, may forcibly escort them along streets and works guarded by police, may confine them in rooms on the premises, and watch over them while they do other people's work. This is the fairness of the law. This is how men are persuaded to work. This is free labour.

SOURCE 8.5   The employers' case from their paper, the *Railway News*

No strike can succeed except by intimidation, which is the striker's only weapon; with picketing impossible, there can be no effective intimidation … this power has been maintained by the peculiar position of the unions, which have hitherto been regarded as outside the jurisdiction of the courts.

SOURCE 8.6   An account of how the union's pickets worked by William Collison, leader of the National Free Labour Association, describing the arrival of his men at Cardiff station

[T]he station was filled with Union pickets, and twenty-eight of my men were forcibly made prisoners, marched to the Union headquarters in Cathays, locked in, and then when the time arrived, marched back to the station and entrained for London.

DISCUSS

1 Explain whether you think the court's judgment in the Taff Vale case was right or wrong. Consider Sources 8.4–8.6, the circumstances of the strike and the legal arguments suggested here.
2 What was the importance of the decision in the Taff Vale case for
   a) employers
   b) trade unions?

B Why did trade unions become more militant, 1900–14?

Growth and recognition of trade unions

Trade unions nearly doubled their membership between 1906 and 1914.

SOURCE 8.7   Total trade union membership and TUC affiliation, 1906 and 1914

	1906	1914
Total trade union membership	2,210,000 (c. 13% of workers)	4,145,000 (c. 25% of workers)
Membership affiliated to the Trades Union Congress	1,700,000	2,682,357

The men outnumbered the women – nearly a third of the male workforce were in unions but only about a tenth of the female workforce. Around 35 per cent of the workers in factories, mines and railways were in trade unions. Union organisation was also expanding in new areas. More office workers joined unions, and some of the new unions from the late nineteenth century at last gained large, long-term memberships. The Gasworkers and General Labourers Union grew from 32,00 members in 1910 to 135,000 by the end of 1913.

In the late 1800s collective bargaining was generally local, but employers and unions increasingly made arrangements to decide wages and working conditions for the whole country. Government involvement in CONCILIATION and ARBITRATION became normal procedure. Under a law from 1896, the Board of Trade's labour department could offer conciliation in a dispute if one side asked for it. People came to expect government action in serious disputes when the Liberals were in power from 1906. A government official, Sir George Askwith, frequently acted as chief conciliator and Lloyd George intervened to avoid strikes on the railways in 1907 and 1911.

Why did trade unions become more militant?

Economic, social and political reasons all help to account for growing trade union militancy.

Economic reasons

- After 1900 real wages do not seem to have risen as fast as they had done from the 1870s–90s (see Source 8.8). Wage demands were the most frequent and obvious cause of disputes.
- A trade boom improved trade unions' bargaining position before the First World War. The best figures we have for unemployment show it fell from 7.8 per cent to 2.1 per cent in 1908–13.

Social reasons

- Education Acts in 1870, 1876 and 1880 had introduced compulsory schooling. Workers were often better educated and more aware of political ideas.
- Since many factories and firms were getting larger, fewer workers knew their employers. More employees worked for companies with large numbers of SHAREHOLDERS. The companies' profits went in DIVIDENDS to people workers never saw.

Political reasons

- The legal decision in the Taff Vale Case was replaced by the **1906 Trade Disputes Act**. Picketing could now include trying to persuade other people not to work, and trade unions could not be challenged in the civil law courts.
- There were 30 Labour MPs in Parliament after the 1906 election, but some workers were dissatisfied with what they achieved, and a small number of syndicalists (see page 149) argued that a general strike was needed to achieve a socialist society.

CONCILIATION
Process of bringing together two sides in a dispute.

ARBITRATION
Procedure for judging and making a decision in a dispute by a person or group not directly involved.

ACTIVITY

1. How important were wage levels in leading to strikes? Consider the evidence in Sources 8.8 and 8.9.
2. Why might
   a) more education, and
   b) larger companies
   encourage more strikes?
3. How would
   a) the 1906 Trade Disputes Act, and
   b) dissatisfaction with Labour MPs
   encourage strikes?
4. Using the answers to questions 1–3, rate each of the six bullet points on the right from 1 (unimportant) to 5 (very important) for their importance in explaining why there were large-scale strikes before the First World War.

SHAREHOLDERS
People who own part of a company by having shares in it and who therefore get a proportion of the profits.

DIVIDENDS
Shares of the profits normally paid to owners of a company.

SOURCE 8.8 Graph showing estimates of real earnings (earnings in relation to prices), 1892–1914, compiled by Bowley before the First World War and Feinstein in the 1980s

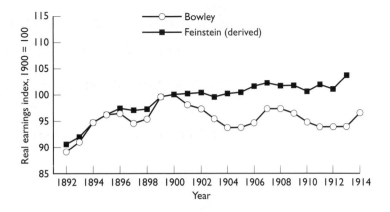

Strikes and industrial unrest 1908–14

There were far more strikes between 1908 and the First World War than ever before. The figures include some lock-outs (where employers shut out their workers) and omit some small strikes, but they give a fair impression of the massive increase in disputes.

SOURCE 8.9 Strike action, 1909–14: working days lost (to the nearest thousand)

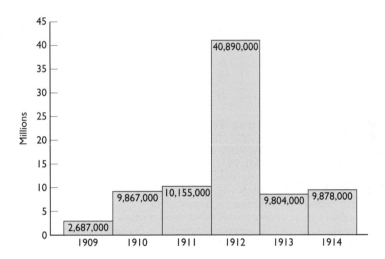

Strikes on the railways and in the coal mines could stop the economic life of the country. A rail strike would quickly paralyse Britain because most goods were transported by rail and long-distance passenger journeys were by train. A coal strike could threaten the country in the long run because trains, ships and many factories were driven by steam. The gas and electricity which lit towns and ran the rest of the factories were also made from coal.

There was a two-day rail strike in 1911, until the Chancellor of the Exchequer, Lloyd George, stepped in and negotiated a compromise agreement.

Coal mines employed over a million men, and miners accounted for half of the working days lost from 1907 to the First World War. There was a national miners' strike in 1912, which accounts for the record total of days lost that year (see Source 8.9). *The Times* described it as 'the greatest catastrophe that has threatened the country since the Spanish Armada'. It ended when the government brought in the Coal Mines Act as a compromise. Local boards were established to fix wages, but they would decide different rates for different regions, and the Miners' Federation of Great Britain (MFGB) did not get the national rate it wanted.

Many people were troubled by the violence during some strikes. Three people were killed in disturbances connected with the South Wales miners' strikes in 1910–11 and another three died in violence connected with disputes at Liverpool.

In 1914 the MFGB, the National Union of Railwaymen (formed from the Amalgamated Society of Railway Servants and others in 1913) and the

SOURCE 8.10 Miners at a South Wales coal mine in 1910. Lads left school at 13 or 14 to go down the pit. By 16 or 17 they could be quite experienced workers

Transport Workers' Federation (including dock workers) set about forming a Triple Alliance, although they did not complete arrangements until the end of 1915. This alliance could organise a crippling general strike among the country's most vital workers. The union leaders would have to consult members of the different unions before taking action, and so the government would have plenty of warning of this, but the threat was there. Union leaders hoped it would get them what they wanted.

During the First World War union activity did not stop, but there appear to have been fewer strikes than in previous years.

ACTIVITY

What would be the main aims for union representatives of the young workers in Source 8.10?

■ 8D The impact of the First World War for unions and employers

DIFFICULTIES

- Skilled male workers had to accept less skilled workers to do parts of their jobs. Some saw women workers as a threat.
- Normal collective bargaining arrangements were often suspended during war.

CHANGES WITH MIXED RESULTS

- Trade union leaders worked more closely with the government.
- Workers in factories and workshops relied more on shop stewards (representatives chosen by fellow workers in factories or workshops).
- Fewer strikes – back to the levels before 1908.

GAINS

- More employer and government recognition for trade unions.
- 1916 – Ministry of Labour established, as Trades Union Congress wanted.
- 1917 – Government committee under J.H. Whitley recommended more collective bargaining committees. National ones set up in many industries (e.g. baking, rubber) where unions had little role before.
- 1918 – Union membership grew from about 4 million to 6.5 million.

CHAPTER 8 REVIEW ACTIVITY

Refer to the graph you compiled for the Focus Route at the start of this chapter. Assess how far the unions were successful in the periods 1850–70, 1870–88, 1888–1900 and 1900–14. You may do this by assessing
a) size of membership
b) success in strikes
c) political influence.

KEY POINTS FROM CHAPTER 8

How did trade unions try to get a better deal for workers?

1 Trade unions were first formed by skilled workers.

2 They faced big problems over legal status and restrictions in the 1860s and 1870s, but they gained rights to hold funds and organise picketing.

3 A new type of unionism developed among unskilled and semi-skilled workers in the late nineteenth century, and there were disputes about the unions' legal rights.

4 Trade unions grew to 4 million members by the First World War and made much more use of strike action.

How important was the Labour Party before the First World War?

CHAPTER OVERVIEW
Workers who were unhappy with their working or living conditions in the nineteenth century might have tried to get a better deal through:

- trade unions gaining improvements from employers
- political parties acting in the workers' interests – and trying to change the laws of the country
- revolutionary action (as occurred in some European countries).

As you saw in Chapter 8, by 1914 many of Britain's workers had taken the first option and joined a union.

This chapter examines the second option. The trade unions, along with various socialist organisations, set up the Labour Party to represent working-class interests in Parliament.

This chapter asks:

A What is socialism? (pp. 149–50)

B Who were the socialist pioneers? (pp. 150–154)

C Why was the Labour Party so slow to develop? (pp. 154–155)

D How and why was the Labour Party created? (pp. 155–159)

E What did the Labour Party achieve 1906–14? (p. 160–162)

F Review (p. 163)

FOCUS ROUTE

In one sentence note the key feature of each type of socialism and place each type on a line like this:

EXTREME ◄————► MODERATE

A What is socialism?

The basic aim of socialism is for the community to control wealth so that it is more equally distributed. Socialists are also interested in people having equal rights in other ways, but wealth is always the main issue.

There are different ideas about how far the equality should go or what means should be used to achieve it. This leads to different kinds of socialism and varied ways of describing them.

Fundamentalist socialism

This means workers or the state on the workers' behalf controlling the means of making wealth (land, factories, trading companies, banks, etc.) to ensure wealth is then distributed more equally. This might be achieved in different ways.

- **Revolutionary socialists** believe that workers should rise up and take over control of government and industry by using **physical force**. The most famous revolutionary socialist was Karl Marx (see Chart 9A).
- **Democratic socialism** means getting people **to vote for** socialism. Democratic socialists try to get power using the current electoral system.
- **Syndicalism** involves workers bringing down the capitalist system by **strike action**. Workers' co-operatives would then run the economy with some central organisation to co-ordinate rather than control it.

150

HOW IMPORTANT WAS THE LABOUR PARTY BEFORE THE FIRST WORLD WAR?

PROGRESSIVE TAXATION
Taxation which falls more heavily on the wealthy, so that they pay a higher proportion of their income in tax than people who are less well off.

Communism

Communism is an extreme form of socialism in which everybody gets equal shares. In Karl Marx's words, wealth goes 'from each according to his ability, to each according to his needs'. It might be achieved by revolutionary or democratic means (see Chart 9A opposite).

Social democracy

Social democracy is a term often used to describe a moderate redistribution of wealth. This can be done by PROGRESSIVE TAXATION – taxes which fall far more heavily on the rich than others. The taxes can then finance welfare reforms which particularly benefit the poor.

Some socialists emphasise changing people's **ideas** of right and wrong and getting them to think more about the community rather than just themselves or their families. They differ very much in how far they want to use the state. Syndicalists, for example, see no role for state power.

DISCUSS

How much did all socialists have in common?

■ **Learning trouble spot**

Left wing and right wing
These terms are used to describe people's political views. Generally left-wingers want big change and right-wingers want to keep the economic and political organisation of the country much the same.

SOURCE 9.1 Henry George

B ## Who were the socialist pioneers?

Many Radicals put forward socialist ideas in the early and mid-nineteenth century. Leaders in the Chartist movement (see page 11) and others argued that workers should get the full value of what they produced without employers making a profit from their work. Land should be returned to the people, and workers should exchange goods between themselves so that traders did not make a profit either. Here, in short, was a socialist vision of a fairer and more equal society. Yet in 1880, although these ideas had been put forward by a few people, there were no significant socialist organisations. Then from 1881 important socialist publications inspired a small number of people to organise, agitate and preach. In the 1880s and 1890s their organisations were still small, but they have attracted historians' attention because they later helped lead to the formation of the Labour Party.

Henry George

Progress and Poverty, by the American Henry George, was first published in Britain in 1881. It argued that land should be returned to the people – a frequent theme among mid-nineteenth-century Radicals – and it sold 109,000 copies in a cheap edition.

DISCUSS

1 Why would Henry George's argument (Source 9.2) be attractive to many people?
2 In what ways could Marx's arguments (Source 9.3) inspire socialists and give them more confidence?

SOURCE 9.2 From *Progress and Poverty* by Henry George, 1881

There is but one way to remove an evil – and that is, to remove its cause. Poverty deepens as wealth increases, and wages are forced down while productive power grows, because land, which is the source of all wealth and the field of all labor, is monopolized. To extirpate [remove] poverty, to make wages what justice commands they should be, the full earnings of the laborer, we must therefore substitute for the individual ownership of land a common ownership. Nothing else will go to the cause of evil – in nothing else is there the slightest hope.

Karl Marx

In the 1880s English translations began to appear of the main works of Karl Marx.

151

HOW IMPORTANT WAS THE LABOUR PARTY BEFORE THE FIRST WORLD WAR?

SOURCE 9.3 From the authorised English version, 1888, of the *Communist Manifesto* by Karl Marx and Friedrich Engels, translated from the original (1848)

Wage-labour rests exclusively on competition between the labourers. The advance of industry ... replaces the isolation of the labourers, due to competition, by their revolutionary combination, due to association. The development of Modern Industry, therefore, cuts from under its feet the very foundation on which the BOURGEOISIE produces and appropriates products. What the bourgeoisie therefore produces, above all, are its own gravediggers. Its fall and the victory of the proletariat [wage-earning workers] are equally inevitable ...

The proletarians [workers] have nothing to lose but their chains. They have a world to win. Workers of all countries unite!

> **BOURGEOISIE**
> Middle-class merchants, industrialists and shopkeepers. Marx and Engels used the word more generally for those who got wealth from workers' labour.

■ 9A Marx's view of the later stages in History

In a CAPITALIST society traders and industrialists control the most important means of making wealth. Both they and the landowners have similar interests in getting profits from the work of the proletariat (wage-earning workers)	As factories develop and machines put people out of work, so there are more and more industrial workers and worse living conditions for the workers. Hardships increase, slumps in the TRADE CYCLE become more severe, and eventually the proletariat, now gathered together in factory towns, rebels	Revolution occurs, workers overthrow the capitalist society and their leaders establish a dictatorship of the proletariat

> **CAPITALIST**
> Referring to a system in which people who contribute or inherit capital (money for investment) control business and get profit.
>
> **TRADE CYCLE**
> Fluctuations in the economy between booms and slumps. Booms come when manufacturers and traders believe there is high demand for goods and so they are keen to produce more and employ more people. Slumps come when demand has been over-estimated or seems likely to fall and so fewer goods are made and fewer people are employed.

Far fewer people read Marx than Henry George – you can see from comparing Sources 9.2 and 9.3 why that might be. But Marx's thinking was much more significant. Its analysis was deeper and its arguments were more compelling to those who could understand them. It influenced the way other socialists thought and wrote. Many readers would come across Marx's ideas in other people's work.

FOCUS ROUTE

Look at pages 152–153. Copy and complete this table by listing the aims, methods, achievements and weaknesses of each organisation.

Organisation	Aims	Methods	Achievements	Weaknesses
Social Democratic Federation				
Fabian Society				
Socialist League				

Social Democratic Federation (SDF)

The first Marxist group in Britain was the Social Democratic Federation, started in 1884 by a businessman, Henry Hyndman. It was small and divided and had difficulties in working out how to follow Marx's thinking. Its members knew they wanted a revolution but did not know if this was best achieved by violence or political means. Hyndman did not want to join with trade union leaders because they were far too moderate and ready to support the Liberal Party.

SOURCE 9.4 (above) Henry Hyndman

SOURCE 9.5 (right) A Fabian Society pamphlet

Although the SDF was involved in workers' demonstrations and disturbances in London in 1886 and 1887, it generally relied more on its own propaganda. The SDF did include some influential trade union leaders, such as the dockers' leaders Tom Mann and John Burns, and many of its members later played an important part in the Labour Party, but it split up and achieved little on its own.

Fabians

The Fabians were another small socialist group begun in 1884, but they were clearer and more practical about what they wanted to achieve. They accepted some of Marx's ideas about how capitalism was working and how change was inevitable, but not about revolution. They were a group of middle-class intellectuals, including the playwright George Bernard Shaw, and Sidney and Beatrice Webb (who wrote *The History of Trade Unionism 1666–1920*). They were going to win support by lectures, books and pamphlets; and they produced hundreds of thousands of them. They saw that socialism might be achieved by NATIONALISATION and progressive taxation. They also believed that Britain was moving towards socialism anyway. The state was providing schools, and local councils were providing public services such as gas and water. They thought they could work through the existing system. If they could gradually replace capitalists by civil servants running enterprises for the good of the people, they would be well on the road to socialism.

What Fabians were not sure about was whether they could achieve this through existing political parties. Several of them, such as the Webbs, could get the ear of Liberal ministers. Did they really need a separate party? The Fabians worked through different parties and organisations, and some historians have argued that they had little importance in the development of socialism or the later Labour Party.

Both the Social Democratic Federation and Fabian socialism developed from economic analysis, but there was another kind based on vision and lifestyle.

NATIONALISATION
Government owning the means of making wealth, for example in major industries such as the mines and railways.

153

HOW IMPORTANT WAS THE LABOUR PARTY BEFORE THE FIRST WORLD WAR?

SOURCE 9.6 Frontispiece of *News from Nowhere*

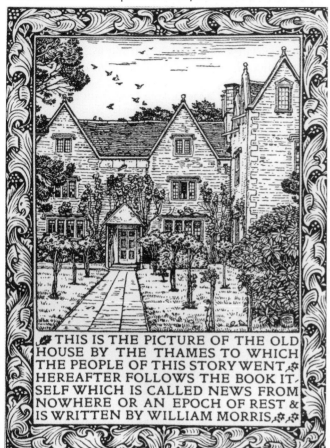

Socialist League

William Morris broke away from the SDF at the end of 1884 and formed the Socialist League. Like the SDF, the League wanted a revolution and could not agree how to get it, but Morris also offered something different. He was a very successful businessman who made money by producing pseudo-medieval tapestries, wallpaper and stained glass windows. He loved traditional craftsman-ship. Capitalist enterprise and mechanisation had destroyed this kind of work. Morris wanted a world where the workers were creative and loved their work.

He wrote about it in *News from Nowhere*, a very imaginative account of a socialist paradise in late twentieth-century London, which he published in 1890. It was an idealistic, religious approach that had much more appeal than pages of statistics.

The *Clarion*

Robert Blatchford was in the Morris mould. He started the *Clarion* newspaper in 1891 to tell people how much better a socialist society could be. There were *Clarion* vans (see Source 9.7) and *Clarion* cycling clubs, and Blatchford's 1895 description of *Merrie England* (see Source 9.8) sold over 2 million copies.

SOURCE 9.7 A *Clarion* van which toured Britain in the 1890s

SOURCE 9.8 In *Merrie England*, 1895, Robert Blatchford shows some of the attractions of the new socialist world

I would make all the land, mills, mines, factories, works, shops, ships, and railways the property of the people ...

I would have public parks, public theatres, music halls, gymnasiums, football and cricket fields, public halls and public gardens for recreation and music and refreshment ...

Then, by degrees, I would make all these things free. So that clothing, lodging, fuel, food, amusement, inter-course [communication], education, and all the requirements for a perfect human life should be produced and distributed and enjoyed by the people without the use of money.

Perhaps it is not surprising that some people talked of their conversion to socialism in the same way as some people speak of a religious conversion.

TALKING POINT

If you had been living in the 1890s which of these organisations would you have been attracted to and why?

ACTIVITY

From reading this section:

1 a) How far are the ideas here a response to practical problems in the capitalist system?
   b) How far are they based on economic theory?
2 What indications are there of socialists linking theories with practical problems?
3 How far would the ways of achieving socialism involve state action?

DISCUSS

'Did the working classes need their own party?' How might
a) a Liberal politician
b) a socialist radical
c) a well-off skilled worker
have answered this question?

SOURCE 9.10 From the cotton workers' paper, the *Cotton Factory Times*, 1890s

If a workman votes for a man with a carriage and pair it is because he believes that his views will be more adequately and effectively represented by him than by his opponent, who may have to do his business on foot.

Socialist Sunday schools

The two approaches of socialism and Christianity fused well in a socialist Sunday school movement which developed extensively after 1900 (see Source 9.9). For example, there was a socialist version of the ten commandments with instructions such as 'love learning which is the food of the mind'.

SOURCE 9.9 Some principles from *Socialist Sunday Schools: Aims, Objects and Organisation*, issued by the National Council of British Socialist Sunday Schools

QUESTION Why is Socialism necessary?
ANSWER Socialism is necessary because the present system enables a few to enrich themselves out of the labour of the people.
QUESTION How would Socialism benefit the people?
ANSWER Socialism would benefit the people as wealth would then be produced for the use of all.
QUESTION On what principle does Socialism rest?
ANSWER Socialism rests on the great principles of Love, Justice and Truth.

C Why was the Labour Party so slow to develop?

The majority of voters in late nineteenth-century Britain were working class so in theory a party that successfully appealed to them could easily gain a majority in parliament and form a government. It could then introduce whatever socialist measures it wished. Many historians have therefore been puzzled by how slow the working class was to develop its own mass party. Most western European countries did have substantial Marxist parties in the late nineteenth century, so why not Britain? There are a number of reasons.

1 The existing parties were popular with the working classes

The Liberal and Conservative parties both had large working-class support. In April 1887 the *Bolton Chronicle* reported nearly 3200 members in the town's 31 Conservative clubs from an overall population of around 110,000. The *Blackburn Times* explained a Radical Labour candidate's poor result in 1885 because 'the operatives and artisans' were 'very strong political partisans' of the Tories and Liberals.

Some groups of London workers supported the Conservatives because of their jobs. Conservative policies to extend the empire and keep the pubs open were more likely to keep workers at the Woolwich Arsenal and London breweries in regular employment.

Many nineteenth-century workers apparently voted on the basis of religion more than class. The Bishop of Manchester referred to the established Lancashire view that 'every Churchman [Anglican] is a Conservative and every Nonconformist a Liberal'.

2 Many workers were not interested in politics or socialism

Stedman Jones' view is that some workers were often too busy with their **pastimes** to have much time for politics. Angling, cycling, breeding pigeons, keeping canaries and growing leeks kept men away from socialism. Some early Labour leaders also helped run Nonconformist churches, but most men did not have the time for both.

3 Many workers were respectful by nature

Where working men did get involved in politics, they accepted the existing system more frequently than they rebelled against it. The extent of working-class enthusiasm for monarchy and empire is debatable, but there does seem to have been a widespread and genuine acceptance of Britain's **parliamentary system**. Politically active working- and middle-class men in large towns joined in local mock parliaments, or Parliament Debating Societies as they were often known.

155

HOW IMPORTANT WAS THE LABOUR PARTY BEFORE THE FIRST WORLD WAR?

4 British governments had treated unions quite well

British governments and employers treated **trade unions** more favourably and respectfully than their foreign counterparts. Trade unions in other European countries could not organise peaceful picketing as British workers could under the 1875 Conspiracy and Protection of Property Act.

5 Labour leaders were happy to work with Liberals

Against this background it made sense for trade unions which wanted parliamentary representation to work through existing political parties. A **Labour Representation League** was set up in 1869, but it simply put forward working-class candidates to stand as Liberals. So trade union-backed candidates went to Parliament as Liberal MPs and were known as Lib–Labs. Two were elected in 1874 and eleven in 1885. About half were miners, as they had the strongest unions and were concentrated in a few areas of the country. Henry Broadhurst, the secretary of the TUC's parliamentary committee, became a Liberal MP, supported Gladstone loyally and had a brief time as a junior minister in his government.

From 1888 this situation began to change. A combination of
• disappointment with the Liberals
• increasing successes for the trade union movement
• the emergence of charismatic leaders
gradually changed the situation and led to the foundation of the Independent Labour Party.

D How and why was the Labour Party created?

There is no single clear date when the Labour Party started. But the key stages of development are outlined below.

> **Overview: the birth of the Labour Party**
>
> **1869** Labour Representation League formed. Union leaders generally put forward working-class leaders to be selected as Liberal Party candidates and the League failed in the 1870s.
> **1885** Eleven Labour representatives were elected as Liberal MPs – the highest number of working men in Parliament so far. They were known as Lib–Labs.
> **1888** Union leaders in Scotland formed the Scottish Labour Party. This was totally independent of any other party. It would put forward its own candidates at elections and they would not join the Liberal Party. Among its founders was a principled and charismatic young leader from the miners' union called Keir Hardie.
> **1892** Keir Hardie elected as MP for West Ham as an Independent Labour candidate. Two other independent Labour MPs soon joined the Liberal Party but Hardie kept to his promise to remain independent. He insisted on wearing the clothes of a working man when he first arrived in Parliament and was accompanied by a trumpeter (see picture, left). He criticised both the major parties – the Conservatives and the Liberals – for ignoring the needs of the working class.
> **1893** The Bradford Conference – Independent Labour Party founded. Keir Hardie and other trade union and socialist leaders called a conference in Bradford which founded the Independent Labour Party.
> **1895** General election. All Independent Labour Party candidates, including Keir Hardie, were defeated in the general election.
> **1890s** Local success. Despite its failure in the general election, the ILP had local successes – 400 of its members were elected to seats on local councils, school boards and other administrative bodies.
> **1900** Labour Representation Committee formed. The ILP, union leaders and other socialist groups together formed the Labour Representation Committee (LRC). This was not a party but a group with the single aim of getting as many Labour MPs as possible into Parliament at the next election.
> **1903** The Lib-Lab Pact or Progressive Alliance. In order to beat the Conservatives the Liberals did a deal with the LRC. Liberals agreed not to put up a candidate in around 30 constituencies where the LRC candidate stood a chance of being elected. In return the Labour MPs promised to support the Liberals in Parliament.
> **1906** General election – 29 LRC MPs elected. In parliament the LRC now called themselves the Labour Party.

ACTIVITY

Draw a timeline 1869–90 and add notes to describe the stages of development of labour representation.

FOCUS ROUTE

Make notes explaining the contribution of the following to the formation of the Labour Party:

a) the 1893 Bradford Conference
b) the Labour Representation Committee.

DISCUSS

Study the overview of the birth of the Labour Party in the box on the right. It is a complicated story. Which of the following dates do you think should be regarded as the start of the Labour Party and why?
a) 1869
b) 1888
c) 1892
d) 1893
e) 1900
f) 1906.
If possible work in groups and each argue for one of the above dates or another date of your choice.

156

HOW IMPORTANT WAS THE LABOUR PARTY BEFORE THE FIRST WORLD WAR?

The Conservative and Liberal parties had been created by leaders in Parliament because they wanted a party organisation outside to support them. The Labour Party was different. It was started by trade unions, labour clubs and socialist societies around the country who wanted to get their men *into* Parliament. In other words it grew from the bottom upwards, not the top down like its rivals. Its origins are therefore more complex.

You are now going to look at the main events and the people involved in more detail, starting with the Bradford Conference of 1893.

The Bradford Conference 1893

In 1890–91 there had been a bitter strike in the silk and wool industries in Bradford. Employers had worked together to defeat the strike. Unions had worked together to support the strikers. The workers had lost. But the experience had created strong support for political action. There were many people in Bradford and West Yorkshire who could see the need for a strong and independent Labour party.

FOCUS ROUTE

1 List the groups that helped set up the ILP.
2 Note the ILP's aims. How far was it socialist?
3 In what ways did the ILP succeed or fail?

■ 9B Organisations and circumstances behind the Bradford conference, 1893

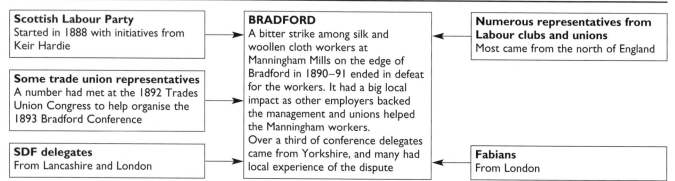

Scottish Labour Party
Started in 1888 with initiatives from Keir Hardie

Some trade union representatives
A number had met at the 1892 Trades Union Congress to help organise the 1893 Bradford Conference

SDF delegates
From Lancashire and London

BRADFORD
A bitter strike among silk and woollen cloth workers at Manningham Mills on the edge of Bradford in 1890–91 ended in defeat for the workers. It had a big local impact as other employers backed the management and unions helped the Manningham workers.
Over a third of conference delegates came from Yorkshire, and many had local experience of the dispute

Numerous representatives from Labour clubs and unions
Most came from the north of England

Fabians
From London

TALKING POINT

The modern Labour Party abandoned its commitment to nationalising industry in 1995. Do you think nationalising industry is a good aim or a mistaken aim in a modern capitalist society?

The main aim of delegates at the Bradford conference was to start a party where socialists and trade unionists could work together and get Labour candidates into Parliament. They were less concerned with working out precise policies as they knew it would be hard to agree on them. They deliberately called themselves a Labour Party, not a socialist one, because that was a way of getting maximum trade union support. Trade union leaders were often suspicious of socialist societies and were divided over how far to back socialist aims, and so they had to compromise.

While not calling themselves socialist, they agreed on the basic socialist aim of gaining 'the collective ownership of the means of production, distribution and exchange'. This was a distant hope for the future. In the shorter term they had economic and political aims on which all were agreed, such as the eight-hour working day, more welfare benefits, votes for all adults and payment of MPs.

What did the ILP achieve 1893–1900?

SOURCE 9.11 As recalled years later by an ILP supporter, some enthusiasts did spread the word like this

The ILP was more successful than the other socialist societies. The *Clarion* newspaper, started in 1891, linked up closely with it, and the party stood for the kind of socialism outlined in Blatchford's *Merrie England* (Source 9.8). It provided a social life for people, setting up Sunday schools and *Clarion* cycling clubs, as well as declaring a set of political aims. Its dominant figure, Keir Hardie, clearly had a certain charisma. He and several of its other leaders had a Nonconformist background, and the party spread a hopeful, religious view of socialism, cycling round the countryside and preaching about a better world.

Keir Hardie 1856–1915

Worked in a coal mine from the age of 10 to 23. Became a trade union leader and Secretary of the Ayrshire Miners Union at 29. Strong Nonconformist, who supported temperance (stopping alcohol), women's right to the vote and self-government for peoples in the empire.

Worked single-mindedly to get labour representation in Parliament and described his priorities in the 1890s, saying: 'Programmes are matters of no moment. It is labour representation which needs keeping to the front'. Inconsistent on policy, but had a talent for speaking and working out compromises. Widely seen as the true founder of the Labour Party.

Worked successfully to get a Scottish Labour Party in 1888, providing an example of what could be done in England. Successfully pressed for the establishment of the ILP in 1893, helped to organise the Bradford Conference and gained wider trade union backing for labour representation.

Having dominated the ILP in the 1890s, he worked out the successful compromise motion for the Labour Representation Committee (LRC) at the conference at Farringdon Street, February 1900.

Was elected the first fully independent Labour MP in 1892, defeated in 1895, but returned to Parliament in 1900. Chairman of the Labour Party in Parliament in 1906–07.

Ramsay MacDonald 1866–1937

Worked in the ILP and then became Secretary of the Labour Representation Committee. Worked out the Lib–Lab Pact in 1903 and became an MP in 1906.

Wrote extensively about the development of socialism.
- Argued for all men and women to have the vote.
- Claimed the government should provide everyone with work and more public services.
- Believed that society was more important than the individual and emphasised the duties people owed to the community.

Chairman of the Parliamentary Labour Party in 1911–14 and its effective leader.

At start of the First World War had to resign because he did not support the war. Became leader again in 1922 and was the first Labour prime minister in 1924 and 1929–31.

At the same time there was increasing dissatisfaction with the Liberals among some Labour leaders. The Liberals did not deliver much for the unions in the 1890s. Although the 1892–95 Liberal governments introduced some useful reforms, they also acted against unions in industrial disputes, as when a gunboat defended strike-breaking labourers at Hull. Local Liberal parties were often reluctant to choose Labour men as candidates. Ramsay MacDonald and Arthur Henderson, the two most prominent early Labour leaders, were both rejected as Liberal candidates.

There are no precise membership figures for the ILP, but it is estimated it had around 35,000–50,000 members in 1895. When all its 28 candidates lost in the 1895 election, membership fell away. By 1900 membership seems to have been around 11,000–13,000. Compared to the Liberal and Conservative parties this was still very small. The Conservative Primrose League had a membership of about 1,500,000 (see page 168).

ILP members also worked actively in trade unions so although the number of members went down, it gradually achieved more influence in the unions. For example, George Barnes, an ILP member, became Secretary of the Amalgamated Society of Engineers in 1896.

Locally, ILP groups were very practical. They worked with whomever they could. They often co-operated with local Liberal parties, as in Bow and Poplar in the East End of London. They frequently worked with local trade union branches and TRADES COUNCILS and did their best to get on the elected councils and boards which provided many local services. There were a lot of these, and in the later 1890s the ILP had over 400 members on local councils, school boards and other administrative bodies.

TRADES COUNCILS
Made up of representatives from different unions or groups of workers in an area and had developed in many large towns during the nineteenth century.

158

HOW IMPORTANT WAS THE LABOUR PARTY BEFORE THE FIRST WORLD WAR?

ACTIVITY

Look back to Chart 9B. Make your own similar diagram to show how and why different groups came together to start the LRC.

Delegates at the Trades Union Congress cast votes for the number of members they represented, which accounts for the thousands of votes recorded.

AFFILIATED
Formally connected.

FOCUS ROUTE

1 To what extent did the LRC depend on the trade unions?
2 How important was the Liberal–Labour Pact made in 1903?

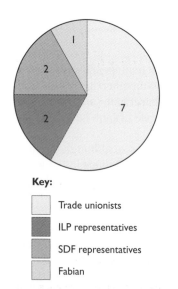

Key:

- Trade unionists
- ILP representatives
- SDF representatives
- Fabian

SOURCE 9.12 Membership of the Labour Representation Committee (LRC)

The Labour Representation Committee 1900

ILP leaders knew the trade union movement was more important to them than anything else, and by 1899 trade union leaders saw more reason for getting their men into Parliament. For example, a demand by the Amalgamated Society of Engineers for an eight-hour day led to a lock-out and an employers' victory in 1897–98. The legal decision in the Lyons v Wilkins case limited the picketing unions could organise (see page 145). The unions wanted laws introducing a maximum eight-hour day and extending picketing rights, and that meant getting MPs to support their cause.

The Trades Union Congress (TUC) voted for action on this in 1899. The initiative came from the Amalgamated Society of Railway Servants (ASRS), and the motion for it was introduced by a union regional organiser who was also a member of the ILP. It called for a special meeting of trade unions, socialist societies and other working-class bodies to devise ways of getting more Labour members in the next Parliament. The motion was passed by 546,000 to 434,000, but unions with about a sixth of the voting strength abstained (chose not to vote).

Keir Hardie and Ramsay MacDonald then planned the conference with the TUC parliamentary committee and delegates from the SDF and Fabians. It met in London at the Memorial Hall, Farringdon Street in February 1900. The trade union delegates represented under half the unions AFFILIATED to the TUC, and there were then delegates from the ILP, SDF and Fabians, as there had been at the Bradford Conference. These groups had very different aims, but they concentrated on organisation, not policy details. Keir Hardie, who had a talent for practical compromises, drew up the agreement for a 'distinct Labour group in Parliament who shall have their own whips (officials) and agree upon their policy'. They would co-operate with any party which promoted legislation 'in the direct interests of labour'. They established the Labour Representation Committee (LRC) of twelve members.

What did the LRC achieve?

The LRC was a federation of different groups, not yet one party. The trade unions and other groups provided money for the LRC to put up candidates. The candidates would come from different organisations and stand as independent Labour ones. There were not yet local Labour parties to join, but some developed over the next few years.

Only two LRC candidates got into Parliament in the general election at the end of 1900. To be more effective the LRC needed money and election workers, and the ILP and socialist societies were too small to provide them. The trade unions on the other hand, which had about two million members, could provide them. They would decide whether or not the committee succeeded.

The Social Democratic Foundation withdrew from the LRC in 1901 because the LRC was not socialist enough and an extra trades council representative was added. By the end of the year the unions had ten out of thirteen seats on the LRC executive.

By summer 1901, 41 unions with 353,000 members had affiliated to the LRC. The final decision in the Taff Vale case (see page 145) in July 1901 gave the LRC an extra boost. By 1903 there were nearly 850,000 affiliated union members. The legal decision in the Taff Vale case, making unions liable to pay damages, was certainly an obvious reason for the extra support, and the unions also agreed to give more money. In 1900 they had given just over a tenth of a penny per member. In 1904 they agreed to a compulsory levy of one penny per member; this later increased to two pennies in 1907.

This level of union support made the committee look much stronger. The Conservatives were in government but were deeply split from 1903 over the issues of free trade and taxation (see page 178). The Liberals, although they had been out of power for most of the time since 1886, saw the opportunity to win the next election but the LRC might stand in their way. A strengthened LRC could expect to get the votes of many potential Liberal voters. Officials in the two parties proposed a pact.

■ 9C Arguments for the pact

HERBERT GLADSTONE Liberal Chief Whip

> Trade union sponsored MPs have sat as Liberals since 1874 and provided valuable support. Many of the LRC people have themselves been Liberals. Surely the party can work with them as they worked with Lib–Labs in the past?

RAMSAY MACDONALD Secretary for the LRC

> The LRC now has £100,000 in its election fund. If Labour candidates stand against Liberals, they will split the anti-Conservative vote, and so Conservatives may win even if they get far less than half of the votes in individual constituencies.

The Liberal–Labour Pact (frequently known as the Lib–Lab Pact and later sometimes called the Progressive Alliance) was semi-secret, as both Herbert Gladstone (Liberal Chief Whip) and Ramsay MacDonald knew many of their own supporters would not like it. About 30 LRC candidates would stand without Liberal opposition, but MacDonald would try to ensure that Liberal candidates elsewhere did not face Labour opposition and that Labour would support a future Liberal government.

The Pact largely worked in the 1906 election. The LRC put up 50 candidates – 40 from trades unions or trades councils and 10 from the ILP. Of these candidates, 29 were elected MPs, and 24 of them had no opposition from Liberals.

Both sides clearly benefited. The Liberals won an enormous majority, and the number of independent Labour MPs increased from 2 to 29. One of the Lib–Labs who had been elected then joined the Labour group making 30. Many historians reckon that most of the Labour MPs would not have been elected without the Pact, but it is impossible to know.

ACTIVITY

The events you studied in Chapter 8 (the growth of the unions) and in this chapter are closely related, but how closely? That depends on your historical point of view.

Some historians, particularly the Marxists such as Eric Hobsbawm, see the Labour Party growing directly out of the development of class consciousness and the resultant success of New Unionism. In Marxist terms the union successes of 1888–90 were an inevitable moment in the development of class conflict and the emergence of a political force to represent labour was also an inevitable part of the same process. This diagram summarises their view on the emergence of the Labour Party.

A The Marxist and more left-wing view
Working-class consciousness develops partly because of the experiences of New Unionism. This necessitates the development of a working-class party.

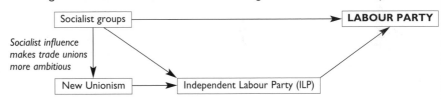

New unions need political power to achieve their aims

Other historians such as Biagini and Reid in *Currents of Radicalism* (1991) stress the continuity that existed between the radical movements of the late nineteenth century. In this interpretation there is nothing special about the Labour Party. The failures or successes of unionism have little impact on most workers' political consciousness. The differences between the Liberal Party and the Labour Party are not that significant. Some men moved between groups. It was practical considerations and compromises, not ideology, that led to the formation of the Labour Party.

B The continuity view
Radicals join different organisations depending on circumstances. With weaknesses and inadequacies in the Liberal Party many join the Independent Labour Party, but this is similar to the Liberal Party in its aims, and the two work closely together.

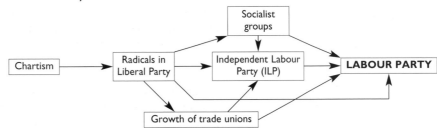

1 From your work on Chapters 8 and 9 choose two pieces of evidence that could be used to support each of the interpretations A and B above.
2 Which of the views do you find most compelling? Write some paragraphs to explain your view and use the evidence you found to support your answer.

160

HOW IMPORTANT WAS THE LABOUR PARTY BEFORE THE FIRST WORLD WAR?

FOCUS ROUTE

1 List the main aims of the Labour Party before 1914.
2 What were the main strengths and weaknesses of the Labour Party 1906–14?
3 To what extent was the Labour Party in 1914 an independent working-class party or a left-wing fringe of the Liberal Party?

MANIFESTO
Public statement of what a party will do if it has power after an election.

PROTECTION
Taxing imported goods to make them more expensive, so that people will buy home-produced goods because they are cheaper than foreign ones. This protects the competitive position of home industries.

Protection is the opposite of free trade (see page 178).

E What did the Labour Party achieve 1906–14?

After the 1906 election the 30 MPs backed by the Labour Representation Committee called themselves the Labour Party.

The conference that set up the LRC in 1900 agreed to work for a 'distinct Labour Group in Parliament', not for a set of policies. It was left up to the Labour members in Parliament to decide on policies when they got there.

In 1906 they did not all want the same thing. Over half saw themselves as socialist, but not all would have been happy with that label. Some historians suggest we should think of the party as a sort of parliamentary extension of the trade unions, working not for socialism but for Labourism – getting workers a fair deal and safeguarding their rights.

MPs may be representative of the country either in their background and social experiences or in the policies they support. Socially these Labour MPs really did represent the working class. All had been born into working-class families; all except three had started as industrial labourers, and none had been to university.

Looking at how elections were fought then, it is also unfair to criticise them for lack of policy. Major parties did not have MANIFESTOS, but the LRC did issue one.

SOURCE 9.13 The Labour election manifesto, 1906

To the Electors –

This election is to decide whether or not Labour is to be fairly represented in Parliament.

The House of Commons is supposed to be the people's House, and yet the people are not there.

Landlords, employers, lawyers, brewers, and financiers are there in force. Why not Labour?

The Trade Unions ask the same liberty as capital enjoys. They are refused.

The aged poor are neglected.

The slums remain; overcrowding continues, whilst the land goes to waste.

Shopkeepers and traders are overburdened with rates and taxation, whilst the increasing land values, which should relieve the ratepayers, go to people who have not earned them.

Wars are fought to make the rich richer, and underfed school children are still neglected.

Chinese Labour [see page 183] is defended because it enriches the mine owners.

The unemployed ask for work, the Government gave them a worthless Act [the 1905 Unemployed Workmen Act, page 178], and now, when you are beginning to understand the causes of your poverty, the red herring of PROTECTION is drawn across your path.

Protection [see page 178], as experience shows, is no remedy for poverty and unemployment. It serves to keep you from dealing with the land, housing, old age, and other social problems!

DISCUSS

1 In what ways did the manifesto (Source 9.13) express 'Labourism'?
2 How far were the statements and complaints in line with socialist thinking?
3 How far were they statements of grievances or policies for action?
4 Examine Chart 9D. How far were Labour aims and policies similar to Liberal ones?
Return to this section when you have studied Chapter 12 and consider
5 What reforms did the Liberal government introduce in 1906–10 to deal with the grievances here?
6 How far could Labour MPs claim credit for any of the reforms?

What were the Labour MPs struggling to achieve beyond the Labour manifesto?

Labour was strongly influenced by Nonconformist traditions. Out of 30 Labour MPs, 18 described themselves as Nonconformists, and about 12 supported teetotalism (not drinking any alcohol). A survey of the books that had influenced MPs showed that Marx had less impact than religious works and novels exposing Victorian social problems.

Chart 9D indicates some of the reforms that Labour MPs wanted and what the Liberals did. It over-simplifies because there were big differences between MPs within the Labour and Liberal parties. For example, one of the most important aims for many Labour MPs was introducing a minimum wage to improve workers' living standards. Most of the Labour MPs wanted this decided by Parliament and put into law. But Ramsay MacDonald, one of the most prominent Labour leaders, wanted minimum wages to be decided by negotiations between unions and employers rather than having a uniform minimum wage laid down by law. Leaders of the Liberal Party, on the other hand, opposed a national minimum wage, yet 25 Radical Liberal MPs supported a Labour motion for it in 1912.

■ 9D Labour Party goals and Liberal Party actions

LABOUR MPs generally wanted	LIBERALS' actions
• Free trade, which meant cheaper food. This would help keep good international relations and therefore world peace.	• Liberals fought 1906 election on the defence of free trade.
• Minimum wage. This was one of the most distinctive Labour policies from the 1890s.	• Liberals introduced this for a number of low-paid workers, under the 1909 Trade Boards Act, and for miners, because of a national strike in 1912.
• Reversal of the Taff Vale decision.	• Liberal government accepted a Labour MP's proposals on this, which became the 1906 Trade Disputes Act (see page 146).
• The eight-hour day.	• Liberal government introduced this for coal mines in 1908, but not elsewhere.
• Nationalisation of mines and railways.	• Some Radical Liberals supported this, but not Liberal governments.
• The right to work. Labour MPs introduced several bills for public works schemes run by government and local councils. These would provide jobs for the unemployed and also boost the economy by giving workers more to spend.	• A few Liberal MPs supported this, but the Liberal government did not.
• Taxes on land. Labour campaigned strongly for these.	• Lloyd George proposed these in his People's Budget in 1909 and his Land Campaign in 1913–14, but was not successful in introducing them.
• School meals. A Labour MP introduced a bill requiring local councils to provide school meals.	• The Liberal government partly accepted the bill. They permitted local councils to provide the meals, but did not compel them to do so.
• Old age pensions. Labour wanted pensions of 10s a week for those over 65.	• The Liberal government introduced pensions of 5s a week for those over 70, if they had below a particular income (see page 197).
• Restrictions on the power of the House of Lords.	• The Liberal government fought a constitutional battle to do this in 1910–11.

How much support did the Labour Party gain?

Greater trade union support was vital to increase party strength, and the decision of the Miners' Federation of Great Britain to affiliate in 1908 (carried out in 1909) was a significant step forward. The miners had a group of MPs who sat in Parliament as Lib–Lab members and these now joined Labour, though many miners still supported the Liberals. In a union ballot in 1908 45 per cent of the miners who voted were against joining Labour.

Most of the former Lib–Lab MPs sponsored by trade unions were now within the Labour Party. By around 1910 50 per cent of the trade unionists were affiliated to Labour. There were legal challenges to this (see page 162) but by 1914 support for the Labour Party was an accepted part of many trade unionists' activity.

162

HOW IMPORTANT WAS THE LABOUR PARTY BEFORE THE FIRST WORLD WAR?

SOURCE 9.14 A three-panel Labour poster for the 1910 elections

Disputes over political funds

W.V. Osborne was a branch secretary of the Amalgamated Society of Railway Servants and a member of the Liberal Party. He did not like some of his union subscription going to the Labour Party and brought a court case about it. The final legal decision in 1909, known as the **Osborne Judgement**, was that unions could not contribute to political party funds. Consequently the Labour Party, which relied on trade unions for money, was in difficulties when there were two general elections in 1910. The **1913 Trade Union Act** allowed unions to have a fund for political purposes if a majority of members voted for it in a ballot, and individual members could choose to opt out of making payments to it. Most unions which held ballots did vote in favour of having the fund and therefore supporting the Labour Party.

The broader picture

Nationally Labour had some difficulties in 1910–14. They had fewer MPs after the 1910 general elections and lost some by-elections. They broadly supported the Liberal government over the People's Budget and House of Lords reform (Chapter 13) and had varied views about the 1911 National Insurance Act (pages 200–201), but they seemed to be taking fewer political initiatives than before.

They had some success in local council elections. They increased their number of councillors from 91 to 171; the exact figure depends on how Labour councillors are defined. Yet they still remained much weaker than the Liberal and Conservative parties on local councils and contested only around 15 per cent of the seats.

Labour was developing more party organisation. Most of the time it still relied on local trades councils made up of trade union representatives. Most constituency Labour parties consisted of delegates from trade unions and socialist societies rather than having their own members, but central Labour parties were started in big cities. Labour was growing, though the members were overwhelmingly affiliated by trade unions. See Chart 13F on page 217.

163

HOW IMPORTANT WAS THE LABOUR PARTY BEFORE THE FIRST WORLD WAR?

"FORWARD! THE DAY IS BREAKING!"

F Review

The Labour Representation Committee, formed in 1900, had a simple objective – to get Labour MPs into Parliament in 1906. They succeeded. Those MPs then formed the Labour Party. Labour MPs gained the Trade Disputes Act in 1906, a compromise measure on school meals and a Trade Union Act in 1913. The Labour Party had a possible influence in encouraging Liberal welfare reforms, which you will study in Chapter 13. On the other hand, Labour succeeded to a great extent because of Liberal help. Most of the Labour MPs were elected without Liberal opposition and they were pledged to support the Liberal government. In Parliament they depended on the Liberals to achieve any legislation. The Labour Party can therefore be seen as either:

- an important and independent working-class party which threatened the Liberals and was bound to take over from them as the main party of the left, or
- a left-wing fringe group to the Liberals which depended on its alliance with a larger partner.

Chapter 13 returns to these issues in greater depth.

CHAPTER 9 REVIEW ACTIVITY

The importance of Labour before 1914 can be judged in three ways:

a) Had they succeeded in creating a viable socialist party to represent the working class in Parliament?

b) Had they brought about improvements for their members by specific legislation?

c) Had they won the support of working people?

For each of the criteria give the party a score out of 5. Explain your score with evidence from Chapters 8 and 9. You may wish to revise your score after you have studied Chapter 13.

KEY POINTS FROM CHAPTER 9

How important was the Labour Party before the First World War?

1 Socialist groups developed from the 1880s, but they generally had few members.

2 Working-class voters in the late nineteenth century generally supported the Liberal or Conservative parties.

3 In 1900 trade unions and socialist groups formed a Labour Representation Committee to get Labour candidates into Parliament.

4 They succeeded in getting 29 candidates elected as MPs in 1906; the party grew.

5 The Labour Party still depended substantially on the pact with the Liberals before the First World War but gained a few of the reforms it wanted.

How did the Conservatives become a successful mass party after 1885?

CHAPTER OVERVIEW

The Conservatives' main purpose in politics had been to conserve or preserve the British way of government, protect the Anglican Church and maintain the power of English landowners. In the mid-nineteenth century they had been in government for only eight out of 38 years between 1846 and 1884. The Third Reform Act of 1884–85 increased the electorate from 3 to 5.6 million so that about two-thirds of adult men could vote. For the first time the working class made up a majority of the electorate. Most expected this to hurt the Conservatives.

SOURCE 10.1 Joseph Chamberlain, the most prominent left-wing Liberal politician in 1885, was enthusiastic about the change

Today parliament is elected by three millions of electors, of whom, perhaps, one-third are of the working classes. Next year a new House will come to Westminster elected by five millions of men, of whom three-fifths belong to the labouring population. It is a revolution which has been peacefully and silently accomplished. The centre of power has been shifted, and the old order is giving place to the new.

In fact the Conservatives were in government for seventeen of the next twenty years. Looking back from the twenty-first century these years seem to have begun an era of phenomenal Conservative success. They won seventeen out of the 30 general elections from 1885 to 2000 and were in government, either alone or in coalition with other parties, for 71 out of 115 years. No other right-wing party in Europe has been so successful. How did the Conservatives defy the odds so spectacularly just after 1885?

■ 10A Ministries 1886–1902

Date	Party in power	Prime Minister	Major developments
1886	Liberal	Gladstone (3rd ministry) 1886	Failure of first Irish Home Rule Bill and split in Liberal Party
1887	Conservative	Salisbury (2nd ministry) 1886–92	
1888			
1889			
1890			
1891			
1892			
1893	Liberal	Gladstone (4th ministry) 1892–94	
1894		Rosebery (1894–95)	
1895			
1896	Conservative	Salisbury (3rd ministry) 1895–1902	Liberal Unionists join Conservative government
1897			
1898			
1899			
1900			} Boer War
1901			
1902			

This chapter asks:

A How did the Conservative Party gain more support? (pp. 166–170)

B Why was the Conservative Party more successful than its rivals? (pp. 171–173)

165

HOW DID THE CONSERVATIVES BECOME A SUCCESSFUL MASS PARTY AFTER 1885?

■ **Learning trouble spot**

Name changes

There are some confusing name changes among both politicians who inherited titles and parties which split and merged.

Lord **Salisbury** was born Robert Arthur Talbot Gascoyne-Cecil. This was his personal name. He became third Marquis of Salisbury when his father died in 1868. At this point he became a peer and sat in the House of Lords. However, before his father's death he was known as Lord *Cranborne* (see page 13), indicating that he was an eldest son who would become a marquis. The title is known as a courtesy title, and Salisbury could sit in the House of Commons when he was Lord Cranborne as he was not yet a full peer.

The same procedure applied to Spencer Compton Cavendish who became eighth Duke of **Devonshire** when his father died in 1891. Before this he was known as Lord *Hartington* but sat in the House of Commons, as it was a courtesy title (see page 93).

Conservatives and Unionists

When the Liberals split over Irish Home Rule in 1886, those who opposed it were called Liberal Unionists because they favoured keeping the full union between Ireland and Great Britain. They worked with the Conservatives, and Liberal Unionist leaders joined the Conservative government in 1895. The Conservatives and Liberal Unionists were then closely bound together, but a separate Liberal Unionist party organisation continued until 1911 when it was amalgamated with the Conservatives to form a united party. As the Conservatives and their Liberal allies were united by their attachment to the union, the two groups sometimes just called themselves plain Unionists both before and after the merger.

■ **10B** The four key figures in the Conservative and Liberal Unionist parties in the 1880s and 1890s

Lord Salisbury
Became leader of the Conservatives in the Lords on Disraeli's death in 1881 and then overall party leader when Queen Victoria asked him to be Prime Minister in 1885. Remained Conservative leader to 1902. For most of the time he was both Prime Minister and Foreign Secretary – his great love in politics was managing foreign affairs

Lord Hartington
Had been leader of the Liberals in the House of Commons 1875–80. Most prominent politician among the Whigs (aristocrats and their supporters who generally wanted moderate rather than radical policies). Refused to join Gladstone's government in 1886 and opposed Irish Home Rule. Inherited the title Duke of Devonshire in 1891 and later joined Salisbury's government in 1895

Joseph Chamberlain
Had been a Radical minister in Gladstone's Cabinet. Put forward a social reform programme in 1885. Most prominent leader of the Liberal left-wingers, but resigned from Gladstone's government in 1886 and opposed Irish Home Rule. After this, generally voted with the Conservatives. Had a passionate belief in expanding the empire and joined Salisbury's government as Colonial Secretary in 1895

Lord Randolph Churchill
Made a name for himself by his sharp criticisms of Gladstone's government in the early 1880s. Briefly in government in 1886. Claimed to be a Tory Democrat, but left no full definition of what that meant and said in a private conversation that it was 'principally opportunism'. Developed syphilis (a painful, mind-distorting sexually transmitted disease), declined and died in 1895

FOCUS ROUTE

1 Divide a page in two vertically. On the left of the page briefly list the reasons for the Conservatives' success in 1886–1902 under these headings:
   a) splits in the Liberal Party
   b) effectiveness in government
   c) party organisation
   d) appeal of imperialism.
Leave space on the right to explain how the Conservatives lost these advantages by 1906.

2 How important were the Liberal Unionists to Conservative success 1886–1900?

BALANCE OF POWER
Situation in which a smaller party was able to decide which of the two main parties could get a majority in the House of Commons to pass laws and govern the country depending on which they supported.

COALITION
A government or other group combining people from different parties.

A How did the Conservative Party gain more support?

Salisbury, the Conservatives' leader from 1885, has not gained the sort of popular reputation that Gladstone and Disraeli achieved, and some historians have criticised his negative approach. There are problems for historians and students in judging Salisbury because his beliefs, values and attitudes were very different from most of ours. He was strongly influenced by religion, dedicated to maintaining the Anglican Church (see learning trouble spot, page 41) and wanted to delay change. His idea of the prime minister's role was also very different. Salisbury saw the prime minister as a chairman of the Cabinet to keep his colleagues together and mediate between them. Prime ministers are now expected to show more leadership qualities and provide stronger central direction.

Many twentieth-century historians criticised him for lack of vision and purpose. Some recent ones believe that his thinking fits in quite well with the ideas of Margaret Thatcher and the modern Conservative Party. Salisbury, like Thatcher and some other recent Conservative leaders, believed in the free market, little government action and avoiding European entanglements.

How did Salisbury and his government increase support for the Conservatives?

1 He made connections with the Liberal Unionists

Salisbury saw the Liberal Unionists were crucial to the political future. They had defeated Gladstone's Home Rule bill in 1886, and Salisbury wanted to win them over to the Conservative side. If they joined up with Gladstone again they could maintain a strong Liberal Party which might keep the Conservatives out of power. For the 1886 general election he made a pact with them, promising that Conservative candidates would not fight Liberal Unionist MPs. The result was that, although the Conservatives did not gain a majority of MPs in 1886, the Liberal Unionists held the BALANCE OF POWER (see Source 10.7, page 171). Either the Conservatives on one side, or the Liberal Party with the support of the Home Rule Party (Irish Nationalists) on the other, could run the country if the Liberal Unionists voted for them in the Commons.

Although Salisbury wanted to maintain a distinct Conservative Party and policy, he believed that for the moment a COALITION with the Liberal Unionists would best achieve his ends. Salisbury formed a purely Conservative government, with the support of Liberal Unionist MPs in Commons votes. They knew they had won their seats with Conservative support and some might be defeated if Conservative candidates opposed them in the future.

When a general election was held in 1892 the Liberals made gains. With their Irish Nationalist allies they had a majority over the Conservatives and Liberal Unionists in Parliament. The Liberals were therefore in government in 1892–95, but the Conservatives returned to office in 1895 and Salisbury formed his third ministry. Five Liberal Unionists joined Salisbury's Cabinet, including their two most prominent leaders, the Duke of Devonshire (previously Hartington) and Joseph Chamberlain. This was the coalition of Conservatives and former Liberals that Salisbury had tried to create from 1886.

2 He chose good Conservative leaders in the House of Commons

At first Salisbury had Lord Randolph Churchill as Chancellor of the Exchequer and Leader of the House of Commons – effectively his second in command. Churchill had gained publicity from his colourful speaking outside Parliament and prestige from his successful point-scoring within it, but he soon proved himself an impossible colleague. In December Salisbury accepted his resignation when Churchill wanted to reduce military spending in order to cut taxes. Churchill had put forward ambitious social reform ideas, which might have been popular, but few Conservatives were ready to weaken the army and navy.

167

HOW DID THE CONSERVATIVES BECOME A SUCCESSFUL MASS PARTY AFTER 1885?

Salisbury replaced Churchill as Chancellor of the Exchequer with Goschen, a clever Liberal Unionist and competent financier, making one of the links he wanted to develop with former Liberals. He appointed W.H. Smith as leader in the Commons. Smith might be dull compared with Churchill, but he was safe and trusted. When he died in 1891 Salisbury replaced him with his own nephew, Balfour, who by then had made himself a great reputation running Ireland and debating in Parliament.

3 The government introduced moderate reforms

The Conservative Party gained much of its support as the one party which would defend property. Many wealthy men feared socialist ideas about taxing the rich to improve life for the poor. The Liberals had brought in reforms which took away rights from Irish landowners and confiscated Church estates. The Conservative Party consequently gained support from large and small property owners who feared these changes and what might follow.

Salisbury did not want reforms that took away money or power from the wealthy and landowning classes, and he knew they could seriously upset Conservative supporters. Yet he also saw reforms were necessary. First, many Liberal Unionists wanted them, particularly the radical ones led by Chamberlain, and their votes kept the government in office. Salisbury wrote privately in 1887 that various government measures were 'payment to Chamberlain'. Second, cautious and carefully drawn-up reforms could appeal to some voters and help win elections. If the Conservatives did not introduce moderate reform, the Liberals might get into power and do something more drastic.

> **ELEMENTARY SCHOOLS**
> Schools teaching reading, writing and arithmetic – some of the teaching now associated with primary schools.

■ 10C The most important reforms made by Salisbury's second and third ministries, 1886–92 and 1895–1902

1888 County Councils Act County councils elected by ratepayers (local taxpayers) would manage local matters in the countryside and small towns, instead of Justices of the Peace (local magistrates appointed from among country landowners and other wealthy men).	**1890 Housing Act** Councils could use rates or borrow money to build houses as well as clear away slums. This was the start of council housing, but it was costly and few homes were built before the First World War; councils owned only 0.25 per cent of cheap rented housing by 1912.	**1891 Education Act** Children's fees at ELEMENTARY SCHOOLS were to be paid from the rates, not by parents.	**1897 Workmen's Compensation Act** Workmen (except agricultural labourers and domestic servants) could get automatic compensation for injuries at work without having to prove it was the employer's fault.

While introducing reforms Salisbury's governments kept taxes down, until the costs of the Boer War in 1899–1902 made increases inevitable. They also resisted demands for protection – taxes on imports so that consumers would buy British goods.

4 Salisbury improved Conservative Party organisation

Reforms were one way of appealing to voters which Salisbury did not much like. Good party organisation was a necessary and better way of getting support. Salisbury had an excellent national agent known as 'Captain' Middleton, who ran a party machine which registered voters, organised CANVASSERS, raised money and distributed pamphlets. As leader, Salisbury oiled the party machine by speaking around the country, writing letters to supporters and giving honours to prominent party workers and donors. 'Died of writing inane letters to empty headed Conservative associations' was, he thought, an appropriate inscription for his gravestone. He hated it, but he did it.

> **CANVASSERS**
> People who try to persuade others to vote for a particular political party or policy.

How did the Primrose League expand the popularity of the Conservative Party?

The Primrose League, named after Disraeli's favourite flower, was founded in 1883, two years after his death and in the same year as the Corrupt and Illegal Practices Act which limited the amount of money and paid workers that party candidates could use at election time. One of its founders said it was 'intended' to get help from volunteers to replace the large number of paid canvassers now forbidden by law.

Of course it's vulgar, that's why we are so successful.

SOURCE 10.2
Lady Salisbury's private opinion of the Primrose League

It arranged events such as tea parties and entertainments. Every concert or party would include a political speaker or lantern slide show, though political speeches were limited to about ten–fifteen minutes.

It gained a massive membership. Large numbers of women and children joined. It was most successful in villages and small towns, though it grew in big cities as well. Its membership of over 1 million in the 1890s seems to have been far larger than any formal political party. By 1910 it was over 2 million.

Entertainments were essential. There might be conjurers, acrobats or brass bands (see Source 10.3)

Primrose League functions were often held in rich landowners' parks with a stately home in the background

The Union Jack emphasised patriotism and national unity

Knife and fork teas were popular

They included people from all social classes. Ordinary members were called associates but many were given mock titles, such as knight, to show they were in the higher ranks of the League

SOURCE 10.3 Poster showing the range of Primrose League entertainments, 1890

PROGRAMME NO. 4.

An Excellent, Enjoyable, and Clever Performance, forming a

POPULAR PRIMROSE ENTERTAINMENT

THE LONDON AND PROVINCIAL

ROYAL ENTERTAINMENT BUREAU

Provides the following at moderate inclusive terms for FETES, GALAS, &c. &c. &c.

ASSAULT-AT-ARMS and Athletic Sports.
BALLOON Ascents and Parachutist's Drop from the Clouds.
CLOWN Cricketers, Conjurers and Characteristic Comic Singers.
DUETTISTS and Dancers, Lady Serios and Gentlemen Comics
EQUILIBRISTS, Balancers, & Boneless Wonders.
FLYING Trapeze and Flying Ring Performers.
GYMNASTS, Acrobats, and Tumblers.
HORIZONTAL Bar Performers, and Vaulters.
INSTRUMENTALISTS, Hand Bell Ringers, and Vocalists.
JUGGLERS, Globe Walkers, and Stilt Dancers
KNOCKABOUT Irish Comics, and Negro Artists.
LAUGHABLE Lilliputians and Living Marionettes.

MUSICAL Grotesques, Clowns and Mimics.
NONDESCRIPTS—A Very Novel Performance.
ORIENTAL Troupe of performing Arabs.
PUNCH & JUDY, Performing Dogs and Monkeys.
QUICK Change and Protean Artistes
ROPE Walkers and Dancers
SENSATIONAL Crack Shot Experts.
TRICK Bicycle Riders and Performers.
UNIQUE Performance with Bantam Fowls.
VENTRILOQUISTS and Farm-Yard Imitators.
WIRE Walkers, Dancers and Balancers.
XELLENT Artists in every other Branch of the Profession.
YIELDING Perfect Satisfaction in every respect.
ZOUAVE Lightning Drill Artists, &c. &c. &c.

CHRISTY MINSTREL TROUPES of from Five to Twenty-five Artistes
BRASS AND STRING BANDS, large or small, in or out of Uniform.
GRAND FIREWORK DISPLAYS, ILLUMINATIONS AND ORNAMENTATIONS, etc.

ACTIVITY

1 What suggests that the Primrose League had any political purpose?
2 Why do you think it was so successful?
3 How could it be useful to the Conservative Party?

5 The Conservatives supported popular causes and appealed to patriotism

Conservatives might not want large-scale reform, but they could make themselves a popular party in other ways.

Many Liberals, for example, wanted to reduce the number of pubs, shorten their opening hours or even stop the sale of alcohol altogether. The Tories would defend the working man's pint and appeal to some of his prejudices as well.

Many northern townspeople resented Irish immigrants, their ways and their Roman Catholic religion. The Tories were the party who opposed Irish Home Rule and supported the main Protestant Church in England (see page 41).

Above all, the Conservatives were the party of empire. Chapter 6 Section B describes the popular appeal of empire. Queen Victoria's diamond jubilee was not a party political event but it could still be useful to Salisbury's government.

Queen Victoria's Diamond Jubilee, 1897

The jubilee celebrations included a giant procession through London, with prime ministers from the colonies, troops from different parts of the empire and an open-air service on the steps of St Paul's Cathedral.

ACTIVITY

1 In what ways do Sources 10.4–10.6 suggest the occasion was
  a) a national thanksgiving
  b) a racist demonstration
  c) a political propaganda stunt?
2 How would such an event have been useful to the Conservative Party?

SOURCE 10.4 The jubilee procession returning from the abbey

170

HOW DID THE CONSERVATIVES BECOME A SUCCESSFUL MASS PARTY AFTER 1885?

SOURCE 10.6   Next day the *Daily Mail* described the troops in the procession

Up they came, more and more, new types, new realms at every couple of yards, an anthropological museum [an exhibition of different races] – a living gazeteer of the British Empire. With them came their English officers, whom they obey and follow like children. And you begin to understand, as never before, what the Empire amounts to. Not only that we possess all these remote outlandish places, and can bring men from every end of the earth to join us in honouring our Queen, but also that all these people are working, not simply under us, but with us – that we send out a boy here and a boy there, and the boy takes hold of the savages of the part he comes to, and teaches them to march and shoot as he tells them, to obey him and believe in him, and die for him and the Queen ... And each one of us – you and I, and that man in his shirt-sleeves at the corner – is a working part of this world-shaping force. How small you must feel in face of the stupendous whole, and yet how great to be a unit in it.

B # Why was the Conservative Party more successful than its rivals?

SOURCE 10.7

■ Election results, 1886–1900

1886	Total votes	Percentage	Candidates	Returned unopposed	Elected
Conservative and Liberal Unionist (LU)	1,520,886	51.4	563	118	393 (incl. 77 LU)
Liberal	1,353,581	45.0	449	40	192
Irish Nationalist	97,905	3.5	100	66	85
Others	1,791	0.1	3	0	0
Total	**2,947,163**	**100.0**	**1,115**	**224**	**670**

1892	Total votes	Percentage	Candidates	Returned unopposed	Elected
Conservative and Liberal Unionist (LU)	2,159,150	47.0	606	40	313 (incl. 45 LU)
Liberal	2,088,019	45.1	532	13	272
Irish Nationalist	311,509	7.0	134	9	81
Others	39,641	0.9	31	1	4
Total	**4,598,319**	**100.0**	**1,303**	**63**	**670**

1895	Total votes	Percentage	Candidates	Returned unopposed	Elected
Conservative and Liberal Unionist (LU)	1,894,772	49.1	588	132	411 (incl. 71 LU)
Liberal	1,765,266	45.7	447	11	177
Independent Labour Party	44,325	1.0	28	0	0
Irish Nationalist	152,959	4.0	105	46	82
Others	8,960	0.2	12	0	0
Total	**3,866,282**	**100.0**	**1,180**	**189**	**670**

1900	Total votes	Percentage	Candidates	Returned unopposed	Elected
Conservative and Liberal Unionist (LU)	1,767,958	50.3	569	163	402 (incl. 68 LU)
Liberal	1,572,323	45.0	402	22	183
Labour	62,698	1.3	15	0	2
Irish Nationalist	91,055	2.6	101	58	82
Others	29,448	0.8	15	0	1
Total	**3,523,482**	**100.0**	**1,102**	**243**	**670**

The 1895 and 1900 election results were the biggest victories the Conservatives won between 1874 and the First World War. One reason why the Conservatives won so decisively in both 1895 and 1900 was that many of their candidates were unopposed and so were some of their Liberal Unionist allies. A total of 163 Conservatives and Liberal Unionists got into Parliament in this way in 1900. These would be in seats they were almost bound to win anyway, but it also reflected the weakness of their Liberal opponents. The 1895 election came about because the Liberal prime minister, Lord Rosebery, resigned when his government, already weakened by internal arguments, was defeated in a House of Commons vote.

172

HOW DID THE CONSERVATIVES BECOME A SUCCESSFUL MASS PARTY AFTER 1885?

The Khaki Election 1900

In 1900 there was an additional factor: the Boer War. Salisbury asked the Queen to call a general election in October 1900 after the British had defeated the main Boer armies in southern Africa (see pages 113–115). Although Britain was still at war, it was believed, mistakenly, that the fighting would soon end. The election contest is generally known as the 'khaki' election, suggesting that the government used the army's success for party advantage.

FOCUS ROUTE

1 Use Chart 10D to compare the Liberal and Conservative parties.
Make your own copy of this table and complete it by giving each party a score out of 5 for each category (1 = weakness and 5 = strength).
When you have completed it:
a) In which category does the Conservative Party score highest
b) Does the Liberal Party score higher in any category?
2 Write your own overall analysis of the main strengths of the Conservatives and the main weaknesses of the Liberals.

	Liberals	Conservatives
Policies		
Leaders		
Alliances and splits		
Party organisation		
Fund raising		
Voter appeal		

■ 10D Comparison of the Liberal and Conservative parties

	LIBERALS	CONSERVATIVES
POLICIES	• Gladstone's main policy from 1886 was **Irish Home Rule** which seems to have been unpopular. • The Liberals were divided over what to do about empire and had no coherent policy on social reform. In 1891 Gladstone endorsed reform proposals known as the Newcastle Programme from a National Liberal Federation Conference, but Liberal governments achieved little of this in 1892–95 because of their own weakness and Lords opposition. The next Liberal leaders, Rosebery and Campbell-Bannerman, avoided reform programmes. • The Liberals had few policies to appeal to the working classes, and proposals to restrict the sale of alcohol were unpopular.	• Salisbury was **opposed to programmes of reforms**. He emphasised **opposition to Irish Home Rule** and practical improvements for working men. • The party would defend property rights, the empire and the Church of England. • After Lord Randolph Churchill resigned in late 1886 no Conservative leaders put forward ideas for social reform.
LEADERS	• **Gladstone** remained leader until he retired aged 84 in 1894. He was the **greatest speaker** and most charismatic politician of the time, but people were expecting him to retire all through the period. • When Rosebery took over as leader in 1894 there were **constant disagreements**, and he resigned in 1896. There was no overall party leader until Campbell-Bannerman was elected in 1899.	• **Salisbury** was already in a **strong position as Conservative leader** in 1886. His position became more secure with his subsequent success, and he remained leader until his retirement in 1902. • He spoke widely around the country after 1880 and was the first party leader in the House of Lords to abandon the tradition that peers did not take part in general election campaigns.
ALLIANCES AND SPLITS	• The **Liberal Unionists** who broke away in 1886 were lost to the party as they worked with the Conservatives and later formed a coalition government with them in 1895. Splits continued over other issues. • Liberal Party workers around the country included many groups with their own policy ideas – causes such as temperance (banning the sale of alcohol), which were sometimes unpopular with the wider electorate. • **Different opinions about** the **empire** brought further splits from 1886, which worsened in the Boer War. Liberal MPs split three ways on a motion of censure against the war in 1900, some in favour of the war, some against and some abstaining (choosing not to vote).	• The Conservatives remained largely united to 1902, and Lord Randolph Churchill's break with the government at the end of 1886 had little impact. • They **allied successfully with both groups of Liberal Unionists** who split from their party – the moderate Whigs led by Hartington and the Radicals following Chamberlain. The Liberal Unionist Goschen became Chancellor of the Exchequer in 1887, and the main Liberal Unionist leaders joined Salisbury's third ministry in 1895 – a coalition Salisbury had been aiming to achieve since 1886.

173

HOW DID THE CONSERVATIVES BECOME A SUCCESSFUL MASS PARTY AFTER 1885?

	LIBERALS	CONSERVATIVES
PARTY ORGANISATION	• Local Liberal parties were joined in the **National Liberal Federation (NLF)** which had an executive committee and held annual conferences. Its resolutions were not meant to be binding on Liberal MPs, but it was hard for leaders to ignore them. • From 1886 an amalgamation of the NLF and Liberal Central Association, under the NLF's Secretary, Schnadhorst, strengthened the party, and a Liberal publications department was established in 1887. • By the 1890s, Schnadhorst's mental powers were declining, and he was going deaf before he retired in 1893. The Liberal organisation was then **less well staffed and organised than the Conservatives' one**, and local Liberal parties were generally much weaker.	• Local Conservative parties were joined in the **National Union** which held annual conferences but had no power, and party leaders were not expected to follow the resolutions. • **'Captain' Middleton** became national agent in charge of organisation in 1885 and remained in the job to 1903. He concentrated on getting voters registered locally and publishing pamphlets nationally. • He tried to get **professional agents** employed to run constituency parties and election campaigns. These were in half of the constituencies in the country by 1900 – a professional strength far ahead of rivals. • The **Primrose League** also gave support.
FUND RAISING	• Many of the wealthiest Liberals became Liberal Unionists, including most of the peers and great landowners. This made it more **difficult to raise money** which led to the decline of some constituency Liberal parties. • Liberal prime ministers were willing to give honours in return for contributions to the party, but they had less opportunity than the Conservatives as they were generally out of office.	• Many industrialists, traders and professional men as well as landowners supported the Conservatives. With far more **wealthy supporters** it was easier for the Conservatives to raise funds than other parties. • As Prime Minister, Salisbury gave peerages and other honours to wealthy men who supported the party.
VOTER APPEAL	• The Liberals' greatest support had long been among Nonconformists. • Some trade union or Labour MPs also sat as Liberals. The party's fight against privilege might appeal to workers, and there was no well-organised Labour Party. • Liberals' working-class connections might also lose middle-class Nonconformist support. In 1897 the minister of Regent's Park chapel commented that 'Trade Unionism and the present position of the Labour Question are driving thousands into the Conservative camp'. They also lost support over Irish Home Rule because of some Nonconformists' distrust of Roman Catholics.	• The Conservatives gained much **middle-class support** in the suburbs of large towns. They also did better when there were more non-resident electors who voted because of property ownership. Conservatives therefore appear to have got the votes of most wealthy men, but they also gained **support from a significant minority of working men**.

CHAPTER 10 REVIEW ACTIVITY

Use the information in this chapter to answer the following essay question: How did the Conservative Party become a successful mass party between 1885 and 1902? Make sure you mention:

a) the issue of Irish Home Rule

b) Liberal Unionist support for the Conservatives and various splits in the Liberal Party

c) Conservative policies and government reforms

d) different ways in which the Conservatives developed a popular appeal

e) Conservative organisation and how it compared with the Liberal Party's organisation.

KEY POINTS FROM CHAPTER 10 **How did the Conservatives become a successful mass party after 1885?**

1 From 1885 there was a large majority of working-class voters in the electorate, but the Conservatives still dominated British politics from then until 1906.

2 This was initially because of the Liberal split over Irish Home Rule and the way the Conservatives gained support from the Liberal Unionists opposed to Home Rule.

3 Conservatives maintained their supremacy mainly because of superior organisation and Liberal divisions and partly because of some attractive policies.

What was the significance of the Liberal victory in the 1906 election?

CHAPTER OVERVIEW

January 1906 was a wonderful month to be a Liberal. The general election contests were spread over several weeks and victories came day after day. Older Liberals thought it was better than Gladstone's great victory in 1880. Younger ones just couldn't remember anything like it. The Tories had thrashed them in 1895 and thrashed them again in 1900. Then the Tories had gloried in the empire and Boer War victories and told the Liberals they were unpatriotic. The Liberals had argued among themselves over the war and could not agree what to say.

SOURCE 1

An artist's representation of the scene at the National Liberal Club when the news of Balfour's defeat was announced

Now in 1906 the Liberals championed Free Trade and cheap food for the workers and accused the Tories of being against the working man. The Tories, who had quarrelled over food taxes for years, could not agree on a reply. So the Tories went down to defeat; even their former prime minister Arthur Balfour lost his seat at East Manchester.

The Liberals won 400 seats and had a massive majority in the House of Commons of 130. It was the first time they had gained an overall Commons majority since 1880. The swing from the Conservatives to the Liberals was 10.6 per cent.

For Liberals at the time it was a great triumph. It is for historians to look more critically and work out the real significance of this event.

There are two major debates:

- How far did this victory prove the Liberals were strong again and how far did they benefit from a lucky set of circumstances including a weak Conservative opposition?
- The election also marked the first significant progress for the Labour Party. They gained 29 MPs and soon had 30. How far were the Liberals under threat from Labour?

PERCENTAGE SWING

This is calculated by adding the number of votes the Conservatives lost (compared with the previous election) and the number the Liberals gained and then dividing by two.

To answer them, this chapter investigates:

A What different interpretations of the election have historians produced? (pp. 175–176)

B Why had the Conservatives become unpopular by 1906? (pp. 177–181)

C What issues were important in the 1906 election? (pp. 182–184)

D How successful were Labour candidates in the 1906 election? (p. 185)

175

WHAT WAS THE SIGNIFICANCE OF THE LIBERAL VICTORY IN THE 1906 ELECTION?

A What different interpretations of the election have historians produced?

Historians view events differently for many reasons, such as their own political beliefs, their varying ideas of what is important or because they use different evidence.

Later developments influence their judgement. The Liberals never again won an overall majority in the House of Commons after the 1906 election, and within twenty years Labour had replaced them as the main left-wing party. This encourages historians to look for signs of Liberal weakness and Labour strength in 1906.

In 1906 some analysts, particularly Conservative ones, were keen to explain the change by the way public opinion seemed to swing from one election to the next. They saw 1906 as part of this cycle. This was the pattern over the previous forty years (see Chart 11A).

■ **11A Pattern of election victories 1868–1906**

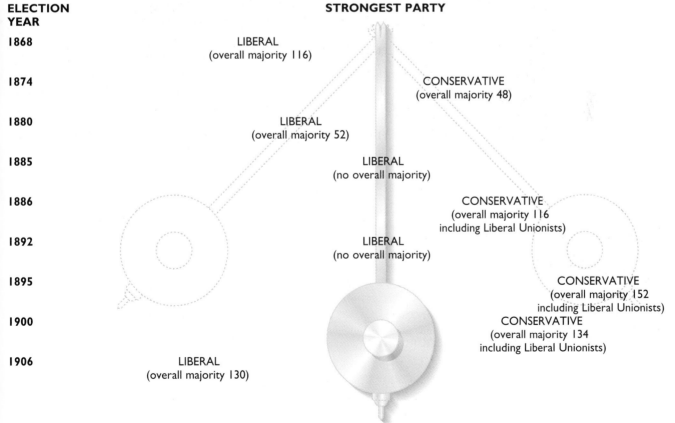

ELECTION YEAR	STRONGEST PARTY
1868	LIBERAL (overall majority 116)
1874	CONSERVATIVE (overall majority 48)
1880	LIBERAL (overall majority 52)
1885	LIBERAL (no overall majority)
1886	CONSERVATIVE (overall majority 116 including Liberal Unionists)
1892	LIBERAL (no overall majority)
1895	CONSERVATIVE (overall majority 152 including Liberal Unionists)
1900	CONSERVATIVE (overall majority 134 including Liberal Unionists)
1906	LIBERAL (overall majority 130)

This was perhaps the simplest of many interpretations given in 1906. Further developments and research have brought more complex and colourful views.

ACTIVITY

Sources 11.1–11.8 are historians' views of the significance of the 1906 election.

a) Which historians suggest the Liberals were strong and what strengths do they identify?

b) Which historians suggest the Liberals were benefiting from lucky circumstances and a weak Conservative opposition?

c) Which historians suggest the Liberals were under threat from Labour?

d) Suggest reasons for the differences in their views.

SOURCE 11.1   George Dangerfield, in his work on *The Strange Death of Liberal England*, 1935, wrote of the Liberals in 1906. The 53 Labour MPs consisted of 29 MPs elected as Labour Representation Committee candidates and 24 MPs who were trade union-sponsored Liberal candidates known as Lib–Labs

[T]he Liberal Party which came back to Westminster with an overwhelming majority was already doomed. It was like an army protected at all points except for one vital position on its flank. With the election of 53 Labour representatives, the death of Liberalism was pronounced; it was no longer the Left.

SOURCE 11.2   Peter Clarke put a contrasting view in *Lancashire and the New Liberalism*, 1971, a study based on intensive research on the north west of England. Clarke himself had a moderate left-wing viewpoint, later supporting the Social Democratic Party (SDP) which allied with the Liberals in the 1980s

[T]he first quarter of the twentieth century saw two sorts of change in British politics. The first sort centred upon the emergence of class politics in a stable form; the second sort upon the effective replacement of the Liberal party by the Labour party. But the first … does not in any simple way explain the second. For one thing, the chronology is wrong. By 1910, the change to class politics was substantially complete. That from Liberalism to Labour had not really begun. Nor were there signs that it must begin …

[T]he Liberals were supported indiscriminately in 1906; but … the most solid element in their support, both then and in 1910, was the working class vote …

Organised labour … which had once been cool towards liberalism, increasingly settled for the progressive coalition [another name for the Liberal–Labour pact] rather than strict independence. Between 1900 and 1910 Liberalism and Labour [the Liberal and Labour parties] drew closer together.

SOURCE 11.3   In West Yorkshire Keith Laybourn (1984) found

The furious assault of Labour in local contests [was] eating into the grass-roots support for Liberalism. All was not well with West Yorkshire Liberalism.

SOURCE 11.4   Paul Thompson (1967) argued that in London

The [Liberal] recovery of the 1900s gave a deceptive illusion of strength, for it was not based on the solution of the Liberal Party's real problems. It still lacked a firm working class basis, a secure financial backing and a coherent political standpoint.

SOURCE 11.5   Duncan Tanner, in a major work on *Political Change and the Labour Party 1900–1918*, 1990, also argued that the alliance between Liberals and Labour, which looked strong in Lancashire, was generally weak

[T]he Progressive Alliance [another name for the Liberal–Labour pact] was a sickly child, the secret offspring of an illicit relationship.

SOURCE 11.6   Neil Blewett, in a study of early twentieth-century elections (1972), stressed the Liberals' strength

[T]he resurgence of Liberalism among all classes and all major groups … underlay the Unionist [see Learning trouble spot, page 165] rout … The swing was neither a middle-class, nor a working-class phenomenon, but was, in fact, universal.

SOURCE 11.7   Michael Bentley (1987) wrote

In the circumstances of 1905 it sufficed to be the Not-Conservative party.

SOURCE 11.8   Geoffrey Searle (1992) concluded

In 1906, then, the Liberals enjoyed popularity with electors from a wide range of social backgrounds. But it soon became apparent that the Liberal triumph had been brought about by an unusual combination of circumstances that were unlikely to recur.

177

WHAT WAS THE SIGNIFICANCE OF THE LIBERAL VICTORY IN THE 1906 ELECTION?

B Why had the Conservatives become unpopular by 1906?

FOCUS ROUTE

1 Turn to the list of reasons for Conservative success 1886–1902 that you compiled for the focus route on page 166. On the right, from reading this section add notes to show how far the Conservatives lost these advantages by 1906 and how factors that had previously led to success later led to failure.

2 Explain how each of the following would have made Balfour's ministry either popular or unpopular:

a) the Boer War
b) 1902 Education Act and other reforms

c) defence policy
d) free trade and protection issues
e) party splits.

The effects of the Boer War

The Conservatives had probably benefited from the Boer War at the 1900 election. It probably damaged them in 1906. Attitudes to the war had changed (see pages 114–115). People thought more about the cost and were often less enthusiastic about imperialism. A ROYAL COMMISSION on the War, chaired by Lord Elgin, reported in 1903 and blamed the early defeats on the government's lack of preparations.

ROYAL COMMISSION
Group set up by the government to investigate and report on an issue.

Balfour's ministry 1902–05

Arthour Balfour became Prime Minister on Salisbury's retirement in 1902 and he resigned in late 1905. His ministry's most controversial reform was the 1902 Education Act.

1902 Education Act

Why? Elementary schools varied a lot in standard. The majority of pupils – three million of them – were taught in VOLUNTARY SCHOOLS which were mainly Anglican and were often short of money.

VOLUNTARY SCHOOLS
Schools run by voluntary organisations (groups of people who chose to give money and set up schools) or set up by wealthy people who gave money for them.

Secondary education was very limited. There were grammar schools, but these were mainly for the middle class. Some locally elected school boards provided secondary education, but judges had recently ruled in a test case (the Cockerton case) that they did not have the legal power to do so. A change in the law was needed just to keep secondary education going in some areas, and in many places little was available anyway.

Effects of the Act School boards (see page 48) were abolished. County and county borough councils now ran the elementary schools previously managed by school boards, though local councils would run them in some larger towns. Voluntary schools, which were mainly Anglican, now got money directly from the rates.

County councils would provide scholarships (free places) for the elementary school children who did best in exams to go to secondary school.

More secondary schools were built before the First World War, though only 1 in 40 children from public elementary schools got free secondary education by 1914.

Nonconformists objected to ratepayers' money going directly to Anglican schools. There was much agitation over this, especially in Wales, and one historian – Blewett (1972) – pointed out that Conservative candidates did considerably worse in BY-ELECTIONS just after the Act.

BY-ELECTION
An election in just one constituency. It is usually the result of the death or retirement of the sitting MP.

1904 Licensing Act

Why? Under the existing law, pub landlords could lose the licence to run their business because there were too many pubs in an area. The government thought this was unfair and interfered with landlords' property rights.

Effects of the Act Landlords got compensation if they lost their licences. Other landlords in the area who might benefit from increased trade would provide money for this. This might seem fair, but TEMPERANCE supporters who opposed the sale of alcohol thought it too generous to landlords.

TEMPERANCE
Belief in self-restraint and in not drinking alcohol.

178

WHAT WAS THE SIGNIFICANCE OF THE LIBERAL VICTORY IN THE 1906 ELECTION?

DISCUSS

What might a modern historian argue were the most important achievements and failures in Balfour's ministry?

■ Learning trouble spot

Free trade describes a system where goods are allowed in and out of a country without any taxes, except for a very few which the government needs to raise money. Such taxes are known as customs duties or sometimes tariffs.

Protection

Some tariffs or customs duties were deliberately used to make imports from foreign countries more expensive than the equivalent home-produced goods. This was designed to protect home producers against foreign competitors, and so was known as protection. In the early twentieth century it was also often called **tariff reform**.

Imperial preference meant that goods from empire countries were imported without taxes or at lower rates of tax than other foreign goods.

1905 Unemployed Workmen Act

Why? There was growing understanding that workmen might be unemployed, through no fault of their own, in trade slumps.

Effects of the Act Distress committees were set up in large towns to help the unemployed find work. Some opened labour exchanges, and they could also help unemployed people to emigrate overseas.

Defence

Balfour thought defending the empire was a top priority. He established a new Committee of Imperial Defence made up of Cabinet ministers and armed service chiefs to plan overall strategy. His government also increased naval spending and decided to build a new and superior type of warship – the Dreadnought (see pages 118–119) – though ministers' plans for army reform were not carried through.

Free trade, protection and imperial preference

Many Conservatives had supported protection when Salisbury was leader. Then in May 1903 Joseph Chamberlain, the Colonial Secretary, made a big speech in favour of it, arguing that it would strengthen the empire. Chamberlain's speech suddenly made protection a hot political issue. He had a great reputation, a flair for getting publicity, a large amount of personal support, especially around Birmingham, and some charisma.

His main proposals, developed in several succeeding speeches, were:

- Taxes (generally known as tariffs) should be charged on foreign imports
- Taxes would not be levied on goods from British colonies, so as to give imperial preference
- Treaties might then be negotiated with foreign countries to lower taxes on their goods if they reduced duties on British imports.

Chart 11B shows some of the reasons why Chamberlain and his supporters favoured protection or tariff reform and why others, paticularly working-class people, doubted them. Britain imported much of its food, and import taxes would make this food more expensive. This fear of higher living costs and less to eat was the key problem that protectionists faced.

■ 11B The pros and cons of protection

ADVANTAGES	DISADVANTAGES
As seen by many Conservatives	**As British workers might see them**
• The government needed more money. Income from import duties could be used for welfare reforms and would pay for old age pensions, which had been widely discussed from the 1890s.	• Would the money be used this way? Chamberlain had talked about old age pensions in the 1890s, but then his government had spent so much on the Boer War that there was no money left for pensions.
• Britain's greatness lay in its empire, and this alone could make it as great as the USA or Russia. Britain should help British settlers already in the colonies and boost their economies so that more emigrants could join them. They in turn would boost British trade and give support in war.	• Was the empire such a great thing? The Boer War, fought to strengthen the empire, was costly and cruel. Southern African gold mines were being worked by Chinese labourers instead of providing jobs for British workers • Colonies might sell more of their produce in Britain if foreign food were taxed, but who would then suffer price increases? The British worker.
• Many British industries suffered unfair foreign competition. All the other advanced industrial countries taxed imports. Britain's main rivals, Germany and the USA, had increased theirs massively in the late 1800s. Britain must retaliate if its industry were to survive and workers keep their jobs.	• Britain was flourishing as a great trading nation and was generally prosperous during Chamberlain's campaign; price increases looked more certain than extra jobs. Employers in some industries might benefit from protection, but would they pass on the advantages to their workers?
• Taxes on imports would help British farming. This would also make the country more self-sufficient at a time when the situation abroad looked more threatening.	• But would the farm workers benefit? As they were generally low paid, higher food prices would hit them hardest • Imperial preference would mean so much Canadian corn or New Zealand lamb entering the country that British farming was unlikely to revive.

SOURCE 11.9 A Conservative poster in support of protection (tariff reform)

SOURCE 11.10 A Liberal poster opposed to Conservative protection policies

DISCUSS

1 What arguments are used in Sources 11.9 and 11.10 for and against protection?
2 Which do you think is the more effective piece of propaganda? Give reasons.

SOURCE 11.11 From a letter from Balfour to Chamberlain, February 1905

The prejudice against a small tax on food is not the fad of a few imperfectly informed theorists, it is a deep rooted prejudice affecting a large mass of voters, especially the poorest class, which it will be a matter of extreme difficulty to overcome.

Chamberlain knew about these doubts. He promised that the duties would remain low, especially on food. Taxes were already levied on some imported items, such as tea, sugar, coffee and cocoa, to bring in money for the government, and he promised that these taxes would be lowered to compensate for duties on other foodstuffs.

Chamberlain's arguments do not seem to have convinced the public. Even a poll by the right-wing *Daily Mail* showed big opposition. Balfour knew the difficulties, which he put to Chamberlain in a private letter in February 1905 (see Source 11.11).

Yet Balfour agreed with many of Chamberlain's arguments and knew that many Conservatives supported them. Consequently, as Chamberlain developed his policies, Balfour developed a compromise version as the official party line.

Balfour's compromise was in two parts:

- **Retaliation** The government should at least threaten to introduce taxes on products from countries which taxed British goods and try to get commercial treaties which would lower the foreign duties
- **'Double Election' pledge** If the Conservatives won the next election they would hold a colonial conference to work out an imperial preference scheme, but they would not introduce it unless they got public approval for the scheme at another general election.

180

WHAT WAS THE SIGNIFICANCE OF THE LIBERAL VICTORY IN THE 1906 ELECTION?

Party divisions

Balfour had to deal with divisions among both party leaders and ordinary members. In 1903 Chamberlain resigned from the government, with the Prime Minister's agreement, so that he could tour the country to get support for his policy. Balfour then virtually tricked three other Cabinet ministers into resigning. They still believed strongly in free trade and thought that Chamberlain was staying in the government and that his policies were going to be followed. The Duke of Devonshire, the old Liberal Unionist leader (see page 165), who also supported free trade, soon resigned as well. Extremists on both sides were now out of the Cabinet, but Balfour looked devious and his government seemed divided and weak.

Chamberlain gained majority support from the Conservative conference, but rival organisations were at work within the party. The Tariff Reform League supporting Chamberlain's policy challenged the smaller Unionist Free Food League, and the argument split many local Conservative associations. This obviously weakened the party organisation, which seems to have declined after the resignation in 1903 of the talented and hard-working 'Captain' Middleton as national agent (see Chart 10D, page 173).

In December 1905, with his party seriously divided, Balfour resigned as prime minister. He thought that, as leading Liberal politicians were divided over empire and foreign policy, Campbell-Bannerman, the Liberal leader, would not be able to form a strong government. He was wrong. Campbell-Bannerman got the support of all the leading Liberals, formed a government and then got the King to call a general election for 1906 so that the Liberals could try to win a majority in the House of Commons.

ACTIVITY

It is 1905. You are Campbell-Bannerman, leader of the Liberals. Your opposite number, the Conservative leader Balfour, has just resigned as prime minister, partly because of splits in his own party. He reckons that your party is also so divided that you will find it difficult or impossible to form a strong government.

It will be a tough job. There has been no Liberal administration for ten years. You were critical of the Boer War but imperialist Liberals, some of the most important people in the party, supported it and are very critical of your leadership.

Asquith, Grey and Haldane would probably like to sideline you but you need to have them in government because they are able and could threaten your position if they are outside the administration. You have to work out how to attract at least one or two of them to join your government. Then you can split them up or, perhaps, get them all to join your administration.

Work on this in pairs.

Stage 1 – Allocate the top jobs
These will be your most influential Cabinet members. They will control the most important policies at home and abroad.
a) Choose your top three.
b) Give them one of the important jobs below.

The big three jobs
• Foreign Secretary
• Chancellor of the Exchequer
• Home Secretary

Stage 2 – Allocate the other important jobs
These jobs are less powerful but still important.

• Colonial Secretary
• Secretary for War
• Secretary for India
• Chief Secretary for Ireland

Stage 3 – Decide what to do about the rest
The people who are left over might still be useful to you. Decide if you will give them a less important job or leave them out altogether.

Stage 4 – Present your team and explain your reasons
Explain to other members of the class why you made the appointments you did. Focus on:
a) who got the top jobs and why
b) who was left out entirely and why
c) any worries you have about your new team.

You can find out who Campbell-Bannerman appointed on page 276.

Herbert Gladstone — Age: 51

Background: Son of the great Liberal leader William Gladstone. Educated at Eton and Oxford.

Political career: Liberal Chief Whip since 1899. Chief Whip's job is to ensure MPs support the party policies. Faced great party disagreements over the Boer War but has kept the confidence of most MPs and avoided major splits. Successfully negotiated an election pact with the Labour Party in 1903.

Comment: Has given you strong personal support. Should have an important job. May be opposed to extending state control which some of your government's reforms may need.

Edward Grey — Age: 43

Background: Educated at Winchester and Oxford, but sent down (expelled) for not working, so he did not get a degree.

Political career: MP since 1885. Parliamentary Under-Secretary for Foreign Affairs in 1892–95 when he did well defending government policy in the Commons.

Comment: Disagreed with you on the Boer War and went further than any other prominent Liberal in supporting the conflict. Strong imperialist who is likely to plot against you with Asquith and Haldane.

James Bryce — Age: 67

Background: Educated in Glasgow and Belfast, then Oxford and Heidelberg universities. Became a lawyer. Was Professor of Law at Oxford University for 23 years.

Political career: MP since 1880. In Gladstone's Cabinet in 1892 and then President of the Board of Trade 1894–95. Unsociable around parliament but a good public speaker. Expert on education.

Comment: Like you he was very critical of the British army's methods in the Boer War and is a friend and strong personal supporter of yours.

David Lloyd George — Age: 41

Background: From a poor family in North Wales. Local school in North Wales. Had no university education but became a lawyer.

Political career: MP since 1890. Inclined to be controversial and outspoken. He has championed Welsh Nonconformist causes, for example opposing extra rights and money for Anglican schools under the Education Act of 1902. Has a big reputation in Wales, but no experience in government.

Comment: Opposed the Boer War because he thought it was an unwise way to settle disputes.

Earl of Rosebury — Age: 58

Background: Educated at Eton and Oxford.

Political career: Never an MP, but has a formidable political record and is a brilliant speaker. Was Foreign Secretary 1886 and 1892–94 and Prime Minister 1894–95, though his ministry was not a success because of divisions in the government. Resigned as Liberal leader in 1896. Showed skills as a negotiator when he successfully mediated to end a coal strike in 1893.

Comment: Strong enthusiast for empire; has been seen as leader of the Liberal imperialists. Strongly opposed to Irish Home Rule. He has refused to co-operate with you as leader and would be unlikely to join the government. But if you could win his loyalty it might greatly strengthen your ministry and consolidate the party.

John Morley — Age: 66

Background: Educated at Cheltenham College and Oxford. Made his name as a journalist editing the *Fortnightly Review* and *Pall Mall Gazette* – journals which were read by many influential people in Britain. Gained reputation as a radical and popular speaker at public meetings in the 1870s and 1880s.

Political career: MP since 1883. Chief Secretary for Ireland in the Liberal ministries in 1886 and 1892–95.

Comment: Devoted to William Gladstone – the former Liberal leader. He published Gladstone's official biography in 1903, presenting a worshipful and uncritical view of the great man.

Richard Haldane — Age: 49

Background: Educated at Edinburgh Academy, Göttingen University (in Germany) and Edinburgh University. Became a successful lawyer.

Political career: MP since 1885. Helped draft and defend complicated budget reforms in 1894. Is able, but has not held high office before.

Comment: Definitely not a personal supporter of yours. He is a prominent Liberal imperialist closely connected with Asquith and Grey.

Herbert Asquith — Age: 53

Background: Educated at City of London School and Oxford. Successful lawyer.

Political career: MP since 1886. Very effective speaker in the House of Commons. Home Secretary 1892–95 and was one of the few Liberal ministers to increase his reputation in these years. He has recently been the most effective opponent of the Conservative government's plans for Protection. Currently has the highest reputation of any of the liberal imperialists.

Comment: Supported the Boer War and opposed you. You have had serious disagreements with him.

John Burns — Age: 47

Background: From working-class family in South London. Left school at the age of ten and trained as an engineer.

Political career: Involved in socialist and radical movements in 1880s and made his name as a leader in the 1889 London Dock Strike. MP since 1892 but has done his most important work on London County Council. Dropped out of socialist movement and later trade union movement and has been working with Liberals as a 'progressive' in London local politics. Has no experience of central government

Comment: Taking him into the Cabinet should help get working-class support and strengthen the Liberal Party against future threats from Labour if the Lib–Lab Pact does not last.

Earl of Elgin — Age: 56

Background: Educated at Eton and Oxford. Landowner

Political career: Never an MP, but has been active in Scottish Liberal politics and Chairman of the Scottish Liberal Association. Was Governor-General in India 1893–98 where he showed some ability in administration but appeared to lack self-confidence. Led a Royal Commission which produced an impressive report on military failures in the Boer War in 1903.

Comment: It is important to have someone in the House of Lords in your Cabinet but not necessarily in a top position.

What issues were important in the 1906 election?

The main parties did not publish national manifestos for elections at this time. Instead individual party candidates had printed election addresses putting forward their policies. A.K. Russell (1973) analysed these in a book about the 1906 election; Source 11.12 summarises his findings.

ACTIVITY

Look at Source 11.12.

a) To what extent did the Conservative and Liberal election addresses seem to deal with the same issues?

b) How far did the Labour election addresses concentrate on similar issues to the Liberal ones?

SOURCE 11.12 Percentage of party candidates dealing with important issues in their election addresses

	Liberal	Conservative	Labour
Protection/free trade	98	98	79
1902 Education Act	86	67	79
Home Rule/Ireland	78	85	79
Chinese labour	75	19	67
Pensions and poor law reform	69	22	81
Trade union law and Taff Vale decision	59	9	88

TALKING POINT

How do these issues compare with the major issues in a recent general election in the UK?

To understand the election we must think of both the individual issues listed in Source 11.12 and of how they influenced particular groups of voters. It is particularly important to understand the meaning of these issues to the **working class** as they were the majority of the electorate. Historians have also stressed the significance of **Nonconformists** in the 1906 election (see learning trouble spot, page 41). In 1906 they probably made up about 600,000 out of around 6 million possible voters in England and Wales. Several historians think they were more important than their numbers suggest, because they formed the bulk of activists who might work for the Liberals, and because many leading Nonconformist ministers campaigned on the Liberal side. Many middle-class Nonconformists had gone over to the Unionists (see Chart 10D, page 173) and might be won back to the Liberals. They appeared as what we might call floating voters. Many Nonconformists were angry about how the Conservatives' 1902 Education Act helped Anglican schools. They also wanted the government to act in a moral way, and many thought government arrangements for using Chinese labourers in South Africa (see page 183) were morally wrong.

How did the issues link together?

Historians and PSEPHOLOGISTS emphasise how particular issues come together to create powerful images in electors' minds and how these can decide how people vote. A.K. Russell (1973) wrote of how 'reasons melt into each other and become hard to distinguish one from another'.

PSEPHOLOGISTS
People who study voting in elections.

ACTIVITY

The following diagram summarises some of the links between the issues mentioned in Source 11.12. Refer to Source 11.12 and the summary of Balfour's ministry on pages 177–178.

1 Which issues encouraged Nonconformists to oppose the Unionists and how are they linked?

2 Which issues most concerned the working class and how are they linked?

3 How important overall was social reform to the candidates and voters in 1906?

The free trade–protection controversy

Many indicators, including election addresses, suggest that this was the main issue.

SOURCE 11.13 The *Manchester Guardian*, on 15 January 1906, wrote of the election in Lancashire

A candidate had only to be a Free Trader to get in, whether he was known or unknown … He had only to be a Protectionist to lose all chance of getting in though he spoke with the tongues of men and angels.

Working-class living standards

Both commentators at the time and later historians have seen this as a key issue which linked with many others. Peter Clarke (1971) found that in Lancashire, where the Conservatives previously had large working-class support, economic issues were taking over from religious ones as the most important discussion points.

Rich v Poor

There were links between different economic issues and working-class consciousness. Suspicion of the very wealthy and powerful was shared by many middle-class as well as working-class people.

SOURCE 11.16 The Conservative-minded *Quarterly Review* in April 1906 summarised much of the debate after the election

It is true that many grievances co-operated to make the Unionist Party unpopular [but] it is also true that most of these different grievances had some common elements … Thus the attack on Chinese Labour, on Protection, and on the Taff Vale judgment, all formed part of an accusation of PLUTOCRATIC CONSPIRACY. *Even the Education Act was represented as a victory for privilege … The issue thus seemed to be Rich versus Poor.*

PLUTOCRATIC CONSPIRACY
Wealthy people in government combining to protect their wealth and power.

The Taff Vale case and trade union issues

Since a legal case in 1900–01 (see page 145) it seemed that trade unions who organised a strike would have to pay employers to cover their losses. As this would make strikes virtually impossible or pointless, most trade union leaders wanted the law altered. The Conservative government had not altered it in over four years, but Liberal and Labour candidates both supported change.

Chinese labour

Many Chinese men worked in southern African gold mines for a fixed number of years, returning to China when their time was up. They lived in special compounds without their families, working 60 hours a week for food, lodgings and two shillings a day. They were forbidden to leave their employers or move around without special passes and were denied normal rights in the law courts. The workers volunteered for this, but the scheme was soon labelled 'Chinese slavery'. It was a gift for Liberal and Labour politicians in turning British workers against the Conservatives (see Sources 11.14 and 11.15).

SOURCE 11.14 As reported in *The Times* on 17 January 1906, David Lloyd George, now a young Liberal Cabinet minister, knew how to make the 'Chinese slavery' issue relevant to his Welsh voters in the election campaign

What would you say to introducing Chinamen at one shilling a day to the Welsh quarries? …
    If they introduced them to one part of the Empire, why not to every part?

SOURCE 11.15 A Liberal poster about 'Chinese slavery', 1906

THE WAR'S RESULT
CHINESE LABOUR

Voice of TOMMY ATKINS
from the shades! —
"Is THIS what we fought for?"

The Tory Government have permitted Chinese Labourers to be imported into the Transvaal, there to work in the mines under conditions which Mr. Seddon described as "SEMI-SLAVERY."

SOURCE 11.17   The 1906 election results

	Total votes	Percentage	Candidates	Returned unopposed	Elected
Liberal	2,757,883	49.0	539	27	400 (60%)
Conservative and Liberal Unionist (LU)	2,451,454	43.6	574	13	157 (incl. 25 Liberal Unionists) (23.5%)
Labour	329,748	5.9	51	0	30 (incl. one originally elected as Liberal) (4.5%)
Irish Nationalist	35,031	0.6	87	74	83 (12%)
Others	52,387	0.9	22	0	0
Total	5,626,503	100.0	1,273	114	670

ACTIVITY

1 How many more votes than the Conservatives did the Liberal Party get?
2 How many more seats did the Liberals get?
3 How strong was Labour?

SOURCE 11.18   As the election results came out, *The Times* on 16 January 1906 saw the key issue as

whether the working classes who form the bulk of the electorate are to dictate the policy they desire, or to go on contenting themselves with choosing between policies offered them by the traditional parties in the State. They have decided for the first alternative.

... Where the working men have run candidates of their own they have returned them by immense majorities, where they have not had their own candidates they have done the next best thing by sinking their differences and concentrating upon the Liberal candidate.

SOURCE 11.19   An artist's representation of the streets of Derby after the Labour and Liberal victory

Other factors

The Liberals' success cannot be explained wholly by their appealing to working-class voters. There was an average swing of nearly 15 per cent away from the Conservatives in some rich London constituencies. Home Rule for Ireland, which had lost the Liberals so much support in the late nineteenth century, now seemed much less important, as the Liberals said that even if they won in 1906 they would not introduce it before another election (see Chapter 14).

185

WHAT WAS THE SIGNIFICANCE OF THE LIBERAL VICTORY IN THE 1906 ELECTION?

D How successful were Labour candidates in the 1906 election?

This was the first election where a significant number of Labour MPs were elected. With hindsight, historians, who know that Labour later replaced the Liberals as the main left-wing party, analyse these results to assess how they achieved this success. Was it largely their deal with the Liberals or was it a sign of the strong groundswell of national support – working men shifting their allegiance from the Liberals to Labour?

In 1903 the Liberal Party and the Labour Representation Committee had made a semi-secret pact not to oppose each other at an election. The agreement was that 30 LRC candidates would stand without Liberal opposition and in return Labour candidates would not oppose Liberals elsewhere. The agreement substantially worked which makes it difficult to tell how strong the two sides would have been in competition with each other. There were a few seats where Liberal and Labour candidates fought against each other. Where **Labour candidates** fought a Unionist and were **not opposed by a Liberal candidate** they gained **58 per cent** of the vote overall and won **24 of the 31 seats** contested. Where **Labour candidates** fought **against a Liberal** in a three-sided contest they gained **29 per cent** of the vote overall and won only **4 out of 18 seats**.

Labour did not yet seem a major threat to the Liberals even in strongly working-class areas. Both Labour and Liberal candidates gained particularly big swings from the Unionists when just one of them stood in a working-class constituency. Whether it was a Labour or a Liberal candidate did not seem to make much difference.

DISCUSS

What do these figures suggest about Labour and Liberal strength?

TALKING POINT

How easy is it for historians to produce opposing arguments by selecting different evidence to support their point of view?

CHAPTER 11 REVIEW ACTIVITY

Read again the historians' statements in Sources 11.1–11.8 on page 176.

1 Which interpretation do you think is more valid – Dangerfield's in Source 11.1 or Clarke's in Source 11.2? Give reasons for your answer.
2 How accurate do you now judge the interpretations to be in Sources 11.5 and 11.7? Give reasons for your answer.
3 What evidence have you found to support or contradict the statements in Sources 11.6 and 11.8?

KEY POINTS FROM CHAPTER 11

What was the significance of the Liberal victory in the 1906 election?

1 The 1906 election was a massive defeat for the Conservatives.

2 The Liberals won a big majority in the Commons, and for the first time a large number of Labour MPs were elected.

3 The working class generally voted against the Conservatives who favoured protection, which many thought would lead to higher food prices.

4 Labour had a pact with the Liberal Party which helped them gain many seats.

Was care for the poor revolutionised by the Liberal reforms of 1906–14?

CHAPTER OVERVIEW

There had been laws about how to treat the poor from Tudor times – from whipping VAGABONDS to providing work and help for more deserving cases. By the early nineteenth century many experts thought the whole system was too generous and discouraged the poor from finding work. The 1834 Poor Law Amendment Act was planned to ensure that fit, poor people who required government help went into harsh workhouses. These were designed to look and feel like prisons so that people would find work rather than ask for help. This system never worked very well. It was much more leniently administered by 1900, but it still seemed unpopular, inhuman and inefficient.

Poor relief (help for the poor) was a matter for local authorities in the ministries of both Gladstone and Disraeli, but by 1900 it was becoming an issue for central government. The increase in working-class voters may be one explanation, but there was also a change in economic and political thinking. Politicians were not so confident that the FREE MARKET worked well on its own or that workers could always find jobs. State welfare measures might be needed to improve the community and make the nation more efficient. A Conservative government would probably have taken some action if it had still been in power after 1905, but it was the Liberal Party who were in power and introduced measures based on a New Liberalism. This chapter investigates how far they revolutionised care for the poor and moved towards a welfare state.

This chapter asks:

A What is poverty? (p. 187)

B How effective were different ways of dealing with poverty in the nineteenth century? (pp. 188–189)

C How did knowledge about poverty improve? (pp. 190–191)

D Why did reforms come in the early 1900s? (pp. 192–195)

E How effective were the Liberal reforms in 1906–14? (pp. 196–202)

F How far did the Liberals create a welfare state? (pp. 202–204)

VAGABONDS
Wandering people who normally begged from others.

FREE MARKET
People exchanging goods, and employers and workers making deals about employment, without the government getting involved.

DISCUSS

Look at these definitions of poverty.

A
The poor are those who do not have or cannot afford the food, clothing, shelter and fuel they need to be fit and healthy. This can be described as not having enough for **physical efficiency**

B
The poor are those who cannot afford things which most other people in the country regard it as normal to have and therefore feel **socially excluded**

C
The poor are those who earn less than half of the average income. This definition is based on **inequality**, not need

a) Which definition do you think is best and why?
b) Which definition would be the most difficult to apply and why?
c) Which definition do you think was normally applied around 1900?
d) Which definition do you think is most frequently applied today?

ACTIVITY

Study Chart 12A.

1 Which of the two sets of views on each issue do you agree with more?
2 Are all your positions on each issue on the same side? If not, why do you have views on different sides?
3 Which views might the following have agreed with in 1900:
   a) an unemployed man with a family
   b) a man with a good job in a factory
   c) the owner of a small business
   d) a teacher in a Church of England elementary school?

■ 12A Arguments about poverty

	MORE LEFT-WING VIEW	MORE RIGHT-WING VIEW
Why is there poverty?	Problems in the way a free market, CAPITALIST economy works lead to unavoidable unemployment and low wages	People do not try hard enough to find work, or spend too much, or do not plan for their futures
Who should help the poor and how?	• We should not allow poverty of any kind in our society • Governments should ensure a minimum wage and improve training opportunities • They should recognise a 'right to work' • There should be state benefits to ensure all have a minimum standard of living	• Individuals must be independent and free to help themselves • Incentives to work are vital, so working people must be better off than those on state benefits • People should provide for themselves through insurance schemes • Charities can help care for people and keep costs down
Should wealth be redistributed?	Governments should ensure a more equal distribution of the country's wealth so no one is poor	Governments should ensure a strong, efficient capitalist economy and a prosperous society
What are the problems in giving benefits?	Employers might support state benefits in order to avoid paying fair wages. Employees should demand the right to a job with a fair wage rather than benefits from the state	State benefits may cost too much, leading to high taxation and discouraging enterprise. Over-generous welfare benefits encourage people to become dependent on the state, taking wealth which could be used for economic investment

CAPITALIST
Referring to a system in which people who contribute or inherit capital (money for investment) control businesses and get profit from them.

TALKING POINT

Why is it likely that views on poverty in the twenty-first century will differ from views on poverty in 1900?

FOCUS ROUTE
1 How were each of the ways of dealing with poverty
   a) useful
   b) inadequate?
2 In what ways did help for the poor increase between 1850 and 1900?

B How effective were different ways of dealing with poverty in the nineteenth century?

■ 12B Dealing with poverty

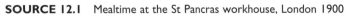

WAYS OF DEALING WITH POVERTY IN THE 19TH CENTURY

State action

The 1834 Poor Law

- Anyone who needed help, apart from medical care, was to go into a workhouse where conditions were to be worse than those for the lowest-paid outside labourer. The workhouses looked like prisons and were intended to deter people from asking for help. Those who received the help, called poor relief (paid for out of local taxes called poor rates), faced humiliating questions, lost the right to vote and were known as paupers.

- Although people were supposed to be refused help outside the workhouse, local records show most paupers still lived at home. It was far cheaper to help them there.

- Treatment for children, old people and the sick improved during the 1800s. Some Poor Law guardians set up hospitals and dispensaries, and the 1867 Metropolitan Poor Act provided for hospitals in London.

- During a trade slump in 1886 the President of the Board of Trade, Joseph Chamberlain, sent out a circular encouraging Poor Law Guardians (people elected by the ratepayers in a local area to fix poor rates there and organise help for the poor) and local councils to set up work schemes for the unemployed.

PROBLEMS RESULTING

Problems with state action

- The money for poor relief and many other local services came from rates (tax payments based on the value of land and houses, made to local authorities). Wealthier people complained about them, and they were a burden on many workers who were ratepayers.

- Each local area had to provide for its own poor, so the most deprived areas found it particularly difficult to raise enough money.

SOURCE 12.1 Mealtime at the St Pancras workhouse, London 1900

WAYS OF DEALING WITH POVERTY

Charities

- Many upper- and middle-class Victorian families thought charitable giving was an important duty. Charities provided more money than the state poor law system, possibly £8 million a year in London alone by the early 1900s – as much as the Poor Law guardians spent throughout England and Wales.

- The Charity Organisation Society founded in 1869 used early statistical information to try to ensure that charities did not duplicate their efforts and believed in helping the poor to help themselves.

- The Settlement Movement involved university graduates from well-off families going to live in poor town areas such as the East End of London, where they worked on educational and social projects.

PROBLEMS RESULTING

Problems with charities

- Help available from charities varied a lot between different places.

- The idealism and sense of duty among charity workers were frequently mixed with a sense of social and moral superiority. This could be irritating and humiliating for those they were attempting to help.

SOURCE 12.2 A drawing from about 1880 in Cassell's *History of England* showing a rich couple visiting a poor family in an East End slum

Insurance

- About 6–7 million people had some kind of medical insurance by the early 1900s. About 5½ million paid weekly subscriptions to friendly societies. These were societies run by their members who paid in weekly subscriptions to get benefits when they were ill and a payment to their families when they died. They were run by their members on a non-profit-making basis, and most men in the upper working class and lower middle class belonged to them.

- The societies normally provided a small payment (around 8–10 shillings a week) when members were sick, paid for doctors and would always provide money for a funeral. Millions more people belonged to burial societies, paying in pennies each week so that the money would be there when death came in the family.

- Friendly societies had many local branches, and large numbers of people collected weekly subscriptions (regular sums of money) for them. They sometimes had a social side and could give mutual support as well as cash.

Problems with insurance

- Many members had to drop out of friendly societies because they could not afford to keep up the payments, particularly if they were ill or lost their jobs.

- Societies had to compete to attract young men and found some difficulties in the early 1900s when they had to pay out sickness benefits to elderly members who were not working for long periods. This was more of a problem as people lived longer, and friendly societies had not calculated on paying out pensions to men who continued living for long after they were able to work.

Family support

- Stories from poor people themselves show the importance of families and neighbours helping each other. People sometimes stayed on in bad housing or lived far from their work because they were surrounded by neighbours who would help out in difficulties.

- Mothers often earned a little extra by working at home – sewing or taking in washing.

Problems with family support

- Relations and neighbours might be too poor to help, and there might be no part-time work for women.

WAS CARE FOR THE POOR REVOLUTIONISED BY THE LIBERAL REFORMS OF 1906–14?

ACTIVITY

When you have examined all the ways of dealing with poverty, work out why all of them together might still not provide adequate help for the poor.

FOCUS ROUTE

1 Summarise in notes what each of the investigations said about poverty.
2 Why might critics and historians have disputed the findings of each investigator?

CARICATURES
Exaggerated and unreal representations.

C How did knowledge about poverty improve?

Many nineteenth-century writers described poverty, but they were not just recording facts. They were propagandists trying to persuade people that more should be done about the poor. Others might therefore doubt how far their accounts were typical, whether they were exaggerated and how far the poor were to blame for their own problems. Some of the most vivid accounts were in novels such as Dickens' *David Copperfield*, *Oliver Twist* and *Bleak House*, but the people in novels might be seen as CARICATURES and the stories as over-dramatised.

Investigations into poverty

Several later nineteenth-century investigators worked in London's East End which had the most obvious concentration of poor and desperate people in the country.

Henry Mayhew

Mayhew was a journalist who wrote a four-volume work on *London Labour and the London Poor* (1861–62). His accounts had a big impact, but there were doubts about his methods.

- He concentrated on irregular workers such as coster-mongers (street-sellers) and on strange occupations such as rat-catchers, snake-swallowers, sewer-hunters and pure-finders (who shovelled up dog excrement used to purify leather).
- He may have selected these because they were colourful and picturesque, not because they were typical.
- He wrote up interviews with the poor, but nobody knows quite how far he led them on or added to their accounts.

Andrew Mearns

Mearns was a Nonconformist minister who wrote *The Bitter Cry of Outcast London*, 1883, reporting an investigation into East End slums and concluding that the people could do little to improve their position.

Charles Booth

Booth, a shipowner and businessman, produced a massive seventeen-volume *Inquiry into the Life and Labour of the People in London* (1889–1903). This suggested 30.7 per cent of London's population were below 'the line of poverty' and showed that this was mostly due to problems in finding work. Many questioned his methods and conclusions.

- He relied a lot on impressions from teachers, clergy, people working for school boards, and various officials, but these were not systematic, well organised or methodical.
- He and the people working for him decided whether people were in poverty by what they saw, not by using income figures.
- Consequently what he means by the poverty line is not clear and seems to have varied during the study.

Seebohm Rowntree

Rowntree, a chocolate manufacturer, improved greatly on Booth's methods when he did a survey of York, reported in *Poverty: a Study of Town Life* (1901). This city seemed more typical of the country as a whole than the East End of London. He calculated a **poverty line** (minimum income necessary to stay out of poverty) using scientific findings about the nutrition people needed and then working out the cost of the food they had to buy. He still had to make unscientific assumptions about what clothing, housing and heating they needed, but he was about as systematic as possible.

Those who did not have the minimum income for this were in **'primary poverty'** and could not afford bare 'physical efficiency'. An average family of two adults and three children needed 21s 8d a week to live on, assuming they bought the cheapest items and wasted nothing. He found that nearly ten per cent of York's population were in this primary poverty.

He distinguished between primary poverty and **secondary poverty** where people were poor partly because they could have spent their money better. Nearly 18 per cent of York's population were in secondary poverty, but he estimated this in a much less systematic way, judging by how the homes and children looked and what the neighbours said. Rowntree's estimate that almost 28 per cent of York's population were in some sort of poverty was striking but much less scientific than his calculations of primary poverty.

SOURCE 12.3 Rowntree's findings about families in primary poverty

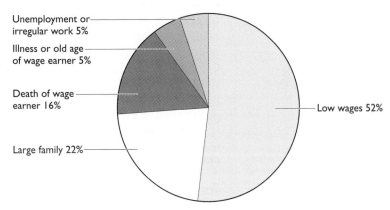

Unemployment or irregular work 5%
Illness or old age of wage earner 5%
Death of wage earner 16%
Large family 22%
Low wages 52%

From Source 12.3 Rowntree concluded that most of those in primary poverty did not seem to be there because of their own faults. He also showed how working families often went through a poverty cycle, as shown in Source 12.4.

SOURCE 12.4 Rowntree's poverty cycle

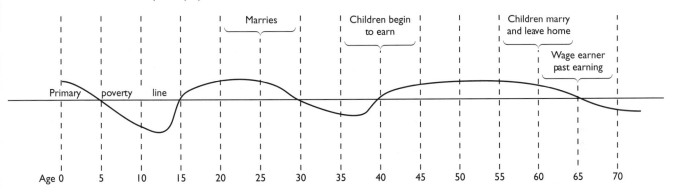

Marries

Children begin to earn

Children marry and leave home

Wage earner past earning

Primary poverty line

Age 0   5   10   15   20   25   30   35   40   45   50   55   60   65   70

ACTIVITY

According to Rowntree, when were families most likely to need help to avoid poverty?

Unemployment

Though workers talked of unemployment from the early nineteenth century, politicians and economists used the word only from the 1880s. It indicated a better understanding of the problems workers had in finding jobs. Chamberlain's circular in 1886 (see Chart 12B) was an early government response to the problem.

Economists discovered more about the issue, and Beveridge published *Unemployment: A Problem of Industry* in 1909. This described the types of unemployment, such as:

- cyclical unemployment, from slumps in the trade cycle
- seasonal unemployment, due to bad weather
- casual unemployment, when labourers were not given work on a regular basis.

People had often been aware of these, but there was now a more systematic economic explanation. It suggested not only that workers could be unemployed through no fault of their own but also that the state might help deal with the different problems in particular ways.

FOCUS ROUTE

Look at the five reasons for reform on pages 192–195.

1 Record and assess each of them using the following pattern.

```
┌─────────────────────────────────┐
│       Summary of reason         │
└─────────────────────────────────┘
              ↓
┌─────────────────────────────────┐
│ Evidence suggesting it was       │
│ important                        │
└─────────────────────────────────┘
              ↓
┌─────────────────────────────────┐
│ How far did it apply to the      │
│ Liberals alone or how far would  │
│ it influence other parties?      │
└─────────────────────────────────┘
```

2 Rate each of them according to how significant an influence you think it was on the Liberals:
   a) very significant
   b) significant
   c) not significant.
3 For each reason, explain your rating decision.

D Why did reforms come in the early 1900s?

The Conservatives introduced the **1905 Unemployed Workmen Act**, which provided for distress committees to deal with unemployment in large towns. They could use money from the rates for public works schemes but action was optional and left up to local authorities, and the Act was to last for only three years.

Also in 1905 the Conservatives set up a Royal Commission to investigate the Poor Law system. The majority of the Commission wanted more action by local council committees and charities but by the time it reported in 1909, the Liberal government was in power and had already introduced many of its own reforms. Had the Conservatives still been in government when the Royal Commission reported, they would probably have taken some action but it would have been different from the Liberal reforms. Most historians do not believe they would have done as much as the Liberals, who came into government in 1905.

To explain the scope and focus of the Liberal measures we must look at a much broader picture. Historians have suggested five main reasons why the Liberals began their welfare reforms.

Reason 1: Increased knowledge of poverty

The work of researchers showed the need for reform. Booth and Rowntree were both campaigning for more government action, and the new thinking about unemployment was important. Consequently there seem to have been some changes in attitudes towards poverty, though people drew very differing conclusions from first-hand knowledge.

SOURCE 12.5 A comment from Margaret Loane, a district nurse whose well-informed descriptions of poor families were published 1905–1911

To speak of a 'living wage' has always seemed to me an absurdity. It is not so much a question of what a man earns, as of what his wife can do with the money.

SOURCE 12.6 Rowntree's conclusion at the end of his study of poverty in York, 1901

[T]he labouring class receive upon the average 25 per cent less food than has been proved by scientific experts to be necessary for the maintenance of physical efficiency . . .

That in this land of abounding wealth, during a time of perhaps unexampled prosperity, probably more than one-fourth of the population are living in poverty, is a fact which may well cause great searchings of heart.

ACTIVITY

1 What does each of Sources 12.5 and 12.6 state about the reasons for poverty or extent of it?
2 How do Sources 12.5 and 12.6 differ in their attitude to poverty?

Reason 2: National efficiency

This was a kind of buzz phrase in the early 1900s. Britain had to be 'efficient' both to keep her empire and to cope with German and American industrial competition. It was partly a matter of education and administration, but it was about national physique as well. Some thought town living was leading to the decline of the British race. Others saw it more as a question of poor environment. Either way, healthy children, good food, public health and welfare measures were at the heart of national well-being and so at the top of the political agenda, not a dull administrative issue.

The empire needed a strong army, but around 40 per cent of the volunteers for the Boer War were rejected as unfit. It was poorer people, not the ones with good jobs, who generally wanted to be soldiers and similar proportions were unfit in French or German industrial towns, but this did not stop British patriots worrying. As one Liberal MP put it, 'empire cannot be built on RICKETY and flat-chested citizens'.

Industrialists relied on skilled or semi-skilled workers being fit to run their machines and contented enough to work hard. Some employers at least saw this as an argument for welfare reforms. From 1906 the Birmingham Chamber of Commerce pushed for a state health insurance scheme like the one already running in Germany. Right and left-wingers were both concerned with physical efficiency, but Liberals were also influenced by some new political philosophy.

Reason 3: New Liberalism

Liberalism had always been about freedom, but some Liberals were changing their views about what kind of freedom they wanted. T.H. Green, an Oxford philosopher and active member of the Liberal Party, developed the idea of 'positive' freedom before his death in 1882 (see Chart 12C). Green also emphasised the importance of community, and L.T. Hobhouse, another Liberal and influential journalist, carried this further as he developed the study of sociology. This thinking – New Liberalism – seemed increasingly relevant to Liberals around 1900 as they became more aware of what government could do and the need to attract working-class electors.

193

WAS CARE FOR THE POOR REVOLUTIONISED BY THE LIBERAL REFORMS OF 1906–14?

■ 12C T.H. Green's idea of 'positive' freedom

'NEGATIVE' FREEDOM
Traditional idea of freedom = safeguards against threats

Individual must be protected from outside interference so s/he can achieve happiness in her/his own way

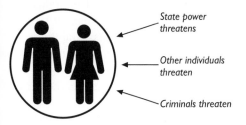

State power threatens

Other individuals threaten

Criminals threaten

'POSITIVE' FREEDOM = help for people to become free

Individual may need strengthening to achieve freedom and happiness

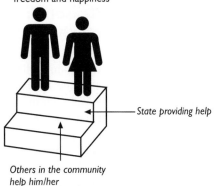

State providing help

Others in the community help him/her

■ **Learning trouble spot**

Individualism and collectivism
The New Liberal thinking was one feature of a change from what historians call individualism to collectivism in the late nineteenth century. Individualism means thinking of individuals, while collectivism puts emphasis on the community or society. It suggests a need for more government action. Whereas earlier in the century people thought every state action needed careful justification as some sort of necessary evil, by 1900 people thought more of a government's duty to improve life for the community.

How did this new approach influence government policy?
The ideas of positive liberty and community had an important influence on a minority of Liberal ministers. They do not seem to have won over the Liberal Party as a whole (see page 216), but they influenced people in power. T. H. Green taught the future prime minister Herbert Asquith at Oxford. Asquith's Chancellor of the Exchequer Lloyd George developed practical schemes to improve welfare. Winston Churchill followed New Liberal thinking most

194

WAS CARE FOR THE POOR REVOLUTIONISED BY THE LIBERAL REFORMS OF 1906–14?

clearly, and he was in a powerful position to influence policy from 1908 as President of the Board of Trade (dealing with the regulation of trade, industry and employment). Chart 12D shows how New Liberal ideas led to government policy with the linkages Churchill suggested. Many reforms were designed to ensure people had the minimum income necessary for a decent life.

■ 12D New Liberalism in practice

Positive liberty meant people needed more than freedom from restrictions. Churchill wrote: *Trade was free. But hunger and squalor and cold were also free and the people demanded something more than liberty.*	The state must help people who did not have adequate opportunities. Churchill wrote: *Mighty trades ... assert the necessity of a labour surplus ... in the streets and round the dock gates. Thousands of children grow up not nourished sufficiently to make them effective citizens.*	They needed a minimum standard of living, and the state must provide this. Churchill wrote: *We want to draw a line below which we will not allow persons to live and labour, yet above which they may compete with all the strength of their manhood.*	Money had to be found for the reforms. Richer members of the community must contribute more for the good of society as a whole.

Government actions

Labour Exchanges, 1909
School meals, 1906

Old Age Pensions, 1908
Trade Boards, 1909
National Insurance, 1911

Higher taxes on unearned incomes from 1907
People's Budget, 1909

ACTIVITY

1 How far was the New Liberal thinking similar to or different from socialism? (See pages 149–150.)
2 Compare the New Liberal thinking outlined here with the Labour Party's ideas for reform (see pages 160–161). What differences and similarities can you find?

Reason 4: Need to win working-class support and beat off challenges from the Labour Party

The argument about New Liberalism was based on political beliefs, but this was about political advantage for the Liberals. The Labour Party had 30 MPs after the 1906 election. The majority of voters were working class, and there was a widespread belief that they wanted social reform although this may have been a mistaken assumption (see box).

Did the working classes support reform?

In a famous article in the 1960s, Henry Pelling showed big problems with the argument that the working class would vote for a party promising social reform

a) Parties had not necessarily won elections because of their social reform programmes:
  • Chamberlain's 'Unauthorised Programme' does not appear to have been successful in the 1885 election (see page 92).
  • Social reform does not seem to have been important for Conservative success at the 1895 and 1900 elections (see pages 172–173).
  • It was a less important issue than free trade, Chinese slavery or church influence in education in the 1906 election.
b) The working class had bad experiences of social reform:
  • Housing reform generally meant slum clearance which destroyed their homes. Replacement housing might be too expensive to rent or heat.
  • Education reforms often included forcing children to go to school which stopped them earning.
  • The Poor Law was hated and may have discredited state action in general.
c) Workers often preferred their own self-help organisations such as friendly societies and were suspicious of state schemes (see page 198). These won support only when benefits were actually paid and people could see the advantages, as with old age pensions.

195

WAS CARE FOR THE POOR REVOLUTIONISED BY THE LIBERAL REFORMS OF 1906–14?

Nevertheless, there is still a case that the Liberals brought in reforms to beat off the Labour challenge:

a) The important issue is not so much what the workers actually wanted as what ministers thought they wanted. Lloyd George claimed that social reforms were one of the things the Liberals must offer if they were to keep support.

SOURCE 12.7 From a speech by Lloyd George in Cardiff, October 1906

But I have one word for Liberals. I can tell them what will make this ILP [Independent Labour Party] movement a great and sweeping force in this country – a force that will sweep away Liberalism amongst other things. If at the end of an average term of office it were found that a Liberal Parliament had done nothing to cope seriously with the social condition of the people, to remove the national degradation of slums and widespread poverty and destitution in a land glittering with wealth.

b) There was some Labour pressure for reform. For example, the TUC and some local trades councils pressed for old age pensions, and the Labour Party supported these.

c) The timing of the reforms at least fits in with the argument that they were intended to counter Labour. There were Labour and socialist by-election successes in 1907–09. Labour's campaign for the 'right to work' came to a climax in 1908, and the Liberals introduced reforms to deal with unemployment in 1909–11.

Reason 5: To keep one up on the Conservatives

The Liberals were probably more worried about the Conservatives getting into power than the threat from Labour. The Liberals wanted to deliver welfare reforms in case the Conservatives won the next general election and so got an opportunity to introduce their own schemes. They worried that the Conservatives would probably then use tariffs (taxes on imports) to finance reforms. The Liberals wanted to show that they could finance welfare reforms by keeping free trade and using progressive taxation.

TALKING POINT

Do you think the Liberals introduced reforms mostly because of what they believed was right or mostly for party political advantage?

■ **Learning trouble spot**

Progressive taxation
Progressive taxation is where taxes (e.g. on income) fall more heavily on the rich than the poor, so that the rich pay a greater proportion of their income. In 2006, for example, people pay no tax on the first part of their income, 10 per cent on the next, 22 per cent on the next and 40 per cent on each £ above a certain amount. This reduces the differences between the incomes of rich and poor.

E How effective were the Liberal reforms in 1906–14?

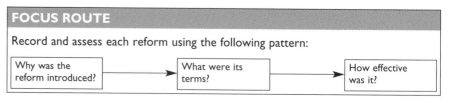

FOCUS ROUTE

Record and assess each reform using the following pattern:

| Why was the reform introduced? | → | What were its terms? | → | How effective was it? |

The first few significant measures helped **child welfare**. Why?

- Children's health and well-being were vital to national efficiency.
- After the Boer War government ministries set up an Inter-Departmental Committee on Physical Deterioration. In 1904 this recommended school meals and medical inspections.

1906 Introduction of School Meals

Why? The Liberal government supported a bill introduced by a Labour MP. This would both help poor families and improve overall national efficiency.

Effects of the Act It was PERMISSIVE. Local councils running schools could use money from the rates to provide meals, and they could give them free to poor children. For the first time their parents could receive benefits without being labelled as paupers and losing their right to vote.

By 1913, 40 per cent of the councils running schools provided meals and 310,000 children got them free. A new law in 1914 compelled councils to provide them.

1907 Medical Inspections for Children

Why? Sir Robert Morant, the Permanent Secretary at the Board of Education and an enthusiast for reform and national efficiency, put the clause requiring inspections into a complex education bill. The government and MPs seem to have taken little notice of it.

Effects of the Act Local councils had to make the inspections but did not have to do anything about what they found. Not all councils acted on the problems they discovered, but many did. Over two thirds were providing some kind of medical treatment by 1914.

1907 Education Act

The Liberals added little to the 1902 Education Act which had already reformed the administration of elementary schools and extended secondary education (see page 177).

The 1907 Act said secondary schools getting state money must take up to a quarter of their pupils from elementary schools rather than private schools if enough passed the scholarship exam at age 11. The numbers of working-class children in secondary schools gradually increased.

1908 Children's Act

Why? It was based on the belief that children had rights and needed state protection.

Effects of the Act It protected children against violence or neglect by their parents and gave councils a duty to check up on this.

A

HOW TO HELP THE YOUNG

PERMISSIVE LEGISLATION
Laws allowing local authorities to do things but not compelling them to act.

197

WAS CARE FOR THE POOR REVOLUTIONISED BY THE LIBERAL REFORMS OF 1906–14?

There was more reform from 1908. Asquith, as Chancellor of the Exchequer, introduced old age pensions. He became Prime Minister soon after and appointed David Lloyd George as Chancellor of the Exchequer and Winston Churchill as President of the Board of Trade.

1908 Old Age Pensions (first paid at the start of 1909)

Why?

Many people worried about having to ask for **poor relief** when they were old, with all the **humiliation** that involved. Forty per cent of those who lived to over 65 had to apply in the last year of their lives, and many more feared that they would have to do so.

Pensions were therefore a **big political issue**. Joseph Chamberlain campaigned for them in the 1890s. Charles Booth, who surveyed the poor of London's East End, founded the National Committee of Organised Labour for the Promotion of Old Age Pensions in 1898. The Labour Party and trade unions now gave them strong support.

The **friendly societies** had opposed pensions because they did not want competition, but they now had difficulties in paying benefits to aged members. In 1904 the National Conference of Friendly Societies voted for state pensions at 65 as long as they were not paid for by contributions which might discourage people from joining the societies.

There were examples of state pensions, paid out of taxation, in **other countries.** Denmark had introduced them in 1891 and New Zealand in 1898.

A pensions scheme had to be **financed by the government** if it were going to be popular. Workers would be unwilling to pay for pensions as they might not even live long enough to get them. Younger men would also be unwilling to contribute if old people received pensions having made no contributions.

Terms of the Act

- Pensions were financed by the government from taxation and went only to people **over 70**.
- They were **5 shillings** a week for each person.
- They went only to the poor. The full pension went to people with under £21 a year (about 8 shillings a week). A lesser amount, which was reduced on a sliding scale according to their income, went to those with between £21 and £31 a year (12 shillings a week).
- The pension was not to go to anyone 'who habitually (normally) failed to work according to his ability, opportunity and need'.

Effects

- The pension was generally paid to people who would otherwise have received poor relief. About 600,000 people, or **45 per cent of those over 70**, got it – a similar proportion to those claiming poor relief before the Act.
- Most old people in workhouses were there because they needed looking after for health reasons. The number of men and women over 70 who got poor relief outside fell from 132,000 to just over 8,000 by 1911.
- The big difference was that old people got the pension **as a right** with no questions asked and no stigma attached.
- The provision about pensioners having worked stopped people getting anything if they had been well-known drunks, been in prison or recently got poor relief, but it was hard to carry out and was abandoned in 1919.
- The 5 shilling sum was small – 2 shillings less than Rowntree thought necessary to support an individual living alone.
- It was enormously **popular** (see Source 12.8).
- But it was expensive and led to **tax increases in the 1909 Budget** (see page 209).

SOURCE 12.8 Pensions were paid at post offices. In *Lark Rise to Candleford*, 1945, Flora Thompson recorded the effect they had on pensioners at the village post office where she worked as a girl

In the 1880s some poorer couples just about held on to their homes but lived in daily fear of the workhouse. The Poor Law authorities allowed people too old to work a small weekly sum – 'outdoor relief'. But it was not enough to live on. Unless they had children to support them, there came a time when the home had to be broken up. When, 20 years later, Old Age Pensions began, life was transformed for these aged cottagers. They were relieved of anxiety. They were suddenly rich. Independent for life! At first, when they went to the post office to draw it, tears of gratitude would run down the cheeks of some, and they would say as they picked up their money, 'God bless that Lord George!' [Lloyd George, the Chancellor of the Exchequer] (for they could not believe that one so powerful and munificent [generous] could be a plain 'Mr') and 'God bless you, miss!' and there were flowers from their gardens and apples from their trees for the girl who merely handed them the money.

The debate about old age pensions

SOURCE 12.9 A friendly society magazine, the *Foresters' Miscellany*, argues against pensions

The establishment of a great scheme of state pensions would legalize and stamp as a permanent feature of our social life the chronic poverty of the age. The desire of the best reformers is to remove the conditions that make that poverty, so that every citizen shall have a fair chance not only of earning a decent wage for today but such a wage as shall enable him to provide for the future ... Man is a responsible being. To rob him of his responsibility is to degrade him.

SOURCE 12.10 A workers' newspaper, the *Cotton Factory Times*, indicated the danger of state benefits in 1890

When people look to the state and receive from it almost everything they get, they will become the strongest supporters of those from whom they obtain their privileges. But they may rest assured that they who pull the wires will take care that in exchange for this the puppet shall not dance to a tune of its own calling. The grip of the state will be gradually tightened until it will be almost impossible for a man to speak except in regulation tones.

SOURCE 12.11 *The Times* condemned the government's old age pension scheme in 1908

By their adoption of the non-contributory basis, the Government are undoubtedly defying the experience of many human generations in which the maxim has held good that free DOLES *undermine the character, while* THRIFT *and* PROVIDENCE *sustain it.*

DOLES
Portions given by charity.

THRIFT
Managing money carefully and not spending much.

PROVIDENCE
Preparing for the future.

SOURCE 12.12 George Cadbury, the chocolate manufacturer, who campaigned for pensions, argued in favour in 1899

I have long felt that as a Christian nation we ought to make some effort to add to the comfort of the aged toilers of our country, of whom it is computed one-third end their days as paupers; whereas if they had a pension by right they would no more be considered paupers than the generals, admirals, judges and ex-ministers of the Crown who draw their pensions. From the intimate connection we have had with working people for many years we knew that the workhouse was looked forward to with great dread by them ...

I think old age pensions would promote thrift. It is now hopeless for a man earning 20s to 25s per week, if he does his duty to his family, to provide for the future, whereas if he was sure of 7s per week there would be an inducement to add a trifle to it, either by joining a Friendly Society, by insurance or by savings.

ACTIVITY

1 What does Source 12.8 show about
   a) how pensions helped old people
   b) how pensions might help the government's popularity?
2 What dangers do Sources 12.9 and 12.10 suggest state pensions involved for workers?
3 a) What criticism does Source 12.11 make of the government scheme?
   b) How far does it appear to agree with the arguments in Sources 12.9 and 12.10?
4 How does Source 12.12 refute the arguments in Sources 12.9–12.11?
5 Write 2–4 paragraphs of argument on how far state pensions increased or decreased workers' dignity, using the evidence in Sources 12.8–12.12 and the sections on the terms and effects of the Act.

Two of the more important early measures were:

• **1906 Trade Disputes Act** – gave trade unions extensive rights and was introduced by a Labour MP (see page 146)
• **1908 Miners' Eight Hours Act** – limited the coal miners' working day to eight hours.

The Labour Party campaigned strongly for these, but the next reforms, setting up labour exchanges and trade boards, were introduced by Winston Churchill as President of the Board of Trade in 1909. They developed out of the work of the Board of Trade's labour department and Churchill's New Liberal thinking (see the quotes in Chart 12D, page 194).

A national system of labour exchanges, 1909

Why? Labour exchanges were an efficient way for employers to find labour and workers to find jobs. Local labour exchanges were established under the 1905 Unemployed Workmen's Act but could display only local vacancies. A national system would be better. The economist Beveridge suggested this in 1907 after seeing how labour exchanges worked in Germany. He joined the Board of Trade in 1908 and introduced the system in 1909–10.

Effects of the Act A national system was set up in 1910 and over 2 million workers a year registered at labour exchanges by 1914. Overall, only a quarter of those registered in 1910–14 found jobs, but the record of the exchanges improved. They filled 900 jobs a day at the start in 1910 but over 3000 a day by 1914.

The exchanges had differing significance for the people using them. Churchill thought they helped the dignity of labour as workers no longer had to go round to different employers. Trade unions suspected they would help employers break strikes and they were used to acquire workers in a rail strike in 1913. Civil servants thought they would help collect statistics and prepare for introducing unemployment insurance which came in the 1911 National Insurance Act.

SOURCE 12.13 Building labourers waiting for hire in London in 1900

SOURCE 12.14 A labour exchange at Camberwell Green, London in 1910

ACTIVITY

How well does a comparison of Sources 12.13 and 12.14 support Churchill's argument that labour exchanges helped labourers' dignity?

1909 Trade Boards Act

Why? It was intended to raise wages in so-called 'sweated' industries – named after the low pay and poor conditions, not the sweat and body odours they involved. The Women's Trade Union League and National Anti-Sweating League had been agitating for this. It fitted in with the New Liberal idea of ensuring a minimum wage and living standard, and the boards were similar to ones in Australia.

Effects of the Act Wages were fixed by boards consisting of worker and employer representatives together with civil servants. At first the Act covered four trades – tailoring, lace-making, box-making and chain-making – with nearly 200,000 workers, including many women. By including other trades it was extended to about 500,000 out of a workforce of around 18 million men, women and young people by 1914.

The state now helped enforce minimum wages for the first time since the early nineteenth century, but the wages varied between regions. The boards allowed for local conditions and the employers' need to sell their goods at a competitive price. They made practical compromises which the state backed up, but there were not enough inspectors to enforce their decisions fully.

The government did want to extend minimum wage arrangements. The 1912 Mines Act introduced them in coal mines as a way of settling a strike, and the government was about to introduce them for agricultural labourers when war came in 1914.

1911 National Insurance Act

Pensions were paid out of taxes, but the 1911 scheme was financed by workers' own insurance payments together with contributions from employers and a government subsidy taken from taxes. Why did Lloyd George, who introduced the Act, do it this way?

- The pensions had cost more than expected, leading to the controversial 1909 Budget (see page 209). Many voters already thought taxes were too high, and the government had to keep spending down.

- Insurance payments were in line with Liberal ideas on individual self-help. Adding a government subsidy combined individual and community action in a very New Liberal way.

The Act introduced two separate schemes for health and unemployment insurance.

Health insurance

Why? The main aim was to prevent hardship in a worker's family if he fell ill. Some workers already belonged to friendly societies.

Friendly societies and insurance companies would have opposed any state scheme which simply replaced their own. Since they had millions of loyal members and policy holders, Lloyd George had to work with them, but they did not yet cover the whole community. Poorer workers could not afford to pay into friendly societies, and many had not kept up their payments. Lloyd George now claimed to cover all workers.

The scheme was developed from the friendly society schemes combined with features from a German system of state insurance against sickness, accident and old age. Lloyd George visited Germany in 1908 to learn from their example, but the British scheme was very different. Workers all made the same payments and got the same benefits, whereas German employees paid and received differing amounts.

Lloyd George never claimed his scheme was a complete solution; it was the best he could achieve for the time being, and he called it his 'ambulance wagon'.

◼ 12E Features and criticisms of the health insurance scheme

TERMS

- Compulsory for all workers aged 16–70 earning below £160 a year (about £3 a week). This included most wage-earning workers.
- Workers could insure through friendly societies, trade unions and commercial insurance companies or buy insurance stamps at the post office.
- The payments and benefits for the basic scheme were laid down by the government, but societies and companies could offer extras including cover for widows and orphans.
- **Payments** each week:
  Worker paid 4d
  Employer paid 3d
  Government paid 2d.

CRITICISMS

- Workers could choose their own insurance company or society and what extras they wanted, but they had no choice over the terms of the basic scheme.
- Everyone started paying in July 1912, but the benefits began in January 1913.

BENEFITS

- 10s a week for insured workmen (7s 6d for women) for first thirteen weeks of illness and 5s for next thirteen weeks.
- Treatment from GP (family doctor) for the insured worker if he were ill.
- Maternity benefit for his wife if she had children.
- Treatment in sanatoria if worker had tuberculosis.
- Long-term benefit of 5s a week if disabled.

CRITICISMS

- By 1914 Rowntree calculated an average family needed 24s a week to maintain physical efficiency.
- There was no medical treatment for wives and children if they fell ill. Only about ten per cent of married women were included in the scheme as they were employed workers.
- General hospital treatment, eye and dental treatment were not covered. No attempt was made to organise the various poor law and voluntary hospitals in any system.

TUBERCULOSIS (TB)

A serious infectious disease, particularly affecting the lungs. It was widespread before the First World War and often fatal, so there were large sanatoria to deal with patients who had the illness

ACTIVITY

Individually or with a partner write or role play an argument between two workmen who support and oppose the health insurance scheme. Remember to discuss the payments and government subsidy, how workers were compelled to join and the extent of benefits.

202

WAS CARE FOR THE POOR REVOLUTIONISED BY THE LIBERAL REFORMS OF 1906–14?

Unemployment insurance

Why? The main aim was to provide money if a worker became temporarily unemployed. The Labour Party and some Radical Liberals pressed for action on this. Better understanding of economics suggested more might be done about different types of unemployment, and some continental countries had unemployment schemes.

Effects of the scheme It covered about 2½ million workers (just under a quarter of the total male workforce) in seven industries where there was a lot of cyclical and seasonal unemployment, such as shipbuilding, engineering and building. Chart 12F summarises the terms.

■ 12F The unemployment insurance scheme

PAYMENTS
each week
- Worker paid 2½d
- Employer paid 2½d
- Government paid 1⅔d.

BENEFITS
- 7s a week for first fifteen weeks of unemployment
- Not paid if workers
  - dismissed for misconduct
  - left jobs 'without just cause'
  - turned down work at a 'fair wage'
  - unemployed because of strikes.

The benefit was not only much less than needed to keep a family but also less than workers normally got from Poor Law authorities or from some trade union schemes.

But significantly unemployment was now accepted as an unavoidable hazard. The government and employers subsidised insurance for many workers in better paid jobs.

F How far did the Liberals create a welfare state?

Many think the Liberal reforms created the foundations for what we now call the welfare state. In December 1942 the *Daily Mirror* referred on its front page to plans for a future welfare state which would be a 'cradle to grave' plan. To what extent did the Liberals create such a welfare state?

Before answering this question we need to define the term 'welfare state'. It is generally taken to mean the government looking after people throughout their lives, that is, 'from the cradle to the grave'. The government must therefore ensure or provide:

- **benefit payments** or other arrangements to help people poor because of unemployment, large families, sickness or old age
- basic services necessary for people's 'physical efficiency', including decent **housing** and **health care**.

To work well it needs:

- education to help children provide for themselves
- a low level of unemployment so that there are enough people earning to provide for others.

Did the Liberal government of 1906–11 successfully lay the foundations of a **modern welfare state**?
Use the following questions to examine this issue. Some points are given to help you.

Universality
1 How far were benefits and services given as a right and did they cover everybody?
   Also think about how they were paid for, as some see financing benefits from progressive taxation (see page 209) as a key characteristic of a welfare state.

Adequacy
2 What level of help was provided?
   Some historians have distinguished between a welfare state providing optimum (the best possible) services and a social service state which provides a minimum.

Central control
3 How far did central government provide uniform benefits and services?
   Whereas nineteenth-century governments generally used local boards and councils for social reform only three out of twelve Liberal reforms – the ones to improve child welfare – were carried out through local authorities.

Modern comparisons
4 How far did reforms create the sort of welfare state established after the Second World War?
   During the Second World War the government asked for a report on how to improve welfare. This was the Beveridge Report published in 1942. As the *Daily Mirror* put it, Beveridge's scheme would look after citizens 'from the cradle to the grave'. His vision became reality in a series of reforms in 1945–48, including family allowances and a National Health Service together with National Insurance arrangements developed from the 1911 scheme.

Responsibility
5 How far should the Liberals take the credit for the reforms they introduced?
   How far were Liberal ministers responsible for reforms and how far did these come because of Labour MPs, civil servants or outside campaigners?

ACTIVITY

Refer back to the activities on definitions and arguments about poverty at the start of this chapter on page 187 when answering these questions.

1 a) Refer to the information on the introduction of school meals on page 196. The children in Source 12.16 were apparently waiting for a dinner provided by some charitable organisation, not a school dinner. How could Source 12.16 be used to criticise the impact of Liberal reforms by 1912?
  b) What other reforms could the Liberals have introduced to help children like the ones in Source 12.16?
2 a) What do Sources 12.15–12.17 suggest about the distribution of wealth in 1911–12?
  b) How effective do they suggest the Liberal government had been in reducing poverty by 1912, using the definitions on page 187?
3 What are the usefulness and limitations of Sources 12.15–12.17 in any study of the impact of Liberal reforms?

SOURCE 12.15   Street scene in the East End of London, 1911

204

WAS CARE FOR THE POOR REVOLUTIONISED BY THE LIBERAL REFORMS OF 1906–14?

SOURCE 12.16 Children waiting for a free dinner in Salmon's Lane, London, 1912

SOURCE 12.17 Ladies shopping in the West End of London, 1912

KEY POINTS FROM CHAPTER 12   Was care for the poor revolutionised by the Liberal reforms of 1906–14?

1   The three main ways of dealing with poverty in the late nineteenth century were:
    a) state action through the Poor Law system
    b) charities
    c) insurance through friendly societies.

2   More knowledge about poverty showed how inadequate these were.

3   Reform came in the early 1900s because of increased knowledge linked with worries about national efficiency, a new approach among some Liberal ministers known as New Liberalism and the Liberals' concern about a challenge from the Labour Party.

4   The Liberal government's welfare reforms included old age pensions and national insurance together with attempts to tackle child poverty, low wages and unemployment.

Was the Liberal Party dying by the First World War?

CHAPTER OVERVIEW

A Liberal ministry led by Herbert Asquith was in power from 1908 to 1915, but this was the last ever Liberal government. Labour was linked with the Liberals in a pact made in 1903 which was used at the 1906 and 1910 general elections, but Labour was then much the weaker partner. At the start of the First World War Labour had 38 MPs against over 260 Liberals. Soon after the War the position was roughly reversed. Labour became the second largest party in 1922 and formed its first government in 1924. By then it was clearly the main left-wing opposition to the Conservatives. At the end of 1924 the Liberals had just 40 MPs. Can such a big change be explained by developments in 1914–24 or were there signs that the Liberal Party was dying by 1914? In 1935 the historian George Dangerfield argued that there were already clear signs of death before the First World War. He entitled his book about the Liberal government's problems in 1910–14 *The Strange Death of Liberal England*. Later historians have heaped criticisms on Dangerfield's work but the phrase about 'strange death' remains in frequent use. Was it already inevitable that in 1914 Labour would break its pact and replace the Liberals as the main left-wing party?

This chapter asks:

A Why do historians argue about Liberal decline? (pp. 206–207)

B Did Lloyd George's 'People's Budget' in 1909 strengthen the Liberals? (pp. 208–211)

C Did their struggle with the House of Lords strengthen the Liberals? (pp. 211–214)

D Did the Liberals achieve much or offer attractive policies from 1911? (pp. 214–215)

E How strong were the Liberals in comparison with the Labour Party in 1910–14? (pp. 216–217)

F Could the Liberal government cope? (p. 218)

G Review: Was the Liberal Party dying by the First World War? (pp. 219–220)

■ 13A Liberal governments 1905–15

1905–08
Campbell-Bannerman's ministry

1908–15
Asquith's ministry

1906 Liberals win overall majority in general election

1908 Old age pensions

1909 People's Budget. Struggle with House of Lords follows

1910 General elections in January and December. Liberals continue in government, but without overall majority in the House of Commons

1911 Parliament Act passed

1914 First World War

Edward VII
1901–10

George V
1910–

FOCUS ROUTE

Summarise the main arguments about the Liberal decline put forward by historians.

 # Why do historians argue about Liberal decline?

Some historians think the decline of the Liberal Party was inevitable.

- Similar Liberal parties in **other European countries** were replaced by more left-wing or socialist parties.
- The growth of **working-class consciousness** meant that workers wanted their own party, not one led by employers or middle-class professional people.
- The Liberal Party was **distinctively nineteenth century** in its thinking. Its belief in **free trade** could not be maintained indefinitely when other states used **tariffs** and trade restrictions. Its work in balancing the interests of different classes and giving people more freedom was completed. The working class no longer needed it.

Other historians say the decline was not inevitable. Since the 1960s a long-standing argument has developed on Liberal decline and shows no signs of ending. Why?

Modern political beliefs

Many socialists and committed Labour supporters believe that workers need a Labour Party to defend their interests and that a Liberal Party just could not do this. Others think the Labour Party should have kept the alliance it had with the Liberals before the First World War and see the split between them as a big mistake. The Labour prime minister Tony Blair once said in an interview that he had 'never given up on' the goal of mending the Liberal–Labour split.

'What if?' questions

Historians rarely accept that anything in history was inevitable, and they argue about what might have been.

- Could the Liberals have maintained their strength if the First World War had not created difficulties for them?
- Without the war the next general election would have been in 1915: would the Liberals have kept their pact with Labour and would they have won?
- Giving the vote to some women and almost all adult men roughly trebled the electorate in 1918. Afterwards there was a long-term Liberal decline and Labour growth, but this was partly because of Liberal splits and trade union growth during and after the War. However, what would have happened if the vote had not been extended to so many more people in 1918 or if it had been done before the war?

Since final answers to 'what if?' questions are virtually impossible, historians work out probabilities and keep arguing.

Interpreting election figures

Historians select those statistics that seem to support their arguments. On the one hand, the Liberals appeared strong at parliamentary elections, whether general elections or by-elections (when the voters choose a single MP), and Labour generally lost in any contests with Liberals. On the other hand, Labour made considerable gains in local council elections and kept increasing their number of councillors. There is almost endless scope for arguing over, or, as historians put it, reinterpreting, the statistics.

■ 13B Liberal Party: dead or alive?

The Liberal Party died in 1910–14

George Dangerfield put the argument vividly in a famous book, *The Strange Death of Liberal England*, 1935

[In 1910–14] that highly moral, that generous, that dyspeptic [indigestible], that utterly indefinable organism known as the Liberal Party died the death. It died from poison administered by its Conservative foes, and from disillusion over the inefficacy [ineffectiveness] of the word 'Reform'. And the last breath which fluttered in this historical flesh was extinguished by War.

The phrasing is typical of Dangerfield's dramatic, extravagant style of writing. His book is largely a story of events in 1910–14, arguing that the Liberals could not handle the agitation by trade unions, suffragettes and different groups in Ireland. They did not understand the forces behind these movements and were doomed to be replaced by the more left-wing and up-to-date Labour Party.

A healthy Liberal Party was knocked out by the First World War

The first important rejection of Dangerfield's view came from Trevor Wilson in *The Downfall of the Liberal Party, 1914–35*, 1966

[The problems from the trade unions, suffragettes and Irish groups were] an accidental convergence of unrelated events.

The Liberal party can be compared to an individual who, after a period of robust health and great exertion, experienced symptoms of illness (Ireland, Labour unrest, the suffragettes). Before a thorough diagnosis could be made he was involved in an encounter with a rampant omnibus (the First World War), which mounted the pavement and ran him over. After lingering painfully, he expired.

■ 13C How historians have developed the argument

Ross McKibbin in *The Evolution of the Labour Party, 1910–1924*, 1974

The **trade union movement** gave Labour increasing support, and its growth ensured the rise of the Labour Party, especially in many mining areas where it made rapid progress up to 1914. The Liberal–Labour alliance was breaking down.

[There was a] growing feeling in the country that the Liberal Party was no longer the party of the working classes, but that in some indefinable way the Labour Party was.

Peter Clarke in *Lancashire and the New Liberalism*, 1971

Lancashire election campaigns and results showed the **Liberals** winning mass support in 1906 and 1910 with progressive policies which included welfare reforms. They gained **mass support from the working class** and it was in working-class industrial areas that they were most successful in holding on to their gains in 1910. The Liberal–Labour alliance was working well for the Liberals.

By 1910 the change to class politics was substantially complete. That from Liberalism to Labour had not really begun.

G.L. Bernstein in *Liberalism and Liberal Politics in Edwardian England*, 1986

Local **Liberal parties** were **very middle class**. They generally accepted welfare reforms, but were most enthusiastic about traditional Liberal causes, especially Nonconformist ones. Liberal organisation was running down, and it would be difficult for them to win a general election in 1915.
Neither Liberal nor Labour members were very keen on the Liberal–Labour Pact.

[The Liberal Party] was not in a strong position to retain the support of the working class electorate in a political world which was moving towards class politics.

Duncan Tanner in *Political Change and the Labour Party 1900–1918*, 1990

Extensive investigations in different regions showed that the **Liberal Party was generally strong and frequently kept working-class support**. There was generally enough agreement between the Liberal and Labour parties to keep their pact going.

[Labour was making headway but] the overall position in 1914 was not much different from that in 1910. Labour had not created a solid class vote ... It had not even the uniform support of trade unionists.

The Liberals looked far stronger and had attractive 'New Liberal' policies, though the leaders who pushed these forward needed to develop their organisation more to support their new ideas.

Keith Laybourn in *Liberalism and the Rise of Labour 1890–1918*, 1984, and a summary of the debate in *History*, 1995

Research in **West Yorkshire** shows a **growing Labour Party well able to challenge the Liberals**.

[Overall] the balance of evidence [suggests the working class switching support from the Liberals to the Labour Party] before 1914 and via the trade union movement.

B Did Lloyd George's 'People's Budget' in 1909 strengthen the Liberals?

FOCUS ROUTE

Sections B–D examine how far the Liberals succeeded in government in 1906–15 and the problems they faced. Their welfare reforms in 1906–14 have already been examined in Chapter 12, and the following sections begin from the 1909 Budget which helped pay for some of the reforms.

Make a large copy of the table below on A3 paper. Use sections B–D of this chapter, and Chapter 12, to record the Liberals' successes and failures.

	Liberal successes		Liberal failures	
	What the Liberals did achieve	**Policies which would appeal to the working class**	**Plans the Liberals did not achieve**	**Problems the Liberals could not tackle adequately or which developed from their reforms**
Summary on welfare reforms 1906–11				
1909 Budget				
Struggle with the House of Lords				
Reforms in 1911–14				
1914 Budget				

When Asquith took over as prime minister in 1908, Lloyd George was appointed Chancellor of the Exchequer. The Chancellor's most important job, then as now, is to present a Budget for the following year, announcing what the government will spend and how it will raise the money.

The 1909 Budget was a particularly demanding one. The left-hand column in Chart 13D shows Lloyd George's problems. Note that these problems were not just about where to find the money. They were also about ensuring support. He needed to keep people voting Liberal and his budget had to go through the House of Lords. The Lords had turned down some government bills in the past. It was generally believed that the Lords had to accept whatever was in the government's Budget but how far could Lloyd George go? The right-hand column of Chart 13D shows what Lloyd George actually proposed.

ACTIVITY

How far did different changes in the Budget do what Lloyd George needed?

1 Draw a sketch of Chart 13D, including only the phrases in bold. Using different colours, draw lines from the problems listed on the left to the tax changes listed on the right which would help solve these problems.
2 Which parts of the Budget would
   a) help win working-class support
   b) appeal to Liberal Party workers?
3 How far would you be pleased or displeased with the Budget if you were a lower-middle-class man earning under £500 a year?
4 What would you say about the Budget if you were a spokesperson for the Labour Party?
5 What complaints would you make about it if you were a working man?

PROBLEMS

A The government must find an extra £10 million in 1909–10 The Cabinet has already agreed to build eight extra **Dreadnoughts** (modern warships).
Old age pensions are expensive. Asquith, the last Chancellor, estimated 572,000 would get the pension; now it seems about 668,000 are collecting it. Pensions are costing £2½ million more than he budgeted for.

B A **trade depression** developed in 1908, meaning more unemployment and less taxes being paid. This looks like reducing government income by £6 million.

C You have ambitious plans for National Insurance to help people when they are ill or unemployed and will need more cash.

D The **Conservatives** say it is impossible to have expensive welfare reforms without **protection**, so that taxes on imports bring in more money. You must prove them wrong – Liberals are committed to free trade.

E Many left-wing Liberals and the Labour Party, which is allied to you, want **taxes on land**. In November (1908) 241 Liberal and Labour MPs signed a petition calling for land values to be taxed in the next Budget.

F The **House of Lords** has masses of wealthy landowners. You must find a way round their opposition.

G Your **Nonconformist supporters** want something done to **restrict or** at least **tax the sale of alcohol.** The Lords has blocked this by turning down a licensing bill in the past.

H Local Liberal parties and a lot of your voters are middle-class small business and professional people, but you must keep large **working-class support**.

I You must not tax the **middle class** too much if you want to keep their votes.

J **Public support is falling**. By-elections in 1908 have gone badly, with a 10% swing against the Liberals, seven seats lost and some Labour gains which show a left-wing threat.

K Plenty of people reckon you will fail. Civil servants are chattering about how you do not do the paperwork. **Show them.**

SOLUTIONS

1 Raise income tax on the rich
- Paid by only about 1 million wealthier people on incomes over £160 a year (roughly 8 million families do not pay it) Kept at 9d (nearly 4%) for each £ earned on incomes £160–£2000.
  Increased for very high incomes to 1s (5%) for each £ on £2000–£3000 and 1s 2d (about 6%) for each £ over £3000.
- Supertax on incomes over £5000 (only 10,000–12,000 of such people).
- Tax of 1s 2d per £ to be paid on all unearned income (such as profits, rents or interest payments) over £700.

2 Reduce income tax for people with children
- People with incomes under £500 not to be taxed on £10 for each child under 16.
- Changes in tax rates for the less wealthy to reduce what people earning under £2000 a year pay overall.

3 Increase estate duty and other death duties (Taxes paid from amounts left by wealthy people when they die)
- Estate Duty (to be increased most sharply) to be paid at the death of about 80,000 of the country's wealthiest people.

4 Start a land valuation
This will be used to collect land taxes:
- Owners selling land to pay 20% of any extra they get for the land above what they paid for it.
- Each year they are to pay ½d for every £ the land is worth if they have not developed it.

5 Increase taxes on alcohol and tobacco
- Taxes on spirits to go up by around 33% and on tobacco by about 25%.

6 Increase the cost of pub landlords' licences
- To take about 50% of landlords' expected profits from selling drink each year.

How fair was the Budget to different classes?

1 Before the Liberals came into power in 1905 about half of government income came from **direct** (e.g. income) taxes which normally fall more on the wealthy. The other half came from **indirect** taxes on goods and services. These generally fall more equally on rich and poor, depending on the items taxed. In 1909–14 the proportion gained from direct taxes went up to over 60 per cent.

2 Under the 1909 Budget the **indirect taxes on alcohol and tobacco** brought in a larger proportion of the government's total income than in any Budget since 1900. Large numbers of working men saw beer and tobacco as necessities of life.

3 Asquith had introduced different tax rates for **earned and unearned income** when he was Chancellor in 1907, but Lloyd George made the difference much greater.

4 The growth of towns had created more demand for land, which pushed up land prices without the owners doing anything. As the community's growth made the land more valuable, should the community not get proceeds in tax? In practice the taxes could not be collected until a land valuation was made. This should have been completed in 1915 but was called off after war broke out. By 1920 land taxes had brought the government about £½ million, but the costs of valuing land and getting this were about £2 million, and the taxes were then scrapped.

Was Lloyd George trying to start a class war?

Lloyd George said his Budget was designed to help the People. It became known as 'The People's Buget'. But the House of Lords opposed and rejected it. Lloyd George responded with famous speeches at Limehouse in east London and Newcastle.

TALKING POINT

The top rates of income tax introduced by the 1909 Budget were 6 per cent and, with supertax, 8.5 per cent on very large incomes. In 2006 the top rate is 40 per cent and the standard rate 22 per cent.

Just before the First World War government spent about 10–12 per cent of national income. In the twenty-first century it spends about 40 per cent.

Does this mean the opposition to the 1909 Budget was unreasonable? How can we explain it?

ROYALTIES
Payments to landowners for coal or other minerals taken from their land.

SOURCE 13.1 A cartoon from the middle-class humorous magazine *Punch*, April 1909

RICH FARE.

THE GIANT LLOYD-GORGIBUSTER: "FEE, FI, FO, FAT,
I SMELL THE BLOOD OF A PLUTOCRAT:
BE HE ALIVE OR BE HE DEAD,
I'LL GRIND HIS BONES TO MAKE MY BREAD."

SOURCE 13.2 Part of Lloyd George's speech at Limehouse in 1909 was about wealthy landowners who gained income as ROYALTIES from coal mines

Have you been down a coal mine? I went down one the other day ...

You could see the pit-props bent and twisted and sundered, their fibres split in resisting the pressure. Sometimes they give way, and there is mutilation and death. Often a spark ignites, the whole pit is deluged in fire, and the breath of life is scorched out of hundreds of breasts by the consuming flame ... yet when the Prime Minister and I knock at the doors of these great landlords, and say to them: 'Here, you know these poor fellows who have been digging up royalties at the risk of their lives, some of them are old, they have survived the perils of their trade, they are broken, they can earn no more. Won't you give something towards keeping them out of the workhouse?' they scowl at us. We say 'Only a halfpenny, just a copper.' They retort 'You thieves!'

SOURCE 13.3   At Newcastle, in 1909, Lloyd George gave vivid descriptions of the peers

The question will be asked whether five hundred men, ordinary men chosen accidentally from among the unemployed, should override the judgement – the deliberate judgement – of millions of people who are engaged in the industry which makes the wealth of this country.

That is one question. Another will be: Who ordained that a few should have the land of Britain as a perquisite [extra reward]? Who made ten thousand people owners of the soil, and the rest of us trespassers in the land of our birth?

ACTIVITY

1 How and why are Lloyd George's speeches effective in responding to the Lords' rejection of the Budget?
2 What could he hope to gain from them?
3 Look at Source 13.1. Do you think Lloyd George would have been pleased or displeased with this view of him?
4 How far would Sources 13.2 and 13.3 stimulate class hatred against the rich?
5 What arguments could be made for and against what Lloyd George was doing? How justifiable do you think it was?

FOCUS ROUTE

Use the information in this section to continue filling in the table you began on page 208.

DENOMINATIONAL
Belonging to one religious group or organisation.

TALKING POINT

There was much opposition to the hereditary peers in 1909–11, yet they kept some power as members of the House of Lords until 1999. Why do you think they survived so long?

C   Did their struggle with the House of Lords strengthen the Liberals?

Why was there a struggle?

The House of Lords rejected the 1909 Budget by 350 votes to 75. The Conservatives and Liberal Unionists together had a massive majority in the Lords, and they had rejected Liberal measures before. In 1893 they had defeated Gladstone's second Home Rule bill, which would have given Ireland self-government, by 419 to 41. In 1906 they had completely changed a Liberal government education bill intended to stop DENOMINATIONAL religious teaching in schools which received money from the rates (local taxes). In 1907 they had defeated a licensing bill which would reduce the number of public houses. Yet voting down a Budget was different. The government could not continue if it could not collect its taxes. There would have to be a general election.

Who was right?

Judging by modern standards of democracy (government by the people) the Lords was plainly wrong. Even a House of Commons elected by around 60 per cent of men and no women had much more right to make decisions than a set of peers who had generally inherited their titles.

Many peers voted against the Budget because of beliefs in tradition, keeping a balance between different parts of government or guarding against over-hasty change. Of course, they would also be hardest hit by the new taxes. Had they a case or were they just being selfish and playing party politics?

ACTIVITY

Study the case on both sides shown in Chart 13E.

1 Which do you think is the strongest argument on each side?
2 In general the Liberal government's case was based on democratic ideas and the Lords' case was based on tradition. Which argument for the Lords is democratic and which Liberal argument is based on custom and tradition?
3 How far might the Lords' arguments be seen in 1909 as a reasonable response to the Liberal government case against them?

LIBERALS' CASE

• The House of Lords readily accepted Conservative government reforms such as the 1902 Education Act. It then rejected Liberal measures such as the 1906 Education Bill which party leaders had put forward at the 1906 election.

  The Conservative leader, Balfour, made no secret that he was using the Lords to resist changes and force compromise. As Lloyd George put it, 'The House of Lords is not the watchdog of the Constitution; it is Mr Balfour's poodle'.

• There was a tradition from at least the seventeenth century that the Lords accepted Commons' decisions about money. Since the 1860s, when modern-style Budgets were first presented, the Lords had always accepted what they contained, even if they had opposed the proposals earlier.

• The Lords was opposing the will of the people. The Liberals had won the 1906 election with an enormous majority. The Lords then stopped them carrying out the measures they had promised in their election campaign and was now making it impossible for them to govern.

• The Lords was selfishly defending its own class interest. Peers wanted more battleships and accepted old age pensions, but now they were refusing to pay for them.

  Richer people could afford to pay. They should not use traditional political power to shift taxation on to the poor who could not afford it so easily.

LORDS' CASE

• The House of Lords had the job, defined by the nineteenth-century CONSTITUTIONAL writer Walter Bagehot of resisting drastic, constitutional or ill-considered change and acting as a 'bulwark against revolution'.

  There were plenty of reasons for thinking the 1909 Budget was drastic and ill-considered.

  Liberal government proposals for new laws, such as the 1906 Education Bill and 1907 Licensing Bill, and the high taxes on pub licences in the Budget were to please some extreme Nonconformists who worked for the Liberal Party, but they were not in the public interest.

• The 1909 Budget had lots of measures 'tacked on' which did not belong in the Budget at all. The arrangements for a land valuation, for example, could not be used to collect any taxes in 1909–10. The licensing measures were an obvious way round the Lords' earlier decisions.

• The Lords was not refusing to accept the Budget if the people wanted it. Such a sweeping measure should be put to the people in a general election before the Lords passed it. The Liberals may have won a big majority in 1906, but by-elections and other indications showed they were now much less popular.

• There were other ways of finding the money, and the Budget was a measure of class warfare. It targeted landowners unfairly. The peers and other landowners had a proud record of service in government and the armed forces. It was dangerous to stir up class hatred as Lloyd George was doing.

> **CONSTITUTIONAL**
> Concerned with arrangements for government.

> **Walter Bagehot**
> Editor of the *Economist* magazine 1860–77. His 1867 book, *The English Constitution*, describes how British government worked in the 1860s and has been used as a reference work for generations.

House of Lords reform

The House of Lords' rejection of the Budget led to a general election in January 1910. After this the Liberals had only two more MPs than the Conservatives (see Source 13.4), but they had a majority with their 40 Labour allies and the Irish Nationalists who would support them to get Home Rule (see page 242). In the election the Liberals emphasised the fight against the Lords and how they must restrict its power, but first they had to get their Budget passed. The Lords, in line with its own arguments, accepted it once the Liberals had a new parliamentary majority.

Prime Minister Asquith now had two other big problems:

1 As the Liberals had lost their overall parliamentary majority, they depended on the support of the Irish Nationalists. These MPs reluctantly agreed to the Budget on the understanding that the Liberals would remove the Lords' powers and introduce Irish Home Rule (Ireland being able to run its own home affairs).

2 The government had to get the Lords to agree to a law which would restrict its powers. The Lords would agree only under pressure, but there was one possible threat. The King – if he were willing – could create enough Liberal peers to get a majority for any Liberal bill. Edward VII said he was willing only if Asquith put a 'particular project' for reform of the Lords to the voters in an election, and in January 1910 there was no such 'particular project' set out in detail. Consequently the Prime Minister could have the new peers – or the threat of the new peers – only if he won another election on the basis of his 'project'.

Edward VII then died, inconveniently. Conservative and Liberal politicians spent a few months having a constitutional conference to try to find a compromise, which never looked likely. The conference failed, and the new king, George V, promised Asquith he would make the peers if necessary on the same conditions as Edward VII.

A second general election in December 1910 produced almost the same result as the first (see Source 13.4). George V promised to create the peers if they were needed, and Asquith brought in a bill to remove the Lords' power to veto new laws.

The Conservative peers had a bitter row about whether or not to accept the bill. The 'diehards' or 'ditchers' stuck to their principles and rejected it, the 'hedgers' abstained (chose not to vote) to let it through, and the 'rats' voted with the government, not because they wanted it but to ensure they did not have the new peers. The dispute led to Balfour's resignation as Conservative leader, but the bill got through and became the 1911 Parliament Act.

The main terms of the 1911 Parliament Act

- A money bill approved by the House of Commons must become law within a month of being sent to the House of Lords whether the Lords approved it or not. The Speaker of the Commons would decide what was a money bill.
- Any bill which the House of Commons approved in three successive sessions would become law even if the Lords rejected it. (A parliamentary session normally lasts about a year from November.) There must be at least two years from the first to the last time the Commons approved the bill.
- A general election had to be held within five years of the last one instead of seven. (This restricted how long the Commons could override the Lords after an election.)

What was the relevance of House of Lords reform to the death of the Liberal Party?

The reform of the Lords' powers was a great triumph for the Liberals. The Lords had frustrated Liberal reforms for 40 years since the 1870 Land Act (see page 231). At the end of his career Gladstone wanted to remove the Lords' powers. Now it was done by a Liberal government, using peaceful, constitutional means in line with Liberal thinking.

So why do some historians think it weakened the Liberals in the end?

- One of the Liberal Party's traditional jobs was gaining reforms against the opposition of powerful, privileged people like the Lords. Was the party so necessary once the Lords' powers had gone?
- Liberals generally wanted moderate, not drastic, reform. What was now to stop left-wingers and more extreme parties getting reforms beyond what the Liberals wanted?
- On the other hand, the Lords could still delay reforms for two years. How far would this stop the Liberals getting what they did want in the next few years?

FOCUS ROUTE

Use this section to complete the table you began on page 208.

D Did the Liberals achieve much or offer attractive policies from 1911?

What reforms did the Liberals introduce?

The three most important reforms the Liberal government achieved were probably:

- **1911 National Insurance Act** (see pages 200–202)
- **1911 Payment of MPs**
  MPs were now given a salary of £400 a year. The Labour Party most wanted this reform.
- **1913 Trade Union Act** (see page 162).

A further three reforms were **delayed by the Lords** as long as possible under the Parliament Act, and were not carried out until after the First World War:

- **Welsh Church Disestablishment**
  In a bill first introduced in 1912, lands and privileges would be taken away from the Anglican Church in Wales. This had long been demanded by Welsh Nonconformists, who far outnumbered Anglicans.
- **Irish Home Rule**
  In a bill introduced in 1912 (see Chapter 14)
- **Abolition of Plural Voting**
  In a bill introduced in 1913, no one was to have more than one vote in an election.

Could Lloyd George's Land Campaign give the Liberals the momentum they needed?

Lloyd George followed up his 1909 Budget with a campaign about land reform in 1913–14 and an attempt to carry out some of his proposals in the 1914 Budget. There was much discussion about the control and ownership of land and the way landowners profited from it. The Labour Party campaigned strongly on the issue, and it seemed to be an important working-class grievance. Lloyd George produced his new policies for the land in a series of speeches and leaflets in 1913–14. Although he had the Prime Minister's backing, it was a personal campaign, not a government one, and the policies were not yet fully worked out by summer 1914 when the First World War broke out.

The main plans were:

1 Minimum wages for agricultural labourers
   These had already been introduced by law for some badly paid workers (1909) and for miners (1912). By July 1914 Lloyd George got Asquith's backing for a general minimum wage, but there was no time to take this further before war broke out
2 Land courts to fix rents for TENANT FARMERS
3 A Ministry of Land and Forests to buy land and build cottages in the countryside
4 Plans for towns including
   a) restricting payments for LEASES
   b) charging RATES on the site value of land.

These policies appealed more in the countryside than the towns, but Liberals argued that rural problems were important to the towns as well. If rural workers were badly paid they might well move to towns and increase competition for homes and jobs there.

How useful was Lloyd George's 1914 Budget in keeping the Liberals popular?

This Budget was to build on what had been done in 1909 and bring in some ideas from the Land Campaign.
   It included:

- higher taxes on the rich, including rises in supertax, the standard rate of tax on high incomes, and death duties
- taxes on the site value of land; lower council rates were to be charged when land was developed.

However good these ideas, they had not been fully worked out, and the land taxes could not be charged until the land valuation was finished in 1915. A number of Liberal MPs who were businessmen voted against them, and parts of the Budget were defeated in the House of Commons.

TENANT FARMERS
Farmers holding their land from other owners.

LEASES
Agreements with landowners to hold land and buildings for a specific period.

RATES
Tax payments, based on the value of land and houses, made to local authorities.

ACTIVITY

Use your completed table on Liberal successes and failures to assess to what extent the Liberals between 1911 and 1914 were as successful or less successful than they were between 1906 and 1911.

How strong were the Liberals in comparison with the Labour Party in 1910–14?

Although the Conservatives appeared to be the Liberals' main rivals before the First World War, historians normally concentrate on the threat from Labour, which later replaced the Liberals as Britain's main left-wing party.

Historians believe the Liberal Party had the following problems:

- **New Liberalism**

This involved welfare reforms and was vital in appealing to voters, but it was largely limited to a few Liberal Cabinet ministers, mainly Lloyd George and Churchill. Although many Liberal backbenchers (ordinary MPs) and journalists were New Liberal in their thinking, most party workers were not. Clarke (1971) found a progressive approach in Lancashire, but many other local studies in the south west, north east, Wales, Yorkshire and Norwich show a much more traditional kind of local Liberalism. Local Liberals accepted the New Liberalism but were more enthusiastic about older Liberal beliefs. Was New Liberalism sufficiently strong in the party to continue to attract voters?

- **Local Liberal parties were very middle class**

They had been reluctant to select working-class candidates. Tanner's (1990) regional studies found local Liberal parties changing, but only slowly. Just before the First World War nearly 40 per cent of Liberal MPs were businessmen. Could the Liberals retain enough working-class support like this?

- **The Pact or 'Progressive Alliance' with Labour**

This had helped both parties succeed. It was used for parliamentary elections but not generally for local council elections. Some historians doubt it could have held, as Labour gained more support in the trade unions.

ACTIVITY

Look at Chart 13F.

1 Which side of the argument is stronger in each of sections 1–5? Why?

2 Rank the five sections in order of importance for judging Liberal and Labour strength.

3 Which points of argument in the chart as a whole do you believe are strongest? Why?

4 How serious would the Labour Party challenge, therefore, have been to the Liberals without the First World War? (If you have answered the Focus route on page 208, this will help you.)

5 What does Chart 13F show about the difficulty of interpreting election figures?

SOURCE 13.4 Results in the two general elections of 1910

January 1910	Total votes	Percentage	Candidates	Returned unopposed	Elected
Conservative and Liberal Unionist (LU)	3,127,887	46.9	600	19	273 (incl. approx. 32 LU)
Liberal	2,880,581	43.2	516	1	275
Labour	505,657	7.6	78	0	40
Irish Nationalist	124,586	1.9	104	55	82
Others	28,693	0.4	17	0	
Total	6,667,404		1,315	75	670

December 1910	Total votes	Percentage	Candidates	Returned unopposed	Elected
Conservative and Liberal Unionist (LU)	2,420,566	46.3	550	72	272 (incl. approx. 36 LU)
Liberal	2,295,888	43.9	467	35	272
Labour	371,772	7.1	56	3	42
Irish Nationalist	131,375	2.5	106	53	84
Others	8,768	0.2	11	0	
Total	5,228,369		1,190	163	670

HOW TO ARGUE

> *Labour was rising and the Liberals were falling*

Parliamentary elections

1 1910 General elections
- Labour had 40 MPs after the January election and 42 after the December one, compared with 29 elected in 1906, plus one who soon joined from the Liberals (see page 159).
- Labour could not get trade union funding because of the 1909 Osborne Judgment (see page 162) and so came out well in the circumstances.

2 By-elections 1910–14
- The Labour vote generally increased in by-election contests compared with the last contested general election.
- The Liberals apparently lost some seats to the Conservatives because Labour candidates stood, showing how much they needed the Liberal–Labour Pact.
- Four Labour by-election losses were largely due to special local circumstances, particularly within the Miners' Federation now affiliated to Labour.

3 Municipal (town council) elections
- Overall Labour gained more town councillors in every year up to the First World War.

4 Trade union support
- The trade union movement was growing fast from 2.6 to 4.1 million in 1910–14 and 1.6 million union members were affiliated to the Labour Party by 1914.
- The Miners' Federation of Great Britain affiliated in 1909, and this was specially important because of the large number of members in coal-mining areas who could decide the outcome of elections there.
- Under the 1913 Trade Union Act, unions which wanted to raise funds for political parties had to hold a ballot on this. Overall, members voted 298,000 to 125,000 in favour of having the funds.

5 How many Labour candidates were going to fight Liberals at the next election?
- The Pact between the two parties worked well in 1910, but Labour was then weak and could not get trade union funding.
- There were significant differences between the aims of Liberal and Labour activists. A list made for Labour's National Executive Committee showed about 120 constituencies where Labour candidates might stand, and there might well be 150–170 candidates by the time of a general election in 1915.

HOW TO ARGUE

> *The Liberals were still the top party and Labour was making slow progress*

Parliamentary elections

1910 General elections
- As Labour had 45 MPs before the elections they actually lost strength. They had more MPs because the Miners' Federation of Great Britain had affiliated (joined up) with Labour in 1909.
- Labour depended almost entirely on the Pact with the Liberals. No Labour MP was elected against official Liberal opposition in January and only two won against Liberals in December.

By-elections 1910–14
- Labour lost four by-elections in constituencies with former Labour MPs. All the Labour candidates who stood came bottom of the poll and got under 30 per cent of the votes.
- Labour came third in contests with Liberal and Conservative candidates. It looked as if they depended on the Liberal–Labour Pact for victory.

Municipal (town council) elections
- Some Labour gains may have come because people were temporarily dissatisfied with the Liberal government, and so were making what is now called a 'protest vote' against the government in local elections.

Trade union support
- Many trade unionists did not support Labour, and some were hostile to it, so trade union growth did not automatically mean more Labour support.
- In contests between Liberal and Labour candidates in mining seats before the First World War most of the miners seem to have voted Liberal, leading to Liberal victories in the 1910 elections and later by-elections.
- Only about 420,000 out of over 1,200,000 members in the unions bothered to vote on funds for political parties. In some unions, members later voted against money going to the Labour Party from wages. In others, members just opted out of making the payments.

How many Labour candidates were going to fight Liberals at the next election?
- Ramsay MacDonald, Labour's leading figure and Chairman of the Parliamentary Labour Party, seems to have favoured fighting the Liberals only in limited areas and might well have negotiated another pact.
- The list of constituencies is misleading as it showed only where Labour might put up candidates. Only some of the constituencies suggested before the 1910 elections had actually been fought.

F # Could the Liberal government cope?

CHAPTER 13 REVIEW ACTIVITY

Part of the debate on whether the Liberals were dying is about whether they could deal with **problems** created by the **Suffragettes**, **trade unions** and **opposing groups in Ireland**. These issues are examined in detail in Chapters 2, 8 and 14. Based on your study of those chapters:

1 Work in pairs. Here are some argument starters. Think how you could develop them, referring to events and evidence from the above chapters. Work out one side of the argument each.

Could the Liberals deal with the Suffragettes? (See pages 30–33)

Suffragette actions were causing the Liberals more and more embarrassment …

But the Suffragettes were losing support …

Could the Liberals cope with the trade union unrest? (See pages 146–148)

Surely the massive increase in strikes shows the Liberals could not cope? …

What about the way they got compromise agreements? …

Could the Liberals handle Ireland? (See pages 241–246)

There were two rival armies ready to fight it out in Ireland …

But there was no violence like the murders in the 1880s …

2 Which of the three problems posed the greatest threat and why?
3 All three involved groups which used some threats, violence or physical force. How similar were they in their methods?
4 Dangerfield (1935) claimed that the Liberals could not deal with these because they did not understand the new forces at work and the methods they used. How far do you support this view?
5 Did the difficulties the Liberal government faced in dealing with these problems suggest that Liberal decline was inevitable?

G Review: Was the Liberal Party dying by the First World War?

What did people in 1910–14 think about the state of the Liberal Party?

Election figures and government performance are two important indicators of Liberal strength, but evidence from people involved in politics is important as well and can help interpret election results.

SOURCE 13.5   A writer in the Labour newspaper, the *Clarion,* commented on the January 1910 general election result

The Labour Party will go back to Parliament weaker in number by half a dozen, and immeasurably weaker in prestige, than they were in 1906.

SOURCE 13.6   A comment on 'The Elections and their Moral' in the Conservative *Blackwood's Magazine,* March 1910

Lancashire and Yorkshire on the whole have given a class vote. The men who applauded a Conservative speaker and heckled a Liberal, when it came to the election day voted not for a principle but for what they had come to regard as their class. The trade union has become not merely an economic but a political organisation. The workman is beginning to stick by his class in politics as for some years he has stuck by it in industrial disputes. The Tory working-man, who used to be common in Lancashire, is fast disappearing. Soon the Liberal working-man will follow suit, and if we are not alive to the danger, the masses will become one vast automatic machine for registering the decrees of the Labour CAUCUS.

CAUCUS
Word for organisers who tried to manage elections or control a political party.

SOURCE 13.7   Beatrice Webb, a Labour supporter and member of the Fabian Society, wrote in her diary, 30 November 1910

The big thing that has happened in the last two years is that Lloyd George and Winston Churchill have practically taken the limelight, not merely from their own colleagues, but from the Labour Party. They stand out as the most advanced politicians.

SOURCE 13.8   C.P. Scott, a leading left-wing Liberal and editor of the *Manchester Guardian,* wrote in his diary in June 1914

I confess I am beginning to feel ... that the existing Liberal party is played out and that if it is to count for anything in the future it must be reconstructed largely on a labour basis.

SOURCE 13.9   Christopher Addison, a Liberal minister who later joined the Labour Party, recorded his feelings on the outbreak of the First World War

Most of us felt that liberalism was already in its grave – at any rate ... that is what I feel like. When one thinks of all our schemes of social reform just set agoing and of those for which plans had been made in this year's Budget, one could weep. Nearly all the things that we have been toiling at for years have come toppling down about our ears. Insurance must go on; the feeding of children is safe; and we must snatch what we can of others. But it is obvious that the war will mop up all the money that has been made available.

ACTIVITY

1 **a)** Which of Sources 13.5–13.9 support the argument that the Liberal Party was dying and which suggest it was in a strong position until the War?

   b) Which, if any, sources could be used to support both sides of the argument? Explain your choice.

2 Sources 13.5 and 13.6 were written for journals which would be on sale to the public but which were read mainly by party supporters. Sources 13.7–13.9 were written in private letters or diaries. How does this affect their reliability and usefulness to historians?

3 Sources 13.5–13.7 were written in 1910. Which developments between then and June 1914 might have convinced C.P. Scott that the Liberal Party was 'played out'?

4 Which source is the most useful for investigating whether the Liberal Party was dying? Explain your choice.

ACTIVITY

Write an essay to answer the question: was the Liberal Party dying by the First World War?

Use the table you have compiled on Liberal successes and failures (see page 208), the answers you have worked out for the Activities for Sections E and F and the answers to the Activity on this page.

KEY POINTS FROM CHAPTER 13 **Was the Liberal Party dying by the First World War?**

1 The Liberals won a big majority at the 1906 general election. They continued in government after the general elections of 1910 but relied on Irish Nationalists for a majority in the House of Commons.

2 Some historians emphasise Liberal strength and how Labour was a small party depending on its pact with the Liberals.

3 Others stress Liberal weaknesses and how Labour had strong support from a growing trade union movement.

4 The Liberals' 'People's Budget' in 1909 paid for old age pensions and new warships by a skilful mixture of taxes which particularly affected the wealthy.

5 The Budget caused great controversy and a struggle with the House of Lords.

6 The Liberal government won this struggle and reduced the Lords' powers, but at some cost.

7 The Liberals produced a number of reforms and policy plans in 1911–14 which pleased many supporters, including working-class voters, but they had mixed success in carrying them out.

8 Although the Liberals were strong in parliamentary elections there were signs of weakness and growing Labour Party support in local council elections and trade unions.

9 The Liberal government faced major problems from armed groups in Ireland, from trade unions and from Suffragettes between 1910 and 1914.

How successfully did political parties respond to the development of democracy and changes in the working class?

■ A British political parties by 1914

The working class has
to choose between

Socialist groups

With only small-scale support and no representation in Parliament

- Syndicalists believed in acting through trade unions and bringing down the capitalist system by strike action
- The British Socialist Party (members of the former Social Democratic Federation and left-wingers from the Independent Labour Party) offered a real socialist alternative rather than the compromises made in the Labour Party

Labour Party

With MPs drawn mainly from working men
Offers:

- More welfare reforms and government action to ensure wealth from land and industry benefits the people
- A party largely from the working class which will govern in the interests of the working class

Liberal Party

With leaders from among landowners and the middle class

- Has provided New Liberal welfare reforms and the People's Budget and curbed House of Lords powers
- Offers a way of gaining reforms using peaceful constitutional means and avoiding class conflict

Conservative Party

With leaders from among landowners and the middle class
Offers:

- Tariff reform to pay for social welfare measures
- Pride in nation and empire which could unite all the peoples of the United Kingdom

Part A

This diagram shows the choices that were available to a working man by 1914. Your task is to choose one party and explain to Joe Worker why he should vote for you and not for the others.

You can write this in the form of a speech to a political meeting or an article for a workers' newspaper, or as a leaflet to be distributed around the workplaces of the cities in Britain. Whichever you choose you must cover three topics:

a) What your party has achieved for the working man.
b) Why the other parties (focus on just one) have let down the working men and failed to respond to their needs and concerns.
c) What you would like to promise Joe Worker for the future.

Part B

Now shift roles and become the historian. You have to rank the three parties – Conservative, Liberal and Labour – according to how successfully you think they responded to the changes in democracy since the third Reform Act of 1884–85. Then write at least three paragraphs to explain your rank – one paragraph for each party.

There were all kinds of different links between politicians and ordinary voters. How people voted depended on lots of things like education and newspapers as well as what politicians themselves said and did. Chart B shows some of the complicated connections between politicians and voters.

■ B Connections between politicians and the public

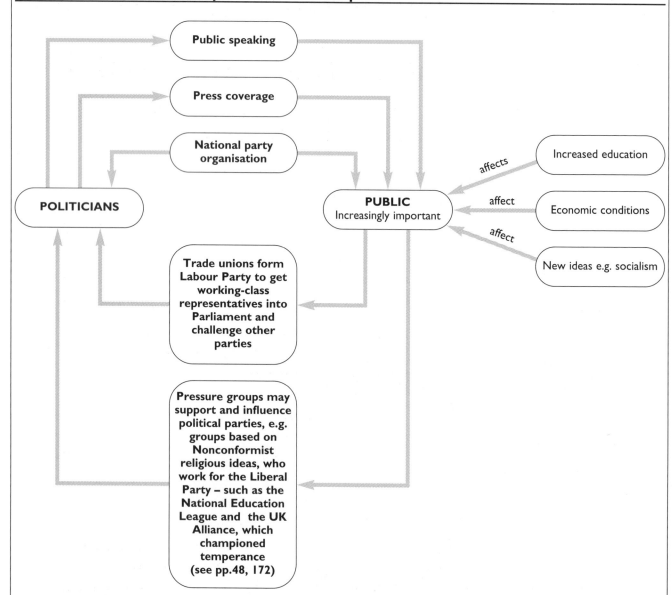

Make a copy of Chart B. Using what you have learned from Section 4, add examples of each influence and add any other influences you can think of.

1 How far did the electorate become more knowledgeable between 1851 and 1914? See pp. 17, 22, 48, 90 and 146.
2 What ways did electors and other citizens use to express their views? Consider particularly the work of trade unions and various pressure groups. See pp. 48 and 141–148.
3 How far did leaders of political parties use citizens to increase their own political power? See pp. 16–17, 64, 92, 167–168 and 173.
4 What differences were there in the relationship between leaders and members in the Conservative, Liberal and Labour parties? See pp. 64, 92, 155–159 and 162.
5 How far was the electoral system democratic by the First World War? Use the three points suggested on p. 7, but add your own if you wish. To make an assessment, use Chart 1F on p. 21; information on the press on pp. 22–23; and tables on pp. 171, 184 and 216 on how votes and House of Commons seats were distributed between parties at elections.

Hitting home – how did events in Ireland and the First World War affect Britain?

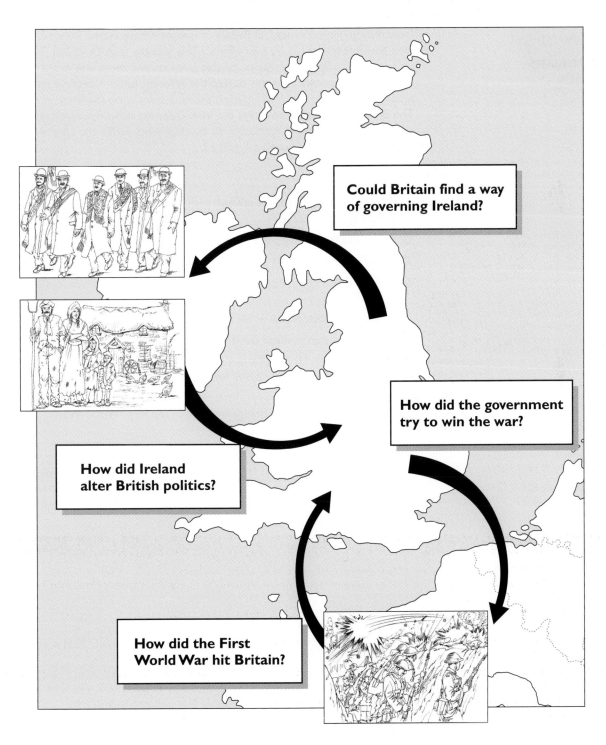

Could Britain find a way of governing Ireland?

How did the government try to win the war?

How did Ireland alter British politics?

How did the First World War hit Britain?

What was the Irish Question and could the British government answer it?

CHAPTER OVERVIEW   Throughout this period the big question facing British governments was 'Could Ireland be governed as part of Britain or should it have Home Rule, i.e. elect its own parliament and run its own affairs?' This was the Irish Question. There was more than one British viewpoint on this question and there was more than one Irish one. Increasingly over this period the different factions became more militant, and by the end of the period the country was on the brink of civil war. The British Parliament also found the Irish Question had a knock-on effect on many domestic issues, in particular on developments within the Liberal Party which you studied in Chapters 5 and 13.

This chapter asks:

A Why was there hostility between Irish people and their British rulers by 1850? (pp. 225–227)

B How was Ireland different from Britain? (pp. 227–228)

C How were the Irish to get a better deal? (p. 229)

D Why did Gladstone not succeed in solving the Irish Question in 1868–85? (pp. 230–236)

E Why did Gladstone fail in his attempt to get Home Rule? (pp. 237–239)

F How serious an attempt did the Conservatives make to solve the Irish Question? (pp. 240–241)

G How close was Ireland to civil war before the First World War? (pp. 241–246)

H How did the problems change because of the First World War? (pp. 247–249)

A Why was there hostility between Irish people and their British rulers by 1850?

■ 14A The unhappy relationship between Ireland and England and how the history affects modern Ireland

Henry II claimed to be lord of Ireland from 1170. The English took over the area around Dublin known as the Pale, but most of the country was controlled by Irish chiefs or Anglo-Norman nobles.

When England became a Protestant country in the sixteenth century the laws about Protestant worship and English monarchs being in charge of the Church were not applied in Ireland. Most Irish people remained Roman Catholic while England became Protestant.
Centuries later the Anglican Church of Ireland owned large amounts of land.

Elizabeth I put down rebellions in Ireland, and the English rulers effectively conquered Ireland.

As Ulster was the most rebellious part of the country, Plantations (settlements) of Scottish and English Protestants were made there in the reign of James VI and I. This created hostile Protestant and Roman Catholic communities within Ireland.

During the English Civil War from 1642 the Irish rebelled. The country was deeply divided and disordered.

In 1649–52 Cromwell and his commanders conquered Ireland.
In 1652 great areas of land were confiscated and handed over to English owners. English landowners now owned much of Ireland.

In 1689 the Roman Catholic James II, who had been turned out of England, went to Ireland. The Roman Catholics were then in control in Ireland. Protestants in the north were besieged in Londonderry and Enniskillen but held out. The Protestant King of Britain, William of Orange, went to Ulster with an army and defeated James at the Battle of the Boyne in 1690. As a result the Protestants got control again.
  William's victory at the Boyne and a heroic resistance at Londonderry led to annual celebrations. The Protestant Orange Order, named after William of Orange, grew in the late nineteenth century. It celebrates the Protestant triumphs in marches every summer.

There was then more discrimination against Roman Catholics and only Protestants could sit in the Irish Parliament.

In 1800 the Irish Parliament was abolished and Ireland then sent MPs to the UK Parliament at Westminster. They were promised that Roman Catholics would then be able to sit in Parliament, but the British did not keep their promise until forced to carry it out in 1829. Ireland was governed from Britain in the nineteenth century. As in India, a viceroy represented the monarch in Ireland. A British minister – the Chief Secretary for Ireland – was in charge of administration.

ACTIVITY

What would be the main grievances the Catholics had against Protestant British rule in the early 1800s?

The English divided Ireland into counties, and the island had four traditional provinces – Ulster, Connaught, Leinster and Munster.

As the early nineteenth century went on, a greater proportion of Britain's growing population worked in industry and went to live in towns. In Ireland a greater proportion of the growing population relied on farming the land. Many fed themselves by growing potatoes on very small plots, so when a European potato blight struck in 1845 there was a disastrous famine.

■ 14B Provinces of Ireland and Protestant Plantations in seventeenth-century Ulster

Key:

The counties included in the Plantations of James I (see 14A)

Additional area settled in the reign of James I

■ 14C The Irish Famine 1845–48

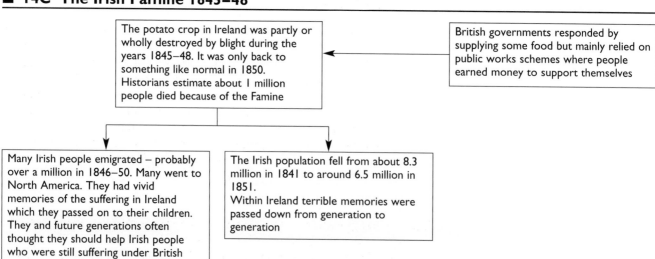

The potato crop in Ireland was partly or wholly destroyed by blight during the years 1845–48. It was only back to something like normal in 1850. Historians estimate about 1 million people died because of the Famine

British governments responded by supplying some food but mainly relied on public works schemes where people earned money to support themselves

Many Irish people emigrated – probably over a million in 1846–50. Many went to North America. They had vivid memories of the suffering in Ireland which they passed on to their children. They and future generations often thought they should help Irish people who were still suffering under British rule

The Irish population fell from about 8.3 million in 1841 to around 6.5 million in 1851. Within Ireland terrible memories were passed down from generation to generation

227

WHAT WAS THE IRISH QUESTION AND COULD THE BRITISH GOVERNMENT ANSWER IT?

SOURCE 14.1 Drawing of a funeral at Skibbereen, County Cork from the *Illustrated London News*, 30 January 1847

SOURCE 14.2 In the twentieth century a woman at Sneem, County Kerry remembered her uncle's story about the suffering of a family called Casey at the time of the famine

There were seven or eight of them, a neat little family; they had white heads. My uncle Mick used to cry when he used [to] be telling the story. The oldest girl went six days of the week to Sneem for soup and came empty. On the seventh day five of them died. I remembered one of them [a survivor] – she was a withered old little woman … The 'ologon' [noise] they ruz [raised] the sixth day, when she came without any food was something dreadful. Years after, my father was ditching near the ruin and found the bones of an old man and a child; the arm of the old man was around the child.

SOURCE 14.3 In 1860 an Irish writer, John Mitchell, claimed in *The Last Conquest of Ireland (Perhaps)*

The Almighty, indeed, sent the potato blight, but the English created the Famine.

B How was Ireland different from Britain?

Ireland was a poor country compared with Britain. The mid-nineteenth-century statistician R. Dudley Baxter thought the average Irish income at that time was just under half of the average British one, but he may well have underestimated the Irish figure, and Britain was the richest country in Europe at the time.

Ireland's population kept falling for the rest of the nineteenth century and much of the twentieth. From 6.5 million in 1851 it fell to 4.4 million in 1911, but this was probably because so many people were leaving – probably about 4 million between 1850 and 1914. Of the people who grew up in Ireland in the 1850s and 1860s, nearly half emigrated, and most of them went for a better life in the USA.

That at least meant that it was easier for the remaining people to get land.

Landownership

Landownership was one of the key parts of the Irish problem in the nineteenth century, and the way the English had confiscated Irish land caused lasting bitterness. Fewer than 800 people owned half of the land of Ireland in the 1860s and 1870s, and people living outside the country owned 23 per cent.

Nineteenth-century Irish landlords have generally got a bad name. The third Earl of Leitrim, who inherited an estate in 1854, really does sound like the 'landlord from hell'. He demolished one village to build himself a new castle, destroyed another to plant a vista of trees, employed a gang of men to pull down a Catholic chapel with crowbars and allegedly forced tenants' daughters to have sex with him, leading one to drown herself in sorrow. After several attempts to kill him, he was eventually murdered, but no one would give evidence against the killers, although they were supposed to be well known.

Most landlords behaved a great deal better, and there is general agreement among historians that Irish tenants were more prosperous by the 1870s than they had been in 1850. With falling numbers of people, tenants generally had larger holdings and most families working on the land had their own farms or gained them between the 1840s and 1880s. The vast majority were rented, but overall rents apparently went up much less than prices.

Differences in religion

After landownership the next most obvious disagreement in Ireland was over religion. About 75 per cent of the Irish people were Roman Catholic – 78 per cent when the first count was made in 1861 and 74 per cent by 1914. The remainder were Protestants. About half of the Protestants – just under 12 per cent of the whole Irish population – were members of the Anglican Church of Ireland, but this was the Established church (see learning trouble spot page 41) of the country, which meant it had great estates and could collect tithes from the population.

Most landlords, many professional men and Ireland's English rulers were Protestants. The Irish language had largely died out. By 1901 only one person in seven knew it and one in 200 used it as their normal language. Therefore, when the Irish wanted to group together as a nation against their English rulers, the Roman Catholic Church helped give them leadership and identity. The problem was that a national identity based on religion excluded a quarter of the people in Ireland.

Government

Britain governed Ireland, but the Irish were well represented in Parliament in proportion to their numbers. The Irish population went down while the British population went up, but Ireland kept 100 MPs at Westminster. In the end, though, it was a British government, depending mainly on British MPs, who decided how Ireland should be run. The Chief Secretary in the Cabinet, the viceroy in Ireland, the civil servants in Dublin Castle and about 20,000–30,000 troops administered the country and maintained British power.

How was Ulster different from the rest of Ireland?

English and Scottish Protestants had come to Ulster with the Plantations in the seventeenth century. As time went on they sometimes intermarried with native Irish people, so there were not two distinct racial groups in the north, but the two communities largely kept themselves apart. They were identified by religion.

In most of Ireland Protestants were a small minority. In Ulster there were large numbers of them, and they made up a majority of the people in the eastern part of the province (the north-east corner of Ireland).

Ulster was also different in having much more manufacturing industry than the rest of the country. Its traditional linen industry expanded in the mid-nineteenth century, and Belfast had shipbuilding yards which developed hugely from the 1880s. Protestant and Roman Catholic workers in the city did not get on well together. They tended to live apart, remembered old rivalries and occasionally attacked each other. Little incidents sometimes led to serious riots.

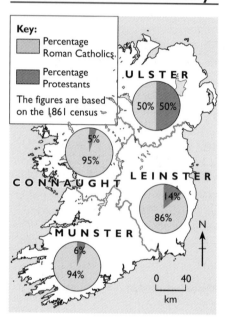

■ 14D Religion in Ireland in the mid-nineteenth century

Key:
Percentage Roman Catholics.
Percentage Protestants
The figures are based on the 1861 census

ULSTER 50% 50%

CONNAUGHT 5% 95%

LEINSTER 14% 86%

MUNSTER 6% 94%

N

0 40 km

FOCUS ROUTE
Briefly summarise what the Irish did to try to get change between 1850 and 1868.

PEASANTS
People working on the land.

TENANT FARMERS
Farmers holding their land from other owners.

C How were the Irish to get a better deal?

TALKING POINT
Economic historians now reckon that Irish PEASANTS generally became more prosperous in the 1850s and 1860s. Why do you think TENANT FARMERS pressed for changes at this time?

■ 14E Options open to the Irish

OPTION 1
Use peaceful and legal means as the British constitution allows

What the Irish did
- Tenant farmers, mainly the better-off ones, formed local societies which joined together in a national Irish Tenant League in 1850.
- The Tenant League put forward three demands generally known as the Three Fs:
  - Fair rent
  - Fixed tenure – safeguards against landlords evicting tenants
  - Free sale – if tenants held their land at a fair rent and could not be turned out, they had valuable rights; free sale meant they could sell these rights to somebody else if they left their land.

Did they achieve anything?
- The Tenant League put forward the demands of the wealthier farmers. They had no success for twenty years, but the British government at least knew what they wanted.

OPTION 2
Use violent and revolutionary means

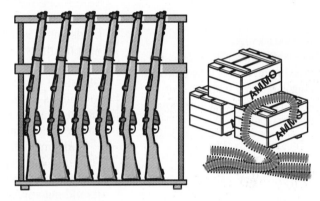

- The English had originally conquered Ireland, and the system of government was imposed from London rather than agreed with the Irish people. It could therefore be argued that the Irish had a right to overthrow it.
- There was already a revolutionary tradition in Ireland. Many looked with pride on risings in 1798 and 1848. The British had crushed them easily, but they showed that some of the Irish nation had the will to fight.

What the Irish did
- James Stephens started the **Irish Republican Brotherhood (IRB)**, normally known as the Fenians, to plan a violent revolution with the help of money from Irish in North America. They recruited up to 50,000 men, but were short of rifles and ammunition. They took oaths of secrecy, but British agents managed to infiltrate the organisation and knew many of their plans.

Did they achieve anything?
- The British soon crushed a Fenian rising one night in 1867.
- Attempts to rescue Fenian prisoners in England probably had more effect on British public opinion. Fenians murdered a police sergeant while rescuing two prisoners in Manchester. An attempt to rescue a Fenian organiser from Clerkenwell Jail in London went badly wrong when an explosion killed and injured residents nearby.
- Three Fenians hanged for the murder of the police sergeant were widely known in Ireland as the 'Manchester martyrs'.

ACTIVITY

1 Why did the Fenians get so much help from North America?
2 Refer to sections A–C.
  Imagine you were a British civil servant in 1868. What advice would you give to a new prime minister about
  a) whether to grant tenant farmers' demands
  b) whether to remove privileges from the Anglican Church of Ireland
  c) whether to set up an Irish Parliament or give the Irish more say in government in other ways
  d) what else should be done to prevent Irish revolutionary activity?

230

WHAT WAS THE IRISH QUESTION AND COULD THE BRITISH GOVERNMENT ANSWER IT?

D Why did Gladstone not succeed in solving the Irish Question in 1868–85?

FOCUS ROUTE

Make a large copy of this table and complete it using the information in this section.

Government action		Irish action	
Action	**Effect**	**Action**	**Effect**
Disestablishment of the Irish Church First Land Act Second Land Act First Home Rule bill		Home Rule movement Land League	

DISESTABLISHMENT

Disestablishing a Church meant removing privileges it had through being connected with the state, particularly land and other wealth. See also page 41.

TALKING POINT

What were the advantages and dangers of Gladstone's way of thinking?

Gladstone was the new British prime minister in 1868, having won an election with the DISESTABLISHMENT of the Irish Church as the main issue. His reasons may have been based more on British politics than the situation in Ireland, but Gladstone worried about the injustices involved in English government of Ireland. As Colin Matthew (1995), the editor of the Gladstone diaries, puts it, 'Ireland was for Gladstone a preoccupation, not an interest, an embarrassment, not an intellectual attraction.'

Gladstone believed major reforms were necessary in Ireland even before the Fenian incidents in 1867, but these made the British public more interested in Irish issues. The time was therefore right for reform. Of course his measures should not appear as concessions to violence, but Gladstone did see Fenian activity as an argument for change. If he gave the Irish some of the reforms they wanted, they would be less likely to support the Fenians. As he put it in a private memo, 'our purpose and duty is to endeavour to draw a line between the Fenians & the people of Ireland, & to make the people of Ireland indisposed to cross it.' At this time he thought only of religious and land reforms, rather than altering the way Ireland was governed.

Gladstone's reforms in Ireland in his first ministry 1868–74

1869 Disestablishment of the Church of Ireland

Why? The Church of Ireland was Anglican (moderate Protestant) in a mainly Roman Catholic country (see page 228). Although the 1861 census showed under 12 per cent of Irish people were Anglican, the Church still had great estates. As most Irish landowners belonged to it and Britain supported it, the Church's privileges were a **symbol** of British power. This was probably much less important to most Irish people than land reform, but removing the symbol could reduce opposition to British rule.

Effects of the Act Commissioners managed Church wealth. About half of this went to Church of Ireland clergy and other officials and some went to schools and schemes to help the poor in Ireland. There was resentment among many strong Anglicans in Britain and Ireland, but one less grievance for Irish Roman Catholics.

1870 First Land Act

Why? Most Irish tenants held their land on a year-by-year basis. Although they were rarely evicted, they wanted more security and had been campaigning for twenty years to get rights over their land. Historians calculate that they were becoming more prosperous from selling their produce and that after rent increases they were around 7.7 per cent better off in 1871–73 than they had been in 1856–58.

Isaac Butt
A Protestant lawyer who became
associated with Irish revolutionaries
when he spoke for them in court,
defending Fenians in 1865–67 and
then campaigning for their release
from prison.
Began the
movement for
Home Rule
and led the
Irish party in the
Westminster
Parliament until
his death in
1879.

Charles Stewart Parnell
Another Protestant lawyer who
became an MP in 1875. Led the Home
Rule Party in Parliament 1880–90. His
'affair' with Mrs Katherine O'Shea led
to his downfall as
parliamentary
leader in 1890.
He then
campaigned for
a more
revolutionary
approach. He
died in 1891.

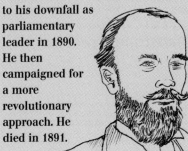

Terms of the Act
- In much of Ulster there was a tradition, known as the Ulster custom, that a
  tenant had rights to his holding which he could sell to a new tenant if he left.
  The law now backed up these rights.
- Elsewhere in Ireland a tenant could get a payment to cover any improvements
  he had made to his holding if he left.
- If a tenant were evicted he could get compensation for being thrown out as
  long as he was up to date with his rent payments. If the rent were 'exorbitant'
  he would get the compensation even if he had failed to pay. (Gladstone wanted
  the word to be 'excessive', but the Lords altered it to the landlords' advantage.)
- Tenants could borrow two-thirds of the money to buy their holdings, but they
  would have to find one-third themselves.

Effects of the Act As landlords now lost some control over their land, the
value of their estates was reckoned to fall by about a quarter to a third. The
compensation made it costly to evict tenants, but landlords might still get rid of
them by increasing the rent so that they could not pay. Very few tenants could
find the money to buy their holdings. The Act removed a few tenant grievances,
but it did not seem to make much difference in the late 1870s when food prices
fell and some tenants had difficulties paying their rent.

What the Irish did
Home Rule movement
In 1870 Isaac Butt, a Protestant lawyer, founded the Home Government
Association to press for an Irish Parliament which could manage many services
inside the country while the UK Parliament kept overall control and ran
foreign policy and defence. At the start, a number of landowners and other
well-off Protestants supported this limited self-government as a way of
preventing more reforms such as the Land Act. As voting was still in public and
they planned an Irish House of Lords, they hoped their own parliament might
be less keen on reform than the UK one in 1870.

The outlook on this changed very quickly. The secret ballot was introduced
in 1872, and the Home Government Association was converted into the Home
Rule League to get mass support in 1873. Fifty-nine MPs supporting Home Rule
were elected to Westminster in 1874, but they had very varied views and
increasingly supported tenants' demands for change.

Some of the MPs also developed new tactics. Joseph Biggar pioneered
'obstruction' as a parliamentary weapon. This meant talking for hours to stop
the House of Commons carrying on its normal business. (There were no
parliamentary rules to prevent this, until they were drawn up a few years later
to shut up the Irish MPs.) It was not necessary for the MPs to say anything
useful. At times Biggar just read interminable extracts from past laws, in a
tedious monotone and with a particularly harsh, grating voice. A few other MPs
used the same methods, notably Charles Stewart Parnell who eventually
became leader of the Home Rule Party in 1880, a year after Butt's death. By this
time Parnell was already taking the party in a new direction.

Land war
In 1878–79 a **Land League** was developed by a Fenian revolutionary, Michael
Davitt, with the long-term aim of turning peasants who worked the land into
owners and the shorter-term aims of stopping evictions and reducing rents.
The League became more significant when Davitt persuaded Parnell, by then
the most prominent MP among Home Rulers, to become its President. Such a
link-up between revolutionaries, using violence in the countryside, and MPs,
using legal means in Parliament, was called the 'New Departure'.

The League was partly a response to tenant farmers' difficulties when food
prices fell at the end of the 1870s. Tenants sold their produce for less and
therefore many failed to pay their rent and some were evicted. On the surface
the League was a response to tenants' hardship and landlords' harshness.

232

WHAT WAS THE IRISH QUESTION AND COULD THE BRITISH GOVERNMENT ANSWER IT?

Recent historians, such as W.E. Vaughan (1996) and Theodore Hoppen (1999), have been very reluctant to see the League in quite this way. After all, farms were now larger and tenants better off than they had been 30 years before. Some tenants were evicted but not very many. Roughly 3–4 per cent appear to have been thrown out over the whole period 1855–80.

What also puzzles historians is the way that so many large and small farmers, farm workers and shopkeepers all joined the League. They wanted different things, but for a time they joined in making demands which would most benefit large tenant farmers. The League seems to have been a triumph of central organisation. MPs, journalists and officials toured the country. Peasants who did not care much about parliaments rallied behind demands for better conditions in their own villages. It was an excellent way of strengthening the Home Rule movement.

While Parnell and his MPs used parliamentary means and public speeches, local Land League members were apparently using terrorist methods. Attacks on unpopular landlords and their agents were not new, but there were now far more of them. It was very dangerous to take a holding from somebody who had been evicted as you might then get a night time visit from 'Captain Moonlight' and his men. A grave dug in front of the house might give you warning or you might get beaten up, have your ears cut off or be murdered.

SOURCE 14.4 An English view of Parnell and his supporters

Parnell openly suggested another method, called 'boycotting' after its first victim, an English land agent named Captain Boycott.

SOURCE 14.5 Parnell described boycotting in a speech in Ireland, September 1880

When a man takes a farm from which another has been evicted you must shun him on the roadside when you meet him – you must shun him in the streets of the town – you must shun him in the shop – you must shun him in the fairgreen and in the market place, and even in the place of worship, by leaving him alone, by putting him into a moral Coventry, by isolating him from the rest of his country as if he were the LEPER of old – you must show him your detestation of the crime he has committed.

When no locals would harvest Captain Boycott's potato crop in November 1880, fifty workers went from Ulster to do so, armed with revolvers and protected by 7000 government troops. The government was taking the threat seriously.

LEPER
Someone with the contagious skin disease called leprosy whom others would avoid.

The government of Ireland in Gladstone's second ministry 1880–85

1881 Second Land Act

Why? Gladstone became prime minister again after the Liberals won the general election in 1880. As there were disturbances in Ireland and Gladstone had introduced reforms in his first ministry, he was expected to propose changes.

The belief that Gladstone responded to pressure brought dangers. Parnell told an Irish meeting in September 1880: 'Depend upon it that the measure of the land bill of next session will be the measure of your activity and energy this winter.' Gladstone himself saw the problem, as he told Forster, his Irish Chief Secretary, how it was sadly true that 'disturbance and fear' had speeded up reform at almost every point in Irish history.

ACTIVITY

How might the figures in Source 14.6 have affected Gladstone's actions on land reform?

AGRARIAN
Agricultural or connected to land.

COERCION MEASURES
Laws to remove some normal legal rights of citizens, such as trial by jury.

LEASES
Agreements with landlords for people to hold land and buildings for a specific period.

SOURCE 14.6 Evictions and crime in Ireland

Year	Families evicted	Total AGRARIAN crime in Ireland*
1877	463	236
1878	1,238	863
1880	2,110	2,590

* This included maiming cattle, burnings, shootings and minor intimidation

In autumn 1880 Gladstone introduced a bill to help tenants who were evicted for not paying their rent, but it was rejected by the Lords. Ministers thought they must bring in so-called COERCION MEASURES to strengthen law and order, but Gladstone did not want to rely on power and punishment alone. He thought granting the Three Fs (fair rent, fixed tenure and free sale) which tenants had demanded from the 1850s, might satisfy the farmers, calm the agitation and reduce support for Ireland's parliamentary leaders, who were using it all to work for Home Rule.

Effects of the Act The Three Fs (see Chart 14E) were granted. There was a kind of shared ownership between landlords and tenants which gave tenants rights and reduced the value of the landlords' estates as they could no longer choose their tenants or fix their rents. Irish farmers got rent reductions from the courts which now decided fair rents. Farmers who had not paid their rents could not use the courts, and up to 20 per cent were in this position. Farmers with LEASES also could not use them as the leases had been freely agreed between owners and tenants and gave the terms of land-holding.

The impact of evictions

Much of the hatred in the land war sprang from the way landlords evicted tenants who could not pay their rent. Irish politicians often referred to evictions, and there were many pictures showing what eviction meant and how it was done.

SOURCE 14.7 A drawing in *The Graphic* showing an evicted family in western Ireland in 1880

SOURCE 14.8 A French paper, *Le Monde Illustré*, showed an eviction in progress in 1881

SOURCE 14.9 The *Illustrated London News* showed how much force might be used in 1881

SOURCE 14.10 A photo from around 1885 shows an evicted family outside their old home with their furniture. The thatched roof had been destroyed to stop the house being occupied again

SOURCE 14.11 *The Graphic* gave this comment on eviction and demonstration in 1886

SOURCE 14.12 *The Graphic* published this picture showing farm workers with pitchforks and clubs before they were evicted from an estate in 1888

SOURCE 14.13 Photo of a battering ram being used in an eviction in 1888. The branches in the windows and doors would make the eviction harder to carry out

236

WHAT WAS THE IRISH QUESTION AND COULD THE BRITISH GOVERNMENT ANSWER IT?

ACTIVITY

Refer to Sources 14.7–14.13 on pages 233–235.
1 Sources 14.10 and 14.13 are photographs. Compare the usefulness of these with the drawings in Sources 14.7–14.9 and 14.11–14.12.
2 a) Which pictures are most obviously posed?
  b) Which, if any, are fictional rather than real?
3 a) In what ways do these sources indicate cruelty by the landowners or by those working for them?
  b) How do they encourage sympathy for those evicted?
4 Which of Sources 14.7–14.13 would you describe as propaganda? Give reasons for your answer.
5 How would you use Sources 14.7–14.13 if you were an Irish nationalist politician who wanted Home Rule?
6 Refer to Sources 14.5–14.13 and the text on pages 232–233 and 236.
  How might you
  a) defend the evictions
  b) argue the problem was exaggerated?
  If you were representing Irish landowners
  c) how might your arguments change between 1880 and 1888?

Events in Ireland after the Second Land Act, 1881–85

Most farmers benefited from lower rents and lost interest in the land war after the Act, but some still had grievances; attacks continued and the government thought Parnell was encouraging them. He was therefore imprisoned in October 1881, but this did not help the crime figures. It may have helped Parnell. He wrote to his mistress, Mrs O'Shea: 'Politically it is a fortunate thing for me that I have been arrested, as the movement is breaking fast, and all will be quiet in a few months, when I shall be released.'

After a few months, in May 1882, the government made a deal with Parnell. It was named the Kilmainham Treaty after the jail where he was held. Parnell would be released and try to reduce the attacks in the countryside. The government would bring in a law to help tenants who had not paid their rents so that they could get the new land courts to reduce them.

The Cabinet minister in charge of Ireland, who favoured a tough policy, then resigned, and a new Chief Secretary, Lord Frederick Cavendish, was appointed. He went for a walk in Phoenix Park, Dublin and was murdered by a gang of assassins with surgical knives. This was a bad start to the new deal, but Parnell condemned the outrage and Gladstone went ahead with the promised help for tenants. Rents fell, the land war subsided, and in October 1882 the Land League was replaced by the **National League**, which was more under the control of the political leaders and more focused on Home Rule. Ireland was less violent, but the Liberal government used some measures of coercion (see page 233) until it fell in 1885.

Parnell's **Home Rule Party in the House of Commons** went from strength to strength.

- Parnell had great qualities as a leader, and his party became the most highly disciplined one in Parliament.
- Money from Irish Americans helped pay MPs and provide for election campaigns and propaganda.
- The Third Reform Act 1884–85 gave the vote to small farmers and farm workers who generally supported the Home Rule Party. Parnell's party gained 85 out of 103 MPs in Ireland at the 1885 election.

237

WHAT WAS THE IRISH QUESTION AND COULD THE BRITISH GOVERNMENT ANSWER IT?

(see page 93)

<table>
<tr><td>FOCUS ROUTE</td></tr>
</table>

FOCUS ROUTE

Make notes under the following headings:

a) When did Gladstone take up the policy of Home Rule?
b) How much power would the Irish Parliament have under his scheme?
c) Why was his Home Rule bill defeated?

E Why did Gladstone fail in his attempt to get Home Rule?

Parnell's greatest success came in December 1885 when it appeared that Gladstone was converted to Home Rule (see page 93). Gladstone formed his third ministry early in 1886 to examine how practical a Home Rule Parliament would be, but the other ministers did not do much examining. Gladstone worked out a package and presented it to them (see Chart 14F).

■ 14F Gladstone's package for Home Rule

UK Parliament
- It would keep **supreme power** – meaning, at least in theory, it could abolish the Irish Parliament.
- It would keep control of foreign policy, defence, trade and a long list of things including shipping movements, customs and EXCISE taxes on goods, the Post Office, and currency. (Ireland would still use UK money).
- There would be no Irish MPs in the UK Parliament.

Irish Parliament
- It would **control other services within Ireland**, such as schools and roads.
- It would consist of two orders:
  – Upper made up of Irish peers and members chosen by voters with a large amount of property (to ensure landlords and Irish Protestants had a say)
  – Lower chosen by the voters who already elected MPs to the UK Parliament.
- The two orders would generally meet and vote together.

Home Rule would be accompanied by a large Land Purchase scheme.

Land Purchase
- The government would lend Irish tenants all the money they needed to buy their holdings.
- This would cost £50 million. (The British navy cost only £12 million a year.) Gladstone disliked the idea of finding so much money, but he thought it necessary to get Home Rule agreed.
- Irish landowners could then sell their estates and take the money, so that they would not have to worry so much about what a new Home Rule Parliament did. There was no knowing what a new Irish Parliament would do about large estates if they remained.

EXCISE
Tax on goods sold within a country.

There was a range of possibilities for giving the Irish more say in running their own affairs, and most politicians at the time thought Gladstone's scheme was at the more extreme end of the range. His Home Rule bill faced serious obstacles (see Chart 14G).

■ 14G The three big obstacles to Home Rule

1 The House of Commons
The Conservatives would oppose Home Rule. Would enough Liberal MPs support it? Joseph Chamberlain and many other Liberals supported more local government in Ireland, but Home Rule went much further than this.

2 The House of Lords
The Conservatives had a big majority and many peers had large estates in Ireland. Gladstone thought they would not dare reject Home Rule if the elected House of Commons supported it. But would they accept it if it passed the Commons on the votes of Irish MPs and most British MPs voted against it?

3 Ulster Protestants
Gladstone thought they should not be able to stop Home Rule if most Irish people wanted it. But Conservative leaders thought they could. One leading Conservative, Lord Randolph Churchill, visited Ulster and stated 'Ulster will fight and Ulster will be right.'

The Home Rule bill fell at the first obstacle, when it was opposed by some Liberals as well as Conservatives in the Commons – 93 Liberal MPs voted against and it was defeated by a majority of 30.

238

WHAT WAS THE IRISH QUESTION AND COULD THE BRITISH GOVERNMENT ANSWER IT?

■ 14H The big debate over Home Rule

HOME RULER'S CASE

UNIONIST'S CASE

1 Britain is ruling the Irish as a subject people. If we respect the Italians' rights to govern themselves as a nation should we not respect the Irish as well?

2 The Irish do not accept rule from Britain. Despite major reforms in land and religion, Britain has been able to govern Ireland only by using coercion, which means depriving Irish citizens of their normal rights to free speech and trial by jury. Laws will be respected in Ireland only if they come from an Irish Parliament.

3 If the Irish get self-government, like the Canadians or Australians, they will become loyal citizens of the empire. Then they will add to Britain's imperial strength instead of weakening it as at the moment.

4 Giving Irish business to a Parliament in Dublin will reduce the Westminster Parliament's workload, and the Commons will no longer be disrupted by Irish MPs who obstruct it to make their points.

5 Would it not be best to give the Irish the Home Rule Parliament they seek rather than making piecemeal concessions and be forced into more later? In many ways Home Rule is a conservative measure. Ireland had its own Parliament in the eighteenth century. What is so worrying about Ireland having a Parliament again? The Westminster Parliament would still retain sovereign power in Ireland.

6 The Protestants are only about a quarter of the population of Ireland and half the population of the province of Ulster. They cannot be allowed to stop Ireland achieving nationhood.

1 The Irish are not a subject people, but are well represented in Parliament. The Irish are not comparable to the Italians and need the civilising and modernising influence of Britain. Britain has given Ireland progressive and ordered government.

2 Agreeing to Home Rule means giving in to terrorist violence. Look at the way Parnell and his friends backed the Land League and their atrocities. However much he appears a fine parliamentarian, think of the men behind him. Only last year Irish bombers were targeting London with explosions in Westminster Hall and the Tower of London. Will these men not think they are winning if we give them Home Rule? (See Source 14.14.)

3 If Britain gives in to violence in Ireland and abandons the men maintaining its power there, what message will this give to peoples in other parts of the empire? What will it tell the Indians?

4 Gladstone's bill would not give Ireland any MPs at Westminster and yet the Westminster Parliament would still impose substantial taxes on the country. That is taxation without representation – just the reason the Americans fought Britain in the 1770s – and look what that led to. Would this Home Rule arrangement not trigger a further agitation for full independence?

5 The Irish Parliament before 1800 was Protestant. Parnell and his party would dominate a modern Irish Parliament and Parnell's National League would be in charge. Ireland's predominantly Roman Catholic rulers would follow their priests. Home Rule means Rome Rule.

6 What about the loyal Protestants who hate the thought of being ruled by a Roman Catholic dominated Irish Parliament? How could the UK abandon Ulster which has supported Britain through good times and bad?

SOURCE 14.14 A British cartoonist's view of Gladstone's decision on Home Rule from *Punch*, 9 January 1886

TEMPTATION OF THE GOOD ST. GLADSTONE.

SOURCE 14.15 An Irish cartoonist's view from the *Weekly Freeman*, 6 February 1886

ACTIVITY

1 How does Source 14.14 suggest that choosing Home Rule would be wrong?
2 What actions in Ireland and by Irish politicians could the cartoonist use to explain or justify his view?
3 What is the point of showing Gladstone reading the imperial constitution?
4 What would be the main arguments in favour of Gladstone choosing Home Rule rather than coercion in Source 14.15?
5 How would you explain why Sources 14.14 and 14.15 take very different views of the decision Gladstone faced over Home Rule?

FOCUS ROUTE

List the setbacks the Home Rule Party faced in 1886–94.

Why was Gladstone unable to deliver Home Rule from 1886 to his retirement in 1894?

When Gladstone opted for a general election soon after the Home Rule bill's defeat in 1886, the majority of the MPs elected were against Home Rule. The opponents were increasingly known as Unionists, indicating that they wanted to keep the full union between Britain and Ireland. Liberal Unionist MPs who had voted against Home Rule drew closer to the Conservatives (see page 166).

Parnell went through spectacular changes in fortune and was brought down as Irish party leader in 1890 because he had been having an 'affair' with a mistress, Mrs Katherine O'Shea. Most of the Irish MPs turned against him, and he died whilst campaigning in Ireland in 1891 at the age of 45. The Irish party remained split until 1900.

Second Home Rule bill, 1893

The Liberals together with Irish Home Rule MPs had a majority in the Commons after the 1892 election, and Gladstone introduced his second Home Rule bill in 1893. The bill was similar to the first one, but this time there were to be 80 Irish MPs in the UK Parliament who could vote on matters concerning Ireland and the empire as a whole, though not on any that affected just Britain. There was no doubt that the bill would pass the Commons, but it failed at the second obstacle – the House of Lords, with its big majority of Conservatives and large landowners, turned it down by 419 to 41. Gladstone retired soon afterwards in 1894, and future Liberal leaders were not committed to the Home Rule cause in the way he had been since 1886.

240

WHAT WAS THE IRISH QUESTION AND COULD THE BRITISH GOVERNMENT ANSWER IT?

FOCUS ROUTE

What appear to have been the Conservatives' main motives when making decisions about the government of Ireland?

F How serious an attempt did the Conservatives make to solve the Irish Question?

Disraeli, the Conservative leader until 1881, largely ignored Ireland during his second ministry in 1874–80. His main interest in Irish affairs was how they would affect Parliament and general elections.

When the Liberals split over Home Rule in 1886, Ireland became the dominant issue in British politics. Salisbury, the Conservative prime minister after the 1886 election, had no overall Conservative majority. He was in power because the Liberal Unionists who opposed Home Rule wanted to stop Gladstone getting back and therefore supported him. The Conservative government got its majority in the Commons and stayed in office because of opposition to Home Rule. The Conservatives were not certain of keeping Liberal Unionist support during their ministry in 1886–92, though leading Liberal Unionists later joined Salisbury's Cabinet in 1895. When they were working out what to do in Ireland they had to think of both the situation there and what the Liberal Unionists wanted.

■ 141 The situation faced by the Conservatives

IRELAND

Parnell's National League started a Plan of Campaign from 1886. They selected estates where the tenants would offer what they decided was a 'fair rent'. If the owner refused to accept it he got no rent at all, and the money went into a fund for tenants who were evicted.

UK PARLIAMENT

The Liberal Unionists were strongly opposed to Home Rule, but they still wanted reforms in Ireland. Chamberlain had worked out his own plan for more local government. If he backed a Conservative government he needed to show his supporters that the Conservatives had at least introduced some of the changes he had campaigned for in 1885.

How did the Conservatives govern Ireland from 1886?

SOURCE 14.16 'Bloody Balfour' supported police who shot protesters

Lord Salisbury said that Ireland needed twenty years of resolute government. His nephew, Arthur Balfour, Irish Chief Secretary from 1887 to 1891, provided it by introducing new laws to stop boycotting and disorder and by backing police who shot rioters at Mitchelstown in 1887. For this, he became known as 'Bloody Balfour'. He also introduced reforms which began the policy known as 'killing Home Rule with kindness' – a phrase used by his brother Gerald, who was Chief Secretary a few years later.

241

WHAT WAS THE IRISH QUESTION AND COULD THE BRITISH GOVERNMENT ANSWER IT?

FOCUS ROUTE

1 How did the Conservative approach to the government of Ireland differ from the Liberals' approach?
2 How great was the effect of Conservative land purchase reforms?

The Liberals and Conservatives had different approaches to the land question in Ireland. Gladstone's reforms gave Irish tenants rights in their holdings so that there was a kind of shared ownership between landlords and tenants. Conservatives disliked taking away landlords' rights without compensation like this and preferred the government lending money to tenants. This gave landlords a better deal, as they could get a good price for their land, and made farmers into small landowners who were more likely to support the existing system.

Conservative land reforms

1885 Ashbourne Act The government would lend tenants all the money they needed to buy their holdings. It was little used because the repayments were considerably higher than the amount of rent they had paid.

1887 Land Act This extended the benefits of the second Land Act (1881), including fair rent, to leaseholders (see page 233).

1891 Land Purchase Act This allocated more money for tenants to buy their land, but the terms were still not attractive enough for most of them.

1903 Land Purchase Act This was worked out by a conference of landlords and tenants in Ireland and then accepted by the government. Tenants could borrow all the money to buy their land and then pay 3.25 per cent of what they had borrowed for 68½ years. This would be less than their normal rent. Landowners would get 12 per cent above the normal market price for the land. The government put in a big subsidy so that both landowners and tenants got a good deal. Far more tenants bought their land than before; 62 per cent of farmers owned their holdings by 1914 and 72 per cent by 1919.

What did the Conservatives achieve?

- The Irish countryside was far more peaceful. Several Irish nationalists deplored this. Archbishop Croke lamented in early 1895 'the country is notoriously and indeed shamefully apathetic (unconcerned). There is no desire for Home Rule.' That was just what Conservatives wanted.
- The Conservatives made a permanent alliance with the Liberal Unionists. Andrew Gailey (1987), who has done the main research on the reforms, argues that this was the point of the exercise. It was 'a British policy for a British electorate and intended to keep the Irish question as the foundation of party structure and of British politics'. This weakened the Liberals and helped keep the Conservatives in power for most of the period from 1886 to 1905 (see Chapter 10).

ACTIVITY

1 Compare the achievements of the Conservatives in governing Ireland in 1886–92 and 1895–1905 with those of the Liberals in Gladstone's second and third ministries (1880–85 and 1886).
2 Did the Conservatives do more than Gladstone between 1880 and 1905 to solve the Irish Question?

FOCUS ROUTE

1 How did the revival of Irish culture before the First World War affect politics?
2 What were the main beliefs of Sinn Fein?
3 Why did the Liberal government introduce the Home Rule bill in 1912?
4 Why and how did Ulster Protestants resist the third Home Rule bill after 1912?

G How close to civil war was Ireland before the First World War?

How did Irish nationalism grow before the First World War?

Only about 14 per cent of Irish people knew their native Gaelic language by the end of the nineteenth century. Strong nationalists were making a deliberate attempt to revive Irish culture, and they wanted it to have political effects.

The **Gaelic Athletic Association** was founded in 1884 to revive Irish football and hurling (a vicious form of hockey) and many Fenians soon joined it. The **Gaelic League** was started in 1893 to stir up national consciousness by getting people to read Gaelic writings. There were also writers, such as W.B. Yeats, who wrote in English and produced plays and poems which were both great literature and appeals to Irish nationalism.

There were other more obviously political groups. Arthur Griffith started the **Sinn Fein** movement. Sinn Fein is probably best translated as 'ourselves' or 'our own thing'. Griffith taught that Ireland could look after itself and he wanted not just Home Rule but complete independence from Britain. He founded a number of clubs which joined together in 1907, but Sinn Fein gained little support before the First World War.

John Redmond Overall leader of the Irish Home Rule Party from 1900 and a key figure in negotiations about Irish Home Rule in 1910–14.

Sir Edward Carson Brilliant lawyer and Conservative minister 1900–05, who became leader of the Irish Unionist MPs in 1910 and effectively led the Ulster Protestant resistance to Home Rule.

Why did the Liberals first delay and then introduce Home Rule?

Liberal leaders after Gladstone were not keen on Home Rule. Sir Henry Campbell-Bannerman, the Liberal leader from 1899, favoured step-by-step moves to self-government. As his Liberal government won a huge majority in 1906, it did not depend on Irish support as the Liberals had done in 1886 and 1892–95. When it introduced an Irish Council bill as a step forward in 1907, the Irish Home Rule Party, now led by John Redmond, rejected it as inadequate.

The situation changed drastically in 1910 when the Liberals lost their overall parliamentary majority (see page 216). They then needed Irish MPs to support the 1909 Budget which imposed new taxes on alcohol and on publicans, who were often influential in local Home Rule parties. Irish MPs would vote for the Budget if Liberals promised to reduce the Lords' powers and introduce Home Rule.

ACTIVITY

1 What argument is Source 14.17 making?
2 How does the cartoon reflect political developments in 1910?

SOURCE 14.17 A Conservative view of why the Liberal government took up Home Rule. The figures (*left to right*) are John Redmond (leader of the Home Rule Party) and the Liberal ministers, Asquith, Lloyd George and Churchill

Third Home Rule bill, 1912

Asquith, the Liberal prime minister, introduced a Home Rule bill in 1912 which was very similar to those in 1886 and 1893. There would be two assemblies in the Irish Parliament, including a Senate, which would at first be appointed by the British government, but the two would vote together if they disagreed on new laws. Ireland was to have 42 MPs at Westminster instead of over 100.

There was a safe majority for the bill in the Commons, and under the 1911 Parliament Act (see page 214) the Lords could delay a bill it opposed for only two years. This meant the bill could get past the first two obstacles to its progress. The big problem was now the third: Ulster.

Why did Ulster Protestants resist?

ACTIVITY

What were the Ulster Protestants' fears about religion and prosperity?

There were two main reasons for the resistance to Home Rule in Ulster.

- Protestants, who were in the majority in the north-eastern part of the province, feared it for religious reasons. Protestants and Roman Catholics largely lived apart with their own schools and shops. Voters divided on religious lines in elections – Roman Catholics supporting Home Rulers and Protestants supporting Unionists. Protestants believed that Home Rule meant 'Rome Rule'.
- Businessmen and workers feared an Irish Parliament would harm Irish industry. It would probably be dominated by farmers or businessmen who dealt with farmers, and they would not understand the type of economy in Belfast or bother about its future. Harland and Wolff, Belfast's largest shipyard, made inquiries about moving to England when Home Rule was proposed in 1893. Many workers thought their jobs depended on Protestant businessmen staying in charge. Serious riots in 1886 are supposed to have been started by a Catholic worker telling a Protestant that Home Rule meant no more jobs for Protestants.

Gladstone's Home Rule bills in 1886 and 1893 sparked off fights between Catholics and Protestants. In 1886 eight people were reported killed and over 120 injured in Belfast. In 1893 Ulster Protestants could rely on the House of Lords to block Home Rule. In 1913 Ulster was the only obstacle, and the danger was real.

How seriously did Ulster resist?

Ulster Protestants were developing a strong sense of solidarity. They revived the Orange Order in the late nineteenth century. Named after William of Orange (see Chart 14A, page 225), this first developed from gang warfare in the Ulster countryside in the 1790s, survived as a set of mainly working-class clubs in the nineteenth century and blossomed from the 1880s as a movement to celebrate past triumphs and bond all classes of Protestant men together against future dangers.

■ 14J The Ulstermen's way to stop Home Rule

1 Developed an organisation
1904–05 Formed an Ulster Unionist Council.
1910 Started looking for weapons. Major Fred Crawford, the Council's agent, wrote round to arms manufacturers.

2 Found a leader and planned alternatives to Home Rule
1910 Sir Edward Carson (see page 242) was chosen as leader.
1911 He told a great meeting of Unionists near Belfast: 'We must be prepared ... the morning Home Rule passes, ourselves to become responsible for the government of the Protestant Province of Ulster'.

3 Won public support
September 1912 Leaders drew up the Solemn League and Covenant pledging to use 'all means which may be found necessary' to stop Home Rule. They claimed over 470,000 signatures.

4 Built up a military force
January 1913 Volunteer groups prepared for military action and joined in an Ulster Volunteer Force (UVF), estimated at 75,000–100,000 men.

5 Bought plenty of arms
April 1914 UVF landed a further 35,000 rifles and 5 million rounds of ammunition at Larne and quickly distributed them across Ulster.

ACTIVITY

1 How do Sources 14.18–14.20 show stages 3–5 in Chart 14J?
2 How might these scenes help to gain support against Home Rule among
   a) Ulster Protestants
   b) the British public?

SOURCE 14.18 Ulster Anti-Home Rule demonstration, Coleraine, September 1912, showing members of the Orange Order

SOURCE 14.19 *Ulster Anti-Home Rule demonstration, Portadown, September 1912, showing naval and ambulance corps*

SOURCE 14.20 *Ulster Anti-Home Rule demonstration, Portadown, September 1912, showing the big gun brigade*

The Conservatives who wanted to prevent Home Rule, for the reasons suggested in the 'Unionist's Case' in Chart 14H (page 238), supported the Ulstermen as a way of stopping it. Bonar Law, the Conservative leader, told a party rally at Blenheim Palace in Oxfordshire: 'I can imagine no length of resistance to which Ulster can go in which I should not be prepared to support them.' There was already much armed drilling in Ulster by the time he said this.

ACTIVITY

What might
a) the UVF
b) the Irish Home Rule Party
have read into Bonar Law's statement?

How did the Nationalists respond?

They learned from the Ulstermen's tactics. As one extremist, Patrick Pearse, put it, 'Personally I think the Orangeman with a rifle is a much less ridiculous figure than the nationalist without a rifle.' The Fenians started recruiting again and hired a shooting gallery for Sunday morning practices.

In November 1913 **Irish Volunteers** were formed to build up an armed force across the country, and a count in May 1914 showed 129,000 of them. They smuggled in more rifles in July 1914, but they had less than the UVF, and the operation went wrong when some members showed the guns too openly on the streets and British army troops killed four of them.

What did the British government do?

- There were now two armed forces in Ulster to fight for opposite things. How was Britain to keep order?
- The Home Rule bill was due to become law in 1914. How was the government to enforce it?

How did the government control Ireland?

Extra guards were put on arms depots in Ulster and battleships were moved to northern Ireland and Scotland for possible use. Preparations were made to use the army, but commanders were hesitant because many officers and men were sympathetic to the Protestants. In March 1914, when the commander at Curragh, the main military barracks in Ireland, asked officers about taking part in action against the Ulstermen to enforce Home Rule, 58 said they would prefer to be dismissed rather than obey orders to act. News leaked out, and it appeared that the British government could not use its army to enforce its laws. If fighting looked impossible, it had to get a compromise – a deal to which both sides would agree.

TALKING POINTS

1 The Conservatives traditionally supported the British constitution and they had been strong supporters of the empire for at least 40 years. How consistent were they being when they supported armed resistance in Ulster?

2 How reasonable was the Conservatives' position in the crisis?

Was there any chance of compromise?

Patricia Jalland, who has written the main work on how Asquith's government handled the crisis (1980), found that it had no clear plans for tackling the situation in Ulster, but still realised it might have to make a deal. The Cabinet told Redmond, before they introduced the Home Rule bill, that they must be free to do what they thought best if they had to make concessions to the Ulster groups. Asquith and the Conservative leader, Bonar Law, discussed the situation in 1913 and agreed that some kind of partition (separating some of Ulster from the rest of Ireland) was necessary, though the Irish leaders then looked unlikely to agree. Carson, the Ulster Unionist leader, wanted to use the resistance in Ulster to stop Home Rule for Ireland as a whole. At first he suggested partition because he thought Redmond, the Nationalist leader, would never accept it, and this would be a way of destroying the entire scheme. By 1914 he realised this was not likely to work and saw partition as the only way of keeping some of Ulster united with Britain.

When the Home Rule bill was going through the House of Commons in spring 1914, on its way to becoming law, the government proposed that each county in Ulster could opt out of Home Rule for six years. Redmond, the Nationalist leader, reluctantly agreed, and the question was then how long the opt-out should last. Carson declared: 'We do not want sentence of death with a stay of execution for six years.'

The King called a conference at Buckingham Palace in late May which broke down without agreement. By the end of July, though, Asquith had decided that the four counties with most Protestants – Antrim, Down, Armagh and Londonderry – must be left out of Home Rule permanently, and he told Redmond this. Asquith offered the deal to Bonar Law, Carson and Craig, the leader of the Protestants within Ulster. The First World War then broke out. Both sides in Ireland agreed to support the war effort and agreed that Home Rule should be postponed. The bill became law as an Act, but Asquith said it would not be carried out until Parliament had an opportunity of altering it.

■ 14K Distribution of Protestants and Roman Catholics in Ulster counties before the First World War

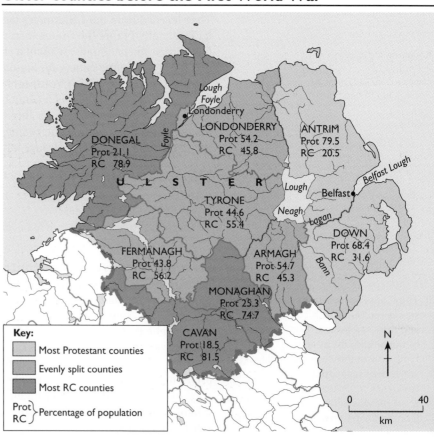

Chart 14L outlines changes in Ireland from the beginning of the war and the developments leading to the Easter Rising in 1916.

REPUBLIC

Type of government without a monarch. An Irish Republic would therefore be completely independent of Britain and its monarchy.

FOCUS ROUTE

Sinn Fein wanted independence for Ireland with its own assembly in Dublin.

1 What reasons would developments in Ireland in 1916–18 give Irish people for supporting Sinn Fein?
2 How did Sinn Fein increase its strength?

■ 14L Developments in Ireland 1914–16

ECONOMIC

> Extra demand for food in war when imports are cut off
> ↓
> Higher food prices benefited farmers

> Need for more workers in war
> ↓
> Less unemployment in all parts of Ireland

> Irish countryside prosperous and quiet
> ↓
> Irish people could no longer emigrate to North America, so young people were stuck in Ireland — but → Less unemployment in all parts of Ireland
> ↓ but
> Workers' wages did not keep up with rising food prices

POLITICAL

> Redmond and Carson both urged their Irish and Ulster volunteers to support the war effort. The danger of civil war disappeared. Large numbers of Roman Catholics and Protestants joined the British army

Asquith offered Redmond a place in the Cabinet in 1915 when he formed a coalition government (combining people from different parties). Redmond turned it down, following the Home Rule Party's tradition of not accepting office in Britain. **But** the Liberals now worked in coalition with the Conservatives, reducing the chances of Home Rule being carried out

Most Irish Volunteers (about 170,000) accepted Redmond's leadership to become National Volunteers.

About 11,000 broke away under Eoin MacNeill (who had started the force) because they disagreed with Irish participation in the First World War. They still called themselves Irish Volunteers. Number of Fenians (IRB men) took leading positions in the Irish Volunteers

Some of the Irish Volunteers under MacNeill wanted a rising against the British government. Patrick Pearse and others believed they could revive the sleeping spirit of Irish nationalism by rising in favour of an independent Irish republic. Even if it failed the blood sacrifice would inspire others

1916 Easter Rising
Plans for the rising went wrong when the British tracked down a ship bringing German arms to western Ireland. MacNeill tried to call it off, but it still went ahead. About 1600 took part in a Dublin rising and declared an Irish REPUBLIC. They held out for a week. Around 450 people (revolutionaries, police, British army troops and ordinary citizens) were killed or wounded

The effects of the Easter Rising

Attempts at a compromise agreement

Lloyd George, acting for the British government, negotiated with the Irish Home Rulers and Ulster Unionists for Home Rule to go ahead. He appeared to get a settlement, but this was partly because he dealt with both sides separately, and they had different understandings about how far the exclusion of six Ulster counties would be temporary or permanent. Southern Irish Unionists influenced Conservative leaders to reject the deal: it could not go ahead without their support as the Conservatives now formed an important part of the coalition government.

Punishments

Soon after the rising the British arrested around 3000 suspected revolutionaries, including many who had taken no part in it. About half were soon released, but the other half were imprisoned, some in England. Ninety were sentenced to death, and in the end fifteen were actually shot.

Significance

At the time the Easter Rising seemed small scale. Most people in Dublin appeared hostile to it, and some cheered British troops acting against the rebels. In the long term historians see it as starting a change in Irish nationalist thinking. Up to 1916 most Irish Roman Catholics had supported the Home Rule Party. Between 1916 and 1918 they changed, so that at the end of the war most apparently supported Sinn Fein. In their view the punishments were seen as disproportionate.

Changes in Ireland in 1917–18

British government initiatives

- In summer 1917 the government restricted meetings and banned groups drilling with uniforms and weapons.
- There were some further arrests of strong Irish Nationalists.
- In spring 1918 the government announced it would introduce CONSCRIPTION in Ireland. British men aged up to 51 were being conscripted, should young Irishmen not go as well? Irish Home Rule Party MPs withdrew from the UK Parliament in protest. The Irish argued that the British government had no right to force Irish men to give up their lives.

From May 1917 to April 1918 an Irish convention, representing people from different parts of the country, tried to negotiate a political compromise and failed. In May–July 1918 the government arrested Sinn Fein leaders, claiming Sinn Fein was conspiring with the Germans – a claim which was not generally accepted in Ireland. Bans followed on the Irish Volunteers, the Gaelic League and other organisations associated with Sinn Fein ideas.

Growth of Sinn Fein

Many Irish revolutionaries released from detention in 1917 formed Sinn Fein clubs which grew to around 250,000 members. Sinn Fein won a number of parliamentary by-elections in 1917 and 1918, some by large majorities and some in areas where the Home Rule Party had been very strong. The Roman Catholic Church showed more sympathy for Sinn Fein and revolutionaries. The Archbishop of Dublin and 200 priests followed the funeral procession of a Fenian who died on HUNGER STRIKE.

1918 election

By the time of the general election in 1918, Sinn Fein stood for an independent Irish Republic rather than Arthur Griffith's original aim of an independent Ireland which would still have a British monarch.

The elected Sinn Fein candidates would not go to the UK Parliament and formed their own assembly (Dail Eireann) in Dublin. It had its own government, law courts and Irish Republican Army (IRA). The British government said these were illegal, and a bitter Anglo-Irish War followed. The Ulster Protestants would never accept the sort of Ireland Sinn Fein wanted. In 1921 a separate Northern Ireland was created from the six more Protestant counties in the north east. Ireland has therefore been divided under two different governments since 1921.

> **CONSCRIPTION**
> Compulsory enrolment in the armed services.

> **HUNGER STRIKE**
> A prisoner refusing food to make a protest.

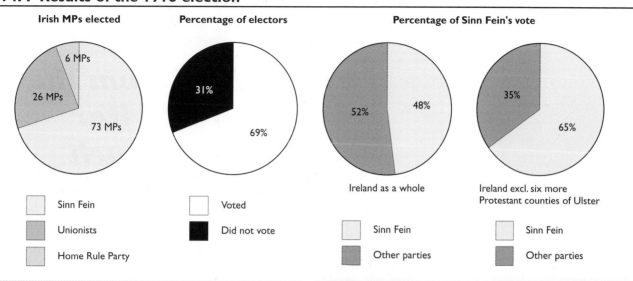

Irish MPs elected

- ☐ Sinn Fein
- ▨ Unionists
- ☐ Home Rule Party

Percentage of electors

- ☐ Voted
- ■ Did not vote

Percentage of Sinn Fein's vote

Ireland as a whole

- ☐ Sinn Fein
- ▨ Other parties

Ireland excl. six more
Protestant counties of Ulster

- ☐ Sinn Fein
- ▨ Other parties

TALKING POINTS

Many people wonder what Ireland might have been by now if different decisions had been made in the late nineteenth century.

1 Gladstone introduced schemes for Home Rule which failed because of opposition in Britain. Could any scheme have been worked out which was acceptable to most electors in Ireland and which the British Parliament would have approved?

2 Could Ireland have remained part of the UK if it had been given substantial self-government when Gladstone proposed Home Rule?

3 Would it have been possible to fuse Roman Catholics and Protestants together in one Ireland if Conservative politicians had not stirred up Ulster resistance or if proposals for Home Rule had included special arrangements for the area?

CHAPTER 14 REVIEW TASK

What was the Irish Question and could the British government answer it?

You have been asked to prepare the entry for a new online encyclopedia covering British government policy on Ireland 1851–1918. You have a strict limit on length: a maximum of 200 words. Within this you have to explain:

a) What was the Irish Question?

b) What were the main strategies taken towards Ireland by the Liberal and Conservative governments?

c) How successful were the Liberals and Conservatives in dealing with this question on a scale of 0–5? Give reasons for your score.

KEY POINTS FROM CHAPTER 14   What was the Irish Question and could the British government answer it?

1 The Famine was a major catastrophe which led to much anti-British feeling.

2 Historians emphasise how much the economy improved in the mid-nineteenth century and are doubtful about how much landlords were to blame for problems in the Irish countryside.

3 They now think the tenants' rights movement from 1850 and the Land League of 1879–82 put forward the hopes and interests of prosperous tenant farmers rather than the views of the Irish nation as a whole.

4 Gladstone attempted to solve problems in Ireland first by Land Acts, which gave tenants more rights in their holdings, and then by trying to introduce Home Rule.

5 Conservative governments attempted to deal with problems in the countryside by using more government money and lending tenants what they needed to buy their own farms.

6 When a Liberal government tried to give Ireland Home Rule in 1912 it was delayed by the House of Lords and effectively blocked by resistance from Protestant Ulster.

7 There was a growth in Irish nationalism from the 1880s.

8 During the First World War Irish Roman Catholics generally turned to the Sinn Fein movement which wanted complete independence. This led to a civil war and further strengthened the Ulster Protestant refusal to live in a self-governing Ireland.

Who gained from the First World War (and how much did everybody lose)?

CHAPTER OVERVIEW

BEREAVEMENT
Losing a close relative through death.

SHELL SHOCK
The effect of being bombarded by shells in the First World War. Men might be dazed and suffer long-term mental illness.

FOOD RATIONING
Restrictions on how much people could buy of certain foodstuffs.

About 750,000 British men were killed in the First World War. Millions more people suffered BEREAVEMENT, often several times over. Some 9000 men suffering from SHELL SHOCK were still in hospital in 1922.

The First World War was a 'total war' – it affected everybody, not just those who fought. Air raids, which killed 1413, showed how war could now come to people at home. Wartime labour demands changed job patterns. War affected people travelling, buying food or looking for favourite foreign goods, and there was FOOD RATIONING in 1918. War was destructive, traumatic and disruptive. How could some people gain from it?

Few people gained from the fighting itself, but there were new opportunities for some people back home in the short term and longer-term advantages that few could have imagined when war began.

- Some groups had more **job opportunities or better wages**.

- War provided a test for national organisation which might **stimulate efficiency** – a country might be better organised at the end of a war than at the beginning.

- Deaths and labour shortages made all workers and children look more valuable, so encouraging **welfare measures**.

- Total war needed widespread participation. The social theorist Andreski stressed the importance of the 'military participation' ratio in the population (proportion of people who took part in the war). He thought that **groups which contributed gained in return** as government rewarded them afterwards.

- A working class who fought for their country deserved, and maybe demanded, a better country afterwards – 'a land fit for heroes' as the prime minister Lloyd George put it. War participation brought **promises of welfare reform later**. The proportion of national income spent on social services rose from 4 per cent in 1914 to 8 per cent in the 1920s.

This chapter examines who gained and who lost from the war. Previous chapters have shown how Liberal and Conservative prime ministers formed governments made up almost entirely from their own party. War needs forced them to combine in coalition governments made up of leaders from all three main British parties. But though war forced politicians to unite, disagreements about the war split parties as well. How politicians responded to the war helped to decide their political future. This chapter examines how the war changed British government and political party fortunes for ever.

Previous chapters have explained how the government controlled, regulated and helped people more. The First World War transformed the role of government. British people would never have accepted so much control or such high taxation if there had not been a major war. A slow increase in government regulation gave way to a rapid government takeover in lots of trades and industries.

Section 4 describes a class structure that changed very slowly. New taxes, new business opportunities and altered working conditions in the First World War changed it very fast. As you read this chapter think how the pace of change quickened, how some lost out and others made long-term gains.

The chapter asks:

A What did it cost in lives and money? (pp. 251–252)

B How did the war change British politics? (pp. 252–256)

C Which political parties gained or lost from the First World War? (pp. 257–260)

D How much more power did government get in the war? (pp. 261–263)

E Which social classes gained or lost in the war? (pp. 264–268)

F Did women gain anything from the First World War? (pp. 268–270)

WHO GAINED FROM THE FIRST WORLD WAR (AND HOW MUCH DID EVERYBODY LOSE)?

FOCUS ROUTE

1 Make a list of the main losses in the First World War.
2 What were the main economic problems created by war?

A What did it cost in lives and money?

SOURCE 15.1 *The Territorials at Pozières on 23rd July 1916* by William Barnes Wollen. This scene was part of the Battle of the Somme, the deadliest battle in British history where over 400,000 British troops were killed or injured

Human cost: how many lives were lost?

What sounds a very simple question brings a very complex and unclear answer. Estimates from the census returns suggest 772,000 were killed, while calculations from the military service records give 722,000. The total seems likely to be between these two – about 9 per cent of men under 45. Far more were injured, and about 1.2 million British ex-servicemen later received disability pensions.

These were the most obvious losers, but those conscripted (called up) into the army clearly lost up to four years of their lives, and their careers or educations were disrupted. There were 3.8 million soldiers by the end of the war and well over 5 million people had served in the army from an overall male population of nearly 18 million.

Financial cost: how much wealth was lost?

This is even more difficult to answer. At its peak the war was taking about half of the total wealth being produced in the country, and the government ran up massive debts. Counting all those contributing to the war effort in industries such as mining or clothing as well as munitions, 61 per cent of the male industrial labour force were estimated to be involved in war work by the last part of the struggle. Government spending rose from under 13 per cent of GROSS NATIONAL PRODUCT (GNP) in 1913 to over 59 per cent in 1918, almost entirely because of the war. Apart from Britain's own army and navy, the government provided weapons and substantial loans to its allies, and much of the money was never repaid.

GROSS NATIONAL PRODUCT
The value of goods and services produced in a state during a year (Gross Domestic Product) together with income from investments abroad minus the amount paid out to foreign investors.

Expenses and losses

- Total government war spending was about £9,420 million.

- British exports fell as it was impossible to reach many foreign countries, and British industries concentrated on war production.
- Imports had to be kept up to provide food and raw materials.

- Britain had to make large payments overseas for imports and for its own war effort. It also lent over £1,500 million to its allies.

> **TRADE BALANCE**
> This is a comparison between the total value of goods and services a country sells abroad (exports) and the total value of what it buys from abroad (imports). A comparison of the goods bought and sold is the visible balance of trade. Services are called invisibles, and the payments for these include interest on loans.

How they were met in wartime

- Under 30% was raised in taxes.
- Most of this was collected from **direct taxes** (paid straight to the government, and mainly falling on the wealthy) rather than **indirect taxes** on goods and services.
- Direct taxes made up nearly 80% of government income at the end of the war compared with under 60% just before. Income tax rose from 1s 2d (about 6%) to 30%.

- Britain had long imported a greater value of goods than it exported. Before the war it had more than made up for this, with earnings from providing services and income from overseas investments, and so had a favourable TRADE BALANCE. By 1918 this had been altered to an unfavourable one.

- Britain stopped investing overseas and had to get large amounts of money back from abroad.
- It ran up a debt overseas of over £1,200 million.

How future generations picked up the bill

- Over 70% was borrowed. The **national debt** (total owed by the government) went up from £650m to £7,435 million. Ten years after the war about 40% of government spending was going on interest on war debt.

- Britain had lost export markets, though France and Germany lost more. Many countries which had previously relied on British exports now made the goods themselves.
- Wartime disruption increased Britain's long-term difficulties in keeping up its exports. There was an unemployment problem in the 1920s.

- Britain ended the war in debt to foreign countries.
- Some of its own loans to foreign countries, particularly to Russia, were not repaid. Former allies still owed Britain £1,500 million in 1926.
- Britain itself had large payments to make to the USA, now the major country that could provide finance to the rest of the world.

Britain had already lost much of its world industrial supremacy to the USA and Germany before the war, and the USA's greater resources were obvious. Britain's economic problems were not just a result of the First World War, but they cannot be separated from the wartime losses and disruption either.

> **FOCUS ROUTE**
> How far was the coalition formed because Asquith's Liberal government had failed?

B How did the war change British politics?

■ 15B Government ministries in the First World War

DATE	PARTY	PRIME MINISTER
1914–May 1915	Liberal	Asquith
May 1915–December 1916	Coalition	Asquith
December 1916–1918	Coalition	Lloyd George

Until May 1915 Asquith's Liberal government continued to run the country and the war with the addition of the famous general Lord Kitchener, who became Secretary for War because he was a suitable national figurehead. In May Asquith brought in other parties to form a coalition government.

**Stage 1:
Liberal
government
weakened**

Ammunition shortages
The country was not producing enough ammunition for fighting on the Western Front. A dispatch from Colonel Repington in *The Times* blamed the government for a shell shortage there

Disaster in the Dardenelles
An attempt to land a British force at the Dardanelles in April 1915 to knock Turkey out of the war went badly wrong. Disagreements between Winston Churchill (First Lord of the Admiralty, minister in charge of the navy) and Lord Fisher (First Sea Lord, the commander of the navy as top admiral) led to Fisher's high-profile resignation

Stage 2:

The Conservative dilemma
Bonar Law, the Conservative leader, found his MPs wanted to attack the government and vote against it. This could bring it down and lead to a general election. The Conservatives might win, but an election could be damaging in wartime, and a purely Conservative government might find it difficult to run the war. Bonar Law feared the consequences

Stage 3:

Bonar Law contacted **Lloyd George**, who had suggested coalition with the Conservatives in a very different crisis over the House of Lords in 1910. Lloyd George thought coalition could bring useful changes in the way the war was run

Bonar Law and **Lloyd George** both tactfully suggested the idea to Asquith, who had probably been thinking about it. He did not want a general election which most people believed would bring defeat for the Liberals

Stage 4:

The Asquith coalition government was formed with a Cabinet of 12 Liberals, 8 Conservatives, 1 Labour leader and Lord Kitchener as Secretary for War. The Irish Nationalists turned down an invitation to join. Lloyd George became Minister of Munitions, and Liberals continued to hold the top jobs

WHO GAINED FROM THE FIRST WORLD WAR (AND HOW MUCH DID EVERYBODY LOSE)?

■ **Learning trouble spot**

Coalition governments

Coalition governments are made up from politicians of different parties. Britain did not fight a major war between 1815 and 1914, and the modern British party system substantially developed between these years. There was therefore no previous example of what a government made up of one party should do in a major war.

Although there were changes in the ministers, and some important disagreements within parties, leaders from the Liberal, Conservative and Labour parties worked together in coalition from May 1915, though most Labour ministers withdrew in 1917. The coalition continued for nearly four years after the war, and politicians formed similar coalition governments in the Second World War.

254

WHO GAINED FROM THE FIRST WORLD WAR (AND HOW MUCH DID EVERYBODY LOSE)?

SOURCE 15.2 Sir Maurice Hankey's views on the existing war committee in his memoirs written later and published in 1961

[T]he Committee was ... failing to keep abreast of its work, and the list of subjects awaiting decision was continually increasing.

HOW DID POLITICIANS USE THE PRESS?

Important newspaper owners had campaigned against Asquith and wanted to remove him. It was Max Aitken, the owner of the Express, who actually brought together Bonar Law, Carson and Lloyd George.

Lloyd George and Carson obviously gave newspapers information at key points in the crisis and must have intended this to strengthen their position. The owner of Reynolds' News, a friend of Lloyd George, spoke to him in the afternoon of Saturday 2 December and then published in the paper on Sunday 3 December news of a resignation letter Lloyd George had sent.

How did Lloyd George become prime minister?

Asquith was prime minister continuously from 1908 to December 1916 but he headed a coalition government from May 1915. Lloyd George had been his most prominent minister as Chancellor of the Exchequer from 1908 to 1915. Then, when there was a crisis over ammunition shortages on the Western Front in May 1915, Lloyd George became the new Minister of Munitions. His energetic action soon helped to increase production and made his reputation as an efficient administrator.

Asquith and Lloyd George differed over their approach to war in important ways. Asquith was concerned to get broad national agreement on wartime measures and thought the Liberal Party, which had long helped different classes work together, had an important role in this. Lloyd George thought little about party. He wanted quick action to solve problems and win the war. He was much readier to introduce conscription than Asquith and got his way in January and May 1916 (see pages 261–262). He became Secretary for War in July after Lord Kitchener was drowned when his ship struck a German mine. Frustrated by the lack of progress on the Western Front, he hoped to alter British strategy but soon found he could do little against the opposition of army generals. By November 1916 he believed that the decision-making arrangements in the Cabinet itself needed reform.

Since November 1915, Asquith's Cabinet had had a war committee but Lloyd George did not think it made decisions quickly enough. He was so dissatisfied that he was thinking of resigning. The Cabinet Secretary, Sir Maurice Hankey (a civil servant concerned with administration, not a politician), also thought it was not quite up to the job (see Source 15.2). He suggested forming a smaller war committee.

Then followed a strange series of events.

a) In late November Lloyd George met with leading Conservatives – Bonar Law and Sir Edward Carson – to discuss setting up a small war committee to take over day-to-day running of the war effort. Carson (leader of the Ulster Protestants before 1914) had resigned from Asquith's government and was his leading critic on the Conservative side. Although the committee's membership was not fixed, the three leaders clearly thought that they were going to man it.

b) To start with, Asquith rejected these proposals. He was not happy with his role (or lack of it) on the war committee. However, on Sunday 3 December he appeared to agree a compromise that would give him some guarantees although he was not a full-time member.

c) On Monday 4 December *The Times* newspaper ran a prominent editorial supporting Lloyd George's proposals.

d) Also on Monday 4 December, Asquith responded to the editorial by rejecting the proposals altogether. He had taken the advice of some members of his Cabinet.

e) On the Tuesday, Lloyd George and Bonar Law both resigned from their jobs in government because Asquith had rejected the proposals.

f) Asquith then resigned as Prime Minister the same day, either because his position as leader was now impossible or as a way of outwitting his opponents as he thought no one else could form a government.

g) Lloyd George himself formed a government and became prime minister.

Asquith was never in government again. Disputes between the two men remained and led to a long-term split in the Liberal Party. With hindsight we can see the dispute as the crucial event that fatally weakened the party. Historians have argued about the events and key politicians' motives ever since. You will do the same.

255

WHO GAINED FROM THE FIRST WORLD WAR (AND HOW MUCH DID EVERYBODY LOSE)?

These are the issues:

- Were the proposals needed?
- Was Asquith's proposed role on the war committee appropriate?
- Did the press have undue influence on the developments?
- And finally, how far can Lloyd George be seen to be acting in the national interest, for the public good, or how far was this a plot to remove Asquith and so achieve Lloyd George's ambition of becoming prime minister?

SOURCE INVESTIGATION

Sources 15.2–15.11 will help you to investigate this crisis.

1 Compare Sources 15.2 and 15.6. According to these sources, why was the committee needed?
2 Compare Sources 15.3 and 15.4. How do they disagree and which do you most agree with?
3 a) What mixture of motives does Frances Stevenson suggest for Lloyd George's actions in Source 15.6?
   b) Why might this information be trustworthy or untrustworthy?
4 What attitude does *The Times* editorial in Source 15.7 take to:
   a) Lloyd George's proposals
   b) Asquith's proposed role?
5 In what ways do Sources 15.9–15.11 indicate different reasons for Asquith's resignation?
6 Using Sources 15.2–15.11
   a) How far do you agree that Asquith was forced out of office?
   b) How far do you think Lloyd George's proposals and methods were right in view of national war needs?
   c) To what extent would you see Lloyd George's actions as
      i) a sordid plot
      ii) a public-spirited move to win the war
      iii) a combination of both?

SOURCE 15.3 Asquith's objections to the war committee proposal in a letter to Lloyd George, 4 December 1916

I have come decidedly to the conclusion that it is not possible that such a Committee could be made workable and effective without the Prime Minister as its Chairman ... I am satisfied, on reflection, that any other arrangement ... would be found in experience impracticable, and incompatible with the retention of the Prime Minister's final and supreme control.

SOURCE 15.5 Asquith claimed in a letter handed to Bonar Law on 4 December that Lloyd George came up with the war committee scheme as a way of replacing him as Prime Minister

[T]here is but one construction, and one only, that could be put on the new arrangement – that it has been engineered by him with the purpose, not perhaps at the moment, but as soon as a fitting pretext could be found, of his displacing me.

SOURCE 15.4 In a reply to Asquith Lloyd George emphasised how the compromise proposals, which had been worked out for the war committee, would safeguard the Prime Minister's position

The Prime Minister to have supreme and effective control of war policy;
The Agenda of the War Committee will be submitted to him; its chairman will report to him daily; he can direct it to consider particular topics or proposals and all its conclusions will be subject to his approval or veto. He can, of course, at his own discretion attend meetings of the Committee.
These proposals safeguarded your position and power as Prime Minister in every particular.

SOURCE 15.6 One good indication of Lloyd George's thinking came from the diary kept by Frances Stevenson, the devoted secretary who later became his wife. These are a few short extracts from her entries for the crisis period

22 November 1916   *D [David Lloyd George] says that the PM is absolutely hopeless. He cannot make up his mind about anything, & seems to have lost all will-power.*

30 November 1916   *If D. strikes alone, it will mean his forming an opposition, but if he & Bonar strike together it will mean the smashing up of the government ... the whole country is pretty sick of [Asquith]. We are receiving countless anxious letters from all parts of the country, urging D to take over affairs. He seems to be the only one in whom the people have any confidence, & I am certain that if he were to resign now he would have the backing of the whole country.*

2 December 1916   *The PM has sent a reply to D's Memo, but it simply proposes an alternative which is if anything worse than the old regime. Moreover he insists on being Chairman of the new Committee, & the vital point of D's proposal was that the PM should have no part in it at all. The PM also insists that the Cabinet shall have the final word in all matters, which of course nullifies (cancels out) everything which might be achieved by the setting up of a new Committee.*

SOURCE 15.7 This editorial appeared in *The Times* on Monday 4 December. The Editor of *The Times* spoke to Carson (who in turn was in touch with Lloyd George) before he wrote it. It showed inside knowledge of proposals for a new war committee which had been agreed on Sunday 3 December

Lloyd George has finally taken his stand against the present cumbrous methods of directing the war ... The gist of his proposal is understood to be the establishment forthwith of a small War Council, fully charged with the supreme direction of the war. Of this council Mr Asquith himself is not to be a member – the assumption being that the prime minister has sufficient cares of a more general character without devoting himself wholly, as the new council must be devoted if it is to be effective, to the daily task of organising victory ... The inclusion of Sir Edward Carson is believed to form an essential part of Mr Lloyd George's scheme, and it is one which will be thoroughly understood.

SOURCE 15.8 Asquith wrote to Lloyd George on the Monday, blaming *The Times* editorial which had obviously been written with inside knowledge

Unless the impression is at once corrected that I am being relegated to the position of an irresponsible spectator of the War, I cannot possibly go on.

SOURCE 15.9 Roy Jenkins (1978) summed up the position in a famous biography of Asquith

In these circumstances immediate resignation was the only course open to Asquith ... He decided to resign, not as a tactical manoeuvre, but because he did not have sufficient support to carry on.

SOURCE 15.10 J.H. Thomas, the Labour leader, wrote in his memoirs

[What influenced Asquith] was the advice of a number of close friends that it was impossible for Lloyd George to form a Cabinet. He himself told me this.

SOURCE 15.11 According to Lord Riddell's war diary, Robert Donald, the editor of a Liberal paper, the *Daily Chronicle*, who saw Asquith after he resigned, told Lloyd George

Asquith was convinced that you [Lloyd George] would be unable to form a Government and the King would have to recall him ... he said, striking his hand upon the table, 'He will have to come in on my terms!'

FOCUS ROUTE

What features of Lloyd George's government would make it more efficient in managing the war?

How did Lloyd George's coalition government change the way Britain was governed?

See Charts 15D–15G for the effects on different political parties.

- A **small war Cabinet of five** replaced the normal-sized Cabinet of about twenty and made key decisions. Its first members were Lloyd George (Liberal), Bonar Law and Curzon (Conservatives), Henderson (Labour) and Milner (a non-party minister and enthusiast for imperialism and national efficiency who had been a colonial administrator).
- Most of the **top jobs were now held by Conservatives**. Addison, the Minister of Munitions, was the only Liberal in a key office apart from Lloyd George.
- A **Cabinet secretariat** made the Cabinet more efficient and business like. It produced regular agendas and minutes for the first time and kept in touch with different government departments.
- More **Cabinet sub-committees** were established on a long-term basis to co-ordinate work between government departments.
- **More government ministries** were now set up for Labour, Shipping, Food and National Service. The number of ministers grew to 88, nearly twice the total before the war.
- The Prime Minister himself developed his own **Prime Minister's secretariat** which could provide him with advice and ideas.

Most of the new ministries were abolished after the war and the full Cabinet was restored. There was also a reaction against many of Lloyd George's methods in the 1920s, so that the Prime Minister's secretariat was scrapped, though the Cabinet secretariat remained and is at the centre of government today.

Which political parties gained or lost from the First World War?

FOCUS ROUTE

Use Charts 15E–15G to compare the parties in the following ways:

1 Which were most divided over the war at the start?
2 Which party's policies would do most to help win the war?
3 Which gained and which lost influence in
   a) the Asquith coalition government
   b) the Lloyd George coalition government?
4 How united or divided were they at the end of the war?
5 Study Chart 15D to compare the election results in 1910 and 1918. Which parties appear to have gained and lost support as a result of the war?

■ 15D The December 1910 and 1918 election results

The December 1910 election was the last before the First World War and the December 1918 election the first after it. Circumstances had changed because the electorate was much larger in 1918 due to the inclusion of women over 30 for the first time and the removal of many restrictions on men voting.

The main issue was whether the coalition government led by Lloyd George should continue. Most Conservatives, a substantial number of Liberals and a few Labour MPs supported the government but all three parties were divided to some extent and Sinn Fein was important in Irish elections for the first time (see page 249). Direct comparisons between 1910 and 1918 are therefore potentially misleading but these election figures are by far the best indication we have of overall changes in national public opinion

SOURCE 15.12 Election results 1910 and 1918

December 1910	Total votes	Percentage	MPs
Conservative and Liberal Unionist	2,420,566	46.3	272
Liberal	2,295,888	43.9	272
Labour	371,772	7.1	42
Irish Nationalist	131,375	2.5	84
Others	8,768	0.2	
Total	5,228,369	100.0	670

December 1918	Total votes	Percentage	MPs
Coalition Conservatives	3,504,198	32.6	335
Coalition Liberals	1,455,640	13.5	133
Coalition Labour	161,521	1.5	10
Total coalition	**5,121,359**	**47.6**	**478**
Other Conservatives	370,375	3.4	23
Independent Liberals generally following Asquith	1,298,808	12.1	28
Labour	2,385,472	22.2	63
Irish Unionists	292,722	2.7	25
Irish Nationalists (Home Rulers)	238,477	2.2	7
Sinn Fein	486,867	4.5	73
Other	572,503		10
Grand total	10,766,583		707

PARTY SITUATION AT START OF WAR

- Many ministers in Asquith's Liberal government had **misgivings** about going to war, but most accepted the need to fight and only two members of the Cabinet resigned.
- The government was facing **severe threats** at the time from opposing groups in Ireland, trade unions and Suffragettes. Suddenly these difficult groups turned to supporting the war effort. Asquith privately wrote a little playlet referring to how 'Luck helped you in external things ... above all (at a most critical and fateful moment in your career) in the sudden outbreak of the Great War.' His luck altered when the war turned out to be so much longer than expected.

POLICIES

- **War needs threatened liberty, the basic principle of the Liberal Party.** Liberals disliked measures such as censorship or imprisoning foreigners which were impossible to resist, but the biggest problems came over **conscription**. Liberals' opposition or hesitancy on these often made them look indecisive or ineffective in fighting the war.
- The decision to go to war and increased government control in national life worsened existing Liberal **party divisions**. Liberals varied between enthusiastic patriotic imperialists and people who wanted Britain to stay neutral in the war. Some had campaigned for much more state action before 1914 whilst others thought the government's wartime controls were wrong. Some of these differences led to disputes between Asquith and Lloyd George, but a number of Liberal MPs thought both had compromised Liberal principles too much.

ASQUITH COALITION

- **Liberal ministers** were in a **majority** and had the **most important jobs,** but the coalition **broke up the 'Progressive Alliance' between Liberals, Labour and Irish Nationalists** that had given them a parliamentary majority since 1910.
- Combination with the Conservatives made it more difficult to carry out Home Rule. The Irish Home Rule Party refused to join the coalition, and Conservative ministers later stopped a compromise agreement for a division of Ireland and the introduction of Home Rule in 1916.
- The Lib–Lab Pact, which had safeguarded the Liberals' position at elections, was now irrelevant.
- Differences within the coalition, particularly over conscription, presented the most immediate problems. Some Liberal ministers supported it, while others opposed it on principle or because they thought that British industry could not supply a larger army with a smaller home labour force.

LLOYD GEORGE COALITION

- The way Lloyd George succeeded Asquith **split the two main Liberal leaders** and their followers. Most Liberal ministers left with Asquith, and most Liberal MPs still saw him as their leader. Asquith and most of the MPs still supported the government in the House of Commons, but Lloyd George increasingly depended on the Conservatives who provided most of his ministers, took the top jobs and gave the government its main support in Parliament.

DEVELOPMENTS IN 1917–18

- Both Asquith and Lloyd George had whips (party officials) and both sides contacted all the Liberal MPs. There was no clear divide between the two groups, but more Liberal MPs came to oppose the Lloyd George government as time went on.
- Local Liberal parties generally stayed united but many seem to have become inactive.

1918 ELECTION

- 159 Liberals stood as government candidates, with letters from the party leaders, Lloyd George and Bonar Law, supporting them (the letters were nicknamed 'coupons' by their opponents). **133 of these Coalition Liberal candidates won.**
- **Independent Liberals did badly** – only 28 won. Asquith himself was defeated.
- Few Liberals won against both Conservative and Labour candidates.
- Many local Liberal parties had declined.
- Labour now emerged as the strongest opposition to the government, which had a Liberal Prime Minister but mainly Conservative membership and a Conservative majority in the House of Commons.

PARTY RESPONSES AT START OF WAR	• **Ramsay MacDonald**, the Chairman and leading figure in the Parliamentary Labour Party, **opposed the war** from the start. Most Labour MPs supported it. **Arthur Henderson replaced MacDonald as leader**. • A strong socialist minority opposed the war, but both supporters and opponents worked together on the party's executive committee.
POLICIES	• Much socialist thinking was internationalist, opposed to wars that boosted imperialism and used the workers as cannon fodder for capitalist governments. When a **majority accepted war** after the invasion of Belgium, the **party was split**. Differences over conscription, again accepted by most Labour MPs, split it again, but, as the war continued, opponents often focused more on measures to prevent future wars which made reuniting easier. • **Increased state control in wartime fitted in well with Labour's aims** for redistributing wealth and power by government action. The Labour Party's *Daily Citizen* welcomed a government Sugar Commission to buy and distribute supplies fairly, saying it showed the nation turning 'to the collectivist experiments urged for so many years by the Labour movement'. State control over railways, mines and shipping all suggested that Labour's policies for nationalising these industries could work.
ROLE IN ASQUITH COALITION	• As the government needed trade union support for the war effort, so it brought **Labour politicians who represented the unions into government**. Arthur Henderson represented Labour interests, and two other Labour MPs were also ministers.
LLOYD GEORGE COALITION	• **Henderson** was now a **member of the five-man war Cabinet** and the number of Labour ministers increased from three to eight. Ministers such as J.R. Clynes, Food Controller for a while, were judged successful administrators. The experience made Labour a credible party to participate in government in the future.
DEVELOPMENTS IN 1917–18	• **Henderson resigned from the government** when other ministers opposed him going to an International Socialist conference at Stockholm in 1917. • He became Secretary of the Labour Party again and leader of the parliamentary group for a short time. He worked with Ramsay MacDonald and other opponents of the war in drawing up a statement of Labour's war aims, so **substantially reuniting the party**. More than any other party, Labour developed new policies that widened its appeal. Henderson built up Labour's organisation for future elections. Constituency Labour parties were now established everywhere so people could join the party directly, and there was a new National Executive elected by the Party Conference to organise Labour nationwide.

Labour's new policies in 1917–18	Possible appeal
War aims • These were intended to make the world more peaceful and democratic and included setting up a League of Nations.	• Appealed to idealistic Liberals and encouraged some high-profile Liberal MPs to join the Labour Party.
Clause IV in the Constitution • To get the fairest possible distribution of wealth by 'common ownership of the means of production, distribution and exchange'. This suggested the party was a fundamentalist socialist one, but Labour governments never carried it out or seriously intended to do so.	• Was it a gesture to socialists in the party? • Was it to show a democratic way to achieve socialism, as an alternative to the violent Russian revolution? • Was it to show how wealth could be found to pay off war debts and get social change?
'Labour and the New Social Order' • Drawn up by the Fabian Sidney Webb and approved by the party conference in 1918. The party now stood for: • **National minimum wage** • **Nationalisation** of the most important industries • **Progressive taxation** (taxes falling more heavily on the wealthy) to get money for better welfare services.	• Showed practical policies for achieving moderate socialism.

1918 ELECTION	• A delegate conference decided the **party** should **resign from the government and fight the election in opposition**. • Labour **gained 63 MPs compared with 38 at the start of the war**, largely because it put up candidates in constituencies it had not previously contested. Individual candidates did not gain a much higher proportion of the poll than they had in 1910, but they had considerable strengths for the future. • Labour was the main opposition party in the House of Commons after the election • Its more internationalist foreign policy attracted some Radical Liberal MPs, and, most importantly, trade union growth brought it far more members. Total affiliated party membership grew from 2.1 million in 1915 to 3.5 million in early 1919.

PARTY RESPONSES AT START OF WAR	• Conservatives supported Britain's entry into the war. Their MPs soon became critical of the Liberal government's war management, pressing for more munitions and measures against foreign goods.
POLICIES	• **Conservative thinking, with its emphasis on patriotism, imperial greatness and practical policies, fitted in with wartime needs.** Troops from DOMINIONS fought in France, encouraging imperialist sentiment, and Conservative PROTECTIONIST policies were now more acceptable. • The outbreak of war suggested Conservatives had been right to call for a stronger navy before 1914. Many Conservatives had long favoured conscription and readily accepted increased state powers to win the war. Some had misgivings about high taxation and there was a certain amount of dispute over where to concentrate military attacks and how to deal with Ireland, but Conservatives had fewer doubts and disagreements than other parties.
ROLE IN ASQUITH COALITION	• **Conservative ministers** were **outnumbered by Liberals** in the Cabinet, and their leader, Bonar Law, had the comparatively minor job of Colonial Secretary. • Ordinary Conservative MPs were increasingly dissatisfied with the government's war management and many campaigned for conscription. • Most of the MPs who were not in the government or armed forces supported a Unionist war committee pressing for greater action and efficiency during 1916. They frequently voted against the government. Carson, the Ulster leader, had been one of the Conservative ministers but resigned from the Coalition in October 1915. He then looked more and more like the leader of the Opposition until Bonar Law joined with him and Lloyd George to get changes in December 1916 which led to Asquith's resignation.
LLOYD GEORGE COALITION	• Conservatives were now **stronger in the Cabinet and held top jobs** in charge of the Foreign Office, Home Office, Treasury, War Office and Admiralty. They did not always get their own way, but they became increasingly powerful.
1918 ELECTION	• The Conservative Party had an **alliance with Lloyd George** who now had a great reputation as a war leader, but it is uncertain how much they needed this. • Over half the British MPs in the House of Commons were Conservatives. They therefore had enough support in Parliament to form their own Conservative government and did not need to work with Lloyd George and his Coalition Liberal supporters. Nineteen Conservatives stood against candidates who had letters of support from Bonar Law and Lloyd George (known as coupons), and five of them won.

DOMINIONS

Countries outside the UK under the sovereignty (supreme power) of the British monarch but effectively having full powers to govern themselves and decide how far they will associate with the UK.

PROTECTION

Taxing imported goods to make them more expensive so that people will buy home-produced goods because they are cheaper than foreign ones. This protects the competitive position of home industries.

ACTIVITY

1 The Conservative and Labour parties were both stronger at the end of the war than they had been at the beginning, in some significant ways.
   a) In what ways was each one stronger?
   b) Overall which one do you think had gained most from wartime circumstances? Give reasons for your answer.
2 The Liberals were weaker at the end of the war. Look back at the work you did on Chapter 13 and to what extent you concluded that the Liberal Party was already dying before the First World War. Using what you have read so far in this chapter together with Charts 15D and 15E, explain the arguments for and against the war being the main reason for the decline of the Liberal Party.

D # How much more power did government get in the war?

261

WHO GAINED FROM THE FIRST WORLD WAR (AND HOW MUCH DID EVERYBODY LOSE)?

Defence of the Realm Acts in 1914–16

These stopped anything that the government thought would harm the war effort. The lists of such things grew and grew, but the main rules were about:

- **blackouts** to stop enemy aircraft seeing towns and villages they might bomb
- **demonstrations** which could distract the police or **alarmist reports** which might upset morale
- **newspaper censorship**, which banned journalists from the Front, ensuring they relied on government briefings and sent tricky items to a government Press Bureau.

Two issues towered above all others.

Issue 1: conscription

Total war with a mass army and full-scale use of national resources poses big problems for any government. Asquith's Liberal ministers often found wartime needs conflicted with their Liberal beliefs (see Chart 15E), and the worst problem of all was conscription.

(see Chart 15E)

Should a fit 22-year-old man without wife or children be allowed to stay at home in safety while fathers of families in their 40s are volunteering and being killed?

Governments exist to protect people against dangers. Forcing people to fight is putting them in the greatest possible danger.

Britain encouraged France to rely on British support if war came. Britain must do everything to stop the fall of France or no one will think Britain is worth having as an ally again.

Governments should protect people's freedom. Conscription takes it away.

If the British allow France to fall, Germany will be so powerful that Britain will never be safe.

Governments should respect individuals' beliefs and not force them to act against their conscience if they do not believe in fighting.

Men have a duty to defend their country. Patriotism is one of the highest virtues.

The government decided to go to war and ordinary people had no say.

Men should be prepared to protect the country's liberties for future generations.

ACTIVITY

Work in pairs to produce a case either **for** or **against** conscription in the First World War, as if you were living in 1916. The question below is how the issue would have appeared to many people in 1915 and 1916. The statements give some of the arguments which well-educated people might have used for and against conscription at the time.

DISCUSS

a) How far was the Derby Scheme a compromise on the conscription issue and how did it help introduce conscription?

b) Professor Marwick (1991) described it as 'a gigantic engine of fraud and moral blackmail'. Think about the pressures men would be under and discuss whether you agree.

Ministers in the government had differing attitudes towards conscription. Generally Conservative ministers were more enthusiastic than Liberal ones, and Lloyd George saw a much more urgent need for it than Asquith.

In October 1915 the government began the **Derby Scheme**, named after its Director of Recruiting, the Earl of Derby. This involved a national register of all men and women aged between 15 and 65, including details of their age and job. Men were encouraged to 'attest' (declare solemnly) their willingness to join the army, and tribunals were set up to decide who should be left out for family reasons or because of their existing jobs. By the end of 1915 just over half the single men – 1,150,000 out of 2,179,000 – and 1,153,000 married men had attested they would serve.

Whatever the original intention conscription was introduced:

- for single men aged between 18 and 41 in January 1916
- for married men aged up to 41 in May 1916
- for all men aged 18–51 in April 1918.

Those who were against fighting in the army on principle could appeal to local tribunals. There were about 16,000 such 'conscientious objectors', but their claims were not normally allowed unless they could give religious reasons based on membership of Christian groups such as the Quakers.

Issue 2: the economy

FOCUS ROUTE

Make your own copy of the table below and, using this section, complete it to show how much government increased its power in different areas.

	How government increased its control	How far and in what ways existing owners maintained their control or business remained in private hands
Industry		
Transport		
Trade in foreign goods		
Food distribution		
Agriculture		

Before the war, government intervened little.

TELEGRAPH
System of wires for sending and receiving messages electronically.

- Apart from the Post Office, TELEGRAPH and telephone systems, and a few naval dockyards and munitions works, businesses were run by capitalist owners with little central government control. The main exceptions were railways and coal mining where more regulations had been introduced for safety reasons and because of the miners' bargaining strength.
- The UK was a free trade country without taxes or restrictions intended to alter the pattern of trade.
- Working hours were restricted for women and young people, though not normally for men except in mines and railways. The 1909 Trade Boards Act and 1912 Mines Act both made a start in regulating wages, but wage rates were not generally under government control.
- Government introduced welfare benefits in the reforms of 1906–14 (see pages 196–202) which meant higher taxes and some direct costs for employers.
- Many local councils ran gas, electricity, water and tramway companies. Local authorities ran schools, dealt with public health and provided limited help for the poor.

Government intervention was therefore increasing by 1914 but this was small compared to its wartime role.

How government intervened more in war

A crisis over munitions supplies in spring 1915 led to much greater government control of trade and industry. The Treasury Agreement worked out with employers and unions in April changed the way munitions factories worked. The Munitions of War Act in July gave the government power to control not only munitions factories but also businesses that provided the raw materials, fuel and transport needed for the war.

Industry
- The Ministry of Munitions started up 250 government-owned national factories by the end of the war.
- Generally the government took supervising powers over businesses which remained in private hands. Existing managers ran enterprises but followed

government guidelines necessary for the war effort. For example, the Ministry of Munitions supervised 20,000 'controlled establishments' by 1918.

- Coal mines were under government control by early 1917. British industry and transport ran on steam so it was necessary to safeguard fuel supplies.

Transport

- Railways, the main kind of inland transport, were under government control from the start. They were run by a railway executive committee made up of general managers from the major lines who followed government instructions. The management of different railway companies was amalgamated for efficiency.
- Ships which provided overseas transport gradually came under government orders. A Ministry of Shipping took over most ships from December 1916, with a management committee from the shipowners rather like the one which managed railways.

Trade

- As the country and the war effort relied on imported food and raw materials, government gradually took control of imports to ensure fair distribution and efficient war production. By 1918 it bought over 90 per cent of British imports.

Food

- Food shortage was the biggest threat. How did the government respond?

> Britain imported most of its food needs, including about 80 per cent of the wheat, 40 per cent of the meat and almost all the sugar that fed the country.

↓

> The government appointed commissions, first sugar and later wheat, to make bulk purchases to distribute goods more evenly.

↓

> Problems increased in 1917. German submarine attacks worsened food shortages, prices rose and public discontent increased.

↓

> The government introduced more general price controls, appealed to people to ration themselves and allowed local councils to introduce rationing schemes.

↓

> Eventually, in 1918 the government had national schemes for rationing items such as meat and butter. At the end of the war 85 per cent of Britain's food was distributed by government-controlled firms or agencies and 94 per cent was sold at prices fixed by the state.

Agriculture

The government tried to get more food grown at home. Agriculture committees of farmers and landowners were set up to ensure more intensive land use, but government control of farming was looser than in industry and trade, relying more on persuasion and having less productive results.

FOCUS ROUTE

Make your own copy of this table and, as you read pages 264–268, list what different classes gained and lost during the First World War.

	Gains	Losses
Upper class (landowners)		
Middle class		
Working class: • Living standards • Bargaining power and social reforms		

E Which social classes gained or lost in the war?

Social historians generally agree that the working class made up about 80 per cent of the British population. These were wage-earners and a small number who got low incomes as street sellers, shopkeepers or piece workers (workers paid by the amount they produced). Of the other 20 per cent most were middle class, but a small minority of wealthy landowners and businessmen formed an upper class.

Some historians think the war brought people together, but this is very uncertain. Men from different classes in the army might mix more than they would back home, but they frequently stayed apart. Junior officers did lead their troops into battle, but the officers, who predominantly came from the upper and middle classes, often lived separately from their men and had their own quarters, canteens, cinemas and even brothels.

Did the upper and middle classes gain?

Deaths

A larger proportion of upper- and middle-class men joined the army than in the population as a whole, normally to become officers. They generally led from the front, which was often fatal. Officer casualties were roughly double those of their men. For example, about 19 per cent of peers (Lords) under 50 who served in the forces were killed, compared with an average death rate for all troops of 11.5 per cent.

This often meant more large death duties to pay in addition to other heavy taxes. After the war landowners held a declining proportion of national wealth and income, and many estates were sold.

Taxes

A new pattern of progressive taxation hit the wealthier classes. The income tax rates, which rose from 6 per cent to 30 per cent, affected them most, and wealthy men who had previously paid under a tenth of their income to the government were now often giving about a third.

Profits

Middle-class businessmen and farmers often benefited from higher profits with wartime demand. Returns in 1916 showed average profits 32 per cent above pre-war levels in the coal, shipbuilding, iron and engineering industries. Farmers' profits appear to have increased five times between 1914 and 1917.

Of course, businessmen were not supposed to benefit so much from others' suffering, and so an excess profits duty, rising from 50 per cent to 80 per cent, was charged on whatever profit they made above pre-war levels. This duty brought in a quarter of the government's wartime income, but many middle-class businessmen still prospered.

Since managerial expertise also seemed more important to a government mobilising the country for war, many business leaders entered Lloyd George's government from 1916.

Did the working class gain economically?

FOCUS ROUTE

1 Make a table with the following headings and complete it using evidence in this section.

What evidence suggests the working class had better living standards?	What suggests they had worse living standards?	What could be used to argue either way?

2 Work out which evidence is most important for deciding whether the working class gained and why.
3 Summarise your findings on working-class living standards and add these to the table you began for the Focus route above.

Some historians argue that working-class living standards rose significantly by the end of the war, but the evidence is so varied it is possible to argue for different conclusions. Jay Winter (1985) stressed how life expectancy increased for men above military age and for many women during the war and how infant death rates went down, but not all historians agree about the strength of his evidence. For instance, he used the Prudential Assurance Company's tables for calculating the life prospects of working-class men, and these may not be representative of the whole population. Yet death rates for children aged up to four did fall sharply before 1918 when a flu epidemic struck, and this is strong evidence of improving prosperity.

Better medical treatment could not account for much improvement. Some 14,000 out of 25,000 doctors were serving in the armed forces by the end of the war, and school medical services were cut back, though there were more health visitors and infant welfare centres. The housing situation also clearly got worse in the war as existing homes decayed and house building had virtually stopped. Taken together with the lower death rate, these changes suggest that living standards must have improved significantly in other ways.

Earnings

Historians then examine how earnings improved. Source 15.13 gives one set of figures for prices and an average from different workers' wages and earnings. Note the difference between wages paid for the normal working week and earnings which reflected the total amount of work done including overtime.

SOURCE 15.13 Index of wages, earnings and prices, 1914–18. These are always hard to calculate. It is necessary to work out an average for wages and then an average for the prices of the goods that workers normally bought with their income (see page 139).

In wartime it is specially difficult to work this out because there were rapid price changes. The prices of different items changed in a very varied way depending on scarcity and government regulations, and workers were likely to alter what they bought as circumstances changed. We have to be very careful how we use any index

Year	Weekly wages i.e. rate of pay	Weekly earnings i.e. allowing for overtime	Retail prices i.e. average cost of what workers usually bought with their wages
1914	100.0	100.0	100.0
1915	107.7	116.0	115.9
1916	117.3	132.0	133.1
1917	138.5	168.0	166.0
1918	178.8	209.0	189.7

Certainly historians have found indications that earnings increased ahead of prices by 1918, but prices had risen rapidly, ahead of some workers' earnings, in 1915 and 1916.

Spending and poverty

Most indications suggest that the total amount of money spent by the whole population did not go up as much as price rises would lead you to expect if people still consumed the same amount. British people seem to have bought about 20 per cent less overall than they would before the war. Some of this fall would have come from the wealthy consuming less. Half of it seems to have been accounted for by lower spending on alcohol and tobacco, which may well have improved people's health. Real spending on food (spending in comparison with prices) fell less, and again the sugar shortage probably did people good as it forced them to eat more healthily. Also, by the end of the war about 1000 canteens catered for over a million workers, and price controls and rationing in 1917–18 probably helped the least well off more than others.

These figures still do not give very impressive evidence of overall improvement, but there are further indications that the poor benefited from

POOR RELIEF
Help given to the poor paid for out of local taxes.

changes. Applications for POOR RELIEF went down and fewer children took subsidised school meals because their families were poor. While the Battle of the Somme raged in France in autumn 1916, the Board of Trade reported 'less total distress in the country than in an ordinary year of peace'.

Different types of work

When there was a big demand for labour, unskilled workers could easily gain higher wages; the differences between their pay and skilled workers' pay (differentials) were reduced. Again historians debate the extent of this. Differentials seem to have been reduced by 14 per cent in engineering compared with about 7 per cent in other heavy industries. Generally all types of workers did much better in industries involved in the war effort, such as munitions and engineering, and less well in those such as building where there was not so much demand for labour.

Overall the demand for labour obviously increased. There was less unemployment, more regular work and more work for women. A lot of people, particularly women, moved into better-paid jobs. Real wage figures would not show this; they give wages in individual jobs rather than how many people had what sort of job. The First World War expanded employment opportunities, and the poorest may have gained most. Many historians think this was the main reason for any improvement in living standards.

Did the working class gain more power?

FOCUS ROUTE

1 Make a table with these headings and complete it using the evidence in this section.

Ways in which the state gained more power over workers	Increased powers for trade unions and concessions from government

2 Summarise your findings on working-class bargaining power and social reform and add these to the table you began on page 264.

The government knew it relied on the workers for the war effort, but it could use patriotic arguments to get co-operation and laws which forced men to serve their country, whether as workers at home or soldiers abroad. Soldiers' sacrifices at the Front were a powerful argument to get workers' sacrifices at home. Lloyd George, who was brilliant at gaining agreements with union leaders, got major concessions over munitions workers' conditions in spring 1915 in the Treasury agreement that formed a basis for a new law – the Munitions of War Act. War workers lost their right to strike and had to accept ARBITRATION in disputes. Trade union leaders gave up all kinds of restrictive practices which protected skilled workers and accepted other less well trained employees doing their jobs. Essential war workers could not change jobs without leaving certificates from their employers. In return for all these concessions government agreed to safeguard workers' wages and restrict employers' profits. The safeguards, though, were not much help when prices soon shot up, and many employers clearly enjoyed huge profits.

ARBITRATION
Procedure for judging and making a decision in a dispute by a person or group not directly involved.

Working conditions and trade unions

Whatever laws or agreements stated, workers were still in a strong position when so much extra war work had to be done and there were so few workers to do it. If workers ignored the law and did strike, they could soon make gains. When South Wales miners went on strike in July 1915 the Minister of Munitions, Lloyd George, and the Labour Party's representative in the Cabinet, Arthur Henderson, were soon on the train to Cardiff ready to meet their demands. The most serious and widespread unrest in 1917, most marked around Glasgow in the Clydeside area of Scotland, soon led to a Commission of Inquiry.

267

WHO GAINED FROM THE FIRST WORLD WAR (AND HOW MUCH DID EVERYBODY LOSE)?

Trade union officials worked with government, and Labour Party leaders were appointed ministers to get workers' support. Of course, the more government used official trade union and Labour leaders to win over and control the working class, the more likely ordinary working men were to seek alternative spokesmen. Shop stewards – representatives chosen by fellow workers in a factory or workshop – often seemed more effective than their national leaders and gained greater influence. Some of these formed a left-wing 'shop stewards movement' which pressed for more rights.

Overall the trade union movement expanded hugely from just over 4 million members in 1914 to over 6.5 million in 1918. The government depended on it more, not only to meet wartime needs but for economic efficiency and social harmony. The Russian BOLSHEVIK REVOLUTION in 1917, socialist uprisings in Germany in 1918 and much smaller workers' protests in Britain, especially on 'Red' Clydeside, showed the dangers.

> **BOLSHEVIK REVOLUTION**
> Revolution which brought the Communists to power in Russia.

Social reform

Many wartime pressures increased the need for social reform (see arguments on page 250) and the government planned improvements in education, housing and health during 1917–18. Educational reform had been promised before the war began in 1914. An Education Act, fixing a uniform school leaving age of fourteen and abolishing remaining elementary school fees, was eventually passed just before war ended in 1918. The 1918 Reform Act gave the vote to all adult men (see Chapter 2) and the state soon took a far greater role in providing housing and unemployment benefits in 1919–20. We cannot know how much war hastened all this or slowed it down.

FOCUS ROUTE

Refer to the Defence of the Realm Acts (p. 261) and Chart 15H.

1 In what ways did the government restrict people's social lives?
2 How big a change did war bring in social life and entertainment?

You may find it useful to add points to the table you began on page 264.

■ 15H The brighter side of life

If you want to have a good time, you could go to ...

... a football match
Forget it. Should fit young men be running round football grounds in wartime?
League football stopped from Spring 1915

... a pub
Still plenty of opportunities, but drunken workers may not be on time next morning, and so hamper the war effort
Pubs generally open later, shut in the afternoon and close earlier at night
Expect weak beer as the government reduces the permitted alcohol content

... a cinema
Plenty of opportunity here. There were already 3000 cinemas in 1914, and the number is growing
You can claim it is your patriotic duty to see the newsreels about the war or the propaganda films the government is putting out
There are a few Charlie Chaplin films and other comedies around. Expect them to be American

... a music hall
Lots of people are still going just as before the war
There are more political propaganda sketches now.
If your idea of fun is laughing at a fat fake German soldier with sausages hanging from his pockets, you should have a good night out

... a club
More people are going to dance halls, and not just toffs
The styles are freer too, and you can find American ragtime and jazz music

... a theatre
More ordinary people are visiting the theatre too
There are a lot of patriotic plays, but there is a wide variety in London

... a concert
There are still opportunities in London and some major cities
Do not expect much German music on the programme and be ready to stand for a series of Allied national anthems

■ 15I People who found life difficult in war

Germans living in Britain
- People wrecked German shops in London's East End at the start of the war.
- Several Germans were killed in riots after a German submarine sank a large passenger liner, the *Lusitania*.
- Over 10,000 Germans were interned in special camps.

Men who refused to join the army
- About 16,000 men were 'conscientious objectors', refusing to join when conscription was introduced.
- Some supported the war effort in organisations such as the ambulance service where they did not need to fight.
- Many had their claims rejected and went to prison or were placed on specially dangerous parts of the Western Front.

FOCUS ROUTE

Draw up a list.

1 a) What kind of gains did women make in the First World War?
  b) How great were the gains?
  c) How far did their gains remain after the war?
2 What did they lose in the war?
3 Women gained the vote during the First World War (see Chapter 2, page 34). Why would this improve their status?
4 Work out which women gained and lost most.

F Did women gain anything from the First World War?

In Chapter 2 you have already examined the process by which the war helped women to achieve the right to vote in general elections. Here we will focus on two other issues.

Issue 1: Did they get more and better jobs?

Famously, as more and more men went into the army from 1915 so more and more women did their jobs. To be more exact, women came in through substitution and dilution arrangements.

- Substitution was simply women doing men's jobs.
- Dilution meant shifting skilled men to the most skilled work and/or getting them to supervise and instruct others while women did the easier and less skilled tasks.

How far women did men's jobs fully it is hard to know. Working men, and particularly their trade union leaders, had reason to claim women were not doing so much or such skilled work because they wanted to maintain their own status and income during and after the war. Employers had an incentive to say the same so that they could pay women less. Where women clearly did the same jobs as men there were claims that they were slower, but it seems impossible to check this.

Numbers of women in different types of work are easier to find out, though note that figures can vary from one source to another depending on how the jobs are defined or the exact dates used. Source 15.14 gives figures for a sample of occupations.

SOURCE 15.14 Numbers of women in work in different employment, 1914 and 1918

	1914	1918	+/−
All employment	5,966,000	7,311,000	+22%
Industry	2,179,000	2,971,000	+36%
Munitions and their suppliers	212,000	947,000	+347%
Commerce (e.g. trading and banking)	505,000	934,000	+85%
Transport	12,000	66,000	+450%
National and local government	262,000	460,000	+76%
Domestic service	1,658,000	1,258,000	−24%

ACTIVITY

Study the figures in Source 15.14.

1 How great is the overall increase in women's employment?
2 Which categories of work given here showed the largest increase
  a) in overall numbers employed
  b) as a percentage?
3 **a)** How great was the decline in numbers in domestic service?
  b) How did the number working in domestic service in 1918 compare with that in munitions?
4 How could you use these figures to argue that women's status in employment improved significantly?
5 How could you use them to argue that change was very limited?
6 In 1915 the *Daily Mail* wrote: 'No woman worker is in greater demand than the shorthand typist.' What does this suggest about women's jobs?

Before the war only about ten per cent of married women had worked outside their homes. During the war some middle-class women who had never worked before took up jobs. Otherwise girls sometimes started work earlier, and married women who had worked before came back into jobs.

What some women saw as improvement might be unwelcome to others. Paid work brought many women money and freedom, but some had a hard time doing boring jobs while still looking after their homes and children.

Many women, including some feminist campaigners, believed that married housewives with children should not have to work for money.

Women gained the vote during the First World War but remember that fighting remained men's work in First World War Britain and never women's. There were female soldiers in the Serbian army, and a women's battalion was recruited to fight in trenches in Russia. In Britain men fought while women grieved, nursed, farmed or made high-explosive shells.

How good were their wages?

Women doing the same work as men were promised that they would get the same PIECE RATES, but not the same rates when they were paid by the hour or the day. Then they appear to have got about a half to two-thirds of what men were paid. Overall historians have estimated that women's average wage was about a third to a half of that of men before the war and around two-thirds at the end.

> **PIECE RATE**
> Payment according to the amount of work done or goods produced.

What happened after the war?

Women who took up new types of jobs were generally expected to leave them after the war. When it finished they were laid off rapidly, urged to let men have their jobs back and to return to looking after their homes or take up traditional women's employment. Many returned to domestic service, but they were less likely to live in with their employers than before. The government would not allow women to continue in civil service and teaching jobs when husbands could provide for them, but they were more likely to hold on to jobs in offices and shops. It is estimated that about two thirds of the women who had entered employment during the war had left it by 1920. Censuses show that the proportion of women over the minimum school leaving age of 14 in employment fell from about 35 per cent in 1911 to 33 per cent in 1921.

Issue 2: How much did the First World War alter the way women lived?

Changes in lifestyle and family relations could not be halted or reversed so easily as the shifts in women's jobs. There are plenty of accounts of how women went out on their own more during the war, visiting restaurants, pubs and theatres, smoking in public, using more make-up and wearing shorter skirts or even, sometimes, trousers. They had gained a greater independence in running their lives which many would not give up, but attitudes varied.

270

WHO GAINED FROM THE FIRST WORLD WAR (AND HOW MUCH DID EVERYBODY LOSE)?

Divorce rates tripled between 1910 and 1920, though only to the low figure of 1629 a year. Contraceptives had been available to some before the war and would certainly have spread anyway, but the war speeded up the process. Some see this as the most important way in which women gained freedom, although others argue that contraception also gave women fewer rights to resist their partners' sexual demands.

ACTIVITY

Rate Sources 15.15–15.19 from 1 to 5 according to their usefulness as evidence on how the First World War changed women's lives and give reasons for your choice. Think about
• the reliability of their authors
• when they wrote
• how significant the subject matter is in the sources
• how typical the experiences were likely to be for large numbers of women.

SOURCE 15.15   Robert Roberts was the son of a corner shopkeeper in a slum area of Salford, west of Manchester. He was born in 1905, grew up during the First World War and wrote about his childhood experiences in *The Classic Slum*, 1971

Many wives of fighting men discovered that they could manage far better on government allowances than they ever did on their breadwinner's meagre wage. Mrs Cassidy with a young brood in a house near the shop now drew nearly three times the amount her usually drunken husband had brought home. 'They can keep Mick for ever!' she said, delighted.

To the shocked stares of the respectable, housewives with husbands away or on night work could now be seen going off in pairs to the pictures or sitting with a glass of stout in the Best Room at the pub.

Bold teenage girls, a type never encountered before (folk were scandalised), earning plenty of money, and foot-loose young housewives began to use face creams – Icilma, Silver Foam – even powder and dabs of rouge. My eldest sister, gone early in the war out of a cotton mill into the rich pickings of engineering, used cosmetics surreptitiously until one evening the old man caught her with a whole 'dorothy' bag full of the stuff. He threw the lot into the fire. The house, we understood, had been defiled. Hadn't Joe Devine (a neighbour), he thundered, 'turned his daughters into the street for using this muck?' Never again must she dare ... Jenny stood unperturbed, 'I either go on using it', she said, 'or you can turn me out too.'

SOURCE 15.16   Robert Roberts describes women's role after their husbands returned from the Front

[W]ith surprise they discovered that husbands, home again, were far less the lords and masters of old, but more comrades to be lived with on something like level terms.

SOURCE 15.17   An 'expert' writing in *The Times* gave a male view on girls' education in December 1918, just after the war ended

Girls [leave] school knowing all about William the Conqueror in 1066, but very little about the method of preparing a first-class steak and kidney pudding.

SOURCE 15.18   Mrs C.S. Peel was a social historian who wrote a history of ordinary life in the war, based partly on her own memories and published in 1929. She described the effect of women's work on their lives

Some women were during the war placed in important positions for which they had neither specialized training nor in many cases the general training in affairs which the public school and the university afford ... But never, although arduous and occasionally dangerous work was demanded of them, did it compare in the smallest degree with that demanded of the fighting men. Yet in doing what they did they found, in spite of weariness and sometimes of personal loss, a happiness which many of them had never known before.

SOURCE 15.19   Sir Robert Bruce Lockhart remembered in 1955

When I left England in 1911 contraceptives were hard to buy outside London or other large cities. By 1919 every village chemist was selling them.

CHAPTER 15 REVIEW ACTIVITY

1 Use a line to mark which groups you think gained or lost most in the First World War. Your line should be drawn like this:

Greatest gain ←――――――――――――――――→ **Greatest loss**

Use the Focus route notes you have compiled for this chapter.

You should include the upper, middle and working classes, men in the army and women in different situations. You may need to sub-divide the groups to show their position sensibly. Note, for example, how working-class experiences differed. The fortunes of men in the army varied from those who were killed to those who were promoted as officers and also survived.

Define your groups, place them on the line and then compare your order with other students. Try to justify your decisions.

2 Look at the main changes you have recorded, whether as gains or losses for different groups.
   a) Which would have come anyway?
   b) Which were hastened by war?
   c) Which were most important in the long term?

KEY POINTS FROM CHAPTER 15   Who gained from the First World War (and how much did everybody lose)?

1 Many people gained better wages, profits or welfare measures as a result of war.

2 The losses were huge. About 750,000 men were killed. The government spent over £9,000 million. About 70 per cent was borrowed and had to be paid back by future generations.

3 The war led to coalition governments.

4 It clearly weakened the Liberal Party but brought some benefits as well as losses to other parties.

5 The upper landowning class generally lost out from war, but other classes experienced a mixture of gains and losses.

6 Women took over many jobs they could not have entered before the war. They often did not retain them afterwards, but there were important changes in women's lifestyles.

Conclusion

Interpretations of the period 1851–1918

Historians' interpretations of what happened in 1851–1918 change over time. This is partly because of new information but also because of their attitudes and beliefs. Historians and political writers in Britain are almost all in favour of democracy. From the Second World War to the 1970s they were also overwhelmingly in favour of more state welfare and economic planning, though there have been much more mixed views since then. Historians' interpretations of the period are inevitably influenced by such fashionable thinking and indeed A level specifications are influenced by it as well. The investigations pursued in this book are not the only stories that could be told about late nineteenth-century Britain but they are significant stories. Now it is time to pull back and review the ground we have covered.

To get you started, try the questions below, then move on to the Review Activity opposite.

FOCUS ROUTE

Study the chart on pages 274–275.

1 How far do you agree with the generalisation that the government regulated the economy less and society more in the nineteenth century?
2 a) Refer to column 5. How extensively did the state regulate working conditions?
  b) What were the important changes in the type of regulations?
3 How extensively did the government provide social services by
  a) 1867
  b) 1900
  c) 1914?
4 Which of these changes would have been
  a) most popular
  b) most unpopular
  among the working class?

We began this book with a picture of Britannia launching blindly into an unknown future. The phrase 'a leap in the dark' had a very specific reference at that time, referring to the unknown impact of giving the vote to working men. Now it is time to draw some broad conclusions about the results of this 'leap in the dark'. Who do you think gained? Who lost?

You are going to look at three main themes:

1 The impact of reform

Make a table with the following headings

The impact of change on:			
Reform	**Upper class**	**Middle class**	**Working class**

a) The chart on the next two pages summarises the main developments you have studied in this book. Choose at least five important **reforms** that you have studied. Try to choose one from each of the five shaded columns of the chart.

b) Complete your table by indicating which groups were affected by them and in what ways.

2 The significance of reform

Some reforms were more significant than others. For example, some reforms affected a lot of people; others only a few. Some reforms represented a big departure from the old way of doing things; others were simply a continuation of an established trend. Which do you think were most significant?

a) Make a set of small cards. On each card write one of the reforms listed in your table for question 1.

b) Arrange the cards in order of significance, starting with the most important reform.

c) Explain your order of priority to the rest of the group, justifying your decisions.

3 The reason for action

Make your own copy of the chart on pages 274–275. Mark on it in three different colours times within the period when each of the following factors affected the way a government acted:

a) changing beliefs among ministers
b) pressure from voters
c) threats from abroad.

Which of these three factors do you think was most important? Give reasons for your answer.

Conclusion: A reply to Lord Derby

Lord Derby's spirit is troubled. From beyond the grave he wants to know how far his fears were realised, where the government's 'leap in the dark' took Britain. Write your own assessment of this period to inform him of how things developed after 1867. Make sure you cover:

a) whether the extension of the franchise led to progress or regress in British politics. Give reasons for your view.

b) whether the extension of the franchise was the most important influence on British politics in this period or whether other factors had more influence and if so which?

CONCLUSION

Change of ministry	Party in government	Prime Minister	Government economic and financial policy	Regulation of work	Education
					How the gove
1851	Liberal	Russell		Women's and children's work in textile mills already restricted	
1852	Conservative	Derby			
1852	Liberal–Peelite	Aberdeen			
1853					
1854					
1855	Liberal	Palmerston			
1856					
1857					
1858	Conservative	Derby			
1859	Liberal	Palmerston			
1860			**1860** Moves to **free trade** by Gladstone, as Chancellor of the Exchequer, largely completed (page 44)		
1861					
1862					
1863					
1864					
1865	Liberal	Russell			
1866	Conservative	Derby			
1867				**1867 Factory Act** extends 10½ hour day for women and children to all factory workers	
1868	Conservative	Disraeli			
1868	Liberal	Gladstone			
1869					
1870					**1870 Education Ac** system of **state elementary school** (page 48)
1871					
1872					
1873					
1874	Conservative	Disraeli		**1874 Factory Act** reduces working day to 10 hours	
1875					
1876					**1876 Education Ac** ensures most childrer school before age 10 (page 68)
1877					
1878				**1878 Factory Act** ensures restrictions enforced in workshops (page 67)	
1879					
1880	Liberal	Gladstone			**1880 Education Ac** completed moves to **compulsory educat** children aged 5–10
1881					
1882					
1883					
1884					
1885	Conservative	Salisbury	**Late 1800s** Governments generally follow **low tax** policy		
1886	Liberal	Gladstone		**1886 Shops Act** introduces restrictions on young shopworkers' hours	
1886	Conservative	Salisbury			
1887					
1888					
1889					
1890					
1891					**1891 Education Ac** ensures children gene educated free in elem schools
1892	Liberal	Gladstone			
1893				**1893 Labour Department** started at Board of Trade and mediates in industrial disputes	**1893 School leaving** raised to 11
1894	Liberal	Rosebery			
1895	Conservative	Salisbury			
1896					
1897					
1898					
1899					**1899 School leaving** raised to 12
1900					
1901					
1902	Conservative	Balfour			**1902 Education Ac** system of state secon schools (page 77)
1903					
1904					
1905	Liberal	Campbell-Bannerman			
1906					
1907					
1908	Liberal	Asquith		**1908 Mines Act** introduces first widespread restrictions on men's working hours (8-hour day in coal mines)	
1909			**1909 People's Budget** raises taxes, especially on the wealthy (page 209)		
1910				**1909 Trade Boards Act** introduces arrangements for fixing minimum wages in some industries (page 200)	
1911					
1912					
1913			**1914–18 First World War budgets** raise income tax to nearly a third of larger incomes (page 252)		
1914					
1915	Coalition	Asquith			**1918 School leaving** raised to 14
1916	Coalition	Lloyd George			

UK		Developments in Ireland	Foreign affairs
health and housing	Poverty and individual welfare		
Artisans' Dwelling Act for demolishing an …thy house (page 70)		1870 Campaign for Irish Home Rule starts	
Public Health Act creates …y authorities with medical …s (page 49) Artisans' Dwelling Act …ages slum clearance …7) Public Health Act gives …verall statement of local …s' responsibilities (page67)		1874 59 MPs elected who support Home Rule 1879–82 Land League develops Land War in support of tenant demands and works with Home Rule party in Parliament in the 'New Departure'	1878 Disraeli attempts to maintain Turkish empire at the Congress of Berlin
		1886 Gladstone converted to Home Rule and introduces first Home Rule bill	1887–97 Mediterranean agreements with Austria-Hungary and Italy. Otherwise Britain has no important alliances with major European powers
Housing of the Working …es Act allows council house …g		1893 Second Home Rule bill passed by Commons but defeated in Lords	
			1899–1902 Boer War
			1902 Anglo-Japanese Alliance 1904 Entente Cordiale (friendly understanding) with France 1905–06 First Moroccan crisis strengthens ties with France and worsens relations with Germany 1908 Scare over German naval building hastens Anglo-German naval arms race 1911 Second Moroccan crisis
	1906 Education Act allows local councils to provide free school meals (page 196) 1907 Children's medical inspections (page 196) 1908 Old Age Pensions (page 197) 1911 National Insurance Act introduces health and unemployment insurance (pages 201–202)	1912 Third Home Rule bill passed by Commons and delayed by Lords 1913 Ulster Volunteers threaten armed resistance	1912 Anglo-French agreements about positioning navies 1914 First World War

Answers to Activities

p. 4
1 b) Almost 21 million in England, Wales and Scotland, compared with near 60 million in the early 21st century.
2 c) Just over half: 54 per cent lived in towns with over 2500 inhabitants.
3 a) About half, according to a count in 1851.
4 b) Up to 35–40 m.p.h. (56–64 km/hr) on some 6000 miles (9600 km) of railway. The record speed was over 60 m.p.h. (96 km/hr), but third-class trains were sometimes as slow as 12 m.p.h. (19 km/hr). Otherwise, horses generally travelled at around 10 m.p.h. (16 km/hr).
5 There are no definitive answers to this but you may have come up with the following:
Ride on a fast train
Read the latest novel by Charles Dickens
Have a punch-up in a disorderly local football match (for men)
See a boxing match
Watch a public hanging (tens of thousands of people went to them; public hangings ended in 1868)
Get drunk (there were more pubs per person in 1851 than in the 21st century)
Have sex, as long as you were happy to have lots of children (there were no contraceptives to buy from shops or machines so you had to improvise if you wanted to avoid reproduction; male homosexual acts were lawful until 1885 but widely disapproved of).

p. 65
Jobs allocated by Disraeli in 1874
Foreign Secretary Earl of Derby
Chancellor of the Exchequer Sir Stafford Northcote
Home Secretary Richard Cross
Colonial Secretary Earl of Caernarvon
Secretary for War Gathorne Hardy
Secretary for India Marquis of Salisbury
First Lord of the Admiralty George Ward Hunt
The other two were in the Cabinet but in less important offices: Lord John Manners was Postmaster-General and Duke of Richmond had no department to run

p. 180
Jobs allocated by Campbell-Bannerman in 1905
Foreign Secretary Sir Edward Grey
Chancellor of the Exchequer Herbert Asquith
Home Secretary Herbert Gladstone
Colonial Secretary Earl of Elgin
Secretary for War Richard Haldane
Secretary for India John Morley
The other two were in the Cabinet but in less important offices:
Lloyd George was President of the Board of Trade
John Burns was President of the Local Government Board
Lord Rosebery never held government office again

Bibliography and Selected Reading

Adelman, P., *The Decline of the Liberal Party 1910–1931*, Longman, 1981

Adelman, P., *The Rise of the Labour Party 1880–1945*, Longman, 1996

Atkinson, D., *The Suffragettes in Pictures*, Sutton, 1996

Bardon, J., *A History of Ulster*, Blackstaff, 1992

Bartley, P., *Votes for Women*, Hodder and Stoughton, 1998

Behagg, C., *Labour and Reform: Working-Class Movements 1815–1914*, Hodder and Stoughton, 1991

Bentley, M., *Lord Salisbury's World: Conservative Environments in Late-Victorian Britain*, Cambridge University Press, 2001

Bentley, M., *The Climax of Liberal Politics: British Liberalism in Theory and Practice 1868–1918*, Edward Arnold, 1987

Bernstein, G.L., *Liberalism and Liberal Politics in Edwardian England*, Allen and Unwin, 1986

Biagini, E., *Gladstone*, Macmillan, 2000

Biagini, E. and Reid, A.J., *Currents of Radicalism*, Cambridge University Press, 1991

Blake, R., *Disraeli*, Eyre and Spottiswoode, 1966

Blewett, N., *The Peers, the Parties and the People: the General Elections of 1910*, Macmillan, 1972

Butler, D. and Butler, G., *British Political Facts 1900–1994*, Macmillan, 1994

Clarke, P.F., *Lancashire and the New Liberalism*, Cambridge University Press, 1971

Clegg, H.A., Fox, A. and Thompson, A.F., *A History of British Trade Unions since 1889*, Volume 1, Oxford University Press, 1964

Cooke, A.B. and Vincent, J.R., *The Governing Passion: Cabinet Government and Party Politics in Britain 1885–6*, Harvester, 1974

Cowling, M., *1867: Disraeli, Gladstone and Revolution*, Cambridge University Press, 1967

Craig, F.W.S., *British Electoral Facts*, Dartmouth Publishing Company, 1989

Dangerfield, G., *The Strange Death of Liberal England*, Serif, 1997 (1935)

De Groot, G.J., *Blighty: British Society in the era of the Great War*, Longman, 1996

Eldridge, C.C., *England's Mission: The Imperial Idea in the Age of Gladstone and Disraeli 1868–1880*, Macmillan, 1973

Foster, R.F., *Modern Ireland 1600–1972*, Allen Lane, 1988

Gailey, A., *Ireland and the Death of Kindness: Constructive Unionism 1890–1905*, Cork University Press, 1987

Garrard, J., 'Parties, members and voters after 1867', in Gourvish, T.R. and O'Day, A. (eds), *Later Victorian Britain 1867–1900*, Macmillan, 1988

Grigg, J., *Lloyd George: The People's Champion 1902–1911*, Methuen, 1978

Grigg, J., *Lloyd George: From Peace to War 1912–1916*, Methuen, 1985

Hamer, D.A., *Liberal Politics in the Age of Gladstone and Rosebery*, Oxford University Press, 1972

Hanham, H.J., *Elections and Party Management: Politics in the Time of Disraeli and Gladstone*, Longman, 1959

Harrison, B. 'Women's Suffrage at Westminster 1866–1928' in Bentley, M. and Stevenson, J. (eds), *High and Low Politics in Modern Britain*, Oxford University Press, 1983

Holton, S.S., *Feminism and Democracy*, Cambridge University Press, 1986

Holton, S.S., and Purvis, J. (eds), *Votes for Women*, Routledge, 2000

Hoppen, K.T., *Ireland since 1800: Conflict and Conformity*, Longman, 1999

Howard, M., *The First World War*, Oxford University Press, 2003

Jagger, P.J. (ed.), *Gladstone, Politics and Religion*, Macmillan, 1985

Jagger, P.J. (ed.), *Gladstone*, Hambledon Press, 1998

Jalland, P., *The Liberals and Ireland: the Ulster Problem in British Politics to 1914*, Harvester, 1980

Jenkins, R., *Asquith*, Collins, 1978

Jenkins, R., *Gladstone*, Macmillan, 1995

Jenkins, T.A., *The Liberal Ascendancy 1830–1886*, Macmillan, 1994

Joannu, M. and Purvis, J. (eds), *The Women's Suffrage Movement: New Feminist Perspectives*, I. B. Tauris, 1998

Joyce, P., *Work, Society and Politics: the Culture of the Factory in later Victorian England*, Harvester, 1980

Judd, D. and Surridge, K., *The Boer War*, John Murray, 2002

Kennedy, P., *The Rise and Fall of British Naval Mastery*, Allen Lane, 1976

Kennedy, P., *The Rise of the Anglo-German Antagonism 1860–1914*, Allen and Unwin, 1980

Laybourn, K., *Liberalism and the Rise of Labour 1890–1918*, Croom Helm, 1984

Laybourn, K., 'The Rise of Labour and the Decline of Liberalism: The State of the Debate', *History* No. 259, 1995

Lee, J.J., *Ireland 1912–1985: Politics and Society*, Cambridge University Press, 1989

Liddington, J. and Norris, J., *One Hand Tied Behind Us: the Rise of the Women's Suffrage Movement*, Virago, 1978

Machin, I., *Disraeli*, Longman, 1995

Marwick, A., *The Deluge: British Society and the First World War*, Macmillan, 1991

Matthew, H.C.G., *Gladstone 1809–98*, Oxford University Press, 1995

Mayer, A., *The Growth of Democracy in Britain*, Hodder and Stoughton, 1999

McDonough, F., *The British Empire 1815–1914*, Hodder and Stoughton, 1994

McKibbin, R., *The Evolution of the Labour Party 1910–1924*, Oxford University Press, 1974

Millman, R., *Britain and the Eastern Question 1875–78*, Oxford University Press, 1979

Murray, B.K., *The People's Budget 1909–1910*, Oxford University Press, 1980

Murray, P., *Poverty and Welfare 1830–1914*, Hodder and Stoughton, 1999

Packer, I., *Lloyd George*, Macmillan, 1998

Packer, I., *Lloyd George, Liberalism and the Land: The Land Issue and Party Politics in England, 1906–1914*, Boydell Press, 2001

Parry, J.P., *The Rise and Fall of Liberal Government in Victorian Britain*, Yale University Press, 1993

Pearce, R., *Britain and the European Powers 1865–1914*, Hodder and Stoughton, 1996

Pearce, R. and Stearn, R., *Government and Reform 1815–1918*, Hodder and Stoughton, 1994

Pelling, H., *Popular Politics and Society in Late Victorian Britain*, Macmillan, 1968

Porter, A., ed., *The Oxford History of the British Empire: Vol 3, The 19th Century*, Oxford University Press, 1999

Price, R., *An Imperial War and the Working Class*, Routledge, 1972

Pugh, M., *Electoral Reform in War and Peace 1906–1918*, Routledge, 1978

Pugh, M., *Lloyd George*, Longman, 1988

Pugh, M., *The March of the Women*, Oxford University Press, 2000

Pugh, M., *The Tories and the People 1880–1935*, Blackwell, 1985

Purvis, J., ed., *Women's History: Britain 1850–1945*, UCL Press, 1995

Read, D., *The Age of Urban Democracy*, Longman, 1994

Roberts, A. *Salisbury: Victorian Titan*, Weidenfeld and Nicolson, 1999

Rosen, A., *Rise up Women! The Militant Campaigns of the Women's Social and Political Union*, Routledge, 1974

Russell, A.K., *Liberal Landslide: the General Election of 1906*, David and Charles, 1973

Saab, A.P., *Reluctant Icon: Gladstone, Bulgaria and the Working Classes 1856–1878*, Harvard University Press, 1991

Scott-Baumann, M., ed., *Years of Expansion: British History 1815–1914*, Hodder and Stoughton, 2002

Searle, G.R., *The Liberal Party: Triumph and Disintegration 1886–1929*, Macmillan, 1992

Shannon, R.T., *Gladstone: Heroic Minister 1865–1898*, Allen Lane, 1999

Shannon, R.T., *Gladstone and the Bulgarian Agitation*, Harvester, 1975

Smith, F.B., *The Making of the Second Reform Bill*, Cambridge University Press, 1966

Smith, P., *Disraeli: A Brief Life*, Cambridge University Press, 1996

Tanner, D., *Political Change and the Labour Party 1900–1918*, Cambridge University Press, 1990

Thompson, P., *Socialists, Liberals and Labour: the Struggle for London 1885–1914*, Routledge, 1967

Vaughan, W.E. (ed.), *A New History of Ireland: VI, Ireland under the Union, II, 1870–1921*, Oxford University Press, 1996

Vincent, J.R., *The Formation of the British Liberal Party 1857–68*, Penguin, 1966

Vincent, J.R., *Disraeli*, Oxford University Press, 1990

Watts, D., *Tories, Conservatives and Unionists 1815–1914*, Hodder and Stoughton, 1994

Watts, D., *Whigs, Radicals and Liberals 1815–1914*, Hodder and Stoughton, 1995

Willis, M.V., *Democracy and the State 1930–1945*, Cambridge University Press, 1999

Wilson, K.M., *The Policy of the Entente 1904–14*, Cambridge University Press, 1985

Wilson, T., *The Downfall of the Liberal Party*, Collins, 1966

Winter, J.M., *The Great War and the British People*, Macmillan, 1985

Index